What are the possible scenarios when I
make up a book? The voices might for
mony. An disturbing treat for the mind
may collide in a cacophonic noise battle.
and thoughts. This book and its voices o.
narios. Put together, these new, creative, a.

.... up a polyph-
ony. Each voice offers something on its own terms, each chapter lingers on
as an individual melody that showcases how subjectivity is key to developing
knowledge about human experiences. And yet, when played together as a
polyphonic orchestra, the individual melodies also offer something much
more. As a whole, the book offers harmony and cacophony. Could you ask
for more?

**Professor Trude Klevan**, *University of South-Eastern Norway*

# AUTOETHNOGRAPHIES IN PSYCHOLOGY AND MENTAL HEALTH

This autoethnographic volume gathers a multiplicity of different voices in autoethnographic research from across psychology and mental health disciplines to address topics ranging from selfhood, trauma, emotional understanding, clinical psychology, and the experience of grief.

Edited by two leading figures, this volume broadens the concept of psychology beyond its conventional, mainstream academic boundaries and challenges pre-conceived and received notions of what constitutes 'psychology' and 'mental health'. This book collects new autoethnographic writers in psychology and mental health from across as diverse a range of disciplines and, in doing so, makes a strong case for the legitimacy of subjectivity, emotionality and lived experience as epistemic and pedagogic resources. The collection also troubles the related concept of 'mental health'. In contemporary times, this is either biomedically over-colonised (welcomed by some but resisted by others), often regarded by lay and professional people alike in terms of an 'ordered or disordered' binary (comforting for some but associated with stigma and othering for others), or, at worst, is reduced to a set of hackneyed memes – the stuff of Breakfast television (well-intentioned and undoubtedly reassuring and helpful for some but patronising and naïve for others). Overall, the volume promotes the subjective and lived-experiential voices of its contributors – the hallmark of autoethnographic writing.

*Autoethnographies in Psychology and Mental Health* will be of interest to psychology and mental health students and professionals with an interest in qualitative inquiry as it intersects with autoethnography and mental health.

**Alec Grant**, PhD, was a Visiting Professor at the University of Bolton, but from May 2024 has reverted to his nonaffilliated title of Independent Scholar. He was the recipient of the ICAE Inaugural Lifetime Contribution Award in 2020 and is widely published in journals such as *Qualitative Inquiry*, *The Qualitative Report*, and the *Journal of Autoethnography*.

**Jerome Carson**, PhD, is a Professor of Psychology at the University of Bolton. He did his Psychology degree at the University of Reading and trained as a clinical psychologist at the University of East London. He was awarded his PhD by King's College London in 2005.

# AUTOETHNOGRAPHIES IN PSYCHOLOGY AND MENTAL HEALTH

New Voices

*Edited by*
*Alec Grant and Jerome Carson*

LONDON AND NEW YORK

Designed cover image: Painting by Alec Grant, 'New Voices,' 2023

First published 2025
by Routledge
4 Park Square, Milton Park, Abingdon, Oxon OX14 4RN

and by Routledge
605 Third Avenue, New York, NY 10158

*Routledge is an imprint of the Taylor & Francis Group, an informa business*

*British Library Cataloguing-in-Publication Data*
A catalogue record for this book is available from the British Library

ISBN: 9781032528908 (hbk)
ISBN: 9781032507606 (pbk)
ISBN: 9781003408963 (ebk)

DOI: 10.4324/9781003408963

Typeset in Galliard
by CodeMantra

# CONTENTS

# ABOUT THE EDITORS

**Jerome Carson**, PhD, is a Professor of Psychology at the University of Bolton. He did his Psychology degree at the University of Reading and trained as a clinical psychologist at the University of East London. He was awarded his PhD by King's College London in 2005. Jerome's main research interests are in mental health recovery, positive psychology, alcohol addiction, bereavement, flourishing in seniors, and autoethnography. While he came to the field of autoethnography later in life, it is a methodology that he has been inspired by. Along with Dr. Freda Gonot-Schoupinsky and Professor Mark Weeks, he has co-developed Positive Autoethnography. Working with Patrick Hopkinson, Andrew Voyce, Dr. Mats Niklasson, and Peter Bryngelsson, he has also co-developed IDCAP (International digital collaborative autoethnography and psychobiography). He is excited by the collaborative opportunities that autoethnography provides. He is affiliated with the University of Bolton.

**Alec Grant**, PhD, was the recipient of the ICAE Inaugural Lifetime Contribution Award in 2020 (https://youtu.be/VXqCw-Tyq0E) and is widely published in journals such as *Qualitative Inquiry*, *The Qualitative Report*, and the *Journal of Autoethnography*. His Routledge co-edited and co-authored books include *International Perspectives on Autoethnographic Research* (2018); *An Autoethnography of Becoming a Qualitative Researcher: A Dialogic View of Academic Development* (2022); *Writing Philosophical Autoethnography* (2024); and *Meaningful Journeys: Autoethnographies of Quest and Identity Transformation* (2024). He was affiliated with the University of Bolton until May, 2024.

# CONTRIBUTORS

**Kevin Acott** is an experienced but still confused educator, clinician, coach, inspector and manager in mental health and social care, with more than 30 years of working in partnership with individuals, groups, families, and communities. His clinical, educational, and research interests are in self-harm, mindfulness and the arts, empathy, social class and economics, and the impact of trauma. He is the developer of the Three-Phase Conversational Model of Communication (TPCM), widely used in practice and in universities. Following a writing sabbatical, he returned to the UK to work with survivors of, and people bereaved by, the Grenfell Tower fire. He later delivered a national trauma training package he would designed for Victim Support, and worked with both adult learners at City Lit and medical students at Barts. He currently leads the Mental Health Nursing team at Brunel University, London.

**Ijeabalum Asike** is an African immigrant living in the UK. She is a UK-registered and practising counsellor (MBACP). She obtained a BSc in Psychology from the Enugu State University of Science and Technology in Nigeria, an MSc in Applied Psychology from Middlesex University Hendon, London and an MSc in Counselling and Positive Psychology from the University of Bolton. She is currently pursuing a PhD at the University of Bolton on the lived experiences of lupus sufferers. Her study aims to collate the lived experiences of lupus sufferers, adapt the CHIME framework to those lived experiences and hopefully develop a positive psychological intervention for people with chronic illness. This is her first publication.

**Robert Balfour** is a survivor of CSA and the North Wales 'looked after care' system, and is the Chief Executive Officer of Ben's Place (Survivors West Yorkshire), which pioneered male sexual violence survivor video counselling in 2015. He's spent 28 years cross-sector working with psychologically distressed groups. These include acquired brain injury, 'schizophrenia', personality 'disorder', and sexual violence. He has commissioned and co-authored academic papers, articles, and reports looking at the service needs of sexual violence survivors since the mid-2000s. He is an independent scholar practitioner.

**Yulin Cheng** is an autistic self-advocate and independent researcher based in Hong Kong. She graduated with a BA in Law and Politics from Queen Mary University of London and an MA in Law from the National University of Singapore. She has worked in the fields of disability rights and suicide prevention research. A PhD candidate in the Department of Social Work and Social Administration, The University of Hong Kong from 2019 to 2023, she decided to withdraw due to unfavourable research conditions leading to burnout. As one of the few openly autistic researchers in Hong Kong doing autism and mental health research from a critical and neurodiversity lens, her research looks at the experiences and impact of stigma and discrimination on autistic adults. She is an independent researcher.

**Amanda Costello**, DEd, is a Fellow, Senior Lecturer and Researcher at the University of Bolton and Programme Lead for MSc Pathways in the School of Nursing and Midwifery. Her research interests include learning disabilities and autoethnography work, assessment literacy, and learner attrition. Additionally, she is involved in university-wide research workshop delivery and facilitation and PhD supervision.

**Nicola Cross** is currently an Intervention Centre Manager at a mainstream secondary school. She is a successful and proud graduate of the University of Bolton, graduating with a BSc in Psychology, Psychotherapy and Counselling, and an MSc in Counselling and Positive Psychology. She was inspired to pursue a career in the educational sector after overcoming her own challenges with dyslexia. She is affiliated with the University of Bolton.

**Freda Gonot-Schoupinsky**, PhD, is interested in laughter and humour, positive psychology, and methodology. Her contributions include the Laughie (Laugh Intentionally Everyday); laughter prescription; Personal Development Theory of laughter and humour; the Humour Laughter Affect model: collaborative autoethnography pragmatic autoethnography, positive autoethnography, and the concept terms 'positive reflexivity' and 'solirisy'. She is the lead author of *The Positive Psychology of Laughter and Humour* (in preparation with Emerald Publishing). She is affiliated with the University of Bolton.

**Joe Hoare's** upbringing in the countryside imbued in him an ever-deepening appreciation of nature, especially by walking in it. His foreshortened formal education in no way diminished his appetite for studying and appreciating the subtleties of human connection and communication. His life's work is fostering this awareness in fellow humans to promote a fairer, more compassionate, and peaceful world. His written contributions include articles for *Resurgence & Ecologist Magazine, Addiction Today, Nursing Standard*, and others. He is the author of *Awakening the Laughing Buddha Within* (2013), *Laughter Yoga and Happiness* (2018), and *Laughter Yoga for Joy* (2022). He is an independent practitioner.

**Robert Hurst** is an Associate Lecturer in Psychology and a registered person-centred counsellor, an area that most of his teaching focuses on. He has published articles on topics such as meaning in life, mental health recovery and positive psychology in journals such as *Psychology Teaching Review* and *Counselling and Psychotherapy Research*. He curates *Remarkable Lives*, a series of first-person accounts of mental health difficulties and recoveries for the journal *Mental Health and Social Inclusion*. He also has a keen interest in the links between creativity and mental health and is the first author of a forthcoming book on the subject, *Creative Mental Health Recovery: An Approach To Healing* (Routledge). He is affiliated with the University of Bolton.

**Adeela Irfan** qualified as a clinical psychologist at the University of the Punjab, Lahore, Pakistan, in 1994. She had received her BA in Psychology in 1990. She went on to acquire a Master's degree in Psychotherapy in 2009 in Ireland. Adeela is a therapist with over 28 years' experience in mental health. She works with both adult and child clients and has a wide range of expertise from autism to PTSD. She works part-time with Pennine Care NHS Foundation Trust as a psychologist/psychotherapist in psychosexual therapy. She is affiliated with Pennine Care NHS Foundation Trust.

**Marcin Kafar**, PhD, is an interdisciplinary scholar working at the intersection of human and social sciences. To express his own voice, he combines the fields of anthropology of culture, education, literary studies, sociology, and philosophy. He is the recipient of internships and is a Visiting Professor in the Department of Communication, University of South Florida, working with Professors Carolyn Ellis and Art Bochner. He promotes autoethnography in Poland. He is affiliated with the Faculty of Educational Sciences, University of Lodz.

**Dariusz Kubinowski,** PhD, is a Full Professor of Social Sciences, educational researcher, qualitative researcher, and choreologist. He is a former lecturer at universities in Lublin, Szczecin, and Słupsk (Poland) and is currently an elected member of the Committee of Educational Sciences in the Polish Academy of Sciences. He is the initiator and all-state coordinator of the Transdisciplinary Network for Qualitative Researchers and the author of over 180 scholarly publications. Among other topics, he has written on education and culture, education through art, philosophy, evaluating educational qualitative research, culture pedagogy, traditional and contemporary dance culture, and cultural animation. He is affiliated with the Committee on Pedagogical Sciences of the Polish Academy of Sciences.

**Kirsty Lilley** currently lives in the North Cotswolds area. Originally from Liverpool, she initially trained as a registered general nurse, continuing her career by undertaking qualifications in occupational health nursing, psychotherapy, and coaching. She has been freelancing for over 16 years, successfully running her own business and undertaking training and consultancy in mental health and wellbeing. Kirsty became interested in autoethnography three years ago, initially as a way of making sense of her own experiences of childhood adversities. She has since gone on to use this approach to add her voice to the growing literature from other survivors, with the aim of improving support and care for others who have experienced similar adversities. She is an independent writer.

**Irene Niklasson** is a former Physical Education Teacher by training and co-founder of the Vestibularis Clinic in Kalmar, Sweden. She later continued her education and expertise in psychotherapy. Together with her husband Mats and a former neuroscientist, the late Professor Matti Bergström, she developed a method for assessments and interventions of sensory and motor difficulties, sensorimotor therapy (SMT). One part of SMT, as it is practiced at the Vestibularis Clinic, is auditory perceptual training (ADT), which has become her field of expertise. She is the co-author of seven peer-reviewed papers, two of which are published in the journal *Frontiers in Psychology* and one in the journal *PLOS ONE*. She is affiliated with Vestibularis Clinic, Kalmar, Sweden.

**Mats Niklasson,** PhD, has an academic background mainly in developmental psychology. He is an associate editor of the journal *Perceptual and Motor Skills*. His interest in autoethnography and mental health has grown in recent years, resulting in his co-authoring a few publications. In 1989, together with his wife Irene, he started the Vestibularis Clinic at the University College in Kalmar, Sweden. The Clinic later became a private enterprise at which he is still active as a sensorimotor therapist. He is affiliated with the University of Bolton.

**Justyna Ratkowska-Pasikowska** holds a PhD in Educational Sciences with a focus on human sexuality, normativity, and death and dying. She specialises in providing psychological assistance in the field of sexology. With 17 years of experience in Higher Education, she has contributed to various publications about literature, femininity, sexuality, and qualitative research. She is affiliated with the Faculty of Educational Sciences, University of Lodz.

**Nawal Saleh**, for over 20 years, has been inspired and intrigued by the world around her and has always aspired to learn as much as she can about things that fascinate me. A factor influencing her pursuit of an academic career and feeding her natural curiosity has been her nomadic childhood. Growing up in multiple countries has given her an appreciation for human diversity. Having interacted with many types of people, her view of what is 'normal' has been consistently challenged from an early age. She is affiliated with the University of Bolton.

**Sonia Soans**, PhD, is a critical psychologist based in India. She is an intersectional feminist whose research interests are in gender, mental illness, nationalism, and cinema. In 2021, she founded the Afro-Asian Critical Psychology Network, which is a space for activists and scholars who have an interest in critical psychology and work in the Majority World. She is an independent lecturer and researcher.

**Colette Szczepaniak**, PhD, is a qualitative researcher and autoethnographer. Her research interests focus on gender, femininity in socio-cultural context, and maritime sociology. She publishes in, among other journals, *Qualitative Inquiry, Cultural Studies ↔ Critical Methodologies*, and *Qualitative Sociology Review*. She is affiliated with the Institute of Sociology, University of Szczecin.

**Oskar Szwabowski**, PhD, is a critical educator, autoethnographer, and unfulfilled writer. He is the author of five books and editor of several more. He has published in journals such as *Policy Futures in Education, Research in Education, Humanity & Society, Journal of Poetry Therapy, Qualitative Inquiry, Cultural Studies ↔ Critical Methodologies*, the *Journal of Autoethnography*, the *International Review of Qualitative Research, Power and Education*, and the *Journal for Critical Education Policy Studies*. He is affiliated with the Department of Pedagogy of Uniwersytet Pomorski in Słupsk.

**Siw Heidi Tønnessen** lecture in professional practices in mental health, substance use, and addiction, alongside currently completing her PhD. She has a background in family therapy, systemic thinking and practice, and a biographical history as an active alcoholic until 2014 when she stopped drinking. In her PhD, she research meaningful everyday life for people in recovery from mental health challenges and addiction. As part of her thesis, she has published an analytical autoethnographic article on the meaningfulness of challenging the controlled drinking discourse. Her chapter in this book builds up on thoughts from this article. She is affiliated with the University of South-Eastern Norway.

**Dr. Marianne Trent** is a Chartered Clinical Psychologist helping aspiring psychologists to develop in their roles. She started her own business in 2019 and, since this time, has been featured by the BBC, Channel 5, and *The Guardian* newspaper. In 2021, building upon her free support sessions for up-and-coming psychologists, she published the highly acclaimed book *The Clinical Psychologist Collective,* and, later, the multiply downloaded podcast, *The Aspiring Psychologist.* Marianne lives in The West Midlands with her husband and two children, where she can often be found drinking herbal tea and reading books in the hanging egg chair in her garden. She is an independent practitioner.

# PREFACE

## Populating Projects with People and Their Autoethnographic Stories

Is the academic discipline of psychology really a science? If you think it is, what kind of science is it? What is its subject matter?

The answer to these questions is complicated. Originally, academic psychology was construed as an experimental science of the mind, an unmediated study of consciousness made possible by applying the rigorous experimental methods of the natural sciences. This ambitious version of psychology may have made sense, at least on the surface, given that the primary goal of psychology was to achieve the status of a unique and independent scientific discipline, different in kind from philosophy, physiology, and biology. But this aspirational goal begged the question of how to gain access to consciousness through the procedures of scientific method. Is consciousness objectively accessible? If so, how? Is it even an object?

The problem, you see, was the murkiness and subjective qualities of consciousness. How was psychology going to become an objective science if it had to deal directly with consciousness, which is subjective, active, aware, and creative? The story that could answer these questions is too long and detailed to tell here. Suffice it to say that psychology as an experimental and primarily quantitative discipline ultimately (though not everlastingly) cast its lot with behaviour (and behaviourism), turning away from the centrality of experience, a person's subjective inner life, and the method of introspection (Adams & Ellis, 2020; Bochner & Adams, 2020; Ellis, 1991). In the 19th and 20th centuries, no experimental science akin to the natural sciences could count on rising to the state of an elite discipline by making sense of the chaos and dynamism. And subjectivity of consciousness.

Academic disciplines, though, are never fixed and unchanging, and neither are the research conventions that define them. Instead, they constantly evolve, not as much in the manner of the 'scientific revolutions' that Kuhn (1970) described, but rather through more gradual processes of reform and extension, growing larger, stronger, and hopefully more appealing and interesting. These changes occur by adding alternatives or new options such as autoethnography (Bochner & Ellis, 2022; Ellis & Bochner, 2000). But those seeking to modify, stretch, or broaden the boundaries, methodologies, and/or writing practices of a field of inquiry inevitably must cope with what the psychotherapist, Jay Haley (1963), once referred to as 'The First Law of Human Relations: *The more change is attempted, the more it is resisted*' (p. 189).

As new goals and practices begin to emerge, researchers identified with older, conventionalised, and formerly irreproachable goals and methods – the ones they were trained to abide by and keep to – may feel as if the discipline's view of the world is being challenged and weakened by the introduction of new approaches, diverse goals, and novel ways of depicting, justifying, and narrating research. Often, this new vernacular feels unfamiliar, abnormal, and unsettling to them. They worry about what will happen to the discipline if these new objectives, methodologies, and vocabularies take hold. How then will the gatekeepers know what counts as significant work? Will the discipline lose its hard-earned respectability as a rigorous science?

Psychology and many of the mental health professions have been particularly slow to loosen what Bochner (1993) once called 'the coercive grip of neutrality'. Under the rules of neutrality and objectivity, the idea of 'blurring borders' or 'bending genres' of representation would not be permitted or condoned in psychological research. Psychology was determined to be a 'data-driven' field emphasising objectivity, value-neutrality, intersubjective verifiability and either environmental determinism, as in behaviourist thought, or mental determinism, as in cognitive thought. A few notably brave holdouts in psychology and aligned disciplines – Ken Gergen, Clifford Geertz, and Charles Taylor – were tolerated, but psychology was obsessively preoccupied with its self-image as an individualist, positivist, largely experimental science dealing almost exclusively with objective truths and snubbing any defiant notions of cultural, historical, or contextual relativity.

What psychology's gatekeepers failed to appreciate was the extent to which, as Laing (1982) once observed, 'what is scientifically right may be morally wrong' (p. 22). Moral and ethical consequences matter. Indeed, the road to scientific truth can lead to the kind of ruthless indiscretions that caused Apter (1996, p. 22) to label psychology 'an intrusive and frequently cruel discipline' that too often contributes significantly to human suffering by manipulating not only variables but also people.

You may wonder whether the discipline of psychology ever had a choice. Actually, it did. 'Psychology did not have to become scientific', observed psychologist Mark Freeman (2016, p. 363), 'certainly not in the way it has ... it could have emerged in a quite different form, more particular, more historical, more cultural, more artful'. For several years, Freeman has issued a clarion call for 'a poetic science of human being that would allow the people that psychologists study – such as those represented by the stories in this book – to live on the page in their difference, their otherness' (2016, p. 359), one that moves from a reliance on argument to that of appeal through the poetic resonance of evocation (Freeman, 2016) as frequently found in autoethnographic storytelling (Bochner & Ellis, 2016).

Throughout the 20th century, however, the failure to consider other options meant that research in psychology rarely focused on issues central to the rousing and severe character of lived existence such as how to empathise with suffering people; overcome racial, sexual, and religious persecution; eradicate systems of oppression; contest and/or prevent global unrest; or express and help people cope with heartbreaks, regrets, abuses, disabilities, sorrows, trauma, chronic illnesses, entrapments, and social injustices. Nor was much attention given to encouraging researchers and practitioners of the psychological sciences to focus not only on *what* to study but also on *ways* of broadening the *forms* by which researchers and practitioners can *express* and *represent* their research.

'Why not?' you may want to ask. The answer is uncomplicated. As heirs of the objectivist tradition of scientific research, most social scientists who had been graduate students prior to the 1990s were unprepared either to recognise that predicting and controlling may not be the only goal to achieve from our research, or that every research monograph need not stick to the same standardised form of narration – namely hypothesis, literature review, methods, results, and discussion. Their training in research methodology was monolithic, which had the effect of narrowing research projects to topics that conformed closely to the technologies of objectivist social science. But how truly 'social' was this kind of social science? And how 'human' could the human sciences claim to be if much of the work produced is 'unpopulated writing' that makes little if any reference to actual people and/or episodes of their lived-through lives (Billig, 2013). On the contrary, most of us regard people as considerably more important to our social lives than things and concepts (Billig, 2013).

Fortunately, by the mid-1980s, a crisis of representation (Clifford & Marcus, 1986; Geertz, 1988; Marcus & Fisher 1986; Turner & Bruner, 1986) had taken hold across the human sciences. This crisis opened new vistas of inquiry, a spirit of experimentation with new research and writing practices, and a turn towards narrative, interpretive, and qualitative approaches to inquiry that emphasise the ways in which research in the human sciences is a relational, political, and moral activity (Denzin, 1997). In the 1990s, the two of us seized upon the term 'autoethnography' (Ellis & Bochner, 2000) to represent a covering term for many diverse genres of first-person, vulnerable writing that calls attention to subjectivity, emotionality, and contingency, encourages 'feeling' contact with the pain and suffering of others, and invites readers to deal with the concrete – particular people in particular places facing particular circumstances of lived-through experience (Conquergood, 1990).

The editors and authors of *Autoethnography in Psychology and Mental Health: New Voices* personify the spirit and character of this experimentation. A number of these new voices have greatly benefitted from the patient and skilful mentoring they received from Alec Grant and Jerome Carson. In their stories, they resist the temptation to distance themselves from their subject matter or dissolve concrete events and experiences in solutions of overly abstract analysis. Instead, they offer readers the companionship of intimate details as a substitute for the loneliness of uncontextualised facts. They want you, the reader, to care about their struggles. Many of these authors choose a binding form of subjective, conversational, and/or performative storytelling that invites a relationship between writer and reader. Instead of speaking in the disembodied prose that dominates writing in the social sciences, many of these writers choose a language more akin to emotional and personal experience. They want you, as the reader, to engage with their struggle with adversity and their heartbreaking feelings of stigma, oppression, and marginalisation. In the process of telling their stories, they inquire into, interpret, make sense of, and/or draw meaning from their memories of what they have lived through, both how it felt then and how it feels now; and they freely express how their struggles have grown ethnographically and relationally out of connections to and/or with other people, organisations, and institutions to which they have been connected.

As exemplified in many of the stories in this book, autoethnography at its best is a reader-centred form of representation and expression of lived-through experiences. Most of these new voices focus on pragmatic issues. They are more concerned with deciding what to do (with their circumstances and their lives) than with devising a social theory to explain the predicaments in which they find themselves. The writers put meanings into motion but ultimately a burden falls on you, the reader, who can choose to sustain the momentum and movement of the story's meanings. As the reader, you carry the weight of the existential question: what do I do now – now that I've taken this opportunity to experience this experience? If these authors were to have their way, you, the reader, would take things slowly, get close to their stories, and resist the temptation to stop yourself if, or when, you experience turbulent emotions rooted in your own lived life.

When we were still teaching courses in autoethnography and narrative inquiry, students would often ask, 'What am I supposed to get out of this story?' Our reply: 'It's not a question of what you should get out of the story, but how you can get into it, how you can make their story yours, and use it for yourself'.

We hope you will take the autoethnographic challenge and follow the autoethnographic mantra: Linger in the story. Prolong your stay. Inhabit the story. Let yourself get into the conversations, dialogues, stories, and essays of these vulnerable and creative new voices and pass them on to others in your life.

Arthur P. Bochner, PhD,
Distinguished University Professor Emeritus,
NCA Distinguished Scholar,
University of South Florida, Tampa, FL

Carolyn Ellis, PhD
Distinguished University Professor Emerita,
University of South Florida, Tampa, FL

## References

Adams, T. E., & Ellis, C. (2020). Practicing autoethnography and living the autoethnographic life. In P. Leavy (Ed.), *The Oxford handbook of qualitative research* (pp. 359–396). Oxford University Press.

Apter, T. (1996). Expert witness. Who controls the psychologist's narrative? In R. Josselson (Ed.), *Ethics and process in the narrative study of lives* (pp. 22–44). Sage Publications.

Billig, M. (2013). *Learn to write badly: How to succeed in the social sciences.* Cambridge University Press.

Bochner, A. (1993). The coercive grip of neutrality: Can psychology escape? *Contemporary Psychology, 38,* 537–538.

Bochner, A., & Adams, T. (2020). Autoethnography as applied communication. In H. Dan O'Hair and Mary John O'Hair (Ed.), *The Handbook of applied communication research: Volume 2* (1st ed., pp. 709–729). Hoboken, NJ: John Wiley & Sons, Inc.

Bochner, A., & Ellis, C. (2016). *Evocative autoethnography: Writing lives and telling stories.* Routledge.

Bochner, A. P., & Ellis, C. (2022). Why autoethnography? *Social Work & Social Sciences Review, 23*(2), 8–18.

Clifford, J., & Marcus, G. (1986). *Writing culture: The poetics and politics of ethnography.* University of California Press.

Conquergood, D. (1990). *Rethinking ethnography: Cultural politics and rhetorical strategies.* Paper presented at the Temple Conference on Discourse Analysis, Temple University.

Denzin, N. (1997). *Interpretive ethnography: Ethnographic practices for the 21st century.* Sage Publications.

Ellis, C. (1991). Sociological introspection and emotional experience. *Symbolic Interaction, 14,* 23–50.

Ellis, C., & Bochner, A. (2000). Autoethnography, personal narrative, reflexivity: Researcher as subject. In N. Denzin & Y. Lincoln (Eds.), *The handbook of qualitative research* (2nd ed., pp. 733–768). Sage.

Freeman, M. (2016). Psychology as the science of human being. In J. Valsiner, G. Marsico, N. Chaudhary, T. Sato, & V. Dazzani (Eds.), *The Yokohama Manifesto* (pp. 349–364). Springer.

Geertz, C. (1988). *Works and lives: The anthropologist as author.* Stanford University Press.

Haley, J. (1963). *Strategies of psychotherapy.* New York: Grune and Stratton.

Kuhn, T. (1970). *The structure of scientific revolutions* (2nd ed.). University of Chicago Press.

Laing, R. D. (1982). *The voice of experience.* Pantheon.

Marcus, G., & Fisher, M. (1986). *Anthropology as cultural critique: An experimental moment in the human sciences.* University of Chicago Press

Turner, V., & Bruner, E. M. (1986). *The anthropology of experience.* University of Illinois Press.

# ACKNOWLEDGEMENTS

We would like to thank Adam Woods, our always supportive, enthusiastic, and responsive editor at Routledge, and the production team. You all work hard and do a great job. Thanks also to all the authors in this volume for making it an engaging international and cosmopolitan read. Finally, we are honoured and privileged to have the preface of the book written by Professors Bochner and Ellis, the pioneers and trailblazers of autoethnography. Thanks to both of you.

Alec Grant and Jerome Carson,
April 2024

# 1

# INTRODUCTION

## The Importance of Autoethnography for Psychology and Mental Health

*Alec Grant and Jerome Carson*

Dear Reader,

We started this volume project with the shared but unspoken assumption that our contributor autoethnographic chapters would conform to conventional understandings of 'psychology' and – therapeutic psychology's stock in trade – 'mental health'. Conditioned by many years of immersion in psychological therapy and critical mental health (Alec), and mainstream and applied psychology (Jerome), it turned out that we were thinking too narrowly. It's an understatement to say that editing this volume has been beneficial in effectively challenging our original preconceived ideas.

The chapters that follow stretch the concept of psychology beyond its mainstream disciplinary limits, and rightly so: there's much more to *psychology* than the academic discipline of psychology (Freeman, 2012, 2024; Teo, 2017). Quite simply, as Mark Freeman (2012, p. 205) writes,

> We have categories and constructs aplenty, inventories and other such sortings. They can be useful. But they tend to obscure the person.

The chapters in this volume also trouble related ideas about 'mental health', which in our times is either biomedically over-colonised (welcomed by some but resisted by others), contextualised by lay and professional people alike in an 'ordered or disordered' binary (comforting for some but associated with stigma and *othering* for others), or is, at worst, reduced to a set of hackneyed memes – the stuff of Breakfast television (well-intentioned and undoubtedly reassuring and helpful for some but patronising and naïve for others).

DOI: 10.4324/9781003408963-1

More than that, the chapters which follow rescue the subjective and lived-experiential voice, which is the stock-in-trade voice of autoethnographers.

## Recruitment

The contributors to the volume came together on the basis of prior or existing collegiate relationships, serendipitous contact, and what's known in qualitative circles as 'snowball' recruitment. Some are our University of Bolton colleagues: *Amanda Costello and Robert Hurst*; MSc students: *Robert Balfour, Nicola Cross,* and *Nawal Saleh*; friends and acquaintances: *Adeela Irfan and Marianne Trent*; and ex-postgraduate students: *Freda Gonot-Schoupinsky,* who got *Joe Hoare* on board, *Robert Balfour* and *Robert Hurst,* and *Mats Niklasson,* who recruited his wife *Irene* as co-writer. *Ijeabalum Asike* is our current PhD student, and we mentored *Kirsty Lilley's* written work until 2024.

Our Polish contributors joined the project during Alec's academic visit to Ustka in June 2023, after taking up Dariuz's invitation for him to present on autoethnography at the 10th Transdisciplinary Symposium of Qualitative Research: 'Critical Qualitative Inquiry for a Better World'. While there, he was fortunate to meet *Colette Szczepaniak, Justyna Ratkowska-Pasikowska, Marcin Kafar, Oskar Szwabowski,* and *Dariusz Kubinowski.*

*Sonia Soans,* from Bangalore, was known to Alec via social media for some years prior to the book proposal. She put us in touch with *Yulin Cheng* in Hong Kong.

*Siw Tonnessen* was recruited via Alec's esteemed sometimes co-author and Siw's PhD supervisor, Trude Klevan.

## New Voices?

How does the recruitment process relate to the phrase 'New Voices', and what does this term mean exactly? In the volume are chapters from contributors fresh on the autoethnographic scene, with some serving their apprenticeship, and a minority already well published and respected members of autoethnographic and related communities. In the case of the latter group, while they are not new to the approach, the nuanced perspectives they give voice to certainly are.

The range of what we mean by 'new voices' inevitably results in the chapters presented to you varying at the levels of: narrative autoethnographic depth of understanding and creativity (Grant, 2023a) and aesthetic sophistication (Grant, 2023a; Richardson & St Pierre, 2018); knowledge of autoethnography as a craft endeavour – relating to the need to develop writer reflectivity, critical reflexivity, self-reflection, and self-awareness by the repeated practice of writing (Grant, 2023a); focus, topic, and style; and care over reflexive choice of language and words (Grant, 2023a; Grant & Young, 2024). Some chapters display tacit assumptions around the use of *autoethnography-as-method* as opposed to *autoethnographicity-as-lived-existential-choice* (Kafar, 2021, pp. 49, 58–61). Whereas the former tends to treat culture as an ordinary given, 'just so' feature of life, and autoethnographic writing as an occasional, 'drop in' endeavour, the latter demands the development of critical cultural sensibilities in autoethnographic writers who are never 'off duty'.

That said, we strongly believe that all chapters are worth engaging with, for several reasons. We predict that readers will be often moved, and emotionally and experientially connect with much of what follows. Autoethnography sophisticates will be able to exercise their critical eyes and will sometimes be pleasantly surprised. Readers steeped in conventional understandings of psychology and mental health will have their discourses profitably challenged and stretched. Novice autoethnographers, and those autoethnographers on a developmental trajectory (which should include all of us), will learn a lot more about their craft. Finally, and hopefully, some potential autoethnographers might be enticed into our methodological communities.

## Rationale for the Volume

Although well-established internationally, autoethnography still has a bad press. Those who are steeped in the research approach and regularly promulgate it – the autoethnographic cognoscenti if you will – can easily rebut constant accusations that it pays little attention to relational and procedural ethics (Grant &Young, 2022; Sparkes, 2024), and that it's a soft option approach for the lazy (Grant, 2023a). None of these criticisms should bother us. In adding autoethnographic writing to trouble the methodological 'begrudger army' who would be pleased to see it contract, we are pleased to be doing our bit to swell the autoethnographic ranks with both absolute beginners and those who have seen action.

The question arises, if you want more people to join an army, when's the right time to let them out on public parade? In answering this, there's what might be regarded as a 'hard line' perspective from within the autoethnographic community that needs consideration. Heewon Chang (2008, p. 54) argues the need to avoid common pitfalls in writing autoethnography. In her view, these are too much:

- Focus on the self in isolation from others;
- Focus on self-narration at the expense analysis of the wider social and cultural context;

- Reliance on memories and recall as the sole data source; neglect of relational ethical considerations;
- Inappropriate labelling of work as 'autoethnography'.

One of us (Alec) is cautiously, and in a qualified way, sympathetic to Chang's listed pitfalls. He does think that what's often written in the name of 'autoethnography' is inappropriately labelled as such, and is solipsistic, naive realist, and lacking in cultural critique and analysis (this relates to the widespread assumption that autoethnography equals story, and anyone can write a story). It's true that relational ethical challenges are often sidestepped, ignored and not acknowledged ('If I'm writing about myself there are no relational ethical considerations'). It's equally true that these challenges are not considered in the round (Sparkes, 2024), or sufficiently critically engaged with, given that relational ethical prescriptions can be presented as dogma, with misogyny creeping in through the back door (Grant & Young, 2022). Moreover, Alec has a longstanding 'beef 'with his perception of a lot of 'autoethnographic' work lacking philosophical adequacy, particularly around the concepts of 'self' and 'culture' (Grant, 2024a, c). However, equally, as a broad orientation to qualitative scholarship rather than simply a specific method or procedure (Grant, 2024a, p. 2), he doesn't hold with autoethnographic writing being over-policed.

Newcomers to the approach deserve encouragement rather than over-censure, and in this regard, we both think it important to display a range of newcomer work in this volume.

And there's more local context to this book project: we want to make the University of Bolton a Centre of Autoethnographic Excellence. In so doing, it's important for us to nurture and build up our international relationships. With a long history of producing autoethnography, since being awarded the title of 'Visiting Professor' at Bolton in August 2022, Alec has had three journal articles published, the aim being to socialise students and staff at Bolton and beyond to the autoethnographic approach (Grant, 2022, 2023a, 2023b). These have been backed up by several conference presentations, workshops, and teaching sessions locally. Jerome came later to the autoethnography party. An early paper by Stevenson and Carson (1995) showed the beginnings of an autoethnographic style. It was to be two decades later that he first read an MSc dissertation based on autoethnography. And it was only during 'Lockdown', that, working with Robert Hurst, he co-produced their first collaborative autoethnographic account (Hurst & Carson, 2021). Since then, he has co-produced a number of collaborative autoethnographic accounts (Carson & Niklasson, 2023; Gonot-Schoupinsky et al., 2023; Qasim & Carson, 2022).

With our Norwegian colleague Trude Klevan, we hope to host an international autoethnography conference at Bolton towards the end of 2024, to include – among a wider range of participants – our Polish and Norwegian friends and colleagues, and our current and past under- and postgraduate students and staff.

## Why Now?

There's also a professional/disciplinary context to this volume. There's never been a better time for it to be released to the world. In *The Psychologist*, the online journal of the British Psychological Society, Miltos Hadjiosif (2023) writes:

> I have studied Psychology for 25 years and I have grown tired of letting it chase my thoughts away like butterflies, of not really knowing what to do with my feelings. I am done spending precious class time teaching brands of qualitative analysis at the expense of truly cultivating foundational research skills such as playfulness, noncertainty... affective fluency, trusting intuition, and refusing to treat the published literature as more worthy of attention than the knowledge that lives in art and rituals, our relationships, and our bodies. I sense my students tiring of the dominance of a handful of approaches, their 'McDonaldisation', mega-franchises eclipsing local alternatives, the textbooks – so many textbooks – with their manualised focus on capturing others' experiences and presenting them as 'analysed data'...Taking autoethnography seriously offered me a way forward without leaving behind a discipline I love... instead of leaving Psychology to pursue autoethnography, it's time to bring Autoethnography to psychology.

While in a magnificent manifesto text where he argues for an urgent need to develop the *Psychological Humanities* to balance the longstanding dominance of mainstream scientific psychology, Mark Freeman asserts that,

> ...Psychology – at its best – is often carried out by people who aren't psychologists. They're writers (and others) who are so fascinated and intrigued by life that they devote their lives to exploring it (our brackets).
>
> *(Freeman, 2024, p. 4)*

Freeman trenchantly argues throughout his text that, although of course necessary and important, scientific psychology has colonised, tidied up, sanitised, and reduced human experience and behaviour to a narrow range to fit with its longstanding presuppositions, assumptions, and disciplinary activities. This leaves much of what we value and celebrates in human living – the richness and the variety of life, from the mundane to the extraordinary, from the actual to the imaginary – out of its purview through being ignored, trivialised, sidelined, and seen as irrelevant or contaminating. In consequence, as we will discuss further below, subjectivity is regarded as an irritant by many hard-nosed psychological positivists, with stories based on lived experience often pejoratively labelled 'anecdata' or (that, dismissive, policing, aggressive, and silencing word) 'BIASED!' Freeman points to the irony at the heart of this state of affairs[1]:

> ...As some of my colleagues in the Psychology Department at Holy Cross have reminded me, for about 35 years now, it's not even clear that I am a psychologist... I continue to think that it's really a weird – and, at times, positively wrong-headed and deplorable – discipline...it's been this way ever since I was an undergraduate, when I learned that the discipline had very little to do with actual people.
>
> *(2024, p. 2)*

## The Importance of Stories

Actual people are stories. As *Homo Narrans* (Fisher, 1987), there seems to be widespread universal, logically underpinned, agreement – accepted within the autoethnographic communities – that being human is a therapeutic and meaning-making, extended narrative condition (Bochner & Riggs, 2014; Christman, 2015; Erdinast-Vulcan, 2019). Autoethnographic inquiry is a storied inquiry. The American poet and social activist, Muriel Rukeyser (in Loy, 2010, p. 3) remarked that 'The universe is made of stories, not of atoms'. After opening his book with that line, Loy, a Zen scholar, qualifies it with an ironic twist (p. 3): 'Not atoms? Of course it is made of atoms. That's one of our important stories'. Loy also asserts that everything from creation myths, television soap operas, how we feel in the mornings, and planning for the weekend are the stories that make our world. Stories are indispensable to us. In an important sense, there is nothing outside of stories, and,

> If the world is made of stories, stories are not just stories. They teach us what is real, what is valuable, and what is possible. Without stories there is no way to engage with the world because there is no world, and no one to engage with it because there is no self.
>
> *(p. 3)*

Moreover, stories are arguably what mark us out as a species. The macro-historian Yuval Harari (2022), for example, asserts, that what makes humans different from all the rest of life on earth is our ability to tell them.

Stories are fundamental to the autoethnographic approach, which is in turn methodologically and schematically situated in qualitative and narrative inquiry (Grant, 2023a). As a form of writing about life-as-experienced, autoethnography has also been impacted by critical and feminist discourses. These have been vital in building sophisticated, progressive understandings of the relationship between subject and object, private and public, and self and other (Marcus, 1994; Oakley, 2010; Renders, 2014; Richardson, 2001).

## Disparaging Subjectivity

Storying life via autoethnography rests on the importance of prizing subjectivity and intersubjectivity (Grant, 2023b). So, some scrutiny needs to be given to why these phenomena have hitherto been accorded a relatively low status in psychological and mental health research:

> Why has so little attention been given to subjectivity…many…feel repelled or threatened by the unruly content of subjective experiences. They shy away from the investigation of subjectivity in much the same fashion that individuals avoid unpleasant or dangerous activities. Subjectivity can be both unpleasant and dangerous: unpleasant because emotional, cognitive, and physical experiences frequently concern events that, in spite of their importance, are deemed
>
> Inappropriate topics for polite society…; dangerous because the workings of subjectivity seem to contradict so much of the rational-actor world-view…
>
> *(Ellis & Flaherty, 1992, p. 1)*

It's easy to see why an investment in 'the rational-actor world-view' continues to hold sway, since much of current mainstream psychology, and conventional understandings of mental health more widely, are premised on this investment. However, the question of why subjectivity is disparaged in favour of (implied) objectivity is still not fully answered in the above quote. Perhaps most pressingly, the question is begged as to what political, economic, and institutional forces are at play in sidelining subjectivity in the service of driving and shaping what is meant by 'objectivity'?

## Political and Economic Forces

Denzin and Giardina (2006) and Goodall (2010) recognise – in Goodall's terms – 'a pattern of bias' (p. 129) against qualitative research in general in the US, the UK, and Australia. These authors link this pattern to the challenge to academic scholarship made by conservative governmental forces in these countries. According to Denzin and Giardina, this gives rise in a circular way to the assumption that what constitutes worthwhile science is that which supports a right-wing political agenda. Good science on those terms mirrors a conservative view of reality while also claiming disinterested objectivity. For Goodall, this is seamlessly linked to the corporate business model of universities, where measurable returns on financial investments are expected. He argues that this model drives 'the engines of change throughout academic culture' for 'programs, faculty, and curricula', with money as the bottom line determining the future, neo-liberalised, direction of universities (pp. 129–130).

Reinforced by what Poulos (2017, p. 308) describes as the 'corporate colonisation of the lifeworld' of autoethnographic scholars by the neoliberal academy, resulting in the autoethnographic voice often being seen to have transgressed the status quo (see e.g., Grant, 2024b, p. 116; Poulos, 2010), such economically and politically driven patterns of bias are still at play internationally. They have an obvious detrimental effect on the perceived respectability and acceptance of much-needed subjectivity- and lived experience-valuing, non-positivist methodologies, including of course autoethnography.

## Autoethnography

So, what is autoethnography?

> Autoethnography is a form of narrative qualitative inquiry (*qualitative inquiry that tells a story*) which values subjectivity, emotions, relationships with others, and epiphany (*important sudden realisations – 'lightbulb moments'*) and other personal experiences as research resources. **The approach connects the autobiographical with the socio-cultural.** This is done in ways that combine the creative aesthetic sensibilities of the humanities (*languages and literatures, the arts, history, and philosophy*) with human and social science respect for (*theory and*) empirical data (*verifiable by observation and experience*).
> 
> *(Grant, 2019, p. 88, brackets and bold print added)*

Let's unpack and expand this definition. Autoethnographic inquiry:

- Belongs to qualitative rather than quantitative-experimental research;
- Is more concerned about feelings, meanings, and values than numbers;

- Aims more for emotional and human connection, hope and social justice rather than the raw fact provision of information – although social and human science theory and empirical data are often included in autoethnographic work, when and where necessary.
- Enables researchers, practitioners, and readers to address and connect with what it feels like, and what it means, to be alive and moving along lived-through experiences.
- Fuses the social and human sciences with the humanities – with literature, art, philosophy, dramatic performance, storytelling, and poetry. It can be text-based – in book, book chapter and article form – or more explicitly arts-based (see, e.g., Grant & Young, 2022).

Turning to what's meant by culture and the social in autoethnography, whereas the social might be understood as society in broad terms – people connecting in random and planned social configurations – 'culture' points more to the specific local ways of meaning-making organised life within which people are entangled – for example families, jobs, work organisations, political affiliations, clubs, etc.

A striking feature of culture is the difference between how things are and how things should be (Grant, 2019). People in general often tend to think that how things are – the descriptive sense of culture – is how things should be in its normative sense. However, for many people, how things are doesn't square with how things should be! Autoethnography gives researchers the opportunity to make the culturally familiar strange; and interrogate and challenge the culturally taken-for-granted.

In challenging culture, autoethnography prizes reflexive writing about lived experience, subjective knowledge, and understandings. It rescues what is sometimes called 'thick', or detailed, descriptions of these aspects of human life from the generalised, abstract accounts conveyed in positivist psychological and mental health research. To that extent it elevates idiographic (subjective and personal) above nomothetic (objective and categorical) knowledge, making private concerns a matter of public awareness, and historical and sociological significance (Wright Mills, 1959).

## Why Is Autoethnography Useful in Psychology and Mental Health?

We are strong of the view that autoethnography is a powerful research approach for phenomenological psychology (what it is like to be...?, what it is like to have this experience?); psychological therapeutics (what it is like to deliver and be in receipt of counselling and psychotherapy?); and critical psychology (what is wrong with dominant models and orthodoxies?; what's the difference between reality 'objectively' described from a third person perspective and lived-through, first person reality?); and for critical mental health (what is wrong with mainstream mental health?; and again, what's the difference between reality 'objectively' described from a third person perspective and lived-through, first person reality?)? Psychologists, and mental health workers more generally, who engage with these questions will hopefully develop a greater understanding and empathy for lived-through experience as a valued and valuable epistemic resource.

What's also clear to us is that – arguably most pressingly important for mental health research – autoethnographic inquiry has a key role to play in remedying the negative impact on the voices of individuals resulting from an over-reliance on objective, at the expense of subjective, inquiry. In this regard, two related concepts stand out as important: *epistemic injustice* (Fricker, 2007) and *misrecognition*. Epistemic injustice refers to the harm done to people when their status as valuable producers of knowledge is undermined. In the mental health context, for example, the framework of epistemic injustice sheds analytic light on the unfair loss of credibility that ensues from people having a psychiatric diagnosis. Moreover, it highlights the lack of a publicly available and fully validated language through which such people can understand their experiences in non-biomedical, non-pathologising terms. All of this links to misrecognition, where people lose viable identity through being trapped in devalued and stigmatised identities.

## Concluding Comments

Having, hopefully, set out the stall of our volume sufficiently, we hope that this entices you into it, dear reader. We resisted the style, often seen in edited qualitative research volumes, of grouping chapters into thematic categories, since each chapter contains multiple themes, with multiple points of intersection between chapters. Instead, we have presented them in alphabetical order, according to author's surname You will, no doubt, form your own category groupings based on your interests and selective reading pattern. This is a book that can be dipped into at any point according to your inclination, or, of course, read from cover to cover. It will be a valuable resource for us and for our contributors for the foreseeable future, and we hope that this will also be the case for you.

## Note

1 Professor Mark Freeman, of the College of the Holy Cross, Worcester, Massachusetts, has made significant contributions in the areas of: narrative psychology; aesthetic, religious, and transcendental experiences; the poetic

dimension of psychological experience – all in the context of developing Psychological Humanities. His work bridges philosophy, psychology, and creativity, enriching understandings of the human experience. (Mark P. Freeman | College of the Holy Cross)

## References

Bochner, A.P., & Riggs, N.A. (2014). Practicing narrative inquiry. In P. Leavy (Ed.), *The Oxford handbook of qualitative research* (pp. 195–222). Oxford University Press.

Carson, J., & Niklasson, M. (2023). The struggle to get a PhD: The collaborative autoethnographic accounts of two journeymen. *Journal of Further and Higher Education, 47*(5), 607–618. https://doi.org/10.1080/0309877X2023.2222363

Chang, H. (2008). *Autoethnography as method*. Routledge.

Christman, J. (2015). Telling our own stories: Narrative selves and oppressive circumstance. In C. Cowley (Ed.), *The philosophy of autobiography* (pp. 122–140). The University of Chicago Press.

Denzin, N.K., & Giardina, M.D. (2006). Introduction: Qualitative inquiry and the conservative challenge. In N.K. Denzin & M.D. Giardina (Eds.), *Qualitative inquiry and the conservative challenge* (pp. ix–x). Left Coast Press.

Ellis, C., & Flaherty, M. (1992). An agenda for the interpretation of lived experience. In C. Ellis & M.G. Flaherty (Eds.), *Investigating subjectivity: Research on lived experience* (pp. 1–13). SAGE Publications, Inc.

Erdinast-Vulcan, D. (2019). Heterobiography: A Bakhtinian perspective on autobiographical writing. In D.L. LeMahieu & C. Cowley (Eds.), *Philosophy and life writing* (pp. 108–125). Routledge.

Fisher, W. (1987). *Human communication as narration: Toward a philosophy of reason, value, and action*. University of South Carolina Press.

Freeman, M. (2012). Thinking and being otherwise: Aesthetics, ethics, erotics. *Journal of Theoretical and Philosophical Psychology, 32*(4), 196–208. https://psycnet.apa.org/doi/10.1037/a0029586

Freeman, M. (2024). *Toward the psychological humanities: A modest manifesto for the future of psychology*. Routledge.

Fricker, M. (2007). *Epistemic injustice: Power and the ethics of knowing*. Oxford University Press.

Gonot-Schoupinsky, F., Neal, M., & Carson, J. (2024). Is laughter really the best medicine? Reflecting on a mental health initiative using pragmatic collaborative autoethnography. *Journal of Applied Social Science, 18*(1), 19–31. https://doi.org/10.1177/19367244231195059

Goodall, H.L. (2010). *Counter narrative: How progressive academics can challenge extremists and promote social justice*. Left Coast Press.

Grant, A. (2019). Dare to be a wolf: Embracing autoethnography in nurse educational research. *Nurse Education Today, 82*, 88–92. https://doi.org/10.1016/j.nedt.2019.07.006

Grant, A. (2022). What has autoethnography got to offer mental health nursing? *British Journal of Mental Health Nursing: Autoethnography and Mental Health Nursing Supplement, 11*(4), 4–11. https://doi.org/10.12968/bjmh.2022.0035

Grant, A. (2023a). Crafting and recognising good enough autoethnographies: A practical guide and checklist. *Mental Health and Social Inclusion, 27*(3), 196–209. https://doi.org/10.1108/MHSI-01-2023-0009

Grant, A. (2023b). In praise of subjectivity: My involvement with autoethnography, and why I think you should be interested. *Social Work and Social Sciences Review, 23*(3), 66–79. https://doi.org/10.1921/swssr.v23i3.2151

Grant, A. (2024a). Introduction: The philosophical autoethnographer. In A. Grant (Ed.), *Writing philosophical autoethnography* (pp. 1–22). Routledge.

Grant, A. (2024b). In search of my narrative character. In A. Grant (Ed.), *Writing philosophical autoethnography* (pp. 114–132). Routledge.

Grant, A. (2024c). Concluding thoughts: Selves, cultures, limitations, futures. In A. Grant (Ed.), *Writing philosophical autoethnography* (pp. 249–269). Routledge.

Grant, A., & Young, S. (2022). Troubling Tolichism in several voices: Resisting epistemic violence in creative analytical and critical autoethnographic practice. *Journal of Autoethnography, 3*(1), 103–117. E-ISSN 2637–5192 https://doi.org/10.1525/joae.2022.3.1.103

Grant, A., & Young, S. (2024). A Scot an' a sassenach scrieve aboot leid: A three pairt scotoethnography (a Scot and an English person write about language: A scotoethnography in three parts). *Journal of Autoethnography, 5*(1), 39–55. https://doi.org/10.1525/joae.2024.5.1.39

Hadjiosif, M. (2023). Let there be chaos: Miltos Hadjiosif makes the case for autoethnography, in its image, and introduces a set of pieces from his students. *The Psychologist,* 9 August 2023. Let there be chaos | BPS

Harari, Y.N. (2022). *Unstoppable us, volume 1: How humans took over the world.* Puffin.

Hurst, R., & Carson, J. (2021). Be honest: Why did you decide to study psychology? *Psychology Teaching Review, 27*(2), 22–35.

Kafar, M. (2021). Traveling with Carolyn Ellis and Art Bochner, or how I became harmonized with the autoethnographic life: An autoformative story. In T.E. Adams, R.M. Boylorn, & L.M. Tillmann (Eds.), *Advances in autoethnography and narrative inquiry: Reflections on the legacy of Carolyn Ellis and Arthur Bochner* (pp. 48–63). Routledge.

Loy, D.R. (2010). *The world is made of stories.* Wisdom Publications.

Marcus, L. (1994). *Autoe/biographical discourses.* Manchester University Press.

Oakley, A. (2010). The social science of biographical life-writing: Some methodological and ethical issues. *International Journal of Social Research Methodology, 13*(5), 425–439. https://doi.org/10.1080/13645571003593583

Poulos, C.N. (2010). Transgressions. *International Review of Qualitative Research, 3*(1), 67–88.

Poulos, C.N. (2017). Under pressure. *Cultural Studies Critical Methodologies, 17*(4), 308–315. https://doi.org/10.1177/1532708617706122

Qasim, K., & Carson, J. (2022). Post-traumatic growth: Does one autoethnographic account make a summer? *Cruse Bereavement Support, 1*(1), 1–9.

Renders, H. (2014). Biography in academia and the critical frontier in life writing. In H. Renders & B. de Haan (Eds.), *Theoretical discussions of biography: Approaches from history, microhistory, and life writing* (pp. 216–221). Brill.

Richardson, L. (2001). Getting personal: Writing-stories. *International Journal of Qualitative Studies in Education, 14*(1), 33–38. https://doi.org/10.1080/09518390010007647

Richardson, L., & St. Pierre, E.A. (2018). Writing: A method of inquiry. In N.K. Denzin & Y.S. Lincoln (Eds.), *The SAGE handbook of qualitative research* (5th ed., pp. 818–838). Sage Publications.

Sparkes, A.C. (2024). Autoethnography as an ethically contested terrain: Some thinking points for consideration. *Qualitative Research in Psychology.* Open Access, online version, 1–32. https://doi.org/10.1080/14780887.2023.2293073

Stevenson, V., & Carson, J. (1995). The pastoral myth of the mental hospital: A personal account. *International Journal of Social Psychiatry, 41*(2), 147–151.

Teo, T. (2017). From psychological science to the psychological humanities: Building a general theory of subjectivity. *Review of General Psychology, 21*(4), 281–291. https://doi.org/10.1037/gpr0000132

Wright Mills, C. 2000[1959]. *The sociological imagination.* Oxford University Press, Inc.

# 2

# US AND THEM

*Kevin Acott*

## Introduction

February 2023. It was cold and wet, and I had a day off. An off day. I was sitting in a coffee shop in Crouch End and looking at the Guardian app. I was feeling particularly middle-class, and, as ever, not quite comfortable with where I was or what I was or who I was. I started reading an article about bailiffs and how their business was booming right now, right now in the middle of this energy crisis, this government-made, Putin-blamed energy crisis. That word – 'bailiffs' – jerked me abruptly back to being eight, nine, ten, and to my mum's tearful, angry yelling at my dad: 'They're coming tomorrow! They'll take all the bloody furniture!' I didn't know what bailiffs were then, but I knew from the tone of her voice they weren't good. And I knew I couldn't imagine life without chairs, or a bed, or a couch, or a table. Or – most importantly – a gramophone. No Sweet, no Slade, no life.

So, I sat there in that caff, thrown back to the early '70s, and then I realised. Life felt like that again. Ever since I'd turned 60 last year, I'd felt – off and on – like I was waiting for the bailiffs to come. Only this time the bailiffs were going to take me away altogether. Or, rather, the singular bailiff. The Grim Bailiff. In a few years (if I was lucky), there would be one last knock on the door and that would be it. They'd take my soul and, presumably, all my memories, all the good I'd done, all the bad, and they'd stick it in a pawn shop, put the better stuff up for auction. My partner, my kids, my mates, my colleagues; they'd all keep some of me. But most of me would disappear.

I wondered then (as I'd been doing more and more over the last year) whether any of my ... what should I call them? ... patients/service users/

DOI: 10.4324/9781003408963-2

clients/people-who-often-seemed-to-be-in-my-life-just-to-teach-me-stuff-I-would-immediately-forget... I wondered whether any of them would remember me. And, if they did, whether, on balance, those memories would be good ones.

The answers lie in stories, I suspect. In the story, Mental Health Nursing tells itself. In the stories, I've told myself and others about Mental Health Nursing. In the ways in which the culture has influenced how I hear and have made sense of the stories the people we call patients have told me. I mention in the third document I'll be looking at here Galen Strawson's ideas about narrative (Strawson, 2004). He says, 'It's just not true that there is only one good way for human beings to experience their being in time. There are deeply non-Narrative people and there are good ways to live that are deeply non-Narrative' (Strawson, 2004, p. 429). I'll attempt to show how trying to understand the shifts between what he calls the 'episodic' and the 'diachronic', has helped me make a little more sense of stories, of the way in which the profession's stories about itself have influenced me and produced both the best and the worst of human interaction. In all three documents/stories to be explored, in all phases of my life, I think, perhaps, I've overemphasised the need for development of a coherent story (the dia-chronic) – *my* story, a past in which I'm the key character – when what matters is the here and now, episodic, experiencing of moments, of interactions, of experiences, the full integration/dissolution of myself with this person, this circumstance, at this time.

So how to describe this to you? I think (and I'm only realising this as I write) the answers lie, perhaps, in dialectics, in the ways in which synthesis can be found in both recognising the need for full experiencing of those episodes (past, present and future) as enough in themselves AND by creating a meaningful story (with a main, linking protagonist (me), with antagonists (Mental Health Nursing) and with plot and conflict and setting and some kind of neat resolution). I was briefly tempted to try to undo some of the tremendous harms I've seen myself and Mental Health Nursing do by playing a game and making a 'patient' – all 'patients' – the main protagonist of this story. But there's a misconception, I think, in the superficially 'person-centred' approaches still hegemonic in Mental Health Nursing (or at least in Mental Health Nursing academia). This is that 'patients' are different, are 'them' and not 'us', that mental health problems automatically both raise someone up to be a better human being than a 'professional' (who, of course, has no mental health problems) and separates them from the economic, political, and ideological chains that bind all of us. They become individuals with an internal life and consequent behaviour that starts off as a mystery, one to be 'assessed' into visibility and comprehension by us experts. The first draft of this Chapter barely directly mentioned patients' experiences. That doesn't necessarily mean I'm a bad Mental Health Nurse, or don't care about 'patients'. But it does mean part of me sees my story as just my story, the key interactions being between me and Mental Health Nursing. But, of course, that's not true.

So, I'm not going to do that, I'm not going to make a 'patient' my central character. But I'm going to use random fragments *and* a timeline to try and shed light on our interweaving journeys: Mental Health Nursing, the people it's meant to help, and me.

## The Stories

I'm coming to the end of my career, a bumpy, rock-strewn, occasionally wonderful trek that started in 1984 when I became (because I wasn't good enough to play for Spurs and because I could never get beyond a clunky G, C, D – and sometimes Em – on the cheap acoustic guitar I've now kept with me for 50 years) a Mental Health Nurse. I'm coming to the end of that career and I'm wondering what the bailiffs – or, maybe more accurately, the house clearance blokes – are going to find to take away with them.

I've wondered a lot over the years if I should have turned round and walked away the moment, I realised there was a callous misanthropy, an inherent sadism amongst many of the nurses I first met at Broadmoor. I wondered whether there was real truth in my lazy half-joke, 'I prefer the patients there to the staff'. And I'm wondering now if I can use this piece – use you, the reader, and my interactions with you – to make some sense out of the mess of experiences, out of the dozen different cultures and the dozen different ways of being me that I crafted and reacted to in order to fit, and to not fit, and to survive, and to 'do good'. I'm wondering if that smugness I half-felt for years – a semi-conscious sense of superiority, because some of the people I went to school with were solicitors, or accountants, or worked in banks or were in IT, were not actually being good and kind or … 'making a difference' – was ever justified.

In this examination of the mess (my own and that all around me, the mess I tried to steal from, the mess that tried to steal from me), I'm going to look at three documents I've produced. First, an article I wrote in about 2006 for a now-long-disappeared Psychology website Second, a PowerPoint slide I put together in 2017 that was attempting to connect the ideas and ideologies that had impacted on my work and on the rest of my life. Third a book chapter I wrote in 2020, in which I tried to examine the impact of Covid, especially the influence of fear and of the key existential human factors of meaninglessness, isolation, freedom, and death.

I look back now on each of these odd creations, and I recognise both truths and lies. Throughout my adult life, I've flirted with a broadly, vaguely humanistic/libertarian left-wing approach to the world and to the game of mental health nursing. In the last few years, I've returned, to much more solidly understand things in class terms, in dialectical terms, in Marxist terms, in terms of seeing the material as more important than the ideal, the superstructure of ideas and culture as being built upon and dictated by the economic base. And I'll be examining my three strange babies through that prism. I've no idea, really, where I'm going with all this, but I think my story will be different at the end. And I hope it makes you feel something. And if you do, that it's a good feeling.

Sometimes I think understanding the world, particularly the world of mental health nursing, is all about resolving tensions, about trying to find syntheses for all these dialectics: optimism/hopelessness; selflessness/self-ishness; certainty/uncertainty; evidence/intuition; art/science; doubt/confidence; theory/practice; nursing/other professions; training/education; acceptance/change ... and a dozen others. I discovered the work of Martin Buber very late on in the writing of this piece. It emerged as I was exploring issues of empathy, trying to find something coherent to say about that awkward, slippery, overused, misunderstood concept. As I've put this together, I've realised that that, perhaps, is the theme that sums up Mental Health Nursing's – and my own – problems: the constant battle between I–Thou relationships and I–It ones. And the constant retelling of stories.

Let's see what happens...

### Story 1 2006.

### Extracts from

### 'Slaying the giant: Mental health nursing: A personal reflection'

*I'm a Spurs fan. They routinely let me down, promising all and delivering little, but I could never stop supporting them, however much I wanted to – it's in my blood. Mental Health Nursing, on the other hand...*

*I've been a mental health nurse for twenty-odd years now. A lot of my closest friends are mental health nurses. Many of the most compassionate, wisest, funniest, and astonishingly effective people I've ever met have been mental health nurses. But I feel I've had enough. Had enough of over-stating the worth of our 'profession'. Had enough of squaring circles, blunting the sharpness of the contradictions. Had enough of sometimes railing against, sometimes just ignoring the poor care we so often provide; the half-hearted education and training we frequently offer and undertake; the absence of any convincing research base to what we do; the passive-aggressive stance we take towards patients and our colleagues in other professions; our determined anti-intellectualism; our lack of curiosity, the obstinately vague 'humanistic' anti-rationalism inherent in so much of what we do. (Each of those things is true – to an extent – of mental health services as a whole, of course. But each is especially true of nurses).*

*The roots of this piece (and of my slowly-deepening ambivalence towards Mental Health Nursing) lie way back in the early eighties and in working with nurses in a Special Hospital who despised the patients they were meant to be caring for, expressing in physical and emotional abuse and a profound institutionalised (and personalised) neglect. My attitude has its genesis in receiving death threats from other nurses after complaining about assaults on patients, and in smaller, but no less telling, experiences such as sitting in a ward round as a student, watching a Consultant humiliated first his (male) SHO and then – with added venom – the (female) staff nurse, who waited till afterwards to regain some self-respect by shouting at a (male) HCA, who bided his time before verbally abusing a (female) 'PD' patient. Yeah – I could tell you a hundred stories: and every mental health nurse reading this – everyone – will have their own tales of witnessing attack and contempt and destructiveness.*

*But this casual abuse and misuse of others – and our own continuing self-abuse – wasn't abandoned there, in the days of Thatcher and Duran Duran. Nor is it by any means the whole story of our failings as a profession…*

> 'I've got no time to listen to patients, I've got too much work to do'.
> A mental health nurse.

*The very existence of 'Mental Health Nurses' had long reinforced, it seemed to me, all that was wrong and damaging and abusive in mental health care, not least its frightened, controlling nature, its territorialism, its racism and sexism, its power imbalances, its insistence on a medical model based on flimsy and illusory foundations. If the most powerful groupings in mental health care – managers, psychologists and psychiatrists – could just incorporate, though, what we nurses always claim we do, and develop mutually-influential relationships founded on a genuine validation of distress, a search for pragmatic solutions, on empathy, warmth, genuineness and respect (with colleagues as well as with 'patients'). If they would only loosen (with our help) their gender- and class-bound arrogance; their obsessive desire to monitor and control; their need to work with people while employing dubious science. And if they would only become more like us … well, then things might improve. Nurses and psychiatrists and psychologists would grow, new professions might emerge, we'd no longer be hidebound by our need to identify with historically-determined, mutually-loathing tribes. Mental Health Nursing would eventually disappear, and mental health nursing – a non-professionally-aligned, intuitive and informed collaborative venture, scientific, caring, curious, informed by empathy and evidence – would replace it, not only in inpatient environments but across the whole field of mental health care.*

*Perhaps. Interviews I undertook for an inpatient research project suggested many patients felt strongly that the most caring and effective people working on that unit – the people most prepared to listen and to respect them and to help them – were psychiatrists and psychologists. The findings also suggested the existence of a disturbing phenomenon we never seem to want to get to grips with: an open (though rarely published or researched) acknowledgement that, in our profession – and among our students – there are many people who just don't care, don't want to care, and who approach their job and any studies with a complete absence of either curiosity or compassion. This dispiriting, denying vacuum is one that seems less overt in Psychiatry and Psychology, and Occupational Therapy and Social Work (though is certainly one mirrored in the often nurse-dominated 'profession' of management), despite those professions' continual stereotyping by nurses as somehow overbearing, arrogant, posh, and uncaring.*

*I had my pat answers for these disquieting phenomena, not least the usual it's-everyone-else's-fault stuff we nurses trot out about a lack of time, a lack of space, a lack of 'support', a lack of supervision: the doctrine of learned helplessness as justification for poor care. 'The Bad Nurse' was – obviously! – an aberration, their equivalent present in all occupations: the old 'bad apple' idea that lets us all off the hook. Plausible psychodynamic explanations – not least Tom Main's expositions of the rage and sadism we all feel (and occasionally act-out) when someone (despite our best efforts) fails to get better – were also on hand to enable me to put all the self-doubt back on the shelf ... But I'm sure, now, I was deluding myself: there's a deeper malaise inherent in the profession, in its very 'nurseness'.*

*I was wrong, then, at least in part, in my reactions to people like Phil Barker's insistence that we should more assertively stand up for our profession. I was denying the compassion and curiosity of our colleagues in other professions whilst minimising the toxins in our own. And it was, perhaps, a typical nurse's self-deception to insist on others changing first: the same results (the development of genuine nursing and the elimination of the profession) would surely emerge from an open dialogue led by nurses, an exchange in which, rather than take on Barker's robust over-stating of our importance, his attempt to solidify our position, we started to acknowledge and address – publicly, openly and honestly – our intellectual and emotional shortcomings. To learn, in other words, from the strengths of others and deliberately, consciously dilute that position, in the process (perhaps) diluting the self-seeking positions of Psychiatry and Psychology and Occupational Therapy and Social Work and enhancing the position of 'patients'.*

\*\*\*

*The question may be this: how can we as a profession best help develop a more caring, more effective mental health system? And the answer may be we can help by ceasing to be a profession that chases an illusory academic credibility; that keeps defending itself; that keeps leaping on government bandwagons; that keeps trying to justify itself with spurious appeals to concepts like 'the therapeutic relationship;' that denies the existence of The Bad Nurse; that clings to a meaningless caricature of Freud or Rogers or Beck. and/or ... the answer may simply be: we can help by ceasing to be a profession altogether.*

* * *

2006. It feels like another lifetime, though Spurs (of course) are still letting me down. I do still agree with a lot of that article. And disagree with some. I'm sitting here now wondering why I'm *still* part of a system so seemingly broken, so malevolent. But, also, I'm wondering why I don't actually care as much anymore if Mental Health Nursing exists or doesn't exist as a distinct profession.

When I first re-read that piece a few weeks ago, 17 years older and a lot balder, I wanted to edit it, to improve the 2006 me, make him less pompous, less didactic, and above all (I think) happier... I wanted to make it look like I'd actually talked much more back then about the experience of the people we're meant to be helping; and I wanted to have talked about my own life, my own fears, my own 'disorders', and how they influenced the care of the people I worked with, the people I was supposed to help. I wanted the reader to think I'd actually talked so much more about the inner experience of the undocumented refugee on my ward who'd set fire to himself; about the experiences of the young man who'd jumped off a tall building and survived, never to walk again; the recently retired man who hanged himself in the woods I used to love walking in; the experiences of the young woman with whom I'd burned the abusive letters her stalker had sent her, and those of the well-known musician who told me I'd saved his life, even though I'd spent 6-hour-long sessions with him while I felt utterly useless, blundering through conversations in which I'd felt overwhelmed by his feeling of being overwhelmed... I fear that I didn't deal with those things in the article enough because of my disquiet that I was part of an oppressive system. And because it's a system, a culture, that says all the right things but rarely acts in the right way, a culture that encourages the disingenuous and the partial. Maybe mentioning those episodes, those intimate connections with others, the good and the bad, 15 years later can help synthesise them into a story – into my story (and your story about me)? And maybe the spareness of my description of those incidents can tell you a little about what Mental Health Nursing can do ... and what it should do. Maybe I can give voice to the man in the woods, whose story I never really knew, but whose pain I'd felt so strongly whenever I saw him?

---

'He's very clever for a nurse'. (Consultant Psychiatrist to a Ward Sister, who proudly passed it on to me).

---

By 2006, I'd shifted from being a Community Mental Health Nurse to 'Practice Development Facilitator' (what a terrible, telling job title!) to a Lecturer in Mental Health Nursing. Alongside the University work, I was still involved in clinical practice, working therapeutically with people diagnosed with borderline personality disorder. I enjoyed the work, the challenge, the sense of being part of a team that worked hard and compassionately, that really made a difference. I felt useful, I knew I was pretty good at what I was doing. I felt this was maybe my niche, this was maybe what I wanted to do with my life. It wasn't nursing, though, as more than one person pointed out, it was, as another nurse suggested, 'more like being a psychologist'. Psychologists do all the girly, fluffy, clever stuff. Nurses do the tough, more macho, more practical stuff. I knew, of course, I could be both, that there was a hard, male, working-class part of me, and that there was a more reflective, softer, sensitive part of me. I was a lower-middle-class kid who went to a grammar school, selected for my brightness/as a well-intentioned piece of social engineering. And that dialectic – there in so many of us, that clash of internalised stereotypes – meant I never felt like I'd fitted, from early schooldays on. My desire to do something that helped others emerged in part, I think, from that tension: most of all, I suspect, I wanted to help myself. I didn't feel 'good enough' to be a doctor or psychologist or historian when I was 18, 19 or 20 (I didn't feel academically clever enough, and I knew I wouldn't quite fit socially with them – I'm not sure which was more important). I wanted to be a music writer, really, but I didn't think I could ever write as passionately and cleverly and confidently as my heroes – Marcus, Bangs, Burchill, Morley, Penman – and so I drifted and drifted until the social worker sister of a girl I fancied told me I should 'do something' with my life...

No degree, no self-confidence, no direction ... so I applied to be a Mental Health Nurse, targeting Broadmoor because ... because it had a certain (macho) glamour AND I could be kind, do good as well. It could, maybe, though I didn't think of it in this way then, help me synthesise those two parts of me. After all, people were weirdly impressed when I said I was going to do my training at Broadmoor ... aren't the Krays there? Isn't the Yorkshire Ripper?

The thing is, I always did genuinely feel more comfortable with patients than with staff at Broadmoor. When I've been helpful in my subsequent career, when I've felt proud to be a Mental Health Nurse, I think it's been because of empathy, because of identification. When I've felt angry and disillusioned, as I did when I wrote that article, it's because I recognise both my limits in terms of empathy, my own uncomfortable sense of power over others AND my own sense of 'mental disorder', of not being whole enough, open enough to the world as it is, functioning enough, happy enough.

What was missing here in the article too was class, I think, and the identification or distancing it leads to. The key difference between the Broadmoor nurse and the Broadmoor doctor: social class. And the key similarity between the mental health nurse and the patient: social class. It explains a lot of the toxic power dynamics in both exchanges. And it explains in part the constant backwards-and-forwards between what Buber (2013), writing in 1923, terms *I–Thou* relationships (in which we leap into the experience of others while staying accessible) and those he says are *I–It* ones (in which we stay detached, separate).

Seventeen years on, the piece exemplifies much of what I still think. I'm still involved. I'm still here, in this bent, twisted system. But that understanding of class is different. I think I was talking back then more about a more liberal view of class. I think now (in an often contradictory, almost-dialectic way) in terms of a more Marxist one. I think we can all be stratified in different ways – according to education, to income, to role and to status – but ultimately there are those with real power, those who still own the means of production and maintain control of it through what the Marxist philosopher Althusser (2014) referred to as both 'repressive' and 'ideological' state apparatuses. My worry is that I've been part of reproducing an often-brutal system that acts on occasion as both repressive (in its use of legal ways of detaining those considered dangerous or threatening) and ideological (in its use of an individualised, pseudo-scientific, placement of distress within damaged individuals, rather than in recognising it as emerging from inequalities in society as a whole).

Soon after writing the article, I ran a workshop on the then-mushrooming ideology of 'Recovery'. There were clinicians, service users, carers, and educators there. I emphasised hope and optimism (the ideology had originally developed as a reaction to the negativity of the medical model that consigned so many, particularly those diagnosed with 'schizophrenia', to a lifelong, 'chronic' condition, in which they would always be somehow less than whole, less than adequate, less than healthy, outside society). A mother of someone diagnosed with schizophrenia became really angry with me that afternoon, asking how I dared to talk about optimism and positivity when she'd seen her son deteriorate gradually, year by year by year, losing his energy, his smile, his sense of fun, his own optimism. I had no honest answer for her apart from trying to acknowledge what she was saying, but that day I shifted a little, felt myself finally letting go of the last of a naïve, hopeful humanism, a 'person-centredness' I'd been clinging on to in the face of knowing there was a black, black heart to so much of mental health care, to 'service users'' lives, to professionals' lives, to human beings. I hope so much that mother and her son are living lives in which there are episodes of laughter and hope. But, as you know, life's not always that positive.

### Story 2: The Big Showoffy Ideas Thing: 2019

So much to say about this one. But I'll just pick a couple of elements (Figure 2.1). I constructed it for me. I'm always – always – trying to create this smooth, diachronic story, one in which I – the hero – progresses, develops, overcomes obstacles, solves everything. But I'm also always – always – uncertain. I showed my younger daughter this once (and soon realised it only meant sense to me), but never anyone else – I think I was trying to explain myself by doing it, and to understand myself simultaneously (just as I'm doing now with this chapter). Every now and then, I've read something, been taught something, stumbled across something, and I've felt – briefly – that this thing, this idea or set of ideas could allow me to fill in the gaps, understand. Those that have been most significant I added to this PowerPoint slide: politics, philosophy, religion, spirituality. I think all these things are inescapable if you're working in Mental Health. And finding that intellectual coherence (whilst accepting uncertainty) should be part of our daily struggle. But it's not, not consciously anyway.

You see, I long so much for clarity, for a single, coherent explanation of the world and my place in it whilst at the same time rejecting the certainties, the easy answers most ideologies in mental health care offer. I envy-ists of any type. I envy those who have strong spiritual or political beliefs. I envy those who believe in a medical view of mental disorder. I envy those who see everything as a plot, that see mental health nurses, say, purely as agents of control. I envy those who have settled into the world with acceptance, those who have made sense, even if that sense is that there is no sense, even if the conclusion is, ultimately, a nihilistic one. And I wonder how much envy informs the whole culture of mental health nursing.

Re-looking at this presentation just now, I felt a bit of a fraud. My first thought (the voice of those around me when I was a kid?) was that I'm showing off (perhaps another reason not to share it with anyone). The second – not entirely true – is that I don't *really* understand any of these models, theories, ideas.

I think perhaps Mental Health Nursing academics have a double, if not triple sense of fraud anyway. We're teaching a non-academic subject to

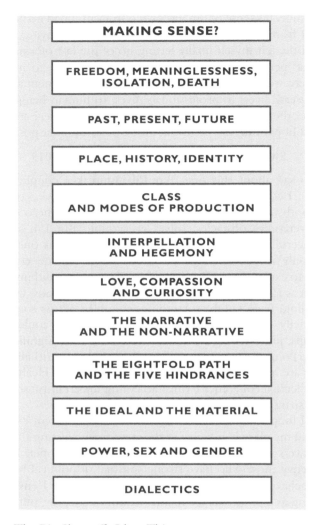

**FIGURE 2.1** The Big Showoffy Ideas Thing.

non-academic students and we really don't belong in academia. Nursing is a cash cow for universities, but it doesn't have academic respect from them, or even from its own profession. Mental Health Nursing is trying to be (actually is, I think) the most *academic* strand of nurse training, but isn't accepted (as it isn't either in practice) even by other nurses as real nursing. Not a proper nurse; not a proper academic. How we, Mental Health Nursing academics, make the most of that sometimes!

And there's something else: a good friend of mine, probably the best teacher I've ever worked with, left clinical work, and became a lecturer. He said he now frequently felt like a World War One general, safe, and well-fed way behind the battlefield, sending young soldiers over the top to do something he could never have done. My friend saw himself as a failure clinically – those who can, do ... but actually he was loved by his patients, and he was the most truly empathic person I've ever met. But he chose to teach well, teach guiltily, because Mental Health Nursing couldn't contain, or support, his passion. (And I saw him, coincidentally, last week and he said 'the best mental health nurses are all a bit odd' and I agreed, absolutely, with him...).

I've decided I'm going to do something different, something out of character, now: I'm a little bit proud of this slide – it's evidence of my continuing curiosity; it's evidence that I'm trying to find ways to understand who I am and how I can be a better person. And its evidence, I think, that those elements are there, in Mental Health Nursing. We just need to make them available to the people who need them.

And now I'm going to move quickly on before I change my mind...

### Story 3: Extracts from 'At Any Instant:
### Fear, Hope and Love in a Time of Fragmentation'. 2020.

I agree with a lot of what I wrote here, too, in a chapter of a book I helped edit. But when I re-read just now it, it helped rescue me from the negativity the first two stories had left me with.

Here are some of the key elements for me now, three years on:

*There are, of course, no easy solutions to the awful emotional, cognitive, social, political, economic, and spiritual dilemmas we find ourselves facing. I certainly don't think we should merely be looking for opportunities, be seeing this crisis as a way of resetting the world, of building the utopia we always dreamed of, nor do I think we should be giving in entirely too some kind of nihilistic despair. Brennecke and Amick's seductive hedonistic phrase, "Life is a gift. Take it, unwrap it, appreciate it, use it, and enjoy it," is cited by Yalom (1980, p. 437), disapprovingly, and my own response to it, as I write these words while feeling like I'm drowning in fear and uncertainty, is one of irritation. And yet, maybe there is something useful we can draw from it, something worth eating in the chocolate box of that phrase?*

*Frankl (2006), who survived Auschwitz, talked about a 'tragic triad', the three struggles of guilt, suffering and death, which we all inevitably face at some point in our lives. Right now, for a lot of us, it seems each of these is both all around us and swimming wildly within us. Whatever we've previously done to try and mitigate the effects of the triad, to push them away, to pretend maybe they don't exist, to turn them into something else, is being massively tested, even ripped apart. How can we do then do what Frankl asks us to, how can we engage fully with these experiences, and begin to affirm ourselves and our reality? How can we turn suffering into a catalyst for some kind of personal progress, build opportunity from guilt, and derive from the certainty of our own death the drive to act more compassionately toward ourselves and toward others? And how can we do this without disappearing back into a pretence that what we've seen and felt and fought – what we continue to see and feel and fight – hasn't really happened, might not happen again?*

*As we struggle right now, individually, and collectively, with these questions, it may start to become clear that there are two levels to each of them, levels that intersect. We're dealing with death as a real, material fact and with its meaning for us, in terms of loss, grief and pain. We're dealing with isolation from each other as a real, material fact and with its meaning for us. We're dealing with 'freedom' as a real, material fact – we have choices, choices, for example, to 'go out' or 'stay in', to lockdown or not lockdown – and we have to engage us with working out the meaning of our decisions. We're dealing with meaning itself and a fear of/knowledge of an ultimate, inherent meaninglessness – the apparent pointless, unjust, random, Godless carnage caused by the virus.*

* * *

Pema Chodron (2007, p. 57) suggests,

> *Most of the time, that warding off death is our biggest motivation … time is passing and it's as natural as the seasons changing. But getting old, sick, losing love – we don't see those events as natural. We want to ward them off, no matter what.*

*In normal times, all this is true. But then a virus comes along and death is no longer just rumbling, just at the outskirts of our lives, and we stop being so willing to let the sand slip through our fingers…*

I was sort of, just about, OK with the Kev I see here. And then I discovered I wrote this:

*Lenin, cited in Kolakowski (2005, p. 727) talks, similarly, about a 'perpetual interplay' between cause and effect, the political and the personal, the universal and the individual, the conflict, and the unity of opposites. This interplay can lead to distress, confusion, and alienation; it can also lead – as we become more conscious and aware – to positive, empowering change, for ourselves and for society as a whole.*

Yes! That's it! I think this is what I'd been searching for throughout this piece. I still feel messed up, but re-reading this has helped me find some peace. It doesn't let me off, but it does allow me to find some synthesis.

How come that passionate, brilliant, murderous man's words, that man responsible for so much mental and material suffering, has helped bring some sense, some meaning? I'd wanted my chapter in the book to act as both acknowledgement of the suffering caused by Covid, and as something that could point towards hope. I told myself I was doing this for the intended reader (health professionals), but I re-read it now and I realise again this was also a dialectic I was trying to synthesise: I want to be acknowledged and understood *and* I want to feel hope:

*Four questions have been dumped on us at birth, and are questions that, overlapping with Frankl's 'triad', we all have to avoid, confront or answer – regardless of our situation – every single day. They come and go, but they're always there, lurking. Right now, they've abruptly re-entered our lives, and intensified, with the arrival of Covid-19. The questions are, essentially:*

*How can I make sense of death?*
*How can I make sense of isolation?*
*How can I make sense of freedom?*
*How can I make sense of meaninglessness?*

*As we confront right now, individually, and collectively, these questions, it may start to become clear that there are two levels to each of them, levels that intersect. We're dealing with death as a real, material fact and with its meaning for us, in terms of loss, grief and pain. We're dealing with isolation from each other as a real, material fact and with its meaning for us. We're dealing with 'freedom' as a real, material fact – we have choices, choices, for example, to 'go out' or 'stay in', to lockdown or not lockdown – and we have to engage us with working out the meaning of our decisions. We're dealing with meaning itself and a fear of/knowledge of an ultimate, inherent meaninglessness – the apparent pointless, unjust, random, Godless carnage caused by the virus.*

*I think we could maybe benefit from trying to apply the four 'givens' to these cold, hard days, applying the challenges of Frankl and Yalom to our struggles, but in new ways. Yalom (2013, p. 31) talks about Heidegger's idea of 'authenticity' and about mindfulness. When we're 'inauthentic', we just float through life, unaware of the 'authorship of our life': it seems to just happen to us. There are times, though, where being 'inauthentic' helps me cope, maybe helps us all cope. If I'm honest, my inauthenticity at times, my avoidance and denial of what's going on has kept me going. There have been times writing this piece where I've felt a fraud: word after word masking my real desperation, the actual confusion and rage I feel. As I write, I'm trying to embrace both the value in doing so and the seeming pointlessness.*

*I know a dialectical approach here – allowing the truth in authenticity and the truth in inauthenticity – can spare us some of this struggle. But it's hard: emotion can suffocate thought almost entirely (Acott, 2020, p. 289)*

It's still a struggle, three years later. At times, *everything* can seem a struggle, emotion suffocating thought again and again, in so many ways – politically, culturally, personally. Mental Health Nursing may well be vanishing as a separate profession and I neither want that nor don't want it. I do want to continue synthesising Strawson's dialectic – his 'episodic' and his 'diachronic'. And I do want to accept myself as the unheroic protagonist in my own story *and* live in the moment.

So, to some extent, I think I've now done what my newly – found autoethnographic friends, Adams et al. (2015, pp. 1–2), would want me to do:

- I've used my personal experience to describe and critique cultural beliefs, practices, and experiences.
- I've acknowledged and valued my relationships with others.
- I've used 'deep and careful' self-reflection to name and interrogate the intersections between self and society, the particular and the general, the personal and the political.
- I've shown 'people in the process of figuring out what to do, how to live, and the meaning of their struggles'.
- I've balanced intellectual and methodological rigour, emotion and creativity.
- I've demonstrated a striving for social justice and to make life better.

I've tried to do all that (though I admit I keep wanting to 'yes but' every positive claim I made). I've related to you an episodic mish-mash: disconnected and in-the-moment and free of protagonists and antagonists. And a diachronic story, too; aware, awake, in the present, yet linking the past and the future through a consistent 'I'. I've attempted a synthesis, I hope, of the two, found truth in each, given voice to old me and new me, to the people we call 'patients', and to the professional culture that's become so much part of me.

Whether (like Strawson) you don't see yourself as a continuous, evolving character in a story, or whether (like me) you do, I hope there's been something here that can help you make sense of whatever you're trying to make sense of. I hope my partner, my friends, my kids, all the people who've accompanied me on this weird road, can get something from it too. And I really hope, when he comes, The Grim Bailiff will be leaving empty-handed.

### References

Acott, K. (2020). At any instant: Fear, hope and love in a time of fragmentation. In A. Odunlade, D. Rawcliffe, & K. Acott (Eds.), *Living with fear: Reflections on COVID-19* (pp. 287–304). Writershouse Consultancy.

Adams, T. E., Jones, S., & Ellis, C. (2015). *Autoethnography*. Oxford University Press.

Althusser, L. (2014). *On the reproduction of capitalism: Ideology and ideological state apparatuses*. Verso Books.

Buber, M. (2013). *I and thou*. Bloomsbury Academic.

Chodron, P. (2007). *When things fall apart: Heart advice for difficult times*. Element Books

Frankl, V. E. (2006). *Man's search for meaning*. Beacon Press.

Kolakowski, L. (2005). *Main currents of Marxism*. W.W. Norton.

Strawson, G. (2004). Against narrativity. *Ratio, 17*(4), 428–452. https://doi.org/10.1111/j.1467-9329.2004.00264.x

Yalom, I. D. (1980). *Existential psychotherapy*. Basic Books.

Yalom, I. D. (2013). *Love's executioner and other tales of psychotherapy*. Basic Books.
*I just noticed: there's not a single Mental Health Nursing book here...*

# 3

# THE SHACKLES OF LUPUS, AND THE REDEFINING PATH OF FAITH AND POSITIVE PSYCHOLOGY

*Ijeabalum Asike*

## Introduction

My story is riddled with the pain of a chronic health condition (lupus) and a terrifying immigration experience. However, it has been redefined by faith, hope, optimism, resilience, and posttraumatic growth (PTG). My story begins with my relocation from Nigeria (my country of origin) to England to join my mother as a student. I had hope and aspirations of starting a family and having a career. Unfortunately, the hope of starting a family ended with a broken relationship and a pregnancy. After the birth of my son, I was diagnosed with lupus. That diagnosis ended my hope of a career. My story details my diagnosis, treatments, and their impact on the entirety of my life. Additionally, I narrate my immigration ordeal, which may have exacerbated my health condition. The fear of being sent back to a country with no medical facilities to manage a chronic illness was a debilitating feeling. Nonetheless, my story reflects on the role of faith in infusing hope, optimism, resilience, and PTG. I highlighted the impact of acceptance and adaptation in improving my life, irrespective of lupus. Acceptance and adaptation to lupus have enabled me to overcome the seemingly towering limitations. I referred to lupus as a cross, and by accepting it I found reasons to be grateful. I found meaning and purpose. Although it has been a tumultuous journey, the story is a tale of acknowledging God's gift of science in ensuring I survive and thrive.

## Relocation to England

In my first year at university, my mum relocated to England, and I moved to my paternal aunt's house for an easy commute to the university. At the end

DOI: 10.4324/9781003408963-3

of the four-year course, I moved to Lagos and lived with my maternal cousin and her family. I started working in a procurement organisation. I tried to visit my mum twice in the UK, but my visa was denied. During this time, I had no major health worries, except for 'normal' malaria, which everyone had. I also had a sensitive stomach, clicking joints, sore back, was always bloated, had swollen fingers (especially when in an air-conditioned room), and had constant diarrhoea. I wasn't worried about them. I took painkillers and avoided some foods to reduce the symptoms. Nonetheless, I wasn't deterred from enjoying life, working, and dating. I was also in my twenties, so I had thoughts of marriage and childbearing because it felt like the next step towards becoming a fulfilled woman (Ademiluka, 2021; Agboola, 2022; Maponya, 2021). Marriage is the juncture where all the people in a particular society gather, the deceased, the living, and the unborn (Agboola, 2022). This makes marriage the centre of existence for many African communities (Agboola, 2022; Maponya, 2021). I pursued a career in banking, but that was a secondary issue because my main prayer intention was to get married. I consciously succumbed to the societal misconception that defines a woman as inferior, sexual, and submissive (Bassey & Bubu, 2019; Szolc, 2022). Mentally, I didn't mind being submissive, all that mattered was getting married and procreating. I had a cousin who would always tease me on my birthday. She would say, 'How old are you now? You are getting old, oh!' We both laughed about it, but it bothered me.

Furthermore, Agboola (2022), noted that in Nigeria an unmarried man is viewed as independent or working hard to make a living after a certain age. In contrast, an unmarried woman is immediately assumed to be having issues and is mocked and pitied (Agboola, 2022; Chukwuokolo, 2019). Nonetheless, my mum wasn't bothered. She welcomed the idea of me getting married but wasn't desperate. According to Gui (2022), parental pressure to marry and interference in adult children's romantic lives are ongoing issues in the lives of women. My mum wanted me to be fully mature emotionally and physically (Agege et al., 2018). Nevertheless, she had her criteria for a prospective suitor. He must be educated, be employed, and most importantly, be a Catholic. On the other hand, she wanted me to join her in England. Hence, we started making plans for me to come and do my master's in human resource management. Thankfully, I was granted a student visa to study International Human Resource Management at Middlesex University in London. However, I switched to Applied Psychology on the advice of my mother. I attended University during the week and worked for 20 hours during the weekend as a healthcare assistant. Whilst doing my master's, I started a long-distance relationship with a friend in Lagos. As our relationship progressed, we started talking about marriage, and that was music to my ears. I told my mum about him and the first thing she asked was, 'Is he a Catholic?'

Disappointingly, he wasn't a Catholic, so my mum vehemently refused. That was the beginning of the feud between me and my mum. She believed he would prevent me from practicing my Catholic faith. According to Eke (2018), the main risk of a mixed marriage in Nigeria is the potential denial of the Catholic party's right (especially the woman) to practice and raise their children in the Catholic faith, or more specifically, the risk of defection from the Catholic faith. That was the least of my worries. All that mattered was being called a 'Mrs' to change my social status (Chukwuokolo, 2019). In agreement with Agboola (2022), it was a societal indoctrination that led me to believe that if a woman is married and has children, then she is successful or deserving of the title 'woman'. Reflecting now, I was not in love. My desperation clouded my sense of reasoning, no doubt further weakened by his height and good looks. Amidst the feud between my mum and myself, I fasted and prayed to get her consent. While she prayed for me to end the relationship. Studies have shown that parents play a significant and important traditional role in a couple's marriage in Igboland (Chukwuokolo, 2019; Ifeanyichukwu et al., 2018; Nwoko, 2020). For instance, a man is not considered married until the bride's father (in this case my mum), hands her over to him, after completing all the requisite customary rites of the land (Ifeanyichukwu et al., 2018). Unfortunately, this period of the feud was extremely stressful. I started experiencing chest pain, joint pain, dry mouth, swollen fingers, and entire body pain. As I had completed my MSc, I decided to go back to Nigeria to get married, regardless of my mum's consent or blessing. My mum was concerned about my symptoms and insisted I booked an appointment with the doctor. I told the doctor I was worried I had serious issues with my joints. He sent me to have a chest x-ray and some blood tests to check for autoimmune disease (AID). I felt everything was fine since I didn't hear back from the doctor. However, en route to the airport, my General Practitioner (GP) practice called asking me to come to the practice immediately. I was already on the train and had no intention of missing my flight.

Nevertheless, the relationship broke down after a few months in Nigeria, but unfortunately, I was pregnant. I had secured a job in the bank so the dilemma was, 'should I abort the baby and resume work, or should I go back to England'. The first option seemed to be better, but I couldn't in good conscience concede to aborting my child. I was worried about the stigma associated with being a single mum. Some cultures in Nigeria reject the concept of single motherhood because of its presumption that the woman is wayward (Alayaki et al., 2021). I was ashamed and devastated. How could I explain my pregnancy to people? Should I make up stories or should I hide from people? I would face stigma in my Igbo community. Nonetheless, stigmatisation is not exclusive to Nigerian or African culture alone. Several studies have investigated and discovered the enormous discrimination and stigmatisation experienced regularly by single mothers (Bradley & Millar, 2021; Choi et al., 2020; Morris & Munt, 2019; Williams, 2021). However, stigma was not my only issue, I also feared the moral implication on my conscience if I aborted the child. I called my mum and informed her of my pregnancy and with no doubt in her voice, she said, 'Don't do anything to the child, come back to England'. Realistically, my only option was to return to England. The image of receiving the call from my GP as I left for Nigeria was lodged in my memory and I had no iota of doubt that I was unwell. Additionally, I had a baby depending on me. Therefore, I needed to know my health status and I knew our chances of survival were greater in England than in Nigeria.

## Tales of Lupus

I returned to England in July 2011, and my due date was 28 February 2012. I had a lot of pain during pregnancy, which I believe was caused by lupus. Nonetheless, my pain was both physical and emotional. Studies have shown that women with medically high-risk pregnancies frequently experience 'anxiety, worries, and depressive symptoms', as well as a strong sense of powerlessness and stress (Dagklis et al., 2016; Meaney et al., 2016; McCoyd et al., 2020). I stopped working in December 2011 due to the pain. On 3rd February, I went for my 38-week appointment. My blood pressure was high, and the midwife asked me to go to the hospital. I was induced on the 4th and at 6 am on 5 February 2012, I welcomed my gorgeous son, and I named him 'Chinkemno' (My God is with me). Although I was happy to see my son, the circumstances surrounding his birth evoked sadness, loneliness, fear, and shame. I had post-natal depression, I couldn't sleep, was fatigued, and lost interest in everything. Rajendran and Ramasamy (2021) stated that the most common type of depression in women is post-natal depression. The onset of depressive episodes following childbirth occurs during a critical period in a woman's life and can last for many years (Rajendran & Ramasamy, 2021). I would wake up in the night crying and asking my mum for forgiveness. She would console me and tell me that she never held any grudge against me. The most important thing for her was that I had my baby, and we were both at home with her. I felt like the prodigal son, returning after squandering his father's wealth and asking for forgiveness. In the parable, his father welcomed his son with open arms, hugged him, kissed him, put a ring on his finger, and threw a big feast to celebrate his return (King James Version Bible, 2022, Luke, 15: 11–32).

Two months after my son's birth, I had an appointment with the rheumatologist Dr H, in Croydon Health Services. She said my tests showed

I had an AID. AIDs are complex diseases associated with chronic or recurring inflammation, altered immune function, and the production of specific autoantibodies (Ciccacci et al., 2019). Mine was called systemic lupus erythematosus (SLE), which caused my body pain, swollen joints, and fatigue. According to Deng et al. (2013), SLE is a model AID associated with the production of autoantibodies, chronic inflammation deposition, and a wide range of diagnostic symptoms. My urine analysis showed blood and protein in it. Therefore, more tests needed to be carried out to find out its effects on my kidney. I was given a leaflet that explained what SLE was, but everything was a blur. I couldn't explain anything the doctor said to my mum. All I could say was that they needed to test my kidneys. My mum said, 'In Jesus' name nothing is wrong with your kidneys'. How I wish that was true.

Additionally, the doctor prescribed hydroxychloroquine twice a day, but one week after starting the medication, half of my face became swollen. I went to my GP who immediately gave me an urgent referral letter for A&E. I took my medication because I thought I was reacting to it. On arrival at A&E, I was transferred to the ward for more tests and waited to see the doctor the next day. A nephrologist came to see me and informed me that my kidneys were leaking protein. Hence, I needed a kidney biopsy and an ultrasound on both kidneys to determine the best treatment. I didn't understand what he was saying, all I wanted was to go home to my baby. The next day I had the ultrasound and the biopsy. Surprisingly, Dr H visited me in the hospital. I told her the hydroxychloroquine made me unwell. She looked at me tenderly and said, 'Ije, you were already very unwell before you started the medication'. I froze, shocked that my present condition was a result of a pre-existing illness and not a side effect of my medication. She informed me that a nephrologist, Dr S, would be taking care of the kidney aspect of my illness. On the same day, Dr S visited me and informed me that my kidneys were enlarged and were indeed leaking protein, which caused the swellings on my face, hands, fingers, and ankles. He explained what lupus meant and gave me some leaflets to read. I was discharged and prescribed more medications.

I was glad to be home, but in less than a week I was readmitted to the hospital. My legs were swollen, I was in agony, and my temperature was high. I spent two weeks in the hospital and had a seizure while on the ward. I got out of bed to use the toilet and when I got back in bed the only thing, I recall was seeing a tiny light. The next thing I remembered was nurses and doctors calling my name and trying to resuscitate me. I woke up and cried but the words coming from my mouth were 'I want my mummy'. The shock of losing consciousness made me call for the only face that made me feel safe. That morning my whole body was covered in a red rash, and it hurt. Every morning, I had a blood test done. However, on that day, even a mere touch from the phlebotomist made me weep. My Uncle Uche who also visited that morning, tenderly stroked my hair saying, 'Nne ndo' (My dear I am so sorry) with tears in his eyes. The phlebotomist tenderly said 'Sorry Ije, you will be ok'. I prayed it would be okay, but I didn't feel like it was going to be okay. I was sent for magnetic resonance imaging (MRI) of the brain because of the seizure.

When the results came out, Dr S invited my mum and my Uncle Uche to explain my health condition to them. He informed them that I had stage 2/3 lupus nephritis and my brain MRI showed I had cerebral vasculitis. This is the inflammation of the walls of blood vessels (Callen et al., 2021). He explained that my immune system was unable to recognise good cells. Therefore, it attacked my cells and organs. That is the reason immunosuppressive treatment is used to manage the condition (Fava & Petri, 2019). Furthermore, he informed them that if my condition deteriorated, I would need to have chemotherapy called cyclophosphamide infusion for six months. He turned to me and said 'Ije, two things you need to take off your mind, are finance and romance'. These can trigger a flare-up because they involve a lot of stress. It felt like my life was over, I can't stress about work or finding a relationship. Why me? I was just 26 and my world was tumbling down. I have a baby and I have a health condition that I would live with for the rest of my life. Dr S saw my bible and said, 'I can see you pray, so when you pray, read Psalm 27'. 'The Lord is my light and my salvation, whom shall I fear?' (King James Version Bible, 2022, Psalm 27). I felt the faith of my doctor, but I was still terrified. I was discharged and an outpatient appointment was arranged. I still looked swollen both from my fluid retention and the side effects of my medication. As my condition got worse Dr S referred me to Epsom and St Helier University Hospital, for the commencement of my chemotherapy. On my first appointment, I met Dr M and Dr H, both consultant Nephrologists. They were very nice and spoke to us (myself and mum) about my diagnosis, the rationale for cyclophosphamide treatment, and the side effects of chemotherapy such as infertility and hair loss. I had no alternative, so I agreed to the treatment.

The chemotherapy helped with my kidneys, but I started developing sore fingers. They were red and tender. I was referred to a rheumatologist in Epsom and St Helier called Dr P and he requested a finger biopsy. The biopsy showed inflammation of the nerves in my fingers which affected blood circulation. Due to a condition referred to as Raynaud's disease (NHS, 2017), they began to ulcerate and get infected. My doctors began trying several treatments, so I felt like a guinea pig. First, was the 'iloprost' infusion. I stayed in the hospital for one week. It is a very painful treatment, from the crown of my head to the sole of my feet was in agony, until the infusion ended. The second was plasma exchange, which was used because 'iloprost' became intolerable. The third was rituximab, but none of them worked. I was in the hospital every fortnight and that was my life in London from 2012 to 2015. My mum worked and took care of my son because most of the time I struggled to get out of bed. We shared a house with my Uncle Uche and his family in London, so he helped care for my son. As my fingers got worse, I also developed avascular necrosis (AVN) on both knees and ankles, which was a side effect of taking a high dose of steroids. AVN occurs when the blood supply to the end of a bone is cut off. The affected bone and the surrounding tissue may begin to die gradually. This can result in bone joint stiffness, pain, and/or a loss of range of motion in the affected joint (Great Ormond Street Hospital NHS, 2022).

Equally, I started requiring a walking aid and became more dependent on my mum and uncle. I was depressed because I was developing different problems with no solutions in sight. I felt like a young soul trapped in an old frail body. According to del Castillo and Alino (2020), suffering can upset life's most stable and appropriate balance. It can shake the strongest foundations of confidence, and sometimes even lead people to despair, while losing their value and meaning in life (del Castillo & Alino, 2020). Sometimes I felt my mum and son were better off without me. I was not suicidal, but I wished I could close my eyes and not wake up. I could not recognise this version of myself. Moreover, in 2015, we moved from London to Bolton due to accommodation issues in London. My mum stopped working and devoted her time to caring for me and my son. Faronbi et al. (2019), conducted a study in southwest Nigeria about the lived experience of caregivers of older adults with chronic illnesses. The research sheds light on the financial burden of caring for older adults with chronic illnesses. Caregivers' dedication to saving lives compels them to continue providing support that may be detrimental to their health (Faronbi et al., 2019). My mum was the first to wake up and the last to go to bed. She cooked, cleaned, and supported me with personal care. She never complained, prayed for me, was with me, and never gave up hope.

Additionally, my medical care was transferred to Salford Royal Hospital, but my doctor read my file and said she could not handle me and transferred me to a lupus clinic in Manchester Royal Infirmary. My medical complications meant that I needed the care of a rheumatologist, nephrologist, dermatologist, orthopaedic specialist, and an ear, nose, and throat (ENT) consultant. My main Consultant is Dr B the head of the rheumatology and lupus clinic. He tried steroids, methotrexate, and rituximab. They didn't work so he applied for funding for a trial biological treatment called belimumab. Once it was approved, he prescribed four weekly infusions, which I have had from 2017 to date. Likewise, I have a quarterly treatment of 'flolan', a five-day treatment carried out before the beginning of any major season (winter and summer) to date. On the other hand, my AVN was getting worse, so I had core-decompression surgery on both knees and ankles in 2016 at Salford Royal Infirmary. Two years after surgery I developed an osteochondral lesion in my right knee. According to Stanford Health Care (2022), an osteochondral lesion is a focal area of damage that involves both the cartilage and a piece of the underlying bone. These can result from severe trauma to the knee or from a bone disorder (Stanford Health Care, 2022). I had a surgery called arthroscopy and microfracture of the right knee.

### My Journey of Faith

I struggled with illness from age 7 and am 37 years old now. It was my mum's reality when I was a child because it was practically her cross. It became my reality in 2012. I was young, full of life and aspirations. Although on reflection those aspirations were limited to my desire to marry, have a career, and be reliant on my strength. Those were good aspirations, but on the career front, I lacked direction, meaning, and purpose. Ironically, my illness made me weak, but made me solely reliant on God's grace and mercy. According to the Catholic church, Christ Jesus is the source of mercy and grace (del Castillo & Alino, 2020). There are challenges that we cannot overcome without the assistance of divine grace and mercy (Benedict XVI, 2008, as cited in del Castillo & Alino, 2020). I came to England as a student in 2009 and after my graduation in 2010, I was given a two-year post-study work visa. I was expected to either go back to Nigeria or find an employer who would renew my work visa. My deteriorating health made those two options impossible. In 2012, my mum made an immigration application for me and my son to remain in England on conditions of exceptional circumstances.

We had to get letters from my doctors and from Nigeria, proving that my medical condition could not be managed in Nigeria. The application was refused, and we appealed. The case was taken to court. The first court date was cancelled and rescheduled. I was admitted to the hospital 24 hours earlier because I became neutropenic. I remember, crying and begging the doctor that I had a court hearing in the morning. He said 'I will write a letter that will be taken to court, but I can't let you out of the hospital. Your body is too weak to fight any infection and I must protect you from further risk'. On the second appointment for the court hearing, my mum and I were grilled with questions. I showed the judge my fingers and how I needed my mum for everything. I explained how my health condition affected my daily living. The judge asked my mum, 'will you go back to Nigeria with your daughter if this application is unsuccessful?' My mum replied

I have no job in Nigeria, and even if I had, there is no health facility available to manage her condition. I won't be able to afford it because this is a lifelong illness. You will be sending her to an early grave if you send her back.

As she said this she began to cry. One week after the hearing, we received the Judge's verdict and his advice to the Home Office. In August 2014, I was granted 'Leave to Remain' in the UK for 30 months, with the provision to renew at the end of the 30 months.

Nonetheless, when we moved to Bolton in 2015, my health became worse, so my mum stopped working. We needed financial help. My immigration status restricted me from claiming benefits, so we were advised to apply for a change of circumstance to enable me to access public funds. We applied and sent in the supporting documents to prove my health status. We prayed and God showed his mercy yet again. I was allowed to apply for Personal Independent Payment (PIP) and Employment Support Allowance (ESA). The ability to access public funds made it possible for my house to be adapted to meet my mobility needs. A stairlift was fitted, a reverberator was fitted in my bed, a walk-in shower was built, and I was given a 'Motability' car. However, towards the end of my 30 months 'leave to remain', I applied for renewal. Unfortunately, my application was caught up during the 'Windrush crisis' and it took more than one year. During that period, I received a letter from the Home Office, notifying me that I was liable to be detained because I had no 'leave to remain'. I was asked to report to the Salford Detention Centre on specified dates.

Those were very dark times. My benefits were stopped, and 'Motability' requested the return of my car. Additionally, I was scheduled for surgery (arthroscopy and microfracture of the right knee), so I pleaded with Motability to be allowed a few weeks to be done with my surgery. Fortunately, they allowed me to return it after my surgery. I prayed for God's help because I was drowning in misery, and I developed a fear of brown envelopes (the Home Office letters normally came in brown envelopes). I remember crying and telling my mum that the best thing was to go back to Nigeria and die peacefully, so that they would have less stress. She replied, 'How do you feel I will cope?' Applying and waiting for a visa renewal was so stressful and made me face the reality that England was not my home country yet. I developed post-migration stressors. Von Werthern et al. (2018), suggest that a post-migration stressor is time spent in immigration detention in the host country, which involves loss of freedom and the threat of being returned forcibly to one's country of origin. I was sad and in despair, but I had no other comfort than to pray. Prayer gave me a glimmer of hope and optimism. Concurring with Frankl (2004), prayer gave me an awareness that my inner values were anchored in higher, more spiritual things and were unshaken by suffering.

My friends and family prayed for me and that gave me comfort. I tried to tell myself one day that a letter will say, 'You have been granted leave to remain', and it will come through the letter box. I attended the Detention Centre for a period of six months until my approval letter arrived, and I felt free again.

At the beginning of any upheaval in my life, there seems to be no light at the end of the tunnel. I feel buried in the pit of darkness, kneeling over with my head on the ground and overcome with fear. No sound outside or inside my head, only the sensation of my heart beating slowly and gradually a faint prayer quietly in my heart;

Oh Lord be gracious to me,
I long for you, be my strength every morning.
My salvation in times of distress.
*(King James Version Bible, 2022, Isaiah. 33;3)*

That salvation may seem far away and my distress unending. However, slowly but surely, God reveals his light at the end of the tunnel. It may be dim at first, but it gets brighter and brighter. As I journey in that part of pain, sadness, darkness, confusion, loneliness, fatigue, and hopelessness, the Holy Spirit subconsciously, reminds me that I am never alone. I reflect on the poem 'Footprints in the sand', though I may turn and ask God, why he has left me to walk on my own bearing the unsurmountable suffering? God reminds me that when the suffering feels unbearable, He is the one carrying me along the footpath and it's His footprints that I see on the sand, not mine. According to St. Paul, God's grace is sufficient for me because his power is made perfect in my weakness (King James Version Bible, 2022, Corinthians. 12:9–11). Therefore, I am solely reliant on God's grace and strength. My pain, fatigue, ulcerated fingers, unstable knees, unpredictable nature of my illness, and physical dependency on my mum, became the building blocks of my faith.

Bennett (2021), reflected on the faith journey of Abraham by asserting four points about faith, that need to be assimilated into our modern world. First, faith must be viewed as a journey, a pilgrimage, undertaken as a response to God. Second, faith encounters God who is largely hidden, especially in modern contexts, but as faith grows, we find ourselves gradually seeing God face-to-face. Third, faith necessitates the formation of a community, that not only demonstrates that God is a God of life, but also nurtures our faithful pilgrimage towards God. Finally, faith will compel us to pursue God's own life. The journey of faith becomes great. We will see that faith truly is like a mustard seed that blossoms into a tree that can accommodate large birds building their nests within (Bennett, 2021).

## My Miracle and Healing

Basinger (2011), defined miracles as occurrences that would not have ensued when and how they did, without the approval of a compassionate supernatural agent (God). Therefore, as a Christian, I believe in miracles particularly because I experienced one as a child. Consequently, I resorted to prayer when I was diagnosed with lupus. I also believed in medical science, so I religiously took my medication, went to mass every day, and prayed on my own. I wanted to walk into the hospital one day and the doctors would say 'Ije, your lupus has vanished'. In the face of stress and psychic suffering, believing in miracles can be a spiritual/religious coping strategy (Leal et al., 2022). My mum always reminded me of the first tumour and believed that God would do it again. My uncle who is a priest in Australia would send me different herbal remedies, probiotic drinks, and shakes. He sent them every month for almost two years. I used all those things to boost my immune system. I did everything by the book, but the miracle was not coming. I spent more days in the hospital than at home because I continually had infections, in my throat, my skin, my chest, and my fingers.

Hence, the future seemed bleak. My mum joked that my vocation was being unwell and sometimes we found comfort in that. While at other times I was full of despair. However, praying and reflection gradually changed my focus from searching for a magic cure to a soul search and self-discovery. I believe my miracle started when I accepted my chronic illness. There is a Nigerian mantra, 'It is not my portion', which is commonly used to reject illness, misfortune, or evil spirits. One day on reflection I laughed and asked, 'Whose portion, is it?' Medically, no healing was occurring but spiritually and mentally I was getting healed. Accepting my disability as my cross to bear meant that I accepted help. Some days I am bed-bound, overwhelmed in pain and my dear mum must wash me, clothe, and feed me. I can remember, a period when I lay in bed for days, unable to walk, a mere touch was agonising. When things get this bad my mum calls a priest to give me communion and anointing of the sick. Father R. came. He prayed, anointed, and gave me Holy Communion. The next day was a Saturday, I got out of bed with my stick and walked out of my room. Walking into my mum's room, my son, four years at the time, was watching TV but he suddenly turned and saw me on my feet. He screamed 'My mum can walk, my mum can walk!' and motioned me to come towards him, like a parent cheering a toddler when they make their first steps. While moving his hands back and forth, he charmingly said 'Come on mummy, come on mummy', his face was filled with utter joy. These are precious moments, so I try to do as much as I can, when I can. Listening to my body, so when it says stop, I stop. I pace myself to avoid breaking down. Keeping my fingers warm and covered. These were my processes of acceptance and adaptation to my health condition.

Moreover, studies show that upon achieving acceptance, adaptation and rediscovery of life can start, allowing a transition from 'What I cannot do' to 'What I can do' (Avvenuti et al., 2016). I vividly remember a disabled man who worked in my aunt's restaurant in Nigeria. There was an argument and there was a demeaning remark about his disability. The man, overcome with sadness, said 'There is an ability in every disability'. This statement was inked into my mind. I may have limited my hopes and dreams, but my illness allowed me to appreciate the little things such as walking without a stick, putting my hands in my pocket, or holding my son's hands. I remember when my son was three (the difficult three), I went to pick him up from nursery. My mobility was declining, so I walked with my stick. My son wanted to go into a shop to get some sweets. I had no money, and I was fatigued, so I said 'No!' He threw himself on the ground, arms and legs stretched out, crying. I lost it! I wailed like a child, shouting his name – 'Kemno, get up'. As I cried on the street, my thought was 'Why me? I am just 29. I can't pick my son up and am unsteady on my feet. Is this my life?' That day I felt helpless and hopeless.

Fortunately, I am looking back on those days with a heart full of gratitude. I may not have had healing that eradicated my pain. However, my miracle is being able to sit and type my story with my fingers. Looking at pictures of sore fingers, and inflamed skin (cellulitis). The gift of having a loving mother, an adorable son, and a house adapted to suit my needs. The availability of medical science working tirelessly to manage my condition. Journeying with lupus, but not being defined by lupus. These are my miracle and my blessings. We have a hymn that says:

*Count your blessings.*
*Name them one by one.*
*Count your blessings.*
*See what God has done.*
*Count your blessings.*
*Name them one by one.*
*And it will surprise you,*
*What the Lord has done.*

Confidently, I testify that God has done amazing things in my life. Reflecting on this ongoing journey, I will say that accepting physical and mental pain and discomfort brought growth into my life. My mum borrows the words of St. Paul, the gift of long-suffering produces perseverance, which produces character, and character produces hope (King James Version Bible, 2022, Romans. 5:2–5). Using positive psychology, I am inclined to say that adversity, produces resilience, resilience produces PTG, and PTG produces hope and optimism. Csikszentmihalyi (2008, p. 193) posed the question 'How is it possible for people to achieve mental harmony and grow in complexity even when some of the worst things imaginable happen to them?' Growth and harmony can be accomplished by adapting and accepting (Avvenuti et al., 2016), consequently, rejecting hopelessness and helplessness (Seligman, 2006). This reminds me of the serenity prayer:

*Lord, grant me the serenity,*
*to accept the things, I can't change.*
*The courage to accept the things, I can change,*
*And the wisdom to know the difference.*

## Final Reflection

I found meaning by focusing on what I can change and am discovering my purpose. My tumultuous journey in life has been a fruitful one. This reflects in my name 'Ijeabalum', which means 'a fruitful journey'. Names are symbolic in the Igbo culture. They are used as an expression of hope, beliefs, fears, joy, grief, and the circumstances of a parent when they birth their child (Anyachebelu, 2015; Salami & Tabari, 2021). My mum may one day tell the story that prompted my naming. While awaiting that day, I believe my name aligns with my path through life. One may choose to agree or disagree. Nonetheless, my life has been a fruitful journey. I have been given a gift of life and I am eternally grateful. I hope my story will encourage people with chronic illness or any disability that life is not over. Circumstances may change and limitations may abound, but there is always a hidden ability that is yet to be discovered.

## References

Ademiluka, S.O. (2021). Marriage as a choice or duty: Considering Nigerian Christians' attitude to singlehood from the biblical perspective. *In die Skriflig*, 55(1), 1–9. https://doi.org/10.4102/ids.v55i1.2674.

Agboola, O.T. (2022). 'Marriageism': The self-identity of the Nigerian woman in selected Nollywood films. *Tropical Journal of Arts and Humanities*, 4(1), 1–12. https://www.researchgate.net/publication/373139801_%27Marriageism%27_ The_self-identity_of_the_Nigerian_woman_in_selected_Nollywood_films# fullTextFileContent

Agege, E., Nwose, E., & Odjimogho, S. (2018). Parents' perception on factors of early marriage among the Urhobos in Delta State of Nigeria. *International Journal of Community Medicine and Public Health*, 5(2), 411. https://doi. org/10.18203/2394-6040.ijcmph20180213.

Alayaki, I.A., Bello, A.A., & Ayodele, K.O. (2021). Stress status and social support as predictors of mother-child interactions among single mothers in Ikeja Local

Government Area, Lagos State, Nigeria. *Babcock University Journal of Education, 7*(2), 127–139. bujed 2021 (researchgate.net)

Anyachebelu, L.A. (2015). Social symbolism of Igbo names in Nza na Obu. *Journal of Nigerian Languages and Culture* (JONLAC). https://ir.unilag.edu.ng/handle/123456789/8723

Avvenuti, G., Baiardini, I., & Giardini, A. (2016). Optimism's explicative role for chronic diseases. *Frontiers in Psychology, 7*(295), 1–9. https://doi.org/10.3389/fpsyg.2016.00295.

Basinger, D. (2011). What is a miracle? In G.H. Twelftree (Ed.), *The Cambridge companion to miracles* (pp. 17–35). Cambridge University Press.

Bassey, S.A., & Bubu, N.G. (2019). Gender inequality in Africa: A re-examination of cultural values. *Cogito: Multidisciplinary Research Journal, 11*, 21–36. GENDER_INEQUALITY_IN_AFRICA_A.pdf

Benedict XVI. (2008*). Apostolic journey of his Holiness Benedict XVI to France on the occasion of the 150th anniversary of the apparitions of The Blessed Virgin Mary at Lourdes.* September 12–15. Available at: http://w2.vatican.va/content/benedict-xvi/en/homilies/2008/documents/hf_ben-xvi_hom_20080915_lourdes-malati.htm

Bennett, J. (2021). On pilgrimage with Abraham: How a patriarch leads us in formation in faith. *Journal of Moral Theology, 10*(Special Issue 1), 20–39. 24525-on-pilgrimage-with-abraham-how-a-patriarch-leads-us-in-formation-in-faith (1).pdf

Bradley, C., & Millar, M. (2021). Persistent stigma despite social change: Experiences of stigma among single women who were pregnant or mothers in the Republic of Ireland 1996–2010. *Families, Relationships and Societies, 10*(3), 413–429. https://doi.org/10.1332/204674320X15919853021486.

Callen, A., Narvid, J., Chen, X., Gregath, T., & Meisel, K. (2021). Neurovascular disease, diagnosis, and therapy: Cervical and intracranial atherosclerosis, vasculitis, and vasculopathy. In S.W. Hetts & D.L. Cooke (Eds.), *Handbook of clinical neurology* (pp. 249–266). Elsevier (Interventional Neuroradiology). https://doi.org/10.1016/B978-0-444-64034-5.00023-7.

Choi, S., Byoun, S.J., & Kim, E.H. (2020). Unwed single mothers in South Korea: Increased vulnerabilities during the COVID-19 pandemic. *International Social Work, 63*(5), 676–680. https://doi.org/10.1177/0020872820941040.

Chukwuokolo, C.J. (2019). Igbo philosophy of marriage: Towards the revival of family values for veritable development of Igboland. *Journal of African Studies and Sustainable Development, 2*(8), 119–140. https://acjol.org/index.php/jassd/article/view/jassd_v2n8_8

Ciccacci, C., Latini, A., Perricone, C., Conigliaro, P., Colafranceso, S., Ceccarelli, F., Priori, R., Contin, F., Perricone, R., Novelli, G., & Borgiani, P. (2019). TNFAIP3 Gene polymorphisms in three common autoimmune diseases: Systemic lupus erythematosus, rheumatoid arthritis, and primary Sjogren syndrome-Association with disease susceptibility and clinical phenotypes in Italian patients. *Journal of Immunology Research, 2019*, 1–6. https://doi.org/10.1155/2019/6728694.

Corinthians. 12:9–11. King James Version Bible. (2022). Available at: https://www.kingjamesbibleonline.org/2-Corinthians-Chapter-12/

Csikszentmihalyi, M. (2008). *Flow: The psychology of optimal experience* (Harper Perennial Modern Classics). Ingram International Inc.

Dagklis, T., Papazisis, G., Tsakiridis, I., Chouliara, F., Mamopoulos, A., & Rousso, D. (2016). Prevalence of antenatal depression and associated factors among pregnant women hospitalized in a high-risk pregnancy unit in Greece. *Social Psychiatry and Psychiatric Epidemiology, 51*(7), 1025–1031. https://doi.org/10.1007/s00127-016-1230-7.

del Castillo, F., & Alino, M.A. (2020). Religious coping of selected Filipino Catholic youth. *Religions, 11*(9), 462. https://doi.org/10.3390/rel11090462.

Deng, Y., Hahn, B.H., & Tsao, B.P. (2013). Systemic lupus erythematosus. In D. Rimoin, R. Pyeritz, & B. Korf (Eds.), *Emery and Rimoin's principles and practice of medical genetics* (6th edition, pp. 1–22). Academic Press. https://doi.org/10.1016/B978-0-12-383834-6.00081-1.

Eke, V.C. (2018). *Spiritual, practical and doctrinal ecumenism in the Anglican-Roman Catholic relations in Nigeria.* Unpublished Doctoral Dissertation. John Paul II Catholic University of Lublin, Faculty of Theology. Vitus Eke_doctoral_thesis_13.02.2018_final ver. (kul.pl)

Faronbi, J.O., Faronbi, G.O., Ayamolowo, S. J., & Olaogun, A. A. (2019). Caring for the seniors with chronic illness: The lived experience of caregivers of older adults. *Archives of Gerontology and Geriatrics, 82*, 8–14. https://doi.org/10.1016/j.archger.2019.01.013.

Fava, A., & Petri, M. (2019). Systemic lupus erythematosus: Diagnosis and clinical management. *Journal of Autoimmunity, 96*, 1–13. https://doi.org/10.1016/j.jaut.2018.11.001.

Frankl, V. (2004). *Man's search for meaning.* Rider.

Great Ormond Street Hospital NHS. (2022). *Avascular necrosis.* Great Ormond Street Hospital Site. Available at: https://www.gosh.nhs.uk/conditions-and-treatments/conditions-we-treat/avascular-necrosis/ (Accessed: 21 September 2022).

Gui, T. (2022). Coping with parental pressure to get married: Perspectives from Chinese "Leftover Women". *Journal of Family Issues, 44*(8), 2118–2137. https://doi.org/10.1177/0192513X211071053

Ifeanyichukwu, C.A., Chukwu, J.N., Nwasum, C.J., & Nwakpu, E. (2018). Winning parental consents in inter-tribal marriages in Igboland: Considering the public relations option. *Ebonyi State University Journal of Mass Communication, 5*(1), 178–195. https://doi.org/10.13140/RG.2.2.27754.16329.

Isaiah. 33:3. King James Version Bible. (2022). Available at: https://www.kingjamesbibleonline.org/Isaiah-Chapter-33/

Leal, M.M., Nwora, E.I., de Melo, G.F., & Freitas, M.H. (2022). Praying for a miracle: Negative or positive impacts on health care? *Frontiers in Psychology, 13*, 1–10. https://doi.org/10.3389/fpsyg.2022.840851.

Luke 15: 11–32 King James Version. (2022). Available at: https://www.kingjamesbibleonline.org/Luke-15-11/ (Accessed: 21 September 2022).

Maponya, D.T. (2021). The African woman's plight of reproduction: A philosophical analysis of marriage, procreation, and womanhood. *Agenda, 35*(3), 82–91. https://doi.org/10.1080/10130950.2021.1972598.

McCoyd, J.L.M., Curran, L., & Munch, S. (2020). They say, "If you don't relax… You're going to make something bad happen: Women's emotion management during medically high-risk pregnancy. *Psychology of Women Quarterly, 44*(1), 117–129. https://doi.org/10.1177/0361684319883199.

Meaney, S., Lutomski, J.E., O'Connor, L., Donoghue, K.O., & Greene, R.A. (2016). Women's experience of maternal morbidity: A qualitative analysis. *BMC Pregnancy and Childbirth, 16*(1), 184. https://doi.org/10.1186/s12884-016-0974-0.

Morris, C., & Munt, S.R. (2019). Classed formations of shame in white, British single mothers. *Feminism & Psychology, 29*(2), 231–249. https://doi.org/10.1177/0959353518787847.

NHS UK. (2017). Raynaud's. Available at: https://www.nhs.uk/conditions/raynauds/

Nwoko, K.C. (2020). The changing nature and patterns of traditional marriage practices among the Owerre-Igbo, a subgroup of the Igbo of Southeast Nigeria. *Journal of Historical Sociology, 33*(4), 681–692. https://doi.org/10.1111/johs.12295.

Psalm 27 King James Version *JV.* (no date). Available at: https://www.kingjamesbibleonline.org/Psalms-Chapter-27/ (Accessed: 6 March 2023).

Rajendran, S., & Ramasamy, R. (2021). Prevalence of post-natal depression and risk factors of depression among women seeking health services in Southern India. *Turkish Online Journal of Qualitative Inquiry, 12*(9), 7970–7976. Prevalence of Post Natal Depression and Risk Factors of Depression among Women Seeking Health Services in Southern India - Search (bing.com)

Romans. 5:2–5. King James Version Bible. (2022). Available at: https://www.kingjamesbibleonline.org/Romans-Chapter-5/

Salami, A., & Tabari, B. (2021). Igbo naming cosmology and name symbolization in Chinua Achebe's Tetralogy. *Folia linguistica et litteraria, 33*, 39–61. https://doi.org/10.31902/fll.33.2020.2.

Seligman, M. (2006). *Learned optimism: How to change your mind and your life.* Nicholas Brealey Publishing.

Stanford Health Care. (2022). *Chondral/osteochondral defect.* Available at: https://stanfordhealthcare.org/medical-conditions/bones-joints-and-muscles/chondral-osteochondral-defect.html (Accessed: 21 September 2022).

Szolc, M. (2022). Violence and rejection: The hegemony of White culture and its influence on the mother–daughter relationship in Toni Morrison's The Bluest Eye. *Polish Journal of English Studies, 8*(1), 25–42. Violence and Rejection: The Hegemony of White - ProQuest

von Werthern, M., Robiant, K., Chui, Z., Schon, R. Ottisova, L., Mason, C., & Katona, C. (2018). The impact of immigration detention on mental health: A systematic review. *BMC Psychiatry, 18*(1), 382. https://doi.org/10.1186/s12888-018-1945-y.

Williams, A. (2021). *Social work practice and systemic stigmatization of low-income, African American, single mothers.* D.S.W. Walden University Proquest Dissertation. Available at: https://www.proquest.com/docview/2572595526/abstract/FE6FA7FE1D7D4CAEPQ/1 (Accessed: 17 September 2022).

# 4

## TELL FEAR, NO

### The Hope Is You (An Autoethnographic Account of a Male Sexual Violence Survivor's Journey Through an Academic Psychology Education, to Understand How to Bring Himself and Others Home Safely)

*Robert Balfour*

### Introduction

My story will weave personal reflection with accounts of sexual violence experienced in my early childhood, and my journey via higher education, to reach a more informed insight into both my own and our culture psychological processes when dealing with such crimes against children and adults. I will use Star Trek TV episodes as metaphors to reinforce my insights. As a child, I found such future-based stories made me kinder.

Like many of the characters we know from Star Trek, my story is constantly evolving (McAdams, 1997). Like Captain Kirk during his death, there are many profound 'Oh my' moments. It's a cliché, but if our minds remain open to new insights the 'wow' moments are a pleasure. As one of the leading autoethnographers observed, the autoethnographic methodology 'emphasizes subjectivity, self-reflexivity, emotionality, dialogue, and the goal of connecting social sciences to humanities through storytelling' (Bochner, 2012, p.156). Some psychologists have argued that the understanding human stories can be as valid as any other scientific inquiry (Balfour, 2013, 2022; Bruner, 2002; Crossley, 2000; Frank, 2012; László, 2008; Sarbin, 1986).

### Preparemus Bellum

During the early 1980s, I served as a Senior Aircraftman on 3 Wing HQ, Royal Air Force Regiment at RAF Catterick. Its motto fits well for my story: 'Preparemus Bellum' – 'Prepare for war'. For it was a form of endless

DOI: 10.4324/9781003408963-4

'frontline combat' that I endured as a child whilst constantly targeted by a series of sexual abusers. As a 'sexual violence survivor activist', the environment I have navigated for nearly a quarter of a century has been one of silencing, especially when advocating for system change. It often feels like a combat zone where one is forced to collude with those who run systems or become a 'guerrilla-partisan' with nothing in between. This was recently evidenced in a report commissioned by the current Mayor of West Yorkshire which evidenced that male survivors are either seen as allies or abusers in the minds of system professionals. However, their victimisation has vanished from system narratives (WYCA, 2023).

Society resists change in relation to sexual violence and ignores the legacies of human distress it leaves behind. As Herman (1992) observed, society finds the reality of sexual violence to be unspeakable. Though systems have an 'endless' thirst for lived experience storytelling, it can feel like entertainment at a Roman coliseum, often with little change being generated as a result, and such thirst for public disclosure being deeply retraumatising for those sharing their stories (Taylor & Clarence, 2021).

Stories need a beginning. So let me 'beam you down' to the landscape of my sexually abused childhood to offer a brief insight into what it was like to navigate what seemed at times an endless nightmare. However, the story was not all darkness; islands of humanness 'attachment' (Maté & Maté, 2022; Perry & Winfrey, 2021) often allowed me to see the positive possibilities of my potential future. Real people offering simple things like compassion and patience made the difference. I mattered to them, and they matter to me to this day, and mattering is important (Prilleltensky, 2014). I will think of them with a big smile in my final moments.

Around the outbreak of foot and mouth disease in November 1967, I would have been seven years old. I found myself living in Bangor, North Wales. I can remember being in my uncle's car one day passing over the old Menai Bridge and seeing the straw placed on the road to hold the disinfectant used to try and stop the transmission of the disease onto the island of Anglesey. We had rapidly moved to Bangor due to the breakdown of my parents' marriage as Bangor was my mother's birthplace. The marriage was not a happy one with lots of conflict between them.

I was born in Wallasey (Merseyside) where I had enjoyed a feral childhood. I lived not far from the ferry terminal at Secombe in a terraced house, which had no indoor toilet or bathroom. Shakespeare Road had survived the bombings during World War Two and lay just across the road from the Catholic church. By the age of four or five, I could often be found wandering alone around the docks of Secombe and walking the promenade to New Brighton. I recall a sense of wonder and excitement as I explored what was still a very busy docks landscape in the early 1960s, filled with lots of warehouse activity and ships, both Royal Navy and Merchant, docked and anchored in the river.

I once bumped into my aunty Pat whilst she was enjoying her lunch break. She was concerned to see me walking on my own down the promenade not far from Wallasey Town Hall. She recalled asking me what I was doing, and I said 'exploring'. She said I should get myself home as I was too young to be out on my own so far from home. She remembered my response with some distress even many decades later. I told her I would rather kill myself than go home. What drives a four- or five years old to spend most of their day walking the streets on their own rather than spend time with their mother, I have asked myself – I have no memory so cannot answer.

*The streets of Wallasey village seemed like a vast city to me. I would investigate the windows of all the shops and return the smiles of the people who I encountered. I had no anxiety as I felt free, and the hours passed quickly. I loved finding pennies on the pavement and on one occasion I found a £5 note which I quickly spent on sweets – it was a big bag of sweets.*

The memories I do recall begin in Bangor, and at times my mother could be extremely violent without any warning.

*I liked the kitchen of the Edwardian terrace we had moved to which people called the railway houses; the old cast iron range dominated the kitchen. It reminded me of the kindness of an Edwardian widow down my street in Secombe who made me a bacon sandwich every Sunday morning. Dipping the freshly sliced bread into the pan she used to cook the bacon on her coal fired range.*

*One day my mother flew into a rage and picked up the cast-iron iron sitting on our range and threatened to hit me on the head with it. I was terrified but grateful there was no money to have coal in the range and the iron was cold. It felt very lonely to have it reinforced on that day that there would be no more Sunday morning bacon sandwiches with Mrs. Ritzen, but I remember what she always told me when I left her on those Sunday mornings – always be kind.*

Humanistic psychologists argue that people are 'meaning making beings' (Frankl, 2011, 2021; Kaufman, 2020). Sadly, I never bonded with my mother but nor do I hold feelings of anger towards her. Instead, I now feel compassion as she was lost in her own mental health issues – she may have been a survivor of her own childhood traumas. Her violence stopped when I was around eight years old following an incident when she came towards me with her hand raised to smash against the side of my head which was her normal strike point.

> *It was exciting to be growing up very rapidly as many people would comment I would grow to be 6 foot 6 inches tall easily. I loved the thought of being grown up. I never did reach such a height but by 10 years old I was nearly 5'7 inches tall.*

I remember grabbing my mother's arm as it swung towards my head and halting its progress in midair. I told her if she ever hit me again, I would hit her back. My uncles in Liverpool had told me never to hit a woman even when she is hitting you. My uncles always treated me well. I do not believe I would have ever hit her. However, I was not willing to be hit anymore. Jung (2015) talks about the parts of us we keep buried and locked away as fearing looking inside the box that holds the buried things we wish to forget. As I look back now over 60 years, I would have liked to have loved my mother but something in my very early childhood stopped that from happening:

> *I feel dissociated when asked what I think was happening to make me leave˙ the house every day. My instinct at such moments of inquiry speaks powerfully to me – somethings are best not known – behind that message I sense a deep fear of hating my mother and I move on quickly.*

She died aged 39, a day before the siege of the Iran embassy in London in early May 1980. It is 44 years since her death. I remember not being able to help carry her coffin. I now understand I could not touch her coffin as I feared triggering my anger and loss;

> *I am at peace with knowing – somethings are what they are. I feel a deep sense of compassion for the young man who was too scared to touch his mother's coffin and for my mother who lived such a short and tough life.*

I did experience a deep and loving attachment with my father's mother, Mavis Balfour (nee Summerville). She was the granddaughter of a released West Indian slave (Thomas Padmore). Thomas married the daughter of a Liverpool harbour master around 1860. She is reported to have been no more than 5 feet tall and a 'force of nature' by all accounts. He is reported to have been a deep ebony black in skin colour and six foot six tall. It must have taken great courage to marry a black man in the mid-19th century. Thomas was an educated man who had worked as a shipping clerk in the Caribbean. He preached in the Methodist church and must have been an imposing sight in a Victorian top hat and tailcoat. My great-grandmother had reportedly single-handedly stopped a runaway horse-driven wagon on one of the docks, whilst bigger and stronger males all around her ran for their lives.

*Sometimes I wonder where my resilience and grit generate from. I smile at the thought that my great grandparents stand beside me holding my hands as I journey for personal meaning and advocate for social change.*

Vulnerability is often situated as a weakness within the sexual child abuse survivor in the reductionist stories our culture tells, blaming them for the sexual crimes committed against them.

*I recall feeling very alone at the age of 7, and I suspect the sex predators' senses registered new prey and they began to hunt.*

## Memento Mori

Recently in one of the latest iterations of Star Trek, the story focuses on the USS Enterprise as they respond to a planetary distress call. On arrival they are faced with a new enemy they have little knowledge of. The Gorn are a reptilian species who feed on other species including humanoid ones (https://youtu.be/gabIdOMrn7k). The ship security officer, La'an Noonien-Singh, having encountered the Gorn previously as a child, is acutely aware of the threat they pose to the crew and states to the command team, 'The Gorn eat your flesh whilst you are still alive' (Liu, 2022).

*I've often reflected that sexual abusers feast on your spirit but leave you alive, with the toxin of their defilement continuing to erode your sense of being human, leaving a deep sense of shame that doesn't belong to you but them. That sense of shaming is often reinforced by people in positions of power if they are aware of your sexual abuse experiences as a child.*

The 'Gorn' is a good metaphor for abusers and for those who collude with the blaming and silencing of male survivors in particular – and as a device to support a quick flyby of my journey through their 'hunting grounds', and my graduation to a metaphorical 'Star Fleet' via a Psychology higher education to, currently, MSc level. I hope to shine a small light on why I believe my journey through a psychology education has enabled me to find a way to a more self-connected 'Dasein' (Heidegger, 2010).

*I smile even when encountering the bullying and silencing that still plays out as I push for change. To paraphrase from Star Trek, I have truly gone where I had not dare go before – home –to recover what was truly never lost – me. Not victim not survivor – just me – and to live a life of honesty and integrity – to 'live long and prosper' indeed.*

For ten years from the age of seven, I experienced four male sexual abusers who would now be categorised as groomers, and one female aged around 14, who introduced me to male–female sex when I was around eight years old. My first male abuser was not investigated. However, I brought the second to justice in 2015. Clifford Jones is a man with a long history of sexually abusing children. He was sentenced to 18 months as he could only be jailed under the laws in place in the 1960s. The North Wales police declined to investigate two other males, but my allegations were recorded as credible. My final sexual abuser, John Allen, who ran one of biggest children's home business in the UK at the time – *The Bryn Alyn Community* (Lost in Care, 2000) – was at the centre of a major inquiry run by the National Crime Agency: Operation Pallial (Towler, 2015).

The female I did not report. She often told me during our sexual encounters about the abuse her Catholic priest was committing against her and how she confessed our sexual activity during her confessions with him. It's my understanding that the priest had targeted her and other children in her family and, led by her, he was brought to justice some years ago. I am told she has found her way home and I am pleased for her.

I spent approximately three years navigating the Bangor hunting grounds of the 'Gorn' and I became extremely difficult to deal with, especially if I encountered males who attempted to control me. I was assessed for admission into a children's mental health unit at Colwyn Bay, just around the corner from the town's zoo. I seem to remember finding that amusing. Following an assessment, it was felt I was not 'mentally ill', and I was not sent there.

*I sometimes find my thoughts turning to what people saw in that young boy who seemingly did not pass thresholds for 'mental illness.' I wanted them to see the nightmare that I could not say the name of. I wonder how many people still look the other way when they see the silent scream for help from children from the corner of their eye?*

I was disappointed not to be labelled 'mad'. The unit had a drama theatre and I recall liking the staff I met. I wanted to spend every day acting in that theatre, I suspect.

*I have on occasion wished I'd explored being an actor – I can see how a life being someone else could be freeing for many survivors. The emotions experienced following abuse would be powerful tools for an actor to use.*

What is not known widely is that many children placed into care during the 1970s were placed via a voluntary order which their parents agreed to. I was one of those children. I wished to escape the 'Gorn' and had advocated for my own placement into care robustly without disclosing why.

> *I would often walk up into the hills above Bangor and wander the lanes and woodland paths. I loved to walk through blue bell carpeted woodlands. Once I found an open gate into a field which was just a carpet of wildflowers. It was a lovely summers day and I lay down in that field of wild diverse colour and watched the clouds pass by wishing I could stay there forever – blue bells are my favourite flower.*

I never told anyone about the 'Gorn' as I feared being shamed and it was easier to be a 'delinquent'.

Aged around ten, I was taken to a children's home called Bryn Alyn Hall just outside of Wrexham in North Wales (Lost in Care, 2000). It seemed like a children's paradise and in many ways it was. Materially it was a very different experience to the poverty of my home. There was no threat of hunger there, but it was owned and run by a very smart 'Gorn' called John Allen, and the next seven years were spent avoiding his sexual hunting.

> *The fear of having a bath if he was around, I could sense him at the locked door. He would ask if I needed anything. I stopped bathing and chose to stink rather than submit.*

I learnt to survive in the hunting ground of the children's home. I was a witness at Allen's trial in 2014 at Mold Crown Court, and he was given a life sentence for the crimes he committed against me and 13 others. He deserved every second of his sentence for the lives he injured.

> *I remember one of the other witnesses bursting into the waiting room just outside the door which led to the box witnesses gave evidence from. He was a big bloke and knew me as he used my name on entering – I was calm but ready for anything. He was wearing a very fluffy large woolen jumper on a very hot summers day. He looked down at me and said, 'Thank you for being here for us.' He was then quickly ushered out of the room by the court staff. I had no recall of him from my childhood – dissociation deletes memories of people as well as the painful events which surrounded them, regrettably.*

The way I learnt to survive often mirrors the personality of Starfleet's Lieutenant La'an;

> *La'an had a spotless Starfleet record, although she found other people challenging. She was used to enduring pain and maintaining her composure.*

*She actually preferred not to be sedated and remain fully aware even during a very painful gene therapy. La'an preferred work and her duties over recreational activities, even in her spare time. She herself credited her painful childhood for not enjoying childish activities. She was a strict teacher when it came to tactical and combat training, especially with cadets. La'an's 'Lessons of Security' included the following;*

- Lesson 1: A Rigelian tiger pounces with no warning.
- *Lesson 2: There are no breaks in security because threats never take breaks.*
- *Lesson 3: Let your tricorder do the investigating.*
- *Lesson 6: Know when to bend the rules.*
- Lesson 7: Leave no stone unturned.

*(Alpha, 2022)*

In conclusion, I shall return to the 'Gorn', La'an, and myself.

I left the Bryn Alyn Community days after my 17th birthday and joined the RAF Regiment, serving for four years leaving with an exemplary record. The next 40+ years have seen me lead a diverse and often successful life; that story will be told elsewhere due to the word count limitation of this chapter. I shall instead explore my journey to achieving a BSc and MSc in Psychology, whilst for the last eight years holding an Honorary Supervisor contract at the University of Liverpool's Department of Clinical Psychology:

La'an:   *Ever the optimist*
Pike:    *'Sometimes, hope is a choice'.*
La'an:   *'Yeah, you've told me that one before'.*
Pike:    *'Maybe I'm just saying it because I need to hear it. It's why we're here, on this planet'.*

*(Vrvillo, 2023)*

## Broken Circle

Broken Circle is a Star Trek episode that sees the main characters of the show grappling with different professional and personal challenges, from Spock dealing with his humanness, to a crew member dealing with the disclosure of her genetic augmented difference, which will see her arrested for lying about her genetic status on enrolment in Star Fleet (Fisher, 2023).

For Star Fleet, given the history of Earth's eugenics wars in the mid-21st century, which saw the rise of super-humans like Khan Noonien Singh, to be augmented is a clear danger (Daniels, 1967). In many ways, this phase of my story mirrors the complex issues playing out for the crew of the USS Enterprise. My survivor status was now public having disclosed following the publication of the Waterhouse Inquiry (Lost in Care, 2000). The research evidence suggests survivors of childhood sexual violence often have enhanced awareness of threat, and like Spock, they struggle to control the emotions that generate from such enhanced sensitivity (Schalk et al., 2023).

> *As my disclosure dispersed into my lived world, it became clear to me that not all responses were positive. Many people seemed triggered by my difference and acted as if I was a threat even if I excelled at my job. I began to feel angry about the responses – in many ways more than the abuse itself – it seemed a double injustice and trauma compounding – especially coming from people who often claimed to be healers.*

There were people who treated me in a trauma-informed way, even though that term would not have been known to them. They knew how to be trauma-informed. They knew how to respond as a human being and still be professional. A week after my disclosure I recall the following conversation with my team leader;

Rob:    '*I think this is the end of my career how can I ever work in mental health again?*'
Kim:    '*Come back to work – we will work it out together*'.

I will always be grateful to Kim. Her response was the right one for me – it saved my life even though at times she must have thought 'Did I make the right decision?' She did, but she could not control the responses of some of her manager peers who were not as trauma-informed in their responses, which at the time was very triggering and nearly undid Kim's insightful – before its time – trauma-responsive approach. Kim was an officer Star Fleet would have wanted in any frontline command team.

> *It was horrifying to feel trapped in work environments where people with power 'other' you for being open about being a survivor. One told me to not talk about it and another advised me to lead a quiet life and return to the silence.*

I believe they meant well. They knew better than me at the time that victim blaming and microaggressions (which do not feel so micro when you experience them almost daily) are really damaging. On occasion they seem aimed to trigger some form of acting out, so allowing 'gaslighting' to be deployed. This is often carried out by people in agencies who claim to work for survivors, but in truth often work for themselves and only tolerate survivors who conform to their agendas (Javaid, 2016).

## Ad Astra per Aspera

In this episode, the Starship Enterprise is dealing with the trial of its First Officer an Illyrian who is genetically augmented. The episode addresses discrimination within Star Fleet; research regularly notes survivors of sexual violence are discriminated against (Reich et al., 2021).

> *I was angry being kept waiting to see someone who could have seen me in a second, but once I said I was looking to create a service for sexual violence survivors, she kept me waiting for nearly an hour and her attitude was dismissive of my plans. It was a bitter taste of what was to come during the next two decades of activism – with few exceptions very few doors have opened proactively to embrace supporting change for male survivors.*

Stigmatisation is a toxic cultural phenomenon which dehumanises people (Goffman, 1990). Whilst my journey through an academic psychology education has been mostly positive, I've also encountered stigma and discrimination. During my BSc Psychology with Counselling, some of the academic and admin staff were less than welcoming. That reinforced the experience I had had with Social Work, having been barred from a course during a short intense episode of depression as I transitioned from my previous married life to a solo one within student halls. It took me back to North Wales and feeling trapped and on my own. It took the head of social work 6 minutes to press the button to eject me when I disclosed depression – no offer of support, no radical empathy.

Even though I assertively fought to return to the course, that pathway was closed and internationally known figures who claim best practice leadership status colluded in keeping the door closed. Stigma is indeed a shaming projection.

However, the shame is the property of the stigmatising.

> *I remember awaking from my depressive state quickly when the speed of her response granting my request registered. Like people who have survived attempting to end their own life report in the moment of actioning death, one wakes up to life. I felt angry – such a response could have triggered my ending, and to come from a social work professional showered with accolades for their work in child protection astonished me.*

My social worker course experience had been at the same University where I achieved my BSc in Psychology. Some academic psychologists were less than welcoming. Thankfully most did not allow my history with the Social Work Department (they had offices on the same floor) to cloud their attitudes towards me. I achieved a 'good' upper second and given the circumstances that's an achievement worth being proud of! Ad Astra per Aspera (To the Stars through Hardship) seems apt. It mirrors the RAF Regiment motto Per Ardua (Through Adversity).

A final reflection on stigma and some psychologists. Just before the pandemic, I applied for entry to a Counselling Psychology PhD course. On paper, I exceeded the requirements for the course both academically and in relation to work experience. I was initially offered an interview but that was cancelled. I then received a rejection letter stating the selection panel felt it would be better for me to pursue a counselling diploma and academic PhD separately. I replied to say that I did not understand the logic of that decision. I was offered a video feedback meeting, and I approached it with a curious and relaxed mindset. The conversation went in circles regardless of the professional representations I made. The lead for the course at one stage leaned in the camera on their computer and stated:

*I'm not being a cunt, you know.*

If I were a police Senior Investigating Officer I would call that the suspect leaking their true intent (Canter & Youngs, 2009). My references in support of my application were from nationally known consultant clinical psychologists. My girlfriend at the time said I should make a formal complaint. I chose not to, as why would I want to study on a course that had such unprofessional people running it.

> *The Federation teaches that if we can find a way to empathize with an enemy, then they can one day become our friends. They're wrong. Some things in this universe are just plain evil, La'an.*
>
> *(Liu, 2022)*

## Tomorrow and Tomorrow and Tomorrow

During the recent pandemic, I studied for an MSc in Counselling and Positive Psychology and whilst this was quite a journey in relation to the Covid restrictions I obtained a good merit overall with a distinction for my dissertation.

I am now a qualified psychotherapist as well as an academically educated psychologist and a graduate member of the British Psychological Society. There are many survivors and care leavers who enter University in later life, often unseen. They do not disclose their 'looked after' care experience, instead focusing on catching up on educational opportunities lost by the systems which should have supported them better (Duncalf, 2010). However, it is sadly true I am a rare example from my 1970s children's home context.

This episode of Star Trek focuses on La'an (Reed, 2023). I reflect on how I am drawn to her character. The stoic will not give like a survivor from a Gorn-feeding planet. La'an finds herself transported back in time to the early 21st century with a mission from a dying future Star Fleet temporal operative and tasked with stopping something that will alter the timeline. She finds herself accompanied by alternative timeline Captain Kirk. In his timeline, the Federation and Star Fleet never formed, and he serves in Earth Fleet. He has never visited Earth as its environment was never repaired after its Third World War (WWIII), as the alliance with Vulcan never happened and it had been their science which allowed Earth's environment to be repaired. The story moves at a fast pace and follows lots of plot twists and jeopardy, including the death of Kirk.

La'an finds the point in time where she must act and save a young boy from being killed by a Romulan agent. That boy is her ancestor Khan who is an augment, and his superior skills at war will lead him to rule one quarter of the earth during WWIII and kill millions. La'an grapples with the dilemma she faces as she understands the power, she holds to change history. She can end her ancestor here and now and save millions of lives in the future.

La'an realises that she doesn't have the right to change history, even though it would mean she was never born and therefore she would escape the horror of the 'Gorn' feeding planet.

*As I watched the scene, I thought what I would do if I could end the lives of my abusers when they were children before they could become 'Gorn.'*

La'an made the right choice – she chose not to change history. We must face the reality of existence and live it well (Frankl, 2021; Van Deurzen, 2012). She could have saved millions of lives. However, she understands that she is more than she was due to the posttraumatic growth she has experienced serving in Star Fleet (Tedeschi & Calhoun, 2004). Changing time could have unexpected consequences and perhaps have led to the death of more people. So, she comforts the boy and then returns to her own timeline where all seems to be as it is meant to be. However, she feels the loss of Kirk and alone with the choice she made;

*As a survivor, I often ponder on loneliness and aloneness and the difference between the two. I am often alone and like La'an I can feel sad. As for loneliness, sometimes I sense that, but I'm lucky as I am never lonely. Either by temperament or nurture, I never worry about solitude as I find it comfortable and, in many ways, intellectually liberating.*

## Among the Lotus Eaters

This episode sees some of the Enterprises crew visit a plant where a unique radiation affects memory and people forget who they are (Row, 2023).

> *For a long time, I struggled with the fact I could only remember the colour of the tiles in the old Victorian public toilets my main abuser took me to, aged 8, one sunny Sunday afternoon, following a day at the seaside. But not what happened in them that afternoon. There was going to be a price to pay for the lovely 'Knickerbocker Glory' I had just been gifted by him. I never went anywhere near him again – all I recall is the vivid blue of the tiles.*

Dissociation is a powerful human capacity (Herman, 2012). It can be a trap filled with chaos or an adaptive behaviour which can be helpful in certain situations where the capacity to dissociate in real time can offer an advantage. This is vividly explored by Barker in her book Regeneration, which is set during the First World War (Barker, 2014). Her main character goes over the top into battle and finds himself almost phased out of time as time seems to slow down for other people around him, but he can move at normal speed around them. I recall my own 'going over the top' moment during a military exercise;

> *It was a cold, clear winter's night – we hung to the grass just in front of the barbed wire which separated the mock Russian special forces team we were playing in the airbase evaluation exercise from our objective. Suddenly the bright halogen lights which flooded the ground in front of the wire and separated us from the aircraft pan which held around six Jaguar fighter bombers went out.*
>
> *I remember it was like a switch went off in my head and I was suddenly up and moving at a sprint towards the low barbwire barrier and vaulting it – it felt like time had slowed and I could move quicker than everyone around me.*

## Subspace Rhapsody

I have learnt much about myself, survivors and the 'Gorn' since I began to study psychology. Of course, the study never ends. Human beings are complex and diverse and not easily categorised by any school of psychology. Like the explorations of the scientific understandings of the dawn of the universe – an ever-unfolding story of new understandings. In this episode (Downs, 2023), the crew of the Enterprise creates a link to subspace. This creates a subspace field, which, when they feel emotional about something, compels them to burst into song and sing the truth of their feelings for each other and their mission.

La'an learns to be authentic in ways that support her growth during this creative musical episode. She listens to No 1 sing;

(https://tinyurl.com/3jcmcezb)

(Downs, 2023)

The final song in the episode is one of my all-time favourite moments in Star Trek. It reinforces a truth that I've learnt during 25 years of education and activism. We can never beat the 'Gorn' unless we all authentically work together;

(https://tinyurl.com/5ekdjxdp)

The lyrics sum up what trauma-informed working should be.

*This is where it all leads – 'The Enterprise' is it 'my' destiny to save us all – No – it's my job to disrupt the chaos find a purpose for us all, We're all rushing around – we are confused and upended – lets refocus now our bond is imperative – let's bring our collective together – as we fight for our lives – Uhura, I really needed to hear that ... our security is only as strong as our unity – We know our purpose is – to protect the mission – our directive – as we work better all together – we overcome – our obstacles – as one.*

(Sweeney et al., 2018)

We all need to sing in harmony to bring progressive change for survivors of all kinds of childhood adversity.

## Hegemony

In the final episode of Series 2 in this iteration of Star Trek, the Enterprise encounters the 'Gorn' again and the stakes could not be higher for individual crew members, Star Fleet, and the Federation itself (Vrvillo, 2023). Increasingly, I see the 'Gorn' rebooting to adapt to a 'trauma-informed' system – using the knowledge as a new weapon against survivors who challenge their cultural hegemony. So, the mission is far from over – so yes tell fear, no: the hope is you indeed...

To Be Continued...

## References

Alpha. (2022). *La'an Noonien-Singh*. Memory Alpha, Fandom, Inc. https://memory-alpha.fandom.com/wiki/La%27an_Noonien-Singh#Personality_and_abilities

Balfour, R. D. (2013). *Narratives accounts: Sexual violence -abuse activists: From Rebel to Sensei'* [Unpublished undergraduate dissertation, University of Bradford].

Balfour, R. (2022). Victim–Survivor–Warrior–Healer: An autoethnographic account of a male childhood sexual violence survivor's activist journey. *Social Work and Social Sciences Review, 23*(2), 103–125. https://doi.org/10.1921/swssr.v23i2.2086

Barker, P. (2014). *Regeneration*. Penguin Books.

Bochner, A. P. (2012). On first-person narrative scholarship. *Narrative Inquiry, 22*(1), 155–164. https://doi.org/10.1075/ni.22.1.10boc

Bruner, J. S. (2002). *Acts of meaning*. Harvard University Press. https://doi.org/10.1177/0891241606286982

Canter, D. V., & Youngs, D. (2009). *Investigative psychology: Offender profiling and the analysis of criminal action*. John Wiley & Sons.

Crossley, M. L. (2000). *Introducing narrative psychology: Self, trauma, and the construction of meaning*. Open University Press.

Daniels, M. (1967, February 16). *Star Trek: The original series - Space seed* (Season 1 (22). NBC. - Search Videos (bing.com).

Downs, D. (2023, August 3). *Star Trek: Strange new worlds - Subspace rhapsody* (Season 2 (9). Paramount +. "Star Trek: Strange New Worlds" Subspace Rhapsody (TV Episode 2023) – IMDb.

Duncalf, Z. (2010). *Listen up! Adult care leavers speak out: The views of 310 care leavers aged 17–78*. Strathprints.

Fisher, C. (2023, June 15). *Star Trek: Strange new worlds - Broken circle* (Season 2 (1). Paramount +. "Star Trek: Strange New Worlds" The Broken Circle (TV Episode 2023) - IMDb

Frank, A. W. (2012). *Letting stories breathe: A socio-narratology*. University Of Chicago Press.

Frankl, V. E. (2011). *Man's search for ultimate meaning*. Rider.

Frankl, V. E. (2021). *Yes to life in spite of everything*. Rider.

Goffman, E. (1990). *The presentation of self in everyday life*. Penguin Books.

Heidegger, M. (2010). *Being and time*. State University of New York.

Herman, J. L. (1992). *Trauma and recovery*. Pandora.

Herman, J. L. (2012). Review of special issue: Guidelines for treating dissociative identity disorder in adults (3rd revision); Rebuilding shattered lives: Treating complex PTSD and dissociative disorders; and Understanding and treating dissociative identity disorder: A relational approach. *Psychoanalytic Psychology, 29*(2), 267–269. https://doi.org/10.1037/a0027818

Illyrian. (n.d.). *Memory alpha*. Retrieved October 15, 2023, from https://memory-alpha.fandom.com/wiki/Illyrian

Javaid, A. (2016). Voluntary agencies' responses to, and attitudes toward male rape: Issues and concerns. *Sexuality & Culture, 20*(3), 731–748. https://doi.org/10.1007/s12119-016-9348-z

Jung, C. G. (2015). *Aion: Researches into the phenomenology of the self* (2nd ed., Vol. 9). Routledge.

Kaufman, S. B. (2020). *Transcend the new science of self-actualisation*. Tarcher Perigee.

László, J. (2008). *The science of stories: An introduction to narrative psychology*. Routledge.

Liu, D. (2022, May 26). *Star Trek: Strange new worlds. "Memento Mori"* (Season 1 {4}). Paramount +. "Star Trek: Strange New Worlds" Memento Mori (TV Episode 2022) – IMDb.

'Lost in Care' Report of the Tribunal of Inquiry into the Abuse of Children in Care in the Former County Council Areas of Gwynedd and Clwyd since 1974. (2000). idoc.pub_lost-in-care-the-waterhouse-report-wales-foster-home-abuse-enquiry-2000.pdf

Maté, G., & Maté, D. (2022). *The myth of normal: Trauma, illness and healing in a toxic culture.* Vermilion.

McAdams, D. P. (1997). *The stories we live by: Personal myths and the making of the self.* Guildford Press.

Perry, B. D., & Winfrey, O. (2021). *What happened to you?* Flatiron Books.

Prilleltensky, I. (2014). Meaning-making, mattering, and thriving in community psychology: From co-optation to amelioration and transformation. *Psychosocial Intervention, 23*(2), 151–154. https://doi.org/10.1016/j.psi.2014.07.008

Reed, D. (2023, June 19). *Star Trek: Strange new worlds - Tomorrow and tomorrow and tomorrow* (Season 2 (3). Paramount +. "Star Trek: Strange New Worlds" Tomorrow and Tomorrow and Tomorrow (TV Episode 2023) – IMDb.

Reich, C. M., Pegel, G. A., & Johnson, A. B. (2021). Are survivors of sexual assault blamed more than victims of other crimes? *Journal of Interpersonal Violence, 37,* 19–20. https://doi.org/10.1177/08862605211037423

Row, A. (2023). *Star Trek: Strange new worlds - Among the Lotus Eaters* (Season 2 (4). Paramount +. "Star Trek: Strange New Worlds" Among the Lotus Eaters (TV Episode 2023) – IMDb.

Sarbin, T. R. (1986). *Narrative psychology: The storied nature of human conduct.* Praeger.

Schalk, T., Oliero, J., Fedele, E., Trouser, V., & Lefevre, T. (2023). Evaluation of multidimensional functional impairment in adult sexual assault survivors, with a focus on its psychological, physical, and social dimensions, based on validated measurements: A PRISMA systematic review. *International Journal of Environmental Research and Public Health, 20*(14), 6373. https://doi.org/10.3390/ijerph20146373

Sweeney, A., Filson, B., Kennedy, A., Collinson, L., & Gillard, S. (2018). A paradigm shift: Relationships in trauma-informed mental health services. *BJPsych Advances, 24*(5), 319–333. https://psycnet.apa.org/doi/10.1192/bja.2018.29

Taylor, J., & Clarence, B. (2021). *Beneficial but triggering: Experiences and support of survivors' speakers in the UK.* Victim Focus Publications.

Tedeschi, R. G., & Calhoun, L. G. (2004). Posttraumatic growth: Conceptual foundations and empirical evidence. *Psychological Inquiry, 15*(1), 1–18. https://www.jstor.org/stable/20447194

Towler, K. (2015). Learning the lessons: 'Operation Pallial.' In *www.dera.ioe.ac.uk.* Children's Commissioner for Wales. 528. pdf (ioe.ac.uk).

van Deurzen, E. (2012). *Existential counselling and psychotherapy in practice.* Sage.

Vrvillo, M. (2023 B.C.E., August 10). *Star Trek: Strange new worlds - Hegemony* (Season 2 (10). Paramount +. "Star Trek: Strange New Worlds" Hegemony (TV Episode 2023) – IMDb.

WYCA. (2023). *Scoping to support the development of a safety of men and boys strategy for West Yorkshire.* westyorks-ca.gov.uk

# 5

# AUTISTIC AND CHALLENGING THE NEOLIBERAL ACADEMY IN HONG KONG

*Yulin Cheng and Alec Grant*

**9 May 2023**

*Yulin:*    Autoethnography is a method that 'interrogates and critiques practices and power imbalances in order to make advances in social justice' (Grant, 2019, p. 88), but what does social justice look like and who are we seeking justice from?

*Alec:*    Good questions! We should pursue this at some point in our chapter.

*Yulin:*    Can we, or should those who hold positions of power, and who are complicit in perpetuating oppressive practices, be held accountable? This is a critical reflection of my experience as an autistic mental health researcher in the neoliberal academy who is also suffering from depression and fatigue. I want to call out the hypocrisies and oppressive workplace practices that contributed to my mental ill health. I turn to autoethnography in an act of resistance to subvert the dominance of the positivist paradigm and to take charge of my own narrative. At the same time, I am increasingly questioning how and to what extent the act of writing my own story can become emancipatory and transformative for myself when a part of me is seeking vindication and redress for the 'wrongs' done by individuals and the system.

*Alec:*    So, it seems that there's both a social justice and therapeutic purpose to your chapter.

*Yulin:*    In preparing for this manuscript, I have read a few autoethnographies for ideas to start with, including autoethnographies written

DOI: 10.4324/9781003408963-5

by autistic researchers of their experiences in the academy, notably Botha's (2021) autoethnography on the treatment of autistic people in knowledge production on autism and Raymaker's (2017) autoethnography on the intersections of marginalizations and privilege as an autistic woman with a professional background in engineering.

However, many autoethnographies I read described life events that focused on a period in the past. This is not to say that those events or past experiences no longer affected their present lives or do not happen now. But these autoethnographies describe key turning points in their lives in which they have emerged in a better shape or position. This is in contrast to my own present situation. I am writing while standing at the crossroads where the events and experiences I am to recount are happening in the present continuing tense. While emotions are useful for autoethnography, and may even be cathartic, there are inherently a lot of emotions – intense, painful, confused, obscured, etc. – to disentangle and process, and my alexithymia may make this process even harder.

I am still submerged in the water, so to say, and have not emerged in a better shape. To write in the present continuing tense is to come face to face with my own insecurities and vulnerabilities, to find myself in a precarious situation where, in coming to face my anger, I have to put up with the pain of revealing what is hidden underneath that rage, which I call *desolation*. My sense of helplessness in what I regard to be a hopeless situation leaves me trembling in fear, and the cognitive dissonance between wanting to live and wanting to die, between hope and despair often leaves me in a state of paralysis.

*Alec:* Take courage and go for this. Don't hold back.

*Yulin:* There is another hurdle to overcome before this can proceed. In coming out as an openly autistic advocate and activist, I put myself in an exposed and vulnerable position. Yet I am required, at the same time, to hold myself up to an ethical standard that requires me to protect and disguise the identity of individuals involved?...

*Alec:* My co-written paper, 'Troubling Tolichism...' (Grant & Young, 2022) will help you here.

*Yulin:* ...Even if I did (and I would), but given my exposed identity, the geographical area and specialized field I am writing from, is this even possible? Does this mean I could only write about my experience anonymously or face direct confrontation with the relevant individuals and institution involved? How is this fair and why should holders of power be able to shield themselves under the academic veil? If universities are to be run like neoliberal organizations, isn't it fair that we should be able to pierce through the corporate (academic) veil? Can we achieve justice without holding them accountable? I am facing a moral dilemma – I am outraged by the oppressive practices that domineered our lives but at the same time risk becoming a version of my worst enemy. Perhaps that is how authoritarian and oppressive systems justify themselves – by provoking dissenters to become like their worst enemy. Are we all victims and oppressors of this system? What does it mean to be a survivor of the system? Are we just going to ignore the failings of the system? Do I have it in me to write a good autoethnography?

*Alec:*   Yes, you do. And I will help you.

*Yulin:*   I could possibly justify myself on the ground that qualitative methods such as autoethnographies hold little appeal in the local academy that is domineered by positivistic and quantitative studies, noting I once took a semester course on ethnography in the hope that it would cover autoethnography but, to my disappointment, was told that it will not be covered in the syllabus because it was not a popular research method.

**9 May 2023 (email)**

Dear Alec,

It was great meeting you (on Zoom) and thanks so much for your feedback. I am really looking forward to doing this and thank you for putting me at ease.

Best regards,
Yulin.
(deadline date for next draft agreed)

*

**5 June 2023 (email)**

Dear Alec,

I'm sorry I missed the deadline... I have many things to do, many things undone, but I've reached a stage where I can no longer keep up with deadlines. There isn't a day I don't think about work, the people I let down and the people that let me down, the guilt and anger. Some days, I'm fuelled by a burning rage, ready to take on the world. But most days, I'm just exhausted, caught in my own flames that I'm too tired to put out, just let it burn, I couldn't care less anymore. I can't survive on anger alone when I'm about to lose my bread and butter as my four-year PhD program comes to an end. Even though I have got a six-month extension, I would no longer be receiving my studentship and that's my foremost worry. At this point, I can almost hear my boss say, 'Don't be ashamed to seek help!' But why would I seek help from someone who can't reflect on their own power and role in contributing to structural oppression? What use is he if he is not willing to help counter systemic disparities?

Why would I seek help from someone who assumes that the problem with poor mental health lies in people not seeking help, and questioning the 'help' that's available or given when this is sought? 'In order to be a crusader, you have to put yourself through it', were the words that were said to me on a previous occasion when I tried to ask for reasonable adjustments. Why do I want to seek help from someone so brainwashed by positivist thinking that they don't recognize the inadequacies and rigidity of positivist research and the related medical model of mental health? Why do I want to be at the mercy of someone who is partially responsible for the difficulties I've had in doing my PhD? 'I don't see you as disabled', is not a compliment, nor is being a high-functioning autistic an achievement to be proud of. At what point does one fall from high-functioning to low-functioning?

Have you worked with someone who is not very good at keeping with deadlines? I could do with more supervision and mentoring. Could you please give me another try?

## 3rd June (email)

Dear Alec,

I am sorry but this is all I could manage to produce after working on it for two days. I thought if I devoted one or two days to thinking and writing my chapter, the inspiration would come and the words would flow. It seems I have to try another method as I can't rely entirely on my inspiration. I recently wrote a 2,500-word essay in two days, but that was after months of unproductive writing, and after a short break in Australia. I can't afford to travel anywhere else in the meantime. How do you deal with writer's block, and could you share your writing habits and strategies?

I would also like to ask for tips on taking notes and memo writing. I wanted to relay conversations I had or heard in the past but am having trouble recalling the exact contents and words that were used – would that be a problem? Have you got any good practice to share for taking notes of conversations in the future?

## 2nd June

### *What It Means to Be Alive*

*Flipping through photos taken back three months ago when I was travelling in Australia after a three-year hiatus due to Covid restrictions, recalling memories of walking along the coastline, it was the most alive I've felt in the past three years.*

*As I now sit in the cafe, finally feeling awake after four shots of espresso, but am still having trouble squeezing words out of my brain, my thoughts are messy, my mind is confused, my heart is weary. I am forgetting what it feels like to be alive.*

*A voice inside me is saying I should go for a walk outside. It has been said nature is the best medicine. But with all due respect to Mother Nature, I have been walking yesterday, the day before, and the days and weeks before. I have been walking in the outdoors nearly every day for the past three years, and my mind is in no better shape. It keeps me physically active; it keeps life in equilibrium, but it doesn't energise.*

*I need more than just a walk in the park. I need access to wilderness, I need access to wide empty solitary spaces, I need access to an environment where individual rights and freedoms are respected, I need to break free from a culture that demands conformity.*

*How do I write stories to connect readers with what it feels like to be alive when I wake up every day in a place that is sucking the life out of me?*

### 7th June (email, after the Second Zoom Meeting)

Alec: Great meeting you virtually again, Yulin! Just to recap, I spoke about the rationale for writing a dialogical autoethnography, and how I thought that would be helpful given the fact that you're still working on your PhD. We also spoke about the mentoring element of doing a dialogical chapter: although I'm the more experienced person, and am taking the lead, you will also be a co-mentor for me.

We talked about the irony of me mentoring you, given the difficulties you describe with your PhD supervisor/manager (which evoke sadness and anger in me, simultaneously). I tried to reassure you about this, and I believe that working dialogically with me will prove to be helpful for you, even though it seems a bit anxiety-provoking for you right now.

You wanted tips and questions. Having never worked with autistic people before, I don't have any tips to give you other than the 'common sense' ones of maybe tackling one writing task at a time and trying to do a little bit of writing every day. I have one question that we can each, separately explore before our next Zoom meeting: *What does the literature say about support for autistic university postgraduate students?* (related to this question you also gave me permission to share our chapter, later in its development, with my colleague and ex-autoethnographic mentee, Dr Seb Shaw).

We agreed on our next Zoom meeting date and the date for you to send me your response in our developing chapter.

## 22nd June (email)

**Yulin:**

Dear Alec,

If we could show our scars and share our innermost thoughts like we show our tattoos, I would show you the cut and scar on my leg, I would talk about the heaviness on my shoulders, the weight of the world.

There's a monumental amount of work on my plate that no matter how much I have achieved during the day, I'm still lagging behind. When you are living on borrowed time, forever playing catch up; when there is nothing left to look forward to, it is wearisome to carry that burden through the day and into the night.

That's how every day goes. My interests become debts. As a researcher, I have to account for the work I do, for the contents I write, for the participants of my research. As an autistic and neurodiversity advocate, I have to account for the interests of the neurodivergent communities. As a student, I have to account for my progress. Life is a cycle of never-ending work, deadlines, obligations, debts, and responsibilities. But these are just the tip of the iceberg.

It's the emotional labour – the anger, the betrayal, and the loneliness I carry, as an openly autistic scholar and advocate (which is rarely heard of where I live) that proves too much to bear. The people I'm up against and resisting, the ones who hold the reins. Consumed by hatred and rage, let down by hypocrisies and bureaucracies, my tattered self and embittered heart have been broken into pieces. Sometimes I feel I have nothing more to give.

In the span of my PhD, I have spent more time advocating and fighting for my rights, educating fellow academics about autism, neurodiversity, and ableism than I have received support from them. I have more enemies than allies and I am socially and intellectually isolated. Yet, even as a struggling student, even in my seeming powerlessness, I am aware that my connection to the academy is, in and of itself, a privilege, and it is through this privilege that I got to know you. I have always wanted to have a mentor, but my relationship with my PhD advisor is akin to that of a boss and subordinate, marked by constant power struggles and resistance (for this reason, I will refer to him as 'Boss' in my writing). I agree that doing a dialogical autoethnography would be more manageable given my circumstances and I like the idea of a dialogue. The Boss seems to have trouble engaging in dialogues or conversations without making jokes that only he finds humorous. When I or others try to convey our concerns to him, in all seriousness, he has a habit of cutting people short and dismissing our concerns, thinking (as the Boss) that he has everything under control (another example of his inability to stand in the shoes of junior staff and students). Sometimes, I think that he is incapable of dialogue. I also think that a dialogue would be a nice break from the style of conversation I am used to that is associated with my advocacy, which tends to be confrontational and adversarial. I hope our joint collaboration will go, in some ways, to mitigate for the loneliness that I felt and the lack of support.

As for my seeming anxiety, I wasn't anxious but confused about your suggestion and arrangement. When you proposed in the email (quoting, 'I'll reply to you, and you reply to me, etc., until we have your chapter?'), I misread your reply to mean that I will continue to work on my own chapter, in addition to the dialogue. Hence, the confusion.[1]

And if you sense my hesitancy, it is because I would still like to, at one point, write an autoethnography based on my experience, about my time doing research in the university, about the betrayals and hypocrisies, about the heartbreak and pain. As you have it in your pinned tweet, 'Why Autoethnography? If you don't control your narrative somebody else will',[2] I know who these people are, and I've seen them do it. I know that if I leave my narrative in their hands, they will control and twist it into something else I did not intend or mean, to keep their power and the status quo unchallenged. This is why I want to write my own autoethnography and have it published, and I am afraid I won't get another chance to write a chapter, or if I did, I would no longer have the benefit of your mentorship.

Thank you for reading. I will send you a link for our next Zoom meeting on 6th July and share the literature I found.

## 28th June

**Alec:**

Dear Yulin,

First, I want to say that it saddens me that you're in so much stress and pain in your current personal, academic, and organizational life. For a long time now, based on my own experiences and the experiences of colleagues and friends, I've come to believe that organizations – including higher education institutions – can be deeply punitive and unpleasant places to work in. I'll talk more about this below.

I'll begin however by saying that I slowly read through our evolving chapter again this morning, noting down all my responses that I intended to use in this reply in markup side bubbles. I began by thinking about a good title for our chapter, and I came up with 'Challenging oppression in the neoliberal academy: A conversational autoethnography'. What do you think of it?

I then turned to the questions you opened the chapter with: 'What does justice look like?' and 'who are we seeking justice from?'. My response at the time you posed them was 'Good questions! You should pursue this'. However, given that we're writing dialogically and conversationally, I now think that 'I' should be 'We'. So, to answer your first question, 'justice' to me looks like accumulated oppositional writing. To paraphrase the title of another chapter I co-wrote a few years back, *we write to resist, and we write to survive* (Klevan et al., 2020, p. 123). To repeat the maxim, if we don't take charge of our own narrative someone else will. Taking charge of our narrative means making it real, making it palpable. Gloria Anzaldúa tells us 'By writing I put order in the world, give it a handle so I can grasp it' (Anzaldúa, 2017, p. 74). My answer to your second question – 'who are we seeking justice from?' – is that we're taking the neoliberal academy, and by implication and complicit association, the neoliberal academic to task. As I wrote a few years back:

> I think the use of … conversation as method …is eminently suitable and appropriate for our chapter. This is because productivity always seems … to be privileged over relationships in our reptilian, neoliberal, new public managed … universities, where the powerful and ruthless triumph over and often – at worst – destroy the nice folk, and where self-interest trumps kindness … *conversation* in *writing* are important and significant acts of resistance to this state of affairs. Moreover, the solidarity and knowledge that co-evolve with the … conversation-writing process is great for maintaining integrity…
>
> *(Grant, in Klevan et al., 2020, p. 123)*

In line with your need to recount your lived experiences in the present, continuing tenses, I think that this is what we're doing together, dialogically, in this co-evolving, co-developing chapter.

I next came to your point: '…I am required, at the same time, to hold myself up to an ethical standard that requires me to protect and disguise the identity of individuals involved?' I mentioned the Grant and Young (2021) article earlier. I'm not sure if you've read this yet (if not, I urge you to do so when you can), but I think I should say a little about it at this point. Susan Young and I argue that it's not always appropriate to over-protect the identity of individuals written into autoethnographies, especially if these individuals are oppressive or abusive. We further argue that relational, and procedural, ethics, and presupposed ethical standards, often function in the service of silencing individuals. We make the point that because patriarchal assumptions inform the development and policing of those ethical standards, silenced or potentially silenced individuals are very often women.

In this sense, you and I illuminate the dark side of the neoliberal academy – in your terms always obscured by its sanitised, corporate academic veil – in our developing chapter. I think the 'corporate academic veil' is a very good image, which points to a moral good. This is why it's important to see through the veil in the interest of advancing social justice. However, I believe that we can only achieve justice and take individuals and institutions to task in a broad contextual sense. At the present time in history, you rightly say that 'qualitative methods such as autoethnographies hold little appeal in the local academy … domineered by positivistic and quantitative studies'. Building on the argument that autoethnography is always politically charged (Denzin, 2014), I made a similar point five years ago:

> …Autoethnography always needs to be understood in the critical context of the politics of knowledge shaping contemporary social and human inquiry more generally … (it) represents sustained resistance against the kinds of mainstream work expected by corporate, new public managed, neoliberal universities, in which positivist assumptions and practices dominate.
>
> *(Grant, 2018, p. 107, my brackets)*

It would be naïve of us to hope that our autoethnographic chapter is going to topple positivism, and with it the neoliberal academy. But, in the company of other oppositional texts, it constitutes a small and important act of resistance. This directly relates to your questions: 'Are we all victims and oppressors of this system? What does it mean to be a survivor of the system?' I think that to the extent we stay in silent complicity with the system, we remain both victims and oppressors. Surviving the system in a positive sense is often achieved through dialogic writing. As well as being as an act of resistance, it functions as a tool for achieving a preferred narrative identity (Grant et al., 2015).

Now, to answer a couple of your more specific points, my own strategy for dealing with writer's block is to try to write my way through it by writing about my writer's block. Do you get what I mean here? And regarding taking (field) notes of conversations, my strategy is to recall conversations from memory. I don't take notes, or record, because – not being a positivist – I'm not after exactitude. Often, emotional recall (how the conversation made me feel) is truer to my narrative identity than the precise and total recall of the words exchanged (Grant, 2023).

Finally, you ask me if I've worked with someone who is not very good at keeping with deadlines and say that you could do with more mentoring. I hope by now that I've convinced you that my intention is to support you while understanding your difficulties in keeping to deadlines. I also hope that our developing autoethnography is functioning as a helpful kind of mentoring resource for you – not least because of the texts I point you in the direction of – and is useful preparation for you producing your own single-authored autoethnographic article before too long. When that time comes, I give you my word that I will continue to offer you mentorship help.

## 24th July (email)

### Yulin:

Dear Alec,

Some days, I feel the heaviness all over my body I can hardly think. I have been feeling a lot like this lately. July used to be a month of restoration and excitement as I planned for my holiday to Australia, but ever since 2020, it only brings hurt and loss. I can vent and write in anger, but writing in pain and the pain doesn't go away.

July was also around the time of year I flew home to Singapore to visit my parents and from where my mum and I would fly to Australia. My mum had always come along with me on these annual trips to Australia, while sometimes I took additional trips on my own. My birthday also happened to fall in July, hence this month had traditionally been for me a time of year I took a break from work, from the summer heat, to refresh myself in wintry Australia and to celebrate with my parents. Even though overseas travel had resumed earlier this year and I had since been back to Australia for a few days, I can no longer afford the expenses due to my impending loss of income as my original PhD candidature comes to an end and the extended period does not cover additional studentship. My perilous financial situation has contributed significantly to my stress and worries. At a time when I need a break, I must push on, and push harder.

During my monthly progress meeting with Boss and co-supervisor on 10th July, he asked if I still worked from home, and I already knew where the conversation was heading. He said he would like to see me interact more often in the office. I declined and told him our fixed monthly meeting works fine. What seemed like a harmless question was in fact loaded with 'ableist' concerns and triggered emotional trauma. He thinks I'm not working hard and fast enough (he blurted 'work harder' at the end of our meeting) and he thinks that has to do with the fact that I am not working in the office. It brought back memories of the days I used to work in his research centre, bearing in mind our research has to do with social work and mental health, and he is the kind of superior who would monitor attendance by requiring his employees to sign in and out manually, and who first refused my request to work from home for fear that it would set an example for other employees to follow. It seems to me that this requirement is in place for him to keep the employees in control and productivity, rather than for the needs of employees.

It also reminded me of the recent newspaper article he co-authored in response to a spate of local incidents involving acts of violence committed by mentally ill persons. The article described those incidents as causing a 'chilling ripple' effect across the community, which I found to be stigmatizing for its association of mental illness with violence. It brought me back to our last meeting where he acknowledged the important contribution of my research critiquing the medical model of autism research in Hong Kong, but then went on to caution me against falling into the self-victimization complex. I subsequently find that this is a common tactic used against individuals who speak up openly about oppression. In so doing, he not only failed to acknowledge the stigma and harm brought about by the medical model and his own role in reinforcing it, but also invalidated my pain. And I responded to him by saying that it was victim-blaming.

It brought me back to one of the earlier meetings we had where I talked to him about neurodiversity-aligned support and mentioned 'universal design' (for learning) (Rose & Meyer, 2002), to which his immediate response was 'Do you know how expensive that would be?' I responded by asking how could he, as a mental health and social work professional, put a monetary value to human life? While he did not reject it outright, he talked about it in terms of cost-benefit. This brought me back again to our recent meeting where I commented about the importance of listening to service user experience in designing mental health policies, to which he asked me to think about it from a policymaker perspective. I thought to myself, 'How dare you ask me to think about policy makers when you are the ones with the power to make decisions that affect us ordinary citizens?' One seemingly innocent question is all it takes to trigger my memories, taking me back to every incident where he said something insensitive, if not offensive, revealing his lack of empathy and regard of others. Time and again, our exchange takes place in the name of facilitating conversation, but regardless of how he thinks he is doing in terms of inclusion, his inability to listen and his tendency to make a joke of everything gives him away. Why then would I want to work in the office and a physical environment like this?

On the other hand, the online environment presents a different reality where I see academics standing up to challenge oppression in the academy, where research informed by lived experiences are shaping institutional policies.

There is now a growing body of Western literature to substantiate my support for neurodiversity aligned principles in universities, but when

I attempt to challenge the deficit narrative in my home institution and country, people have implied that I am self-victimizing, that I am pursuing a personal agenda, that the principles of neurodiversity are incompatible with Chinese culture. In my review of the literature on supporting autistic students in higher education, universal design is often recommended as an approach that would 'enhance equality of opportunity and potentially benefit anyone' (Martin, 2021), with its emphasis on commitment to equality and planning for diversity (Martin, 2020). In contrast, in the report of a local study on autistic university students that was published this year, while universal design was also recommended, its emphasis or selling point was on the benefits it brought for all students ('...not only cater for students with SEN (special educational needs) but in fact benefit all students'), and only makes cursory mention of equality issues in its introduction (Lam, 2023). The report further recommended that universities adopt a strengths-based approach 'to capitalize on the unique strengths and abilities of each student', which reeks of neoliberalism (Chapman, 2021). When I confronted the author about his deficits-oriented framing in his report, he said a descriptive and positivistic approach was chosen (as opposed to a more critical framework) because he did not have a personal agenda for the study. The discord between my physical reality and online experience is hard to ignore.

Do you see how one question snowballs into an avalanche that is toppling me over?

I know people who are reluctant to come out as autistic or to openly criticize researchers for fear of repercussions. While I acknowledge their predicament, a part of me feels embittered that they are in some ways contributing to the maintenance of the status quo by choosing to remain silent (and, so to say, be both victims and oppressors). On the other hand, I probably would have chosen to remain silent if it weren't for the fact that I've reached a point in my life where the benefits of speaking up weighed against the risks, or rather, I stood to lose nothing. Much has been written about supporting autistic students in higher education. However, the texts written from a clinician's perspective have been criticized by autistic scholars (Milton & Sims, 2015). I was one of the research participants in the local study mentioned above (Lam, 2023), and the author of the report is a collaborator I'm working with but who has betrayed my trust.

Tolich (in Grant & Young, 2021) wrote about anticipatory ethics, and I would argue that positivistic researchers who use stigmatizing and pathologizing language should be subject to the same. Should they not anticipate that their study would be read by their participants? If my autoethnography ever gets published, I will not be afraid to show it to those mentioned so they can see for themselves the hurt they caused, and I would love to hear how it makes them feel to read what I've written. Does it not hurt? Does it not anger? Does it not feel unjust? Does it feel victimizing? At this juncture, I don't quite know where this conversation is heading and how to end this. I have so much more to say, but my thoughts are all over the place. I don't want to just be venting my anger and end up with a piece that has 'little or no analysis, theory, or socio-cultural interrogation or implications' (Grant, 2019).

## 25th July (email)

**Alec:**

Dear Yulin,

Before I respond properly, I need to check out a couple of housekeeping issues with you. The first: I've changed the title a little, adding 'Autism' to it – I think that this is important in future literature searches, and trust that you're okay with this?[3] Secondly, (we agreed earlier about this) I think the time is right to send our work to Dr Seb Shaw for his feedback. I mentored Seb in his early autoethnographic work and we've maintained a good collegiate relationship for several years. He's a neurodivergent physician, and among other roles is the: Research Lead of Autistic Doctors International; Co-Chair of the UK Autistic Health Research Network; PhD supervisor in Critical Autism and Disability Studies at London South Bank University; and Editorial Board Member of the SAGE journal, *Neurodiversity*. We can talk more about this at our Zoom meeting tomorrow.[4]

Now for my response: I'm so sorry that you continue to be in so much pain, and to hear again about your financial situation, and I get your sustained anger – not only about the distanced, sanitised, implicitly defensive research on autistic people, carried out by non-autistic researchers. Your developing description of your Boss, and his 'blind and deaf' participation in organizational double messages and contradictions, must be incredibly difficult for you to keep 'stomaching'. From your description throughout this chapter, he seems to be clearly displaying his own insecurities. I read that, ironically, his mistrust of your integrity and commitment stands in violation of his own assumed integrity.

More than anything, I applaud and very much appreciate your bravery in coming out, in whistleblowing. You will be a beacon for many others, and I think you've said much more than is sufficient.

Your mention of the research literature supporting neurodiversity-aligned principles in universities stands out for me as vitally important, especially – as I understand it – in terms of the universal design ethos of flexibly matching environments to people. From the international perspective of objective demographics, not enough is known about autistic people in higher education (Vincent & Ralston, 2023). Much more pressing, I believe, is the need to hear and read about the subjective experiences of autistic students – hence the importance of our chapter, especially your voice within it.

In relation to universal design, you speak of equality issues. This prompted me to revisit the questions you pose at the opening of our chapter: 'What does (social) justice look like and who are we seeking justice from?' To bring things full circle, so to speak, my second answer to these questions is: from a neo-Aristotelean philosophical perspective, social justice is that which allows people the capacity to flourish (Hursthouse in Warburton, 2005, p. 180). Who are we seeking justice from? From institutions and organizations, and sometimes people within organizations. They need to be called out to bring about progressive and positive changes to the lived experiences of autistic people worldwide, including autistic students in higher education. I repeat: hence the importance of our chapter, especially your voice within it.

## 9 August 2023 (email)

### Yulin:

Dear Alec,

Already, we are wrapping things up, but I feel like I have barely scratched the surface. You asked how important I think my voice is in the face of challenging neuro-normative oppression. In this neoliberal academy where productivity prevails over quality, where individual achievement triumphs social justice advancement, where our morals and integrity are at stake, it is against this very desire for justice that I question whether I have done enough to trouble the neoliberal academy and to pierce through its veil? Have I been fair in my pursuit of justice to challenge epistemic power and critique positivistic assumptions?

If this is an interview by a positivist researcher about my experiences in the academy, I know how my narrative will be used as evidence of my 'deficits'. They will report these experiences as miscommunication and attribute my trauma to excessive rumination. They will pay lip service to raising awareness then ignore what I say about the harm caused by their positivistic research. Instead of highlighting the conditions of the neoliberal academy and their own role in sustaining inequalities, they will stress the importance of interventions to improve my resilience. I say 'Pardon me, your interventions are pointless if you don't recognize your complicity in the silencing of our voices. You can't help if you refuse to redress the power imbalances and systemic failings of our system'. That the academy rationalizes and legitimizes this form of oppression is despicable and insidious because it leaves the marginalized minorities to bear the brunt of the harmful consequences.

If you are autistic, it is crucial to surround yourself with the right people in order to survive and thrive in academia (Jones, 2023). When you are geographically isolated and surrounded by ableist research, and academics hell-bent on pathologizing and twisting your narratives, the only way I could get myself heard is through taking charge of my own narrative. The only way I could get the voices of Asian autistic people across is by doing the research myself. I'm vulnerable by being *out* as autistic and to critique positivist research in an academy and society steeped in hierarchy and seniority, particularly so in a political climate where academic freedom is at threat (Cheng et al., 2023). I wish our conversation doesn't have to end here but I hope our collaboration is testament to the solidarity and creativity that is needed to foster dialogue between transnational scholars, to put right what is wrong.

As an autoethnography taking place in the present, I can't tell how my story is going to unfold, how I'm going to emerge. Being in no better frame of mind and situation than where I was at the beginning, I can't speak to the therapeutic purpose. Re-reading our conversation, I am mortified by the number of times I repeat myself. How am I supposed to write when in pain? How could I write when I don't even know how I'm going to survive? I can only hope that I have done justice to my first attempt and to our conversation.

### Notes

1 This chapter was originally intended to be Yulin's individually written autoethnography. By this point in the dialogue, and the working relationship that was developing between them, she agreed with Alec to make it a co-written piece of work.
2 Pinned tweet, @DrAlecGrant.
3 We negotiated several changes to the title of the chapter along the way, as it developed.
4 We sent the chapter to Dr Shaw, and to Dr Sonia Soans, chapter contributor to this volume. We would like to thank them for their valuable and positive feedback.

### References

Anzaldúa, G. (2017). Speaking in tongues: A letter to Third World women writers. In J. Browdy (Ed.). *Women writing resistance: Essays on Latin America and the Caribbean* (pp. 69–81). Beacon Press.

Botha, M. (2021). Academic, activist, or advocate? Angry, entangled, and emerging: A critical reflection on autism knowledge production. *Frontiers in Psychology*, September 28: *12*, 727542. 12. eCollection. https://doi.org/10.3389/fpsyg.2021.727542

Chapman, R. (2021). Neoliberal, Marxist, and intersectional justice approaches to neurodiversity. *Culture & Psychology*. Online first. https://doi.org/10.1177/1354067X231191489

Cheng, Y., Tekola, B., Balasubramanian, A., Crane, L., & Leadbitter, K. (2023). Neurodiversity and community-led rights-based movements: Barriers and opportunities for global research partnerships. *Autism*, *27*(3), 573–577. https://doi.org/10.1177/13623613231159165

Denzin, N.K. (2014). *Interpretive autoethnography*. 2nd edn. SAGE Publications, Inc.

Grant, A. (2018). Voice, ethics, and the best of autoethnographic intentions (or writers, readers, and the spaces in-between. In L. Turner, N.P. Short, A. Grant, & T.E. Adams (Eds.). *International perspectives on autoethnographic research and practice* (pp. 107–122). Routledge.

Grant, A. (2019). Dare to be a wolf: Embracing autoethnography in nurse educational research. *Nurse Education Today*, *82*, 88–92. https://doi.org/10.1016/j.nedt.2019.07.006

Grant, A. (2023). In search of my narrative character. In A. Grant (Ed.), *Writing philosophical autoethnography* (pp. 114–132). Routledge.Grant, A., Leigh-Phippard, H., & Short, N. (2015). Re-storying narrative identity: A dialogical study of mental health recovery and survival. *Journal of Psychiatric and Mental Health Nursing*, *22*, 278–286. https://doi.org/10.1111/jpm.12188

Grant, A., & Young, S. (2021). Troubling tolichism in several voices: Resisting epistemic violence in creative analytical and critical autoethnographic practices. *Journal of Autoethnography*, *3*(1), 103–117. https://doi.org/10.1525/joae.2022.3.1.103

Grant, A., & Young, S. (2022). Troubling Tolichism in several voices: Resisting epistemic violence in creative analytical and critical autoethnographic practices. *Journal of Autoethnography*, *3*(1), 103–117. https://doi.org/10.1525/joae.2022.3.1.103

Jones, S.C. (2023). Advice for autistic people considering a career in academia. *Autism*, *27*(7), 2187–2192. https://doi.org/10.1177/13623613231161882

Klevan, T., Karlsson, B., & Grant, A. (2020). Writing to resist; Writing to survive: Conversational autoethnography, mentoring and the new public management academy. In J. Moriarty (Ed.). *Autoethnographies from the neoliberal academy: Rewilding, writing and resistance in higher education* (pp.123–134). Routledge.

Lam, G. (2023). Exploring the experiences and needs of college students with autism spectrum disorder (ASD). *Research Report*. Faculty of Education, Chinese University of Hong Kong. Research Report_FINAL_May23.pdf (eoc.org.hk)

Martin, N. (2020). University through the eyes of autistic students and staff. In D. Milton, S. Ridout, D.K. Murray, N. Martin, & R.A. Mills (Eds.). *The neurodiversity reader: Exploring concepts, lived experiences and implications for practice* (pp. 287–308). Pavilion.

Martin, N. (2021). Universal design for learning (UDL) in higher education: A UK, USA comparison. *Journal of Inclusive Practice in Further and Higher Education*, *13*(1).

Milton, D., & Sims, T. (2015). A review of mentoring guidance for students on the autism spectrum. In B. Morris, T. Perry, & M. Hand (Eds.). *Papers from the Education Doctoral Research Conference Saturday 29th November 2014* (pp. 124–130). Birmingham: University of Birmingham.

Raymaker, D.M. (2017). Reflections of a community-based participatory researcher from the intersection of disability advocacy, engineering, and the academy. *Action Research*, *15*(3), 258–275. https://doi.org/10.1177/1476750316636669

Rose, D.H., & Meyer, A. (2002). *Teaching every student in the digital age: Universal design for learning.* Alexandria, VA: Association for Supervision and Curriculum Development. ERIC - ED466086- Teaching Every Student in the Digital Age: Universal Design for Learning.

Vincent, J., & Ralston, K. (2023). Uncovering employment outcomes for autistic university graduates in the United Kingdom: An analysis of population data. *Autism, 28*(3), 732–743. https://doi.org/10.1177/13623613231182756

Warburton, N. (Ed.) (2005). *Philosophy: Basic readings.* 2nd edn. Routledge.

# 6

# MY CHANGING JOURNEY

*Amanda Costello*

## Introduction

This chapter is intended to show a changing journey of my lived experience of my sister with a brain injury, and my desire to become a learning disabilities nurse and later, teacher and leader. The relational ethical ethos held by my sister and I, are marked by mutual respect and trust, and we have shared lived experiences of Catherine's journey to rehabilitation. My sister's rehabilitation and my own professional footprint in the field of learning disabilities and beyond constitute pivotal times in my life. Catherine is part of this changing journey and has given her consent for her own lived experiences to be re-storied in this chapter.

## The Wedding

> *It's summer, 2012. My sister Catherine is marrying a lovely man who used to be an accountant. Having met at 'Headway', a brain injury support group, he has similar disabilities to Catherine. As her new relationship flourishes, it helps Catherine heal the wounds of losing our mother. Catherine and Steven have much to share with each other and because of this have decided to tie the knot – as a family we are so excited for them both! Their own lived experiences have brought them together and they are becoming more agentic.*

My father was able to see Catherine get married in the local Catholic church. It was such a happy time, and as a family, we ensured that both Catherine and Steven received the support that they needed in their new

DOI: 10.4324/9781003408963-6

home. We started to put the wheels in motion to find them a supported living place in a good community. Catherine had lived with my parents all her life, my father was in his 70s and in poor health, and now she and her partner wanted to be together. This was a turning point in Catherine's life, and she had slowly weaned herself off the anti-depressants with the support of myself and my husband. My husband and I then turned to looking after my father, who sadly passed away a year later.

> *My dad, a strong man, is 6 feet and 4 inches in height. He has cared for my sister since her accident at age 15 years. Seated in his big wooden arm chair, he slowly picks up his long shoehorn from the floor. He pushes the shoehorn into the back of his shoe and pulls on his left boot. Leaning down to shoehorn his right shoe, he sits back up and says 'I can't do this anymore – moving and handling Catherine is making my arthritis worse, each day I ache from head to toe, I have no respite. But I don't want Catherine to end up in White Windows'.*

That armchair now resides in my lounge window, with a memory cushion of my dad's old checked shirt. 'White Windows' is still today a Nursing Home for people with disabilities and head injury rehabilitation. My dad didn't want Catherine to live anywhere else other than our family home.

As I remember, my dad finally pulled on his right shoe and shouted to Catherine….

> *I won't be a minute and we will get off to the shops.*

My memories to this day still make me feel emotional. My dad had said to me 'I'm a creaking gate, I will go on forever'. He never asked for help as his inner strength always prevailed, and, sadly, no one outside the family home ever offered to help him because he was, visually, a big strong man, a tower of strength, who always cared for Catherine.

Catherine and Steven were fortunate to find a provision in a nice area, a downstairs inner flat, leading to a lovely big flat patio and grassed area. The quality of life for Catherine and Steven improved but, for Catherine, she has never forgotten how much support and rehabilitation her dad gave with unconditional love … a different love that she had found with Steven.

## My Journey as a Learning Disabilities Nurse

It was in the 1980s that I decided to become a learning disabilities nurse. This decision was connected to Catherine's horrific road accident. It left her with a brain injury and hemiplegia. Her best friend died in the same accident. Caring for my sister and supporting my devastated mother and father at the age of 16 years was a harrowing task. I could say that I was a young carer at the time, however, in the 1980s this was not culturally really recognised or talked about. At the time ignorance was bliss and I didn't want to become a victim of idle talk. I matured fast and had to cope with street comments such as, 'Will your sister walk again?' 'Does she have brain damage?' These comments coming from mature people the same age as my mother and father. I suppose at the time it was easier to ask me than upset my parents. However, on reflection, it did really upset me. I would often cross the road, and in my head, I was saying 'Fuck off and leave me alone!' I felt interrogated and compromised. I was still a child. It was not our fault. Why couldn't people just be kind? I also felt that my family were becoming victims of gossip. The worst experience was when the local newspaper pasted a picture of myself and Catherine in happier times (a photograph that I handed to the journalist, who knocked on our door when my parents were visiting my sister, who at the time was in a coma). The reason why my mother hated the press so much at the time was because of them sensationalising our family's misfortune; 'My sister's horrific accident'.

I began to realise, as my sister started her rehabilitation, that we would show people that being disabled is not an obstacle to a good quality of life, things just needed to change, readapt, and our sense of self needed to be different. So, we did! We went to pubs and nightclubs. We did wheelchair dances. We had fun. We let the world know that Catherine was learning to live with the changes to her new life as a non-ambulant person. We both became more agentic and learned to laugh again.

In February 1984, I entered Bradford School of Nursing. I was ready to embark upon a new journey. I was shy entering a new world of professionalism, but I was also feisty and confident, due to my lived experiences with Catherine. I was determined to conquer the world of learning disabilities and ensure that everyone I met along the way would know how important it is to live a fulfilled life with a disability.

At the time, I felt elated and ready to support the human rights of others unable to advocate for themselves. I told myself, until you walk 1000 miles in someone else's shoes it is more difficult to become empathetic. So, empathy became my new mantra, I would show by example how to uphold other people's rights and respect. I would stand in front of a non-ambulant person and say, 'Hello it's lunchtime and I am going to help you to the dining room', proceeding to manoeuvre the wheelchair slowly to the dining room, talking to the person cheerfully as we started to travel.

So, the journey began...

My first lesson in the School of Nursing was an examination of the Mental Health Act 1983, which originated in the 1950s. It was explained that since the outdated review of the Mental Health Act, the way that services are provided has changed from the early 1980s. It was stated explicitly, that the current laws had failed to protect the public, patients and staff. At the time I felt an overwhelming feeling of anger. 'How could this have happened to people? Why didn't anyone speak up?' Alarmingly today, the existing Mental Health Act results in people having the power to treat patients if in hospital for treatment, assessment, and for prolonged periods. These compulsory acts do not consider that the majority of patients are treated in the community. The history from the 1950s tells us that health services for people with a learning disability was based in large institutions with over 55,000 people being institutionalised (Davis & Giraund-Saunders, 2006).

My first few lessons received as part of my nurse training were starting to ring alarm bells. I thought at the time that things really do need to change. We are talking about failures in government legislation for people who need care, compassion, kindness, and overall to be treated as individuals and to be part of society living a good quality of life (Race, 1994).

The initial taught block was completed; I was placed in my first ward in a long-stay hospital.

## My Experience in a Long-Stay Hospital as a Student Nurse

Working on the wards in a long-stay hospital was an experience I will never forget. The unlocking of ward doors with double locks and nurses with keychains linked to their sterile white uniform pockets. The stench as I walked through the first unlocked door was overwhelming; urine, faeces, sweat, and boiled eggs. I felt nervous and unaccustomed to the amount of noise – a mixture of high pitch screaming and repetitive language. I saw a woman slapping her head, others were rocking in chairs placed in an outward square around the day room. The chairs were squashy vinyl in different colours. I also observed one woman with no clothes on openly masturbating. I felt uncomfortable, I didn't know where to look (I later learned that masturbation alleviates boredom, loneliness, and stress). The ward sister told me not to worry. I would 'get used to the environment'.

> *It's just after lunch and I'm outside in the courtyard of the ward, outside four large walls and one locked door back into the ward. I walk up to an elderly woman carrying a doll in her arms, rocking slowly and pulling the doll further towards her in the cold wind. She's trying to protect the doll, as if protecting a real, live baby. I ask her if she would like to come inside to keep warm. She replies, 'My baby needs fresh air', continuing to rock the doll in her tightly closed arms.*

The woman had her real baby taken away from her at birth for having a child out of wedlock. Her hospital notes stated she was sentenced indefinitely under the 1927 Mental Deficiency Act, classified as a 'moral imbecile' (Thomson, 1997). She had a further classification, 'ineducable', introduced by the 1944 Education Act (Barber, 2000). Language used later in her case notes described her as 'subnormal'. Such labelling of people with a learning disability was commonplace. My feelings at the time were so intense; I felt the woman's anxiety and loneliness.

I also didn't like the language used in the woman's case notes and thought to myself, 'You label jars not people; this is not humane'. I was shocked that a person had been detained simply because she had a baby out of wedlock – institutionalised with unmet needs and unaddressed mental health issues. I felt sad for her. Her detainment was morally, socially, and emotionally wrong. She spent a lifetime yearning and grieving the loss of her baby, whilst being deprived of her human rights; the right to have brought up her own child.

I worked hard on my placement and asked many questions about long-stay hospitals and the effects on people's lives. I could clearly see that society and culture were not sufficiently developed to uphold the rights and respect of people as individuals.

## Grenoside Grange Hospital as a Qualified Nurse

Grenoside Grange Hospital, set in a rural part of Sheffield, was a beautiful building with a huge courtyard, and an open stone arch at the entrance, which was welcoming. I was allocated Coniston Lodge, a ward with low dark and dingy ceilings and corridors. Again, the doors were locked and secure. Coniston Lodge was the long-stay ward for people referred from the Home Office and detained indefinitely under the Mental Health Act. Many had challenging behaviours, and the environment sometimes felt unsafe. There were no CCTV or security cameras for observation of residents in the corridors, and at times, behaviour and aggression went unseen. Many were on a polypharmacy drug cocktail, resulting in some being unable to communicate effectively, appearing lethargic and salivating from the mouth. It was a difficult environment for 16 men to live together in these conditions. The environment was uninhabitable – dark, smelly, and dingy – and most of all the men did not have any reasonable quality of life. I became vocal about my observations, I wanted to have my voice heard. My questions were discussed in ward meetings and with senior staff; 'What can we do about this inhumane situation?'

The hospital was eventually identified as a building that was not fit for purpose and became part of a long-term plan in-line with the National

Health Service and Community Care Act (Legislation.gov.uk, 1990). The first phase of the hospital plan was to create community homes for the men living in Coniston Lodge. The plan gave hope for the men living in such difficult conditions. Culturally and morally the planning for supported living felt, to me, like an epiphany. It looked as though at last people with learning disabilities and mental health would have their individual needs considered and would also be given an informed choice of how they would like to live.

## Care in the Community

The closure of long-stay hospitals was well under way and this type of provision was no longer an option for parents with children or adults with a learning disability. Children and adults diagnosed with a learning disability or an acquired brain injury were to be cared for by their families, with a supported, independent living option as the child became an adult.

I refer back to my sister Catherine at this point. Her care was provided by my parents since her accident, and my parents were not offered any support in the home, even though she was non-ambulant and required regular physiotherapy – a massive injustice that contributed to my parents' health problems, and as I reflect on this I feel angry. Instead, my father would do all the moving and handling. As I said earlier, because he was such a tall and strong man, nobody ever offered to assist him with the moving and handling. My mother, on the other hand, was slightly built and small in height, and because my sister was taller there was no way my mother could handle my sister safely. It was ironic that back then in the 1990s, the hospital would arrange for my sister to have physiotherapy. It would take place just the once, then it was over to my parents to loosen her contractures on a daily basis. Catherine would cry in pain at such movements. To be honest, I don't think my parents really understood if the movements to her limbs were being carried out properly.

In the end, Catherine was offered a cocktail of muscle relaxants and anti-depressants to help both her and our parents cope with the daily routine and the social aspects of their life. As life 'rolled on' my parents were becoming older and less able to support Catherine's social needs. My father had his first heart attack at age 59. We were devastated as a family. He had been the main rock in Catherine's life and my mother couldn't cope. The strain was too much, and she ended up on valium. The first time I knew there was something wrong was when I found her sitting in her car outside the family home, unable to move or leave her car. As I reflect, it was so heartbreaking to see my mother looking so frail and helpless. My dad was in hospital recovering from his heart attack, and my mum was broken. Dr Aske, our family Doctor, did a home visit and my mother rested for three weeks. By now, I had two young children of my own, and I was 'holding the fort'. Now you'd think at this point that with my own knowledge and understanding of health services I would be able to organise more help and support. We had a meeting with social care and Catherine received a daycare provision for two days a week (it did help). Transport was also arranged. Bingo! However, there was no additional physiotherapy which Catherine desperately needed. There was no lifting hoist, and both myself and my husband carried out the moving and handling of my sister for six weeks. We were her care in the community.

## Impact of Community Care

This chapter will now turn to the shift in my experience to a more socially based model of care. I will use insider knowledge to explain and analyse my own lived experiences of my sister, my role as a nurse, and a special needs teacher and leader over the last three decades, referring also to those cared for by their families. I will also endeavour to highlight the gaps in service provision and the key concerns that led to people with a learning disability and mental health issues being arrested, charged and convicted of crimes through lack of listening, ineffective communication, or exploitation.

My own professional lived experiences from my nursing at Grenoside Grange and my parents' experience of lack of support, gave me a good insight into the gaps in service provision, especially for those men and women needing forensic services. I observed the gaps in service become wider, with devastating consequences for some people with a learning disability and their families. I felt so helpless at the time, feeling also an increased need to protect my sister.

My career journey started to change, as I retrained to become a teacher and started to work in special schools. I observed a vast amount of change in both supported living for people with a learning disability and also positive changes to the National Curriculum.

One of the special schools where I was fortunate enough to have a teaching and leadership position, was based on a social, education, and medical model. The school had education running through the middle, and the personal care and medical facilities were placed within and around the school. The walls were curved for easy observation and ceilings were high with lovely big skylights. A sensory room with fantastic lighting effects and interactive flooring made a world of difference to a child with multiple health care and learning needs. There were floor mats and wedges to support interactive technology in a new digital world. A dentist and nurses were on site, and a visiting doctor, and finally a hydro pool with digital lighting for an atmospheric experience. This truly was an amazing building. The design of the school met young people's learning disability needs, in all aspects of education, health, and care.

I used my experience in my first special school to invest growth into my second special school. I was excited about the prospect of making much-needed improvements to the new learning environment, using my knowledge and understanding of what a strong learning environment looked like. In this school, I became Headteacher and had an essential tool in my teaching and learning toolbox; the introduction of the 2014 Children and Families Act (Legislation.gov.uk, 2014). It was a revolution for young people with a learning difficulty and their families. At last, there was a real piece of legislation to make a difference to the lives of children and to hold professionals to account for their service delivery. I felt uplifted at the time as there hadn't really been any positive changes to the caring services for the last decade. Unfortunately, the changes were too late for my sister, who had already been failed by the services and had missed an essential aspect of her education; being able to sit her 'O' levels.

I did, however, become extremely motivated, to ensure that the local authority was on board with the changes. The new Educational Health Care Plan (EHCP) was born (Legislation.gov.uk, 2014). On reflection, it was a huge piece of work to undertake. Some 165 pupils with Special Educational Needs and Disability statements (SEND) converted to EHCPs. We started with Years 6 and 9 and then worked our way through the 'quagmire'. I was determined to complete the conversions in record time. It took two academic years of grit and determination, to complete the conversion process.

A good team of professionals supported the period of change, that changed the lives and services for children with a learning disability. For example, children were, at last receiving the correct number of allocated hours in speech and language therapy, and assessments for identifying a dual diagnosis were starting to take place, ensuring children had the correct amount of funding for additional support in the classroom. What a fabulous feeling! It took a vast amount of emotional intelligence, inner strength, and at times the need for difficult conversations with other services. Leading and managing the EHCP process of conversion as a Headteacher of a special school was illuminating. I learnt so much about people and their professional accountability. I further learnt that the best source of information about the young person with a learning difficulty was the parent. We listened and we learnt, then transformed each package of education and care so that every child mattered. In doing so, I used my lived experiences of supporting my sister to champion the way forward.

### What Happened to Care in the Community for Adults with a Learning Disability and Mental Health?

Shockingly, there were gaps in services for people with a learning disability and mental health. The future planning for adults with learning disabilities living with older parents started to gather momentum. But, unfortunately, these notions were not followed through. I saw for myself that many families had started to give up hope of any future planning. This was another sad moment in my career, as the gaps were becoming gulfs and it appeared that only lip service was being paid to elderly parents. The situation raised so much anxiety. A culture of a lack of local authority services and housing had begun and the failings were massive. For over a decade, there was no progress made in planning supported living or independent living for elderly parents with an adult with a learning disability.

I remember feeling anxious for parents, knowing that government austerity was creating an issue for their future planning for their loved ones. My mood was one of upset, as a crisis unfolded for my sister Catherine. My mother sadly passed away, leaving my father with a dilemma. Could he cope with Catherine on his own without my mother's unconditional love and support?

### Where Does a Person with a Learning Disability Live If Their Main Carer Dies?

Sadly, a person with a learning disability may find themselves in the family home and alone once a parent or carer dies. If an adult with a learning disability is able to live either on their own or with support, the services add a package of care to ensure the person has their needs met on a daily basis (Legislation.gov.uk, 2014). This sounds like a great plan. However, due to the lack of planning by statutory services, the lack of government funding and suitable housing, and the lack of elderly parents' trust and confidence in the services, the placing of a person with a learning disability in suitable housing can become problematic.

According to Healy (2020), people with a learning disability have no informed choice of housing or area. Healy argued that the lack of control over housing was exacerbated because of austerity politics resulting in local authority cutbacks. This has meant that disabled people, particularly adults with learning disabilities, are being housed in areas of high deprivation – often with a social history of poverty – because of the rising cost of housing and shrinking local government budgets (Macdonald et al., 2021). It is shocking to know that austerity not only results in a lack of affordable housing but is partnered with a reduction in adult services. Therefore, people with a learning disability have been placed in housing where they've become isolated and vulnerable, and exposed to the risk of harm. This has increased safeguarding risks for them.

Furthermore, disabled people's homes are being occupied ('cuckooed') by local perpetrators and/or county lines organised criminal groups.

Researchers in the last few years have collected data and their findings demonstrate that 'cuckooing' predominantly occurs at a local level perpetrated by local people (Coomber & Moyle, 2018). A fictional example of this was used by the BBC in 2020, demonstrated by actor Tommy Jessop in the BBC drama, 'Line of Duty'. It explicitly showed Tommy's part as a person with Down's syndrome being exploited in his own flat (Slough Borough Council, 2021).

The drama highlighted drugs and alcohol misuse, weapons including guns and knives hidden away in the flat, and the comings and goings of local gang members, playing loud dance music and taking over Tommy's flat. The fear of finding a mutilated and dismembered body in his fridge, left a disturbing image in viewers' minds. Tommy was observed to have little expression and limited communication. He was being coerced by a gang member who, before Tommy was due to be questioned by the police regarding a high-profile murder, said to him, 'You know I'm still your best mate. Everything is going to be fine as long as you keep your mouth shut'.

Tommy's story depicted in the BBC drama was not dissimilar to research findings, suggesting that cuckooing occurs because disabled people often find themselves socially isolated within their communities, which leaves them at risk of exploitation. Alarmingly, the research by Thomas (2011), illustrates that this form of crime occurs through a lack of adult services, arising because of nationally driven austerity policies. The cuckooing process leads to people with learning disabilities being identified as 'easy targets', who have homes that are valuable resources for others to use. Home takeovers seem to be more common than previously presumed, and these are often perpetrated by local people who see disabled people's homes as commodities to use and exploit. This form of exploitation is heightened when county lines organised criminal gang takes over the drug supply within a particular location or geographical area. This process has been confirmed in disabled people's accounts of cuckooing, and by professionals with experience of working with people who have been cuckooed.

## Mate Crime and Cuckooing

My time spent in the community as a nurse and later as a teacher and leader led me to believe that mate crime and cuckooing are prevalent in many communities. On a personal level and since my father passed, I have always feared for Catherine's safety in the community and I visit her and her husband on a regular basis as they are both vulnerable. Unfortunately for some people with a learning disability and mental health issues, they do not have regular checks by family members or friends.

There is a relationship between localised forms of cuckooing exploitation, and county lines criminality, and research in the field of 'mate crime' (Doherty, 2020; Thomas, 2011, 2013). 'Mate crime' occurs when a person or group of people befriend someone with a disability, with the sole purpose of exploiting, humiliating, or taking control of their assets. When examining the phenomenon of cuckooing, highlighted by Tommy's story in the 'Line of Duty', the victim's home becomes the focal point of where exploitation, violence, and abuse occurs (Doherty, 2020; Macdonald et al., 2021; Thomas, 2011). As Doherty (2020) demonstrates, 71% of mate crime cases occur within the victim's home.

Researchers have identified that the experiences of loneliness and isolation create a space where exploitation can occur, leaving the person with a learning disability at risk of experiencing mate crime (Healy, 2020; Thomas, 2011, 2013). As Thomas (2013) discusses, one of the key features of mate crime is that the person with a learning disability often does not realise that they are being exploited by the perpetrators. They see the perpetrators as friends and welcome them into their homes. Once their homes have been taken over, they can be trapped in a coercively controlled environment, where emotional abuse and violence can become part of the victim's daily routine (Coomber & Moyle, 2018). The effects of 'mate crime' can be devasting for a person with a learning disability. If the crime is eventually uncovered, they can be arrested and charged, either by association or activity within the crime.

## No Self-Advocacy, Unheard Voices, and Liberty Taken Away

With little self-advocacy and having a learning disability, people's lives are determined and restricted by the rate at which they are expected to interact with professionals. Gormley (2022), highlights that those classified as vulnerable or a risk to others and or themselves can find themselves in a quagmire of systems and control. Since the closing down of long-stay hospitals and the evidential gaps in community care, a new kind of institution has formed for people with a learning disability, whereby their liberty is taken away due to their own lack of self-advocacy, unheard voice, or exploitation. Gormley (2022), is explicit regarding the lack of disability research and the unheard voices of people with a learning disability. The lived experiences of being arrested, and attending court as an accused or 'convicted' person are undocumented. The specific impact, challenges, and the consequences of involvement with the justice system and imprisonment of people with a learning disability can therefore be devasting.

Gormley (2022), carried out research in Scottish prisons between 2013 and 2014. The research findings reflected the lived realities of people with a learning disability in prison. The structural and social conditions that caused harm to the people in the study are still in place in prisons today. A really important point highlighted by Gormley is that the lived experiences of a person with a learning disability and mental health have not been heard through research or any other means. Therefore, their experiences of prison and of wider criminal justice processes has given misconceived ideas about how people with learning disabilities interact with the criminal justice system. Unfortunately, a person with a learning disability who once lived in the community with their parents, can in today's society find themselves in a new cultural phenomenon of abuse within their communities, if their liberty has been taken away as a consequence of victim crime.

There are no reliable records to trace the patterns and levels of imprisonment of people with learning disabilities. However, it is presumed that they are overrepresented and misunderstood (Talbot, 2010), and their needs left unmet (Brooker et al., 2009). Evidence cited in The Prison Reform Trust document highlighted that people with learning disabilities experience discrimination in personal, systematic, and routine ways within UK prisons (Talbot, 2010). They found that people with learning disabilities were more likely than their non-disabled prisoners to be bullied, experience anxiety and depression, be subject to control and restraint techniques, and spend more time isolated and in segregation.

## Conclusion

This chapter has taken the reader through my journey of change, through the lens of my own lived experience of being a support to my sister with a brain injury, a learning disabilities nurse, special needs teacher, and leader, throughout periods of change. I have been able to reflect and gaze through the different trends and practices in the field of learning disabilities and mental health and my own sister's journey of rehabilitation. I am empathetic, thoughtful, and at times frustrated by the lack of provision and planning for people with a learning disability. I am also mindful of the effects on a person's mental health and the difficult life changes some have experienced.

Moreover, as I reflect on the position of a person with a learning disability on the basis of my own experiences, I feel a level of sadness that they may be alone when an elderly parent passes away. How difficult must it be for the person to go through a living needs and housing assessment knowing that they may have to move away from their community. More often, the person may be placed in an area of high deprivation and become isolated and lonely. This is not care in the community and a good quality of life. The gaps in service provision have become wider causing an increased risk of harm and exploitation. I reflexively ask why are there no safeguarding measures in place, and how can the government allow further risk of harm and exploitation?

A cuckooing phenomenon has arisen as a result of the emptiness, isolation, and feeling of being alone for a person with a learning disability. The process of cuckooing makes me feel incredibly sad and helpless as a practitioner. *I am truly thankful my sister is safe in her supported living.* The lack of government funding has given perpetrators, as loneliness-alleviating new mates arriving on the scene, the opportunity to exploit disabled people in their own homes.

The lack of adequate services and support for people with a learning disability and mental health issues in their community is a significant concern. Despite the calls for a 'needs led' approach to service provision (Legislation. gov.uk, 2014), the reality is that a lack of planning, support, and supported living, creates anxiety for elderly parents and carers. This highlights the need for continued efforts to improve services for them, and minimise the chances of people with learning disabilities becoming exploited through crime, and imprisoned, due to isolation and loneliness in their community. I also ask myself the question; how can a lack of adult services and supported living accommodation allow criminals to enter someone's home and exploit them and involve the person in their crimes?

## References

Barber, M. (2000). *The making of the 1944 Education Act.* Continuum.

Brooker, C., Gojkovic, D., Sirdifield, C., & Fox, C. (2009). Lord Bradley's review of people with mental health or learning disabilities in the criminal justice system in England: All not equal in the eyes of the law? *International Journal of Prison Health, 5*(3), 171–175. https://doi.org/10.1080/17449200903115847

Coomber, R., & Moyle, L. (2018). The changing shape of street-level heroin and crack supply in England: Commuting, holidaying, and cuckooing drug dealers across 'County Lines'. *The British Journal of Criminology, 58*(6), 1323–1342. https://doi.org/10.1093/bjc/azx068

Davis, J., & Giraund-Saunders, A. (2006). Support and services for young people with learning disabilities and mental health problems. *Mental Health Review Journal, 11*(3), 8–15. https://doi.org/10.1108/13619322200600025

Doherty, G. (2020). Prejudice, friendship and the abuse of disabled people: An exploration into the concept of exploitative familiarity ('mate crime'). *Disability & Society, 35*(9), 1457–1482. https://doi.org/10.1080/09687599.2019.1688646

Gormley, D. (2022). The hidden harms of prison life for people with learning disabilities: *The British Journal of Criminology, 62,* 261–278. https://doi.org/10.1093/bjc/azab061

Healy, J. C. (2020). 'It spreads like a creeping disease': Experiences of victims of disability: Hate crimes in austerity Britain. *Disability & Society, 35*(2), 176–200. https://doi.org/10.1080/09687599.2019.1624151

Legislation.gov.uk. (1990). *National Health Service and Community Care Act, 1990.* National Health Service and Community Care Act 1990. legislation.gov.uk.

Legislation.gov.uk. (2014). *Children and Families Act, 2014.* Children and Families Act 2014. legislation.gov.uk.

Macdonald, S. J., Donovan, C., & Clayton, J. (2021). 'I may yet be left with no choice, but to seek an ending to my torment': Disability and intersectionalities of hate crime. *Disability & Society, 38*(1), 127–147. https://doi.org/10.1080/09687599.2021.1928480

Race, D. (1994). *Services for people with learning disabilities: Historical development of service provision.* 2nd edition. Routledge.

Slough Borough Council. (2021). *Are you being used like 'Line of Duty's' Terry?* Are you being used like Line of Duty's Terry? – Slough Borough Council (accessed 9 March 2023).

Talbot, J. (2010). Prisoners voices: Experiences of the criminal justice system by prisoners with learning disabilities. *Tizard Learning Disability Review, 15*(3), 33–41. https://doi.org/10.5042/tldr.2010.0403

Thomas, P. (2011). 'Mate crime': Ridicule, hostility, and targeted attacks against disabled people. *Disability & Society, 26*(1), 107–111. https://doi.org/10.1080/09687599.2011.532590

Thomas, P. (2013). Hate crime and mate crime: Hostility, contempt, and ridicule. In A. Roulstone & H. Mason-Bish (Eds.), *Disability, hate crime and violence* (pp. 135–147). Routledge.

Thomson, M. (1997). Family, community, and state: The micro politics of mental deficiency. In D. Wright & A. Digby (Eds.), *From idiocy to mental deficiency: Historical perspectives on people with learning disabilities* (pp. 207–230). Routledge.

# 7

# MY LIFE WITH DYSLEXIA

## An Autoethnography

*Nicola Cross*

### Introduction: Dyslexia and Positive Psychology

Dyslexia is a widely known specific learning difficulty, affecting fluent reading and accurate spelling, while not being reflective of levels of intelligence (National Institute of Neurological Disorders and Stroke). There is not a clear cut-off point between dyslexics and non-dyslexics, so dyslexia should be thought of in terms of a continuum (British Medical Association, 2009).

The rise of positive psychology produced an important association between a 'good life' and identity (Seligman & Csikszentmihalyi, 2000). This association was highlighted further by establishing and understanding character strengths in the service of people experiencing increasingly more fulfilling lives, with such strengths regarded as morally valued personality traits (Peterson, 2006; Peterson & Park, 2003).

### My Childhood

As a young child, I always struggled in the education system of the nineties and noughties eras. My main struggles included, but were not exclusive to, retaining information, not being able to listen to the teachers and write down information, spelling what felt like complex words, and being unable to read long text while keeping my focus. This squares with literature from the British Medical Association (2009) relating to dyslexia primarily impacting fluent reading, writing, and spelling. An early memory was of me getting frustrated reading the same line in books over and over again, and often getting into trouble for not reading fast enough for the teacher to move on.

DOI: 10.4324/9781003408963-7

I quickly developed a coping mechanism, which was to 'pretend' to read text and hope for the best. During my time at primary school, my Mum had requested me to be tested for dyslexia, however, my Year 6 teacher didn't have much experience in the area and deemed it not needed. From that early encounter, I felt I was on my own and just needed to try harder. People with dyslexia are often perceived to be lazy or unintelligent and are thus left feeling misunderstood (Thompson et al., 2015).

I really valued my primary school teacher and spent time with her and with the local police officer taking part in open days and day trips to the police station. This would meet the requirements for the character strength of 'curiosity' as despite my difficulties with reading and spelling I was curious to learn about other interests (Peterson & Seligman, 2002). I was so inspired and determined to join the police as it felt like a hands-on job and one which, in my ten-year-old mind, did not involve writing.

Reflecting back now to those times, I knew I would not want a job which included writing as this added anxiety, and in some ways still does now. To add some context, home computers were not around, and if you were lucky enough to use a computer the software was nowhere near as good as it is now. If I needed to know how to spell a word, I had to look it up in a dictionary. This seems reasonable but when all you know is the first letter of a word it takes a long time to find the word you are looking for. Then I had to read to check it was in fact the correct word, so many times I gave up looking. A way I found to overcome this challenge was to spell words phonetically and hope for the best. However, more often than not, they would be missing a letter or be completely the wrong spelling. When the teacher would mark my work the spelling errors were clear as day and something I would fixate on, often without the correct spelling being given. This meant that I was still in the same situation of not knowing the correct spelling and therefore not being able to correct my ways of learning.

Away from primary school my home life was more settled. Being a big sister at the age of ten years old, my parents were preoccupied with a small child, and I was deemed to be of an age to work independently. My Dad worked long hours and would often be very tired when he returned home from work. As a young child stories were read to me and I would enjoy this, but I mainly focused on the pictures to tell the story. I would not follow the words on the page, although I knew if the story was read incorrectly and often corrected the reader if they read it differently to how I remembered the story. At such a young age I must have been a learner through spoken words, and the vast amount of teaching would be verbal.

The expectation of being able to read and spell was still prevalent, meaning I was not being assessed to show my best work and ability. During spelling tests, which were mandatory, I was grouped with a student who was being kept back a school year, as my spelling ability was lower than others in my class. This added a sense of worry that I too should have been kept in primary education for an additional year. From the age of 10 or 11 years, I felt as though I was behind academically, and this impacted my self-esteem. Burden and Burdette (2005) highlight that within the education system, students are expected to achieve a standardised educational goal. More recent research has found that people with learning difficulties find reaching these goals harder. This strongly suggests a need for variations in educational practice to accommodate differences in neurological processing, rather than focusing on deficits in individual students (Berger & Lorenz, 2016; Lackaye & Margalit, 2006).

## Teenage Years

Secondary school followed the same pattern, but it became clear that my coping mechanisms would need to be changed somewhat. I would forget where I needed to be, and remembering what my homework was became more and more difficult, especially as I was starting to become conscious of writing in front of others. So, I tried hard to rely on my memory but came to realise that my memory had its strengths but also its limitations. I could remember what the teacher had said but trying to put my thoughts down on paper soon became a challenge. My handwriting changed when I struggled to spell a word and often my sentences made little sense as words were missing, or I went off track without realising. As the demand for working memory increases during secondary school age, cognitive processing skills are required more and more for those with dyslexia. That this can be a particular challenge (Humphrey, 2003; Singleton, 2002) and affects the developing self-concept (Burden & Burdett, 2005).

In the lessons where there was less writing to complete, I was excelling in subjects like technology. which was hands-on, and I loved it. Maths was a strength and I moved quickly up sets as my ability was improving. I was very creative in my Art, and Religious Studies opened my mind. By not shrinking from the challenge of school life I embraced other subjects, showing bravery to continue learning by utilising my character strengths. It was no surprise to me that English was harder the further I progressed into my educational life. One English teacher would help me, especially with my spelling, and made the lesson fun – marking my work and showing me the corrections clearly without drawing attention to me. Long gone were the spelling tests I would dread, and reading out to the class what your score was. At this point, dyslexia was still not well known, but my English teacher had noticed my challenges and supported me.

It was during my time at secondary school that I needed to complete my General Certificate of Secondary Education (GCSEs), sitting in a hall answering questions through writing, with no one around to ask how to spell a word. During the practice tests I would re-phrase whole sentences of ideas and answers using words I knew confidently how to spell. This meant it took me a long time to finish tests and at times meant I did not answer all the questions, missing out on marks. This is in keeping with 'character strengths', most importantly 'creativity and open-mindedness', and I found alternative methods of passing my exams which was a strength that continued into adulthood (Peterson & Seligman, 2002).

One difference at that time was that there were more computers around, and when I was around 15 years old my parents were able to buy a computer for the home. Although the software was basic this gave me the opportunity to not have to write my ideas down on paper. All the books we read were ones with white paper with black fonts, and it was only when I was in secondary school and asking a friend did the words 'move on the paper', did I realise that there might be something different with what I saw. It was during secondary school that also I needed to complete typed-course work. I used my grandparents' electronic typewriter, and this was probably one of the first times I used an electronic device to complete work. 'Brilliant', I thought, 'finally I don't need to practise my handwriting'. Well, that was short-lived as there was a delete button that somehow removed the last letter, and typing was so time-consuming. My mum read over my work and highlighted spelling errors. Where I had missed words out, missed punctuation, and so on. There was no way to change it, so I had to start again, having to repeat this at least three times.

It was at this moment that I realised I was determined and resilient. I received my grades for my GCSEs and to my upmost surprise I got a 'C' in English Language. I also passed other subjects which gave me four GCSEs above Grade C. I received a D in Maths, which I found disappointing, as I knew I was working to a higher standard, but I still passed English. My mum took me to school to collect my grades. I was 'over the moon', but my mum did not show the same joy, and the car journey to college to enrol was met with a lot of shouting and her telling me how disappointed she was. I soon felt happy no longer.

## Work Life

After college, I worked full-time for many years in different roles, ranging from payroll administrator, finance caseworker, supervisor, innovation analyst, nursery cook, and pre-school team leader. Looking back, I can see that my roles were all so different, and up until starting work at a nursery, all my jobs were office-based. I loved working in payroll, and while in this role felt I could manage my dyslexia well. The manager and supervisor would always be on hand to help me and check my spelling. I worked on setting up new clients, and for tax purposes names and addresses needed to be correct. The management was fantastic and supportive, and this first experience in work life led to me naïvely assume that all workplaces would be this amazing. Such early work experiences helped me to develop moral self-awareness and a more positive identity as I was able to demonstrate my skills and build confidence from learning through experience, which is pivotal in combating dyslexia (Burden & Burdett, 2005). More informal adjustments and positive management strategies that were applied to my working environment also helped me develop my career (Beverton et al., 2008; Riddick, 2003; Riddick & English, 2006).

## Assessment for Dyslexia

Once I moved jobs, I started to look into completing my Maths GCSE as I worked with Maths daily and knew I could pass it even as an adult. At Bolton College, I was finally assessed for dyslexia at the ripe age of 30. It was here that I realised how much I might see and experience the world a little differently from non-neurodivergent people. I was disappointed with what was classed as 'support' there. I felt it made no difference to me and in no way supported my needs. I felt like they were just ticking a box to say they were inclusive. I worked hard to complete my Maths GCSE exam and passed it with a Grade C.

This was the start of me thinking how I could do better. An internal opportunity became available when I was working at the time as an innovation data analyst. I had worked on projects with this firm before and had a lot of knowledge about my job. I knew I would enjoy the challenge, so applied for it. I was successful and quickly moved to the department, but it was here where I experienced discrimination and my mental health really started to decline. Upon working on a project, I was asked to design power points outlining what the intent was, how we expected to make savings, and so on. I sent my project leader what I had produced, and at no point did anyone offer any training or advice. I wasn't the only new starter, but I noticed that I was left out and rarely spoken to. It became apparent that I did not fit in this department, and I went from an employee who received bonuses based on performance to a member of staff who was no longer achieving.

During the quarterly performance meeting, it was brought up that my work was not to the required standard. When I explained that I was dyslexic, I was told I was not suitable for the role, but I knew that this was not the case. Further conversations took place where I was told that they were going to inform Human Resources as I should have told them about my dyslexia on my application form. I would have told them had the application form asked, and as this was an internal role, I had disclosed this when I originally applied to work for the company. It was then I knew I was going to return to a previous role with a team that knew me and my abilities. That did mean taking a pay cut, but I knew my mental health was more important than a small increase in my wage. This experience left a very bitter taste, and when the option for redundancy came, I jumped at it and subsequently left working there. Reflecting on this work experience it is clear to me that the lack of positive management impacted on my mental health and ability to flourish in my career (Beverton et al., 2008; Riddick, 2003; Riddick & English, 2006).

Finding myself unemployed, I applied for a role in a nursery as a cook, which at the time I saw only as a temporary move. It was here that I knew I wanted to work with children. I was never judged and was excelling, which led to my employer recognising my natural ability in working with children and putting me forward to complete my Level Three in Childcare. Once enrolled, I started working with a tutor who would always compliment my writing, and my work observations always resulted in fantastic feedback.

I quickly became a room leader, which meant having to organise the room through planning, and my creativity shone through. My manager would meet with me regularly and believe in my ability. This reignited my passion for learning, something I thought would not happen again. I was able to demonstrate my ability not only in a written format but also practically. I would always express that I worked better as a hands-on person. I stayed at this employment for three years and felt empowered to further my career. My tutor suggested that I would be more than capable of going to university and started to think in terms of courses and what I wanted to do long term as a career.

## University

I started my search looking at University open days and courses, focusing on distance from my home. As a busy mum of two children, being close to home so that I could still take them to school was important to me. My first open day was at the University of Bolton looking around the Psychology department. I had always enjoyed psychology but never really studied it before in any detail. I liked the look of the Psychology, Psychotherapy, and Counselling degree, as I could also complete a Level 2 and 3 Diploma in Counselling, so felt I would get more out of the course. My mind was set on becoming a teacher in a primary school setting, but I was very nervous about obtaining a place. I took my younger sister with me to the second open day and loved the feel of the University, and due to its size felt that it was right for me.

I started the application process and felt both excited and nervous as I knew how determined I was to start a degree. I was quickly accepted and, fast forward to my first day, I was filled with joy. That feeling did not last long after my first lecture. I felt totally out of my depth, and that the lecturers said words that not only did I not know, but also had no idea how to spell when making notes. Instant dread followed, leaving me thinking have I made the right decision? I had given up work, had no income and my family depended on me to complete this course. However, I shared my feelings with nobody. Burden and Burdett (2005) argue that dyslexia affects physical, social, and emotional awareness, as well as reading, writing, and spelling. Reflecting back, it was then I realised that my emotional life and confidence needed work.

A few weeks later and my assessment was booked in for what support I needed to receive. This process was massive for me and a life-changing experience. The assessor was very abrupt in her questions and never have I felt under the spotlight like that before. A lot of the challenges I struggled with, and I remember thinking why can't I do this? All the old feelings from school came flooding back, spelling tests and all. After the assessment ended, the lady told me what help could be put in place. I expressed that I was worried I was not able to do well in my degree. She told me not to worry, that many people with dyslexia can only achieve at best a 2:1, but that it would be hard, and I would require a lot of support.

A few weeks later I was paired up with a support worker whom I met with three times for two hours each time. She spent the vast amount of time talking about herself and jobs she had worked, none of which helped me. By this time, I was now in self-destruct mode and thinking I can't do this. I'm going to fail as my first assignment was fast approaching, and I was sinking fast. I contacted the company and expressed my concerns about the support worker, and they assigned me another. I was slightly worried, thinking please don't be like the last one, and then after meeting Mandy I quickly realised how professional she was and felt relieved. It was clear that I required support tailored to my own difficulties. This has been demonstrated in research on how support is important to people with dyslexia, and when a more positive approach is applied this enables a student to function to the best of their ability (Beverton et al, 2008; Riddick, 2003; Riddick & English, 2006).

My first assignment was submitted, and the long three-week wait started. The results came in and I received 70. I didn't know what that meant until I asked my friend who informed me this was in fact a first. I was over the moon to say the least and this led to a feeling I never had before – I want a first-class degree. The challenge was on, and now with Mandy by my side, I set off making sure that I understood what was being asked of me. I also received other support like software for my laptop to record the lectures, so I didn't need to focus my time on writing notes. I could listen, really listen, and if I needed to make notes I could on the recording software. Due to some mobility problems, I also received a standing desk which I am currently working on and love, an ergonomic chair, an electronic pen which I could pull over words in a book I didn't know.

In my eyes, I had 'hit the jackpot'. This was the support I had never received before and am eternally grateful for. Lecturers knew my name; I asked questions, not for clarity now but to link concepts I had read to what they were teaching. When I started university, I had very few books, and now my friend rings me to ask, 'Do I have a book on…?' I actually love reading. Who would have known? This doesn't just stop at books. I enjoy reading about research and this was showing in my writing style.

I met with my support worker weekly, and she would challenge my thinking and writing in a constructive way, never judging my ability. This shows that although I had not learnt about positive psychology at this point it was clear that character strengths played a part in my experience, especially my love of learning. This enabled me to embrace new knowledge and new skills with zest as I was full of excitement and energy (Peterson & Seligman, 2004).

It was at university that I fully experienced and gratefully accepted wonderful support. There were still some internal challenges I faced – for example, the Disability Team sent me a digital sticker to put on my work to highlight to the lecturers that I was dyslexic, so that I would not be penalised for spelling errors. For most of my first year, I did not put this digital sticker on my work as I wanted to improve my writing and wanted to receive feedback in my eyes fairly. Well, that was what I told myself and others, but deep down I still held onto to shame and did not want to be treated differently. My grades were still hovering at a high 2:1 and a first, and I had now become hungry for a first-class classification and started to pile the pressure on achieving high grades.

By now I was no longer feeling that I could not do it in lectures, but as soon as I started to write for my assignments it would take me a while to get into what I wanted to say and how to structure my work. The structure became a sticking point for me, as I was reading so much, I could not work out how to put everything down and for it to flow correctly and make sense. As my relationship with the lecturers grew, I felt confident asking for help, and there was never a lecturer who would not help and guide me. I knew that I had found the right University for me and my needs. I will forever be thankful to each and every lecturer at the University of Bolton.

My final year. I had been planning my dissertation from the end of Year 2 and had already approached a potential supervisor with my ideas. Richard was enthusiastic about my ideas, and this drove me to keep at it. I chose a subject about allergies and quickly started to read medical research in this area. I was confident in asking Richard what some of it meant and whether it was relevant. Richard would guide me with my reading and explain the concepts so well.

We were now in the midst of Covid, and all learning had moved online, so meetings were virtual as well. This was in some ways perfect for me as the lectures were recorded, which was what I had been doing from the start anyway, so I did not feel I was at a disadvantage. Richard and I would meet online, and when I started to show him what I had written for my introduction he commented on how impressed he was. I worked very closely with Mandy, and I was so grateful when she read out some of the words I had written because although I could read them, saying them was a whole different matter. When I reflect back, I was now no longer the person who would re-write work because I could not spell a word. I was now the person who tried hard to learn the spelling and meaning of words, but my pronunciation was still not there. However, I am at peace with the fact that some words I just cannot say correctly, and this is part of me and my dyslexic story.

The race was on for getting all my work submitted on time and apart from one occasion I was able to submit my work by the deadline. I had done it. I had finished all my work and was waiting for my grades. I felt like I had given my all and loved the experience immensely. I knew I wanted to continue studying so applied for a master's in counselling and positive psychology at the same University. It felt like forever until my final award came through and the words 'FIRST CLASS' were there in black and white. I cried and cried, my Mum cried, my husband was over the moon, and so were the rest of my family. I had done it and achieved not only a degree but a first-class degree! It is worth noting that I know I would not have been able to do it without the support of my family, the lecturers and, most importantly, Mandy. It was during this time that I had started to link together resilience and my disability, in keeping with Seligman and Csikszentmihalyi's (2000) need for having an identity.

## Master's Degree

September 2022 fast approached to start my Masters. My first challenge was to ask if Mandy could be assigned to me again. Fortunately, the agency said 'yes'. Next, I was on to getting back into university life – learning, reading, and being mentally ready for a new challenge. All of this left me feeling like my younger self and thinking, 'Am I able to do this, am I capable, have I stretched myself too far?' I was now working part-time, and worrying about finances and spreading myself too thin, but I was hungry for success. The financial stress also started to mount up along with my son finding school life hard. It was during the start of my course my son was tested and was also diagnosed with dyslexia. I struggled with this mentally as I was becoming concerned about his school life and future career, even though my experience had been relatively settled.

I was really worried about him. He was very upset when we told him of his diagnosis, and in honesty, I felt guilty that I had passed this on to him. I felt guilty that I had added to his academic life in such a negative way. I knew deep down this was not the case and that, although I could be a role model for him, I felt everything but someone to look up to – more that I was someone who was also the cause of his struggles. Some of those feelings have reduced in prominence but they are still there.

Starting my master's qualification meant that I would need to be writing at a higher level. I was not sure I was able to and asked one of the lecturers (Charlotte) to tell me honestly if I was capable. She really helped and assured me that I was more than able, and that set me off completing the work. It has been through this course that I have seen my grades with a mixture of classifications, but one will always stand out to me. I had to deliver a positive psychology presentation about a film. It was during this time that I tested positive for Covid-19. I was really unwell but wanted to get it out of the way, and although I passed it was not my best work. I felt like I had let myself down and this showed in my grade. Covid-19 was a worry for me as I have previously had two blood clots in my lungs, and I was scared that I would need to be hospitalised or in the worst case die from this already deadly illness. Fortunately, I escaped with symptoms which meant I could stay at home although still unwell. I knew that I was ill, and that this would have impacted my grades, but I felt the failure hard.

In the latter part of my master's, like the rest of my peers, my trainee counsellor placement started. I was nervous, but excited as I knew listening was definitely my strength. My biggest challenge started; remembering what I had learnt, what I needed to say for contracting, and what my client said. Over time my confidence grew but it was here that I really noticed issues with the pronunciation of words, which would then leave me feeling like I was not giving my clients the service they needed. That was until I started to be congruent with myself, and since then I have more understanding that my client does not need someone who can say words correctly all the time. They need me to be present, listen, empathise, and so on.

During a placement at a secondary school, I saw a full-time position available in a dream job. I jumped at the opportunity to apply. My story around my master's course has still not finished, and being given the opportunity to complete this work has really inspired me. I have gone from someone who was ashamed of my disability to someone who sees my ability to share my experiences.

## New Career Path

As I have said, I applied for a role at a secondary school. This was not any secondary school. This was *my* secondary school, where I learnt skills, felt happy, and understood. What better reason to apply for a job here!? The role was Intervention Centre Manager, which entailed delivering emotional wellbeing, social skills, body image, and behaviour interventions to the students. I had experience in this field and started my application, and only a few weeks later I was offered an interview with two of the senior leadership team. The interview took the format of delivering a 20-minute session to some students, a writing exercise about my vision for the Centre, and a formal interview. Understandably nerves set in, but I thought outside of the box for my 20-minute session and made it interactive, using computer software for slides. I felt that it went well; the students engaged with me, and the timing was perfect. I had already disclosed my dyslexia status on my application form, but next came the vision exercise, writing on paper which would then be sent to the senior leadership who were interviewing me. I worked hard on that and knew I had made spelling mistakes. It maybe didn't make much sense to anyone, but to my saving grace I presented this, and this gave me the opportunity to really show my knowledge. The interview followed quickly after, which seemed to go well, and after three hours it was all over. The call came later that day. I was successful. Never have I been prouder of myself. As I shared the news with others, one colleague questioned my ability to do the job. Yes, I was a school cleaner applying for a manager job.

Currently, I have been in the role for seven months, and I feel like I have never been away from the school even though I left 20 years earlier. Many may ask how my disability has helped me in this role and the answer for me is clear; I can form trusting relationships with others. I support their needs. I am inclusive to all my students. I listen, and I can relate to those who are struggling. Yes, my difficulties are still there just as intense as ever, but the students don't care when I say words wrong, and they don't care if I write a word incorrectly somewhere. They care that I'm there, and that I support them. The relationships I have built have seen me refer students to receive outside support. I've tackled and challenged them on behaviour, and, emotionally, I'm a member of staff they trust. I have learnt that what you plan to do and what happens can be very different, but I do not need to be in control all the time as life is not like that.

## References

Berger, R. J., & Lorenz, L. S. (2016). *Disability and qualitative inquiry: Methods for rethinking an ableist world.* Routledge.

Beverton, S., Riddick, B., Dingley, E., English, E., & Gallannaugh, F. (2008). *Strategies for recruiting people with disabilities into initial teacher training.* Research report to the training development agency for schools. Durham: Durham University.

Burden, R., & Burdett, J. (2005). Factors associated with successful learning in pupils with dyslexia: A motivational analysis. *British Journal of Special Education, 32*(2), 100–104. https://doi.org/10.1111/j.0952-3383.2005.00378.x

British Medical Association. (2009). *Equality and diversity in UK medical schools.* London: BMA Marketing & Publications.

50410 EOC report SCIED 2010: Layout 1 (nuffieldtrust.org.uk).

Humphrey, N. (2003). Teacher and pupil ratings of self-esteem in developmental dyslexia. *British Journal of Special Education, 29*(1), 29–36. https://doi.org/10.1111/1467-8527.00234

Lackaye, T. D., & Margalit, M. (2006). Comparisons of achievement, effort, and self-perceptions among students with learning disabilities and their peers from different achievement groups. *Journal of Learning Disabilities, 39*(5), 432–446. https://doi.org/10.1177/00222194060390050501

Peterson, C. (2006). *A primer in positive psychology.* Oxford University Press.

Peterson, C., & Park, N. (2003). Positive psychology as the even-handed positive psychologist views it. *Psychological Inquiry, 14*(2), 143–147. https://www.jstor.org/stable/1449822

Peterson, C., & Seligman, M. E. (2004). *Character strengths and virtues: A handbook and classification* (Vol. 1). Oxford University Press.

Riddick, F. A. (2003). The code of medical ethics of the American Medical Association. *Ochsner Journal, 5*(2), 6–10. PMC (nih.gov).

Riddick, B., & English, E. (2006). Meeting the standards? Dyslexic students and the selection process for initial teacher training. *European Journal of Teacher Education, 29*(2), 203–222. https://doi.org/10.1080/02619760600617383

Seligman, M. E., & Csikszentmihalyi, M. (2000). *Positive psychology: An introduction* (Vol. 55, No. 1, p. 5). American Psychological Association.

Singleton, C. (2002). Dyslexia: Cognitive factors and implications for literacy. *Dyslexia and Literacy, Theory and Practice* (pp. 115–129). Wiley.

Thompson, C., Bacon, A. M., & Auburn, T. (2015). Disabled or differently-enabled? Dyslexic identities in online forum postings. *Disability & Society, 30*(9), 1328–1344. https://doi.org/10.1080/09687599.2015.1093460

# 8

# LAUGHTER, JOY, AND MENTAL HEALTH

## An Autoethnographic Case Study of Joe Hoare

*Joe Hoare and Freda Gonot-Schoupinsky*

### Introduction

In this chapter, Joe and Freda explore the use of laughter for mental health from research, practitioner, and lived experience perspectives. Joe Hoare is a laughter practitioner of 20+ years, based in Bristol. Freda has a PhD in psychology, investigating laughter prescription, from the University of Bolton. Centre stage of this chapter is Joe, as he will be sharing his personal battles with mental health, and his laughter journey. Freda introduces, concludes, and poses ten questions to Joe to harness even more insight into how to unleash the power of laughter and joy in our lives.

### Laughter and Mental Health

My research into laughter started in 2017 during an MSc Health Psychology study of the oldest-old. Laughter was not part of that study, but what struck me was how important it was seen to be. That inspired me to develop a practical and accessible way in which laughter could be harnessed intentionally for wellbeing, including in the immobile and bedridden. I conceived the Laughie (Laugh Intentionally Everyday) one-minute laughter prescription, and found it was feasible and effective (Gonot-Schoupinsky & Garip, 2019). The Laughie was influenced by Laughter Yoga, and Joe will talk about Laughter Yoga in more detail. The two differ in a number of ways, with the Laughie intended as a practical way to harness one minute of laughter alone or with others. Merv Neal, the head of Laughter Yoga Australia, used the Laughie in a year-long mental health initiative, and

DOI: 10.4324/9781003408963-8

links to his demonstrating it are found in the references (Neal, 2023a, 2023b).

Joe first contacted me in 2019 after having read about my Laughie laughter prescription research. Joe's enthusiasm for the healing potential of laughter, and his ability to reach out to learn from and unite, laughter researchers, practitioners, and enthusiasts all over the world, is inspiring. As a gelotologist (gelotology is the study of laughter) and a positive autoethnographer (I see positive reflexivity as integral to the autoethnographic discourse), I was keen for Joe to tell his story. Reflexivity is culture-bound (Grant, 2010b), and a cognitive and agentic process that can fundamentally change human emotions (Rosenberg, 1990). Positive reflexivity involves intentional positive thinking with the purpose of drawing out meaning and insight from past experiences in order to inspire and nurture positive emotional and behavioural responses. Thus, positive reflexivity may be leaned on to assess, address, and realign previous negative cycles.

Joe's life is now filled with laughter and joy, but he has traversed some serious mental health battles. Joe is humble and down-to-earth. Yet, and perhaps unusually for a narrative on mental health, as family wealth can be protective (Ettman et al., 2020), Joe comes from a wealthy background. Stourhead, a neo-Palladian house in Wiltshire bequeathed to the National Trust for the benefit of the nation, was commissioned by Joe's ancestor, the son of the founder of what is now the oldest bank in the UK.

Despite the inverse relationship between wealth and depression (Ettman et al., 2022), the lived experiences of people can diverge from the statistics of those they are supposed to represent. We know that adolescents and young males are at a particular risk of suicidal ideation and suicide (King et al., 2020). Joe was 16 when his troubles began and was in his early 20s when he first attempted suicide. Following Joe's story, we will learn more about his thoughts on laughter, joy, and mental health in a question-and-answer format. These questions are adapted from those previously used in investigating the topic of laughter and mental health with laughter experts (Ben-Moshe & Gonot-Schoupinsky, 2023; Kataria et al., 2023; Neal & Gonot-Schoupinsky, 2023;).

Joe has alluded to his life journey in *Awakening the Laughing Buddha Within* (Hoare, 2013). More recently he has written *Laughter Yoga for Joy* (2022). The beauty of autoethnography is that it enables us to reflect on, and share, individual experiences that can add even more depth and understanding. Our many discussions about autoethnography with Zoom and emails over three months, and shared reading materials (Grant, 2010a, b; Grant, 2023; Gonot-Schoupinsky, Weeks, & Carson, 2023), gave Joe a range of new tools to reflect on and share his story in detail.

## Joe Hoare: My Story

### *How Did I Get Here?*

I am living such an unusual life and yet I am somehow living beyond the life of my dreams. I find my life has become more than I ever imagined – it is freer, more rewarding, lovelier, and fuller of day-to-day joy than I previously conceived possible.

I am now aware of, or maybe from, the core of my being that we have the potential to find the 'thank you' in every experience, and that when we do, life improves. It can be difficult to do this when we are struggling and suffering, and yet when we do, we shed a skin and we grow into a kinder, calmer, more serene life. In fact, the most difficult experiences are our best teachers and open us to a greater empathy than before. Life becomes increasingly joyful.

Mine started with privilege and considerable material comfort. I had a private education and for the first half of it I was a star student. As it turns out, this was the seed of a major disappointment for me later in my education but at first learning and getting excellent results were both easy. I was lulled into thinking I was very clever. I also had an inquisitive streak. This meant I was always testing the limits. At prep school, this was naturally pretty harmless, but it got me into many scrapes when I went to Eton and led to my early departure.

I was expelled when I was 16.

The reason I was expelled was because I was the one who always got caught. My infractions were pretty mild – smoking, drinking, breaking out of the house at night, all of which led me to receive a final warning which, when I ignored it, led to me being summarily expelled.

This was very upsetting for all those around me, but not for me. To start with I was still too young and privileged to appreciate what a problem it was for everyone else.

Secondly, it led to one of the most important moments in my personal evolution, a whisper from my soul about my life's purpose.

Dad was driving me to see a Vocational Guidance Counsellor to help me find my way after my troublesome expulsion, and he asked me if I had any idea what I wanted to do with my life. Unbidden, the words that came out of my mouth at the age of 16 were 'I want to help people'. This was not a conscious thought and I had never entertained it before, but the words just popped out of my mouth. 'You mean, like a psychiatrist?', Dad asked? 'No, it's not quite like that I said', and then lapsed into silence because I didn't have a concrete idea, it was just something that popped out.

I have looked back at that moment many times in my life and every time I am struck by that first conscious stirring of my soul and how that early awareness has underlain the whole of my life. Even now I still have a vivid memory of sitting in the car, uttering those words, not knowing what they meant but knowing they were important.

Of course, as a teenager, those words promptly disappeared from my life, particularly as I started a new educational path and felt like a displaced person. I had one term in an international school where I felt out-of-place all the time as it was so different from Eton and its unwritten privileged assumptions. I had never before experienced the awkwardness of not-belonging, nor have I since, and nor would I wish this experience on anyone. In retrospect, it started to open an inner door to empathy and understanding because I can still remember the loneliness and the wistful wanting-to-belong that were present almost all term. To my surprise, even in my navel-gazing unhappiness, there were several other students who both liked me and showed kindness but somehow this added to my confusion. I am glad I only had one term there.

Millfield was the opposite. I found my place here. It was both international and co-educational. I was in a boarding house with fairly strict rules and, fortunately, few opportunities for misbehaviour. Everyone in my boarding house was a fellow misfit so we all got along. I had the happy experience of one or two teachers I understood and felt inspired by. I had my first proper girlfriends. I did well academically. I got good enough 'A' level grades to be accepted at Cambridge. I thrived.

Thrive comes before a fall. While at school I had been a 'First' student, at Cambridge I was definitely only 'Second'. Although that was a shock, it was manageable until I started to explore extra-curricular and illegal activities. I drank and unlike others, I did inhale. I did both to excess and instead of taking my Part 1 exams, I found myself semiconscious under a bush. I realised I had flunked my exams and my future looked unremittingly bleak. I saw no other option than to end my life.

I tried three times. Luckily my failure was my biggest success.

## The Next Crisis

I found attempted suicide exhausting. I had to wind myself up into a frame of mind where the despair overrode my will to live. I found it required a conscious and sustained application of bleakness and having failed three times, I lost the will to die. I ended up going back home.

Fortunately, my parents gave me space. They didn't fuss, they didn't ask questions, they just allowed me to quietly go about my own self-mending. This suited me perfectly. I was living in the countryside surrounded by forest and farmland. It was quiet and peaceful. My parents had a new Labrador puppy who I took for endless long walks and who therefore adopted me. At first, I had minimal social interaction which gradually increased, and bit by bit I started to mend.

In fact, my recovery worked perfectly for me. I spent more and more time outdoors, walking in the woods, being out in nature in all weathers with its quiet, its sounds, its smells, and its quality of just being there. Nowadays I don't know if this recovery process would be allowed but for me it was perfect and it allowed a love and appreciation of nature to flourish in my soul, more so than I realised at the time. It led to me starting my first career, managing forest operations. I started managing the family woodlands on Stourhead (Western) Estate and found I loved it. I loved the hard physical work, the sales and marketing, and the relationship between solo time and team time. The only cloud on my horizon was an imminent forestry meeting I knew I'd have to organise where representatives from all sectors of the forest industry would get together. I dreaded it as I would have to stand up and lead a group of 50 or more people on a day's walking excursion around the woodlands.

After two years this day arrived. I planned a careful excursion where the topics of conversation would naturally flow from one site to the next. To my horror, about 80 people turned up from all sectors of the forest industry. These included senior members of the National Trust, the Forestry Commission, the Nature Conservancy Council, the District and Local Council, the Countryside Commission, as well as my own professional colleagues and peers. It was a prestigious and daunting group which wanted to see the latest developments in the prestigious woodlands I was managing.

To my surprise, I loved the day. I loved the experience of facilitating the flow of information and accessing the group intelligence. I loved eliciting responses from people who might otherwise have remained quiet and not shared their insights. To my even greater surprise, everybody loved the day too. I had discovered facilitative and presentational skills about which I had no previous inkling. I knew I had found a gift I didn't realise I had, and which continues to inform my life today. From that moment on, I knew I needed to communicate.

## And the Next Crisis

My next and most important formative experience was 18 months of insomnia. I refer to it as 'insomnia hell' because it was dreadful. It was a form of 'imposter syndrome' because I was confronted by my deep and lurking fears that I couldn't do my job. There were personal factors too as my relationship was not working out as I had expected. I became increasingly stressed and tense. I still have a vivid recollection of coming downstairs one evening, seeing the clock on the wall telling me it was 8.20 p.m., and not knowing how I would get through that night. I was desperate.

However, time passed, and I survived and gradually I self-mended again. One thing I happened to discover, and which has served me well ever since, was that if I massaged my shoulders for about five minutes, I'd then relax and go to sleep. This was a relief almost beyond description. It was also an early pointer to the effectiveness of body–mind medicine, and although I didn't realise that at the time this accidental body–mind discovery has become a cornerstone in all my subsequent wellbeing work.

Once my ability to sleep properly returned, I realised I had learnt an important lesson. Although I had been well-educated, was well-trained and competent in my work, and respected by my professional colleagues, I had no personal wellbeing skills. I realised I had learnt a vital lesson, that our personal wellbeing is essential and needs to be at the centre of our life.

I became a voracious wellbeing student and many changes happened in a short time. All of them were profound and two of them dramatic. I started to explore the world of invisible energy, starting with emotion. I had been brought up in the era of the Rational Man and was therefore cut off from my emotions and my inner world. Living in my head was a major cause of my insomnia. The journey into my emotional world was both troublesome and magical.

'Learn to breathe' was the first advice I was given. At the time this meant nothing to me but shortly after I came across diaphragmatic breathing and understood what I'd been told. I practiced diligently and learnt to breathe properly again.

I discovered Chi Kung with its focus on mastering the art of internal strength. I developed a daily practice and continued this every day for several years. It is a never-ending practice and one I still use 30 years on as it is based on standing and breathing, being calm and grounded, and remembering to smile.

Although these threads were important, they were overshadowed by two cataclysmic events. I opened my heart and found my voice. Both were irrevocable changes that shattered my former life and pointed it in its current direction. Fortunately, both were breakthroughs and not breakdowns, but they were unexpected and life-changing.

My heart-opening happened in a split second in a healing circle. Earlier in the circle, I had felt a welling up inside me that I desperately tried to push down but suddenly it erupted. It was cathartic because in that instant my old self died, and my new one was born. I experienced the reality and healing power of human connection. I made a transition from 'me' consciousness to 'we' consciousness as my heart burst open and I started to feel. Friends described me as seeing the world for the first time, and that's how it felt. It was almost overwhelming but fortunately, both my rediscovered diaphragmatic breathing and my Chi Kung helped me stay grounded as I started to come to terms with my new life. From that instant, I knew I had come 'home' and returned to my teenage insight of 'I want to help people'.

In the same way many years before when I knew I wasn't a presenter until my forestry meeting, I also knew I wasn't a singer. I had shut down my voice many years earlier and had all the usual 'I can't sing' complexes. However, I was at a Mind Body Spirit festival in London and heard an exquisite sound coming from the group at the main stage. I immediately stopped what I was doing and went to join them. The sound I heard was a group starting a voice warm-up exercise and this touched my soul. I joined in and found my voice. I discovered I had a beautiful voice, a free and natural one that was capable of producing lovely sounds and could also sing in tune. I discovered we all have this ability, that our voice is unique, and we can access its beauty through simple exercises.

I was ecstatic. This was the third time my life had been turned on its head. The first time being when presenting to the forestry group, and the second time with my heart-opening experience. I now felt I had not only the insight but the tools to make 'I want to help people' a practical reality.

## A Laugh Is a Sound on the Breath

I started teaching 'Free your natural voice'. I practiced my voice release exercises and trained until I felt competent to start passing these skills on. I loved these sessions because they used all my skills from open-hearted group connection, through bodywork to free vocal expression. A by-product of the process was gales of uninhibited spontaneous laughter. This was never an intention, but it happened every time because of the open-hearted group connection and the vocal relaxation process. People started commenting and suggested I run laughter workshops, but I was not ready. I enjoyed opening a space where natural laughter flowed freely but I didn't feel competent intentionally to run such sessions.

In 1996 I read an article in the 'Funny old world' section of Private Eye about laughter clubs in India which were being run by Dr. Kataria. He was a practising General Practitioner (GP) who started a laughter club so people could experience the benefits of laughter. I still have a copy of that article, November 1996, page 18! It is a brief article, but I found it an intriguing, sufficiently so that I kept the article although I still didn't feel ready to run laughter workshops.

After 20 years I finally left the forest industry and moved into providing personal and professional wellbeing sessions. I ran British Medical Association-endorsed stress management sessions which included physical relaxation and movement, breathwork and sighing, visualisation and meditation, and positive communication. The sessions were called 'Stress management with a difference' and when people asked what the difference was, my reply was 'laughter'. As with the free your natural voice sessions, the laughter was allowed to happen naturally and spontaneously rather than as a focused activity.

However, I ran my first deliberate laughter workshop in 1997. It was a qualified success, qualified enough that I didn't feel ready to run another one. I continued with my previous approach of allowing the laughter to happen unexpectedly and therefore freely and spontaneously.

All that changed in 2002 when I met Dr Kataria, the Founder of the Global Laughter Yoga Movement. He'd come to the UK, and I happened across a workshop he was running, so I immediately signed up. It was a life-changer. First, he gave us permission to laugh. He gave us both the medical background and the yoga tradition and combined these into a comprehensible and accessible package. Secondly, he demonstrated the power of eye contact. This was the missing piece in my jigsaw because when we have eye contact with a fellow human, we experience a direct connection. When this is done in a context of playfulness and laughter, it opens us to good-natured, open-hearted laughter.

I had now fully come home.

## Yoga Benefits through Laughter Practices

Laughter yoga has the same split personality that yoga does. Both can be defined either by their 'what?' or by their 'how?' This means laughter yoga can be described either by its benefits or how it is practised. Both are accurate and valid, but it is helpful to realise the core practice is in intentional laughter. As with yoga, the benefits include reductions in stress and anxiety, improvements in mood and energy levels, and increased resilience and the sense of being more in control of life.

It is essential to realise it is not entertainment nor based on jokes, humour or comedy but is the practice of laughter for its own sake. It is an intentional wellbeing practice, done for its benefits, in the same way, people might go running or practise mindfulness. This is an important cultural shift for those brought up in the Western mindset who view laughter as something we do when we find something funny. In many ways, laughter yoga is based on the psychologist William James' insight in the 1880s that 'We don't laugh because we're happy, we're happy because we laugh'. Laughter yoga gives us a way of doing this.

In my early laughter yoga days, I focused on the laughter. Now that I realised the importance of eye contact, I threw myself into laughter yoga and founded the Bristol Laughter Club. Clapping and chanting are part of traditional laughter yoga and are well received in Asian cultures but from my first session, I realised that a significant proportion of participants are uncomfortable with them. They evoked resistance. I realised I needed to find a different approach, and this has been my own laughter yoga journey ever since.

I started to adapt and innovate. Instinctively I prefer natural and spontaneous laughter. My quest became how to generate this as simply as possible, within a laughter yoga context. I still love and use standard laughter yoga exercises with their eye contact and inherent playfulness, but I prefer to elicit the spontaneous laughter that comes from pleasure and enjoyment. The monthly laughter club was a valuable resource as it allowed experimentation and creativity. Most of all it showed me the value of movement and body-based laughter yoga.

Shortly after starting the Bristol Laughter Club, I began venturing into festivals like the Glastonbury Festival, the Big Green Gathering, and the World Yoga Festival. These are ideal opportunities for creativity and off-the-wall laughter yoga activities and my evolving style suited this environment perfectly. In particular, festival sessions allowed full scope for movement and the physicality of laughter yoga including touch, dance, Chi Kung and healing, hugging, and full body contact. These sessions allowed me to explore my own creativity and spontaneity. I developed an increasing trust and confidence in my ability to allow ideas to emerge from the group and create activities accordingly. I loved this and so did the groups because they became co-creators of the experience. This fluid, spontaneous style has become a trademark of my own laughter yoga and continues to serve me well.

Simultaneously I started running laughter yoga sessions in professional environments, for teams and conferences. The style was different but the core elements of connection and experiencing laughter yoga benefits were always present, even if not through traditional laughter yoga exercises. I found that in team and conference settings people wanted mind–body as well as body–mind. They wanted information as well as the experience, so I was able to draw on insights from resources like Appreciative Inquiry and NLP (neurolinguistic programming) to provide an intellectual framework. This proves to be a good combination.

As I continued to develop my own approach to laughter yoga, I became aware of benefits beyond the standard ones. I realised that not only do we usually enjoy the experience of free, natural, spontaneous laughter but also usually how this makes us feel. Very occasionally this provokes a catharsis which in these settings tends to be mild and which can be handled gently and allows for a calm and happy resolution. In most cases, we feel freer, lighter, and infused with dynamism and optimism. The shorthand version is we feel alive, and we feel the joy of being alive. It took me several years to realise that although we instinctively feel this, we need to be aware of it to register that we're experiencing it.

I also realised that simple laughter yoga practices can connect us with our joy. I discovered that simple exercises are best because when we focus on the experience rather than the exercise, we become more readily aware of our experience. After years of experimenting, I realised that the simplest exercise is to smile and that the smile is a gateway to joy. Simple, warm-hearted smiling is a good experience for us as well as for others. Smiling in this way is a form of self-acceptance and develops a healthy relationship with ourselves. It also creates healthy interactions with people even if we don't know them and creates a positive contagiousness that nurtures everyone, including ourselves.

The importance of joy is that it is an antidote to life's troubles. It is a dynamic serenity that elevates us, so we rise above life. As it is an emotion that is hardwired into us, we can experience it irrespective of our circumstances, even when they are dire. *Laughter Yoga for Joy* focuses on connecting us with our inner world and with this joy inside us. The more we practice connecting with it, the more we joy we experience.

'Joy is the purpose of life', commented Satish Kumar. *Laughter Yoga for Joy* gives us the tools.

## Ten Questions for Joe

### What Do You See as the Key Benefits of Laughter to Mental Health?

Laughter brings us into the present moment, which means we get out of our head. 'Mental health' issues often involve overthinking and therefore coming into the present moment is always an improvement. Laughter also helps us change our internal biochemistry by triggering the production and release of dopamine, oxytocin, serotonin, and endorphins. These all help improve mood, raise energy, decrease stress, and lower anxiety levels.

When laughter is intentional as in laughter yoga and laughter therapy – and also the Laughie – it is also psychologically empowering.

When laughter is experienced with others, either in a social setting or in a class or similar, there is also the element of group connection. As many mental health issues include a sense of isolation and disconnection, this group laughter dimension is an added benefit.

### Have You Had Any Depressed Clients, and How Do You Advise Them?

I have had a few. Different clients respond to different stimuli. The key is always to help them break out of their head and overthinking. For some, embodiment is the key. This involves body awareness and developing an ongoing practice where they become familiar with reconnecting with the body.

For others, the practice of smiling is their key. I find it essential to listen carefully to help with suggestions that might work for them.

### How Do You See the Differences between Laughing with and Without Humour?

Intentional laughter does not require humour and is therefore a body–mind activity. Humour has an intellectual component because it must be funny. The biggest difference is that intentional or self-generated laughter is an internal process. Humour-based laughter means we are laughing because something 'outside' or external makes us laugh. Although both instances involve laughter, the intentional, self-generated laughter in laughter yoga, some laughter therapy, and the Laughie, means we are deliberately working on changing our inner world and how we respond to life around us. Although reactive laughter can change our inner world, intentional laughter specifically looks to do so. In this respect it is helpful to consider intentional laughter as a wellbeing practice, something we choose to do because we want the benefits it brings us. An analogy is exercise where sometimes we take exercise not because we feel like it but because we know we will benefit.

This is at the heart of all intentional laughter practices.

### What Are Your Thoughts on Prescribing Laughter for Health and Wellbeing, for Example, with the Laughie or Other Modalities?

I hope this will soon become prevalent! The benefits from all intentional laughter practices are so clear, immediate, cost-free, and easy to access that it is an obvious prescription. However, prescribing laughter for health and wellbeing requires a change in our cultural, social, and medical mindset, and these are formidable barriers. These mindsets ignore evidence until the mindsets change as there is already substantial evidence of the efficacy of laughter practices.

Prescribing laughter for health and wellbeing fits completely with health promotion. Fortunately, health promotion is gaining momentum through social prescribing whose activities include a range of activities. It is not beyond hope that intentional laughter will be added to this list even if to help make the other activities even more enjoyable.

### Your Own Approach to Laughter Yoga Is Somewhat Personal, Can You Explain How It Differs?

I am often asked this question and I find it hard to answer, so I asked people who'd experienced it when researching my latest book 'Laughter Yoga for

Joy'. The answer seems to be that it is active and body-based rather than based on laughter exercises. It is based on our personal wellbeing and not in group connection. In the approach I have developed, we make a point of connecting with our bodies. This is always the first step and mindfulness practitioners recognise this as an excellent way of getting out of our heads. The approach is non-prescriptive which means everyone finds their own way of doing it. This itself is freeing because it means there is no right or wrong way, just your own way with increasing emphasis on making the process as enjoyable as possible. When we start relaxing into our body in this way, almost invariably we start to feel better, and our mood improves. When we add a good-natured smile to the process, it becomes even more enjoyable and genuine, natural laughter starts spontaneously. Acknowledging and appreciating everyone else is a natural, flowing development that allows group connection and encourages the natural contagiousness of laughter. Therefore, the approach is to start with yourself, enjoy the process, and share your enjoyment with everyone else.

### How Can Social Laughter Be Encouraged in People Who Feel Anxious About Social Situations?

One simple instruction helps such people – find your own level. In my experience, when people realise there are no external expectations for them to laugh, they immediately start to relax. When they relax, they start to enjoy themselves more and be more open and receptive to the group experience. Again, the process of connecting with their bodies as described above is helpful and because it is non-prescriptive, everyone finds their own way of doing so. This creates an open and free space for everyone to enjoy their own experience and with gentle coaxing and encouragement, laughter naturally and easily flows. Once this has started, it can be easy and enjoyable to encourage connection and mutual appreciation which helps the laughter flow more strongly. The key is always to start gently.

### Is Laughing Alone, or Solitary Laughter, Important, and Why?

In *Laughter Yoga for Joy*, intentional solitary laughter is essential. It is an exercise in positive choice. It relates back to the Viktor Frankl observation from his time in the Nazi death camps, that our ultimate freedom is the freedom to choose how to respond to any given set of circumstances. The choice of intentional solitary laughter for joy is life-affirming as it is an act of self-empowerment. It is wonderful that this intentional life-affirming act also changes our internal chemistry and therefore supports the experience. It puts us firmly in control of our own response to life and is not dependent on groups or any external stimuli. Consequently, this is personal freedom which for some people is essential to their wellbeing.

### What Do You Recommend to Those Who Feel Too Depressed to Even Think About Laughter?

I have never worked with people who feel too depressed even to think about laughter. My general advice is always to keep breathing, just take one more breath. I also like to support and validate people's experience as I have found this is constructive and helpful. It is different when they are open to the possibility of improving their current experience. In such circumstances, besides checking they have a proper and effective support network, I take them gently through the move, breathe, smile *Laughter Yoga for Joy* process and encourage them to keep practising. This approach usually leads to moments of genuine, spontaneous laughter and for some, this opens an inner door. They realise they have an additional tool for their wellbeing toolkit.

### Can You Tell Us More about the Importance of Joy and How It Relates to Laughter?

Joy is inside us. It is independent of external circumstances. It is a transcendent state we can train ourselves to experience more frequently and more intensely. We know it when we experience it and it is a quality that lifts our spirits, irrespective of life's vicissitudes.

Laughter yoga can help us access this inner state. *Laughter Yoga for Joy* focuses on it. Laughter yoga classically uses activities to help access joy but *Laughter Yoga for Joy* uses our awareness. In all the Global Joy interviews I've conducted, one prevalent comment is that joy is in the present moment. It is an inner experience, in the present moment. When we follow this approach, we realise that joy is potentially available almost all the time and is independent of activity. Any activity can be a joyful one when experiencing joy from the inside out. Activities to stimulate joy might work but they are an outside in approach and the experience of joy is linked to the activity.

When we realise we can connect with our inner joy whenever we choose, our life becomes more joyful and we have an improved experience of being alive.

### You Have Met Many Fellow Laughter Experts, What Is the Best Advice They Have Shared?

Funnily enough, the piece of advice that most sticks in my mind is 'Don't repeat nonsense!'. There are many pseudo-scientific claims about laughter which discredit the genuine benefits that laughter practices deliver. Other key comments include being kind. Laughter practices can be an intentional force for kindness, peacefulness, and open-hearted living. The practice of laughing at oneself, or 'lightening up not tightening up' is another excellent piece of advice. It is also an excellent stress-busting tip because we can train ourselves to laugh kindly at our foibles. An example is when we feel technology-induced rage or frustration and have expressed it in our own particular way, remember to complete the experience by laughing. This simple-but-not-easy practice reduces the emotional tone. Above all, practice intentional solitary laughter. In the words of Anne Frank; 'How wonderful it is that nobody need wait a single moment before starting to improve the world'.

## Conclusion

Failure, especially when it relates to failed suicide, is as Joe recounts can be an excellent thing. In this candid narrative, Joe shares his recovery journey, from suicide and despair, to starting and running a laughter club, which is still going strong 20 years on. Joe explains how we can harness laughter intentionally to bring joy into our lives, and how laughter can open the way to positive emotions such as kindness and gratitude. Intentional laughter may take practice and there may also be a need, for many, to change our mindsets about how laughter 'should' occur. The insight Joe shares is valuable both for those new to the practicalities of harnessing laughter for well-being, and for those keen to deepen their understanding of it.

## References

Ben-Moshe, R., & Gonot-Schoupinsky, F. (2023). Laughter, mental health, and cancer: A case study of Ros Ben-Moshe. *Mental Health and Social Inclusion*, Vol. ahead-of-print, No. ahead-of-print. https://doi.org/10.1108/MHSI-11-2022-0071

Ettman, C. K., Adam, G. P., Clark, M. A., Wilson, I. B., Vivier, P. M., & Galea, S. (2022). Wealth and depression: A scoping review. *Brain and Behavior*, 12(3), e2486. https://doi.org/10.1002/brb3.2486

Ettman, C. K., Cohen, G. H., & Galea, S. (2020). Is wealth associated with depressive symptoms in the United States? *Annals of Epidemiology*, 43, 25–31. https://doi.org/10.1016/j.annepidem.2020.02.001

Gonot-Schoupinsky, F. N., & Garip, G. (2019). Prescribing laughter to increase well-being in healthy adults: An exploratory mixed methods feasibility study of the Laughie. *European Journal of Integrative Medicine*, 26, 56–64. https://doi.org/10.1016/j.eujim.2019.01.005

Gonot-Schoupinsky, F., Weeks, M., & Carson, J. (2023). "You can end up in a happy place" (Voyce): A role for positive autoethnography. *Mental Health and Social Inclusion*. 27(4), 380–391. https://doi.org/10.1108/MHSI-02-2023-0021

Grant, A. (2010a). Autoethnographic ethics and rewriting the fragmented self. *Journal of Psychiatric and Mental Health Nursing*, *17*(2), 111–116. https://doi.org/10.1111/j.1365-2850.2009.01478.x

Grant, A. (2010b). Writing the reflexive self: An autoethnography of alcoholism and the impact of psychotherapy culture. *Journal of Psychiatric and Mental Health Nursing*, *17*(7), 577–582. https://doi.org/10.1111/j.1365-2850.2010.01566.x

Grant, A. J. (2023). Crafting and recognising good enough autoethnographies: a practical guide and checklist. *Mental Health and Social Inclusion*, *27*(3), 196–209. https://doi.org/10.1108/MHSI-01-2023-0009

Hoare, J. (2013). *Awakening the laughing Buddha within*. Amazon.

Hoare, J. (2022). *Laugher yoga for joy*. Amazon.

Kataria, M., Ben-Moshe, R., & Gonot-Schoupinsky, F. (2023). Laughter and mental health: A case study of Dr Madan Kataria. *Mental Health and Social Inclusion*, *27*(3), 220–229. https://doi.org/10.1108/MHSI-03-2023-0032

King, T. L., Shields, M., Sojo, V., Daraganova, G., Currier, D., O'Neil, A., ... & Milner, A. (2020). Expressions of masculinity and associations with suicidal ideation among young males. *BMC Psychiatry*, *20*(1), 1–10. https://doi.org/10.1186/s12888-020-2475-y

Neal, M. (2023a). *How to create a Laughie by Merv Neal*. [Video]. YouTube. https://youtu.be/ANGA8jnxlnQ

Neal, M. (2023b). *How to laugh with your Laughie by Merv Neal*. [Video]. YouTube. https://youtu.be/AeLy2FaEZec

Neal, M., & Gonot-Schoupinsky, F. (2023). Laughter and mental health: A case study of Merv Neal. *Mental Health and Social Inclusion*, *27*(4), 407–416. https://doi.org/10.1108/MHSI-06-2022-0039

Rosenberg, M. (1990). Reflexivity and emotions. *Social Psychology Quarterly*, *53*(1), 3–12. https://www.jstor.org/stable/2786865

# 9

## A GRIEF ODYSSEY

*Robert Hurst*

**24 March 2022**

I sit in the coffee shop, a big grin resting on my face. The espresso-scented steam rises from my cup as I close my laptop. Flights booked, accommodation sorted – I am off on holiday for the first time in 18 months, and it is also my birthday. Does life get any better?

**24 March 2023**

Copenhagen sprawls out before me. The takeaway cup in my hand is rapidly cooling in the crisp, damp, spring air. As I breath in salt, the tears on my cheek blend with the rain drops and sea spray.

**24 March 2022**

Stepping out of my mother's car and walking the short distance to my grandparent's front door, I am contented. Based on the cars parked outside, we are the last to arrive. We walk into a room filled with smiles and joy. Happy Birthday! Not just for me, either. I have always felt very lucky to share a birthday with my grandpa. He's there, sitting next to my grandma, as always. My two aunties walk over to hug me, and my brother pokes his head out from the kitchen – he had been telling everyone that he couldn't make it for the double birthday, but he was actually planning to surprise us.

DOI: 10.4324/9781003408963-9

## 24 March 2023

My mum puts her arm around me in the art gallery, as we sit facing a painting of a mourning woman beside a grave. She pulls me close, our tears and grief mingling. I think back to the previous year as I lost myself in the brushstrokes. So much has changed. Last year, on our birthday, was the last time that the whole family was together smiling. Though grandpa's breathing was getting worse, we weren't sure how bad things were. We made sure to squeeze all the happiness we could out of that day, in case it was his last birthday. We were wise to. While his pain was clear, grandma's was not yet. By August, it had rapidly gotten worse, and she had gone. By the following February, grandpa had followed her.

Now, my 25th birthday is my first without him. Grief is so often littered with 'firsts', marked by milestones. Christmases and birthdays – huge days carved into the calendar, dripping with meaning and significance. Immovable occasions on which it is impossible not to think of those that you miss. These, to me, feel inevitable. A part of the process, even. Yet what I found within me was a longing to disrupt this, to accept what grief had in store for me, but sprinkle in the unexpected and adventure. Grief is a journey, so they say. As a lover of travelling, I wanted to take that further. Did my physical, geographical journeys impact my grief journey? How so? What will this teach me along the way?

## Sibiu/Brasov, Romania – September 2022

We never specifically said we were going away together to deal with our grief. Yet, on the night of grandma's funeral, there we were booking flights to Romania. My brother Dan and I are both explorers at heart, though in different ways. Our wanderlusts ignited by many trips abroad with our grandparents that we were lucky to be taken on.

As we entered Liverpool airport, it struck me that this was the first time I had been here since we had gone to Italy with them eight years ago. Looking around I was hit by a wave of deep sadness. She was gone. And here we were, running away. I had not even consciously thought that this was what we might be doing, escaping the world of pain that we had so quickly entered. Grandma had not even been to see a doctor yet, three months ago – she was just having a bit of pain. Now she was gone, and here we were waiting to fly away somewhere completely new. Unknown territory, with rolling hills and Dracula's Castle. I realised that I was running away.

Another dimension to this trip was that I had just applied for a job, a big job. To be an Associate Lecturer at a university. My current job was in customer experience. It felt as though huge change was swirling all around.

Sitting on the plane, it hit me just how much travelling reminded me of those childhood trips with my grandparents. Why had I never noticed this before? I suppose I never had to think too much of it. Yet here, as the safety announcement was read out, grandma appeared next to me, offering a sweet to suck on before take-off. It helps stop your ears from popping, she said. The pain I was escaping from had followed me; it had come along for the ride. With one final check of my phone, I saw an email inviting me to interview for the job. The following is what I felt compelled to write down on that flight.

Joy and excitement mingled with anxiety as I switched my phone to airplane mode. Should I be going for this job? Will I be allowed to rearrange my interview, or will I have to do it from a Transylvanian Airbnb?

These worries I could do nothing about. Not yet anyway. I consoled myself with the idea that I could scribble some ideas for my 15-minute micro-teach presentation while in the air. I had the entire row of seats to myself (thanks, Ryanair!), so I could plug in my headphones, listen to music, and work in relative peace. Fears abated for now, an action plan in place, my sense of pride was allowed to swell.

Absent-mindedly watching the safety demonstration, I realised that for the next 3 hours, I couldn't share my achievement with anyone except for my brother — and even he would have to wait until the fasten seatbelt sign went out.

I thought of who I needed to tell, constructing a mental list as the plane began to taxi down towards the runway. Yet I immediately hit an obvious snag. The harsh reality dawned that grandma would never hear this huge news. She was not here for this big moment in my life.

The plane was beginning to gather pace, the engines humming furiously. The song in my earphones was doing the same, rising in crescendo to the chorus. The wheels lifted from the ground, and the key shift into the chorus coincided with it. This combination of the music and the physical sensation was euphoric, and highly emotionally charged. Mixed with the sorrow I was experiencing, this resulted in the strangest of feelings. Perhaps the most powerful wave of grief I had experienced yet.

I ascended into the sky. As close to The Above as gravity allows. Here, in the heavens, the tears poured down my cheeks. I had never physically *felt* myself cry in this way. My eyes and cheeks were searing, as though on fire. It was a wonder that my tears did not turn to steam as they cascaded down. They say that a unit of alcohol on the ground is equal to four units up in the air. The effect is enhanced. From my experience, I have to say that I think the same is true of grief. Amplified by the altitude.

Now, thousands of feet in the air, I feel for the first time that I am sitting with my grief. We are still wary of one another. Not yet well-acquainted.

In the end, after this initial swell of emotion within me, the trip felt like one where I could absorb lots of beauty while feeling a kind of presence with me. With each knew experience, I was wondering what grandma would have made of it – looking at it through my eyes and attempting to do so through hers.

There was plenty to marvel at. From buildings to scenery to food, from days sitting in the sunshine of the main square to adventures up to castles, we did a little of everything. I felt a deep nourishment of the soul. In between the fun, I found lots of time to think. To sit with a coffee in a park and be *with* my thoughts. To feel present in a way that hadn't felt possible in my usual surroundings. It felt healing.

In terms of our relationship, it felt as though me and Daniel grew closer over those ten days. We talked around our grief. Showed each other that we cared without needing to directly talk about what had happened. Except for one evening.

R:    *Do you remember the night of grandma's birthday?*

D:    Oh god, yes. That night really stood out.

R:    *Everyone back home was doing a 'Midnight Memories' walk to raise money for the local hospice. I remember finding out the date of it, and simultaneously thinking 'Oh, that is perfect because it is on grandma's birthday', and also 'I am going to be away that date. I wish I was there to take part'.*

D:    I was trying to just … forget about it. I was trying to not feel it and stop myself from crashing and ruining the holiday. I was trying not to crumble. Not even consciously … it's like my brain had put a big block there to stop it all getting to me. Unconsciously, those emotions were just not getting through.

R:    *I think seeing messages in the family chat talking about grandma's birthday and then the pictures of everyone on the walk really brought it home to me. We had been on this fantasy journey, a big adventure to literally Dracula's fucking castle.*

D:    It was such a random experience, which helped it all feel less real to me. The places we were going to were completely removed from normal life, and we weren't physically there around everyone for it to hit me.

R:    *It had been a way of escaping and processing maybe, but that meant that when reality hit me it hit hard.*

D:    Yeah, you were almost catatonic. It seemed to me like it really slammed into you. You were listening and receptive to what I was saying, but it was like you were refusing to move. But also, you weren't really letting me in.

R:    *I remember feeling as though it was impossible to move. I was laid in bed, and I physically could not move my muscles such was the overwhelming sense of grief that washed over me. In that moment, I felt I needed to be still and feel that.*

D:    At first, I just thought you were knackered! But then when I realised, I was really concerned. Mainly because I just really wanted you to enjoy the holiday … wanted you to be able to escape it all like I was doing. I was really confused because you were reacting in a totally different way to me. 'I'm fine, so why are you not fine?' So, I was trying to pep you up and get you up and out for some food.

R:    *It didn't help that we were hungry! But I clearly remember being hit by a flash of anger at you but being able to justify it instantly. 'He is trying to help; he's just doing it in a way that isn't what you need right now'. That is something I felt with grief more than any other thing I have experienced – there are so many conflicting thoughts and emotions going on in parallel with each other.*

D:    It was the exact same for me. I needed to be moving, and you needed to be still. We were taking massively different approaches. I just wanted to get on with it, whereas it seemed like you really needed to just let things out and feel the emotions. In the end, I accepted that even if it took all night that would be ok, but it was strange. I was just glad in the end when you got up.

## Copenhagen, Denmark – March 2023

And just like that, I was back down again. Within six months, grandpa was gone too. While he had been living with a terminal condition for some years, the compounded grief was furious in ravaging my mind. Now two were gone. Their home would be sold. They were always a close couple, so while we all wanted them to be together, a life where we were left without the two of them was horridly unthinkable. Yet it was so.

Two months into the new job, with all the swirling change brought by it quickly piling atop my grief, I needed a remedy. Naturally, I looked to what had helped me feel some healing before – travel. With that shared birthday approaching, and a sense that I could not face doing it alone, I organised a trip with my mum and my girlfriend.

Copenhagen was the cheapest option. It was also somewhere my grandparents had visited – 'bloody cold', I'd heard. To be with two of the best people in my life, in a new place, to celebrate Our birthday. It seemed like a win. In many ways though, it felt like too much too soon. In Copenhagen, there was not the openness of scenery that had given me space to breathe in Romania. I had a distinct sense that I was trying to force this. After a long day of tourist-ing where I had not felt like I was 'with' grandpa on our birthday, I slunk away alone and tried to find him. This is what I wrote:

As darkness begins to pull in, I break off from our group. The day has been long, and my feet hurt, but I feel compelled to walk and reflect. Other than a moment of sadness in the museum, there has been too much to do for me to take the time to think and reflect and be 'with' grandpa. Somehow, I feel as though I am neglecting him on our shared birthday. I get a cup of tea from the corner store and find a bench on which to perch and set my thoughts free.

But there is a block. Whether it be physical tiredness, whether it be a kind of grief burnout, I just can't think. I can't connect. Can't engage with that part of me. This only adds to my frustration. As one last roll of the dice, I put on my headphones and play some Queen. This helps – they were one of his favourite bands. Listening to their *Greatest Hits* album always takes me back in time to road trips with him, driving to Edinburgh. As my frustration reduces, my sadness increases. Is this normal? Having to relax into grief?

*Another One Bites the Dust* begins to play, and I cannot help but smile. When trying to settle on a song for my grandma's funeral, Mum had Googled what other people had done to try and find inspiration. My grandpa had usually taken an attitude of, 'When I go, you all do whatever you need to for the funeral, I'm not bothered. It's for you lot, not for me!' However, Mum jokingly told him about this person who had played *Another One Bites the Dust* at their funeral. My grandpa laughed at this, laughed more than he had since grandma had been taken unwell. 'I want that one at mine', he said, serious through his laughter. It summed him up. His musical taste, his sense of humour, and his desire for us not to wallow but to celebrate his life. We honoured this and were able to laugh through the tears as we said goodbye. It is his laughter that I hear now, alongside the song. His daft laugh that I so miss.

The moon above is waxing, very slender. Due to low levels of light pollution, you can see its dark part. The backstage, private part that it intends to hide from us. It is nearly finished, ready to start its cycle again. Ready to show itself to the world. There may be meaning in that ... but I'm far too tired to unpick it. Looking upwards, I notice something burning brightly beside the moon in the inky sky. Despite my limited astrological knowledge, I can tell it isn't the Northern Star. I choose to think that it's grandpa, appearing in the sky to say hello on his birthday. Our birthday. Burning brightly.

I fidget with grandpa's ring, which I have taken to wearing, as a way of comforting myself. Looking down, I remember the pattern embossed on its surface.

A star.

And at last, there I am. Crying, in the happiest city on earth.

## London, UK – April 2023

My first season ticket at Bolton Wanderers was in 2009. I missed out on the team's glory days under Sam Allardyce by just two years. Yet, those games with Daniel and grandpa were massively formative. I became obsessed. I would spend every waking hour thinking about football. Over time we stopped going, as performances (and finances) dipped. Yet we would always speak about the latest results with grandpa. Exactly two months after he died, the Wanderers were in a cup final at Wembley. It may have only been the Papa John's Pizza Trophy … but it meant everything. Despite the expense, me and Dan made our pilgrimage down to the capital. Once more without saying it, we were grieving together with a journey as the pretext.

It felt as though grandpa was with me the whole time. I had noticed I'd brought a lot more of his phrases and words into my own vocabulary, particularly one of his favourites – 'gobshite'. Google tells me that this word is Irish, but to me, it is just grandpa. As we approached the famous arches, we put our pickle and cheese sandwiches into our bags, hoping we could smuggle them in. Just like grandpa would have. With the words we said and the things we did, we were embodying him, bringing him to the stadium with us.

As the match kicked off, I felt a flurry of nerves. This was more than just a game. We needed this. I kissed grandpa's ring, watching on anxiously.

We won 4–0.

We won the fucking cup.

Here, there were positive emotions. Let me stress, I was grieving hard. Yet it was joyous. Celebratory. Judging by social media posts I saw over the following days, we were not the only ones. Others celebrated the victory while paying remembrance to those who would have loved to be there.

Grief is confusing. Sometimes it is weeping. Sometimes it is belting out football anthems at the home of football, surrounded by Boltonians.

## Whitby, UK – April/May 2023

On the way to Romania, I began to read Adam Scovell's novel, *How Pale the Winter Has Made Us*. It partly inspired the idea for this chapter. Briefly, the story follows a woman (Isabelle) who, upon learning of her father's suicide at home in London, bunkers down for the winter in Strasbourg. The story maps her journey into the history of the city, the famous inhabitants that it has housed, and the folklore that surrounds it. To my mind, this character is using her training as a historian as a lens through which to explore her grief. Is that not what I am doing with autoethnography? The book also speaks to me in the way that journeying and grief can co-exist. Though this is where

Isabelle and I differ – for her, it was a means of avoidance, whereas for me it was a means of facing the grief head on … sometimes. The book had been difficult to read, however. As such, it served as a companion as I began to heal, then was thrown into turmoil again. A book I would keep in my bag most days but not feel brave enough to pick up. I sensed that Isabelle's story was a cautionary tale. I do not want to become so lost in my researching and writing that I over-intellectualise my grief, that I find myself avoiding the real work of it. However, on the days where I felt brave enough to pick up the book, I found valuable insights within.

For example, I discovered the concept of *fernweh*. It is a German word, in some ways the opposite of homesickness. It translates directly to 'far-woe'. As well as feeling woe at being far away, is it perhaps that moving far away helps to get away from woe, to leave it behind briefly?

This is on my mind when my friend asks if I would spontaneously like to take a trip to Whitby. It is funny the coincidences and meanings that we find. Whitby is a town that I visited with my grandparents, and one that is intrinsically linked to the part of Romania I explored via Bram Stoker's Dracula. My friend is from there, and the trip has been a long time coming despite only having two days' notice before embarking upon it. She is also called Isabel. It was with all these threads of meaning flying around in my mind that I realised I was becoming too much like the Isabelle of the book. I had written myself into a character and become lost in words and story. Overwhelmed by potential meanings on which to draw. Disconnected from actual feelings, my grief itself feeling distant.

> In the shadow of the ruined Whitby Abbey, a place that has inspired writing and creation for thousands of years, I question my own approach. Am I forcing this work, or feeling it? Is this exploration or avoidance? As I look out across the harbour and the bay beyond, I consider Scarborough Castle, and whether I will go there to recreate a childhood photo that I have with my grandpa. Why am I compelled to do this? Am I craving catharsis or just performing by re-living childhood memories? Is this journey the inciting incident that gets me to change my approach, or a realisation that this is a failed experiment? The middle point or the conclusion? Do I need to step back and allow myself to feel? Give it up altogether?
>
> Is the solution to my desire for space to be found within me rather than on the Ryanair website?

Reading back on my words from this time, it is clear just how unsure I was that autoethnography would suit my grief. Yet ultimately, by noticing this and stepping back, I was able to allow feeling to return and begin to start piecing back my Self. I was looking for a starting shot to get me moving again. It came in a flash...

### Traversing Stages in Grief

#### *Liverpool, UK – May 2023*

Music has always been a key part of my life, whether listening to it or playing it. Whenever I find myself listening to music without *feeling* it, I know something is wrong. Up until this point, only listening to music that my grandparents liked seemed to bring me close to tears. Looking backwards. Then, my favourite band released a new record. They had been through their own hellish bereavements. Their drummer died suddenly in 2022, and the frontman lost his mother not long after. Most fans, myself included, expected them to call time on the band. Yet, unbelievably, one day I was sat looking down at a new Foo Fighters song right there on my phone. 'Under You'. Knowing that it might cut close to the bone, I hit play.

This song helped to unlock tears and feelings that had felt distant until the moment I heard the lyrics. So far, I have not been able to listen to *Under You* without crying. This is an important song, for the band but for me too. When I hear it and its lyrics of loss, I connect in two ways. I hear a man, grieving his best friend and mum. A man whom I have idolised for over a decade, vulnerably sharing his pain. Then also I relate the lyrics to my own life, to my loss.

It has hurt me in the most important way. It has shocked me back to life. The pain from this has picked me up. It has unlocked another stage of my grief, gotten me to look at myself and reconnect with the hurt. Now, when I listen to other music I can *feel* it again.

This coincided with me playing music again. A friend got in touch and asked if I would like to play bass for his band at the Cavern Club in Liverpool, as I had done four years previously. My answer was, of course, yes. As I began to play music again with purpose and direction, suddenly I started feeling further connected. Paired with the new Foo Fighters music, this became a virtuous cycle. I found myself writing more music than I ever had in my life, like an emotional dam had burst.

As I took to the stage where The Beatles made their name, I thought of all the hours spent with my grandpa listening to their songs. How he would often whistle 'Here Comes the Sun'. I remembered how impressed he was the last time I played here. His ring glistened as the stage lights hit it, a beacon firing out across the crowd with each note that I hit.

## Bolton, UK – July 2023

Bolton is my home, so should it really be in this chapter? While the graduation stage is a relatively short journey, it is one with significant meaning attached. I was returning to the Albert Halls for my master's graduation, with two important people missing since my last visit for my Bachelors. The evening before, I felt their absence keenly. Fortunately, by now I had a full album from my grieving companions in Foo Fighters as my soundtrack to help me through. A realisation came to me that night. Looking back, it is surprising that it took so long to arrive in such clear words. I had spotted a pattern in my grief in Romania – that travelling could help – and extrapolated it as a rule. I had tried to tailor all my subsequent grieving around that. Yet, as I had found, I cannot grieve one-dimensionally. You cannot shortcut through grief. You can do things that might help, but there are no guarantees. Sometimes, the big milestones like a graduation loom ahead, and when they arrive you must look grief in the eye.

The next day, I made that short but significant journey across the stage. They were there with me.

A butterfly on my lapel, a ring on my finger, and a photograph in my pocket.

## Wroclaw, Poland – June 2023

As the seasons changed, Dan and I felt in the air a need to travel once again. We chose to go somewhere that nobody we knew had ever been, much like we had with Romania. The intersection of cheap flights and mystery lead to us stepping off a bus in the centre of Wroclaw, Poland. A month before, we couldn't even pronounce the name of the bloody place. There, I found many interesting metaphors. It is known as a city of change – it has passed through the hands of many kingdoms. Sometimes this change is artificial – the majority German population was evicted as World War Two ended, with ethnic Poles being shipped in from Lviv. Buildings that had been destroyed were rebuilt in a traditional Polish style, instead of as they once looked. What looks like a historical city square is less than 100 years old. It is a construction, literally and philosophically.

Yet, does the truth of the past matter? To an extent, yes. But the reconstructed square tells its own story. One of reclamation. This patch of land survived great trauma, and those who found themselves in charge of it chose to tell a story that made sense to them. On that level, I can relate. Despite this artificiality, this enforced meaning, it is working. People live here, the city thrives. As communism was falling, a movement here sparked genuine political change across the country. The meaning became actuality. In the same way, when I shifted my meaning from trying to find a chapter from my experiences of grief, to experiencing both life and grief and allowing the story to present itself from the base I had created, things began to happen.

Also, the communist revolution that started there involved people dressing as gnomes, shouting 'Down with the gnome king', to get around laws that suppressed free speech. Grandma and grandpa would have found that hilarious.

In terms of the relationship between Dan and I, it felt as though we were adapting, forming new traditions from the chaos. Stories can't *just* happen. Yes, you must let them run their course. But sometimes you must shape them. The Poles shaped the physical space of Wroclaw to represent a new direction in the history of this city. Similarly, Dan and I are creating new customs for ourselves. Indeed, taking a trip like this is a sure way to shape a story, take it somewhere new. Amongst fresh surroundings, one might discover new directions, or at the very least escape the ones back home.

R:   *For me, I felt both grandma and grandpa were 'with' me in Wroclaw, but I was in a completely different mental space than I was in Romania*

D:   Me too. I'd gone through a whole year of uni as well. I think I was just burnt out from all my coursework, as I hadn't had a chance to properly grieve yet. I felt very vulnerable in myself. It was like I wasn't sure how to be around anybody. But I felt more at peace with that grief within myself. I really felt them there, too. It's different from being at home because I associate them so much with travelling. They did it so much, and I know they would have been proud of us getting away together and exploring and growing closer. When we were both teenagers, we wouldn't have imagined doing it! I imagined them there seeing us having a good time. So, when we did something interesting, I thought that they would have liked that we were doing that.

R:   *It was nice to keep up the traditions that we have found ourselves falling into. Climbing big church spires (despite my mild vertigo!), trying new foods, getting a bit too drunk on the local stuff. It's like, since Romania, we have begun developing new customs within our travels. As traditions from our childhood are altered, partly from the bereavement, we have built new ones for when we spend lots of time together.*

D:   I think that's the way we bounce off each other as well. After having a long time where we didn't interact (once the hormones kicked in), it's like we've started learning about each other and what we enjoy doing together. And part of that is feeling like we're on an adventure. Even when you are hungover – it's different on holiday! We always seem to do a daft accent when we spend that time together, too! We seem to unconsciously choose a different one each time. It's like we are choosing to spend more time together to deal with the trauma. After such a hard thing in such a short space of time, we had to navigate that somehow. We both always loved travelling, geography, culture. Going having fun abroad together in a way that we enjoy is great, especially knowing how much they would have wanted us to do that, too. So those traditions have sped up and solidified quite fast because of the grief. We needed them to.

Returning from this trip, I was beginning to feel more put-together. The bursts of creativity I had experienced after beginning to play with the band intensified and accelerated at a pace I had never experienced. In the past, writing four songs in a year would be a pretty good output. A week after returning from Wroclaw, I wrote six songs in four days. This creativity was liberating. It felt like an expression of my mental state – the pressure had finally lifted enough that now an outpouring of emotion could flow via music. The songs I was writing were not about my grief, not directly anyway. I tackled all sorts of scenarios from my life, and writing music about them boosted my mood overall. It brought me to a better place to look the grief in the eyes. Now we had gotten to know one another, I felt more equipped to tackle it.

The culmination of all of this was a song called Whitby. Reflecting on my time there, I had realised that it was a huge turning point in my grieving journey. A spontaneous and unplanned trip, which shattered any delusion I had that I could heal just by going to far-flung lands and adventuring. It could help, but I needed to stop trying to force myself to find meaning in everything, and instead try to find joy in life. To let the healing happen as a parallel process. The more I had made it the object of my intention, the further it slipped from me. In Whitby, I had let this all go and started to try to 'sit with' my grief and my grandparents. Their continuing bond that was within me. I sat above the sea, and watched it breathe beneath me, and found myself breathing again. In, then out. One wave of breath at a time. Knowing that they had taken me there many years before made me feel 'close' in a way I could not feel in Copenhagen.

One evening, I found myself with a tune and a set of words in my head. This scene from Whitby had been playing through my mind. Unable to sleep, I got up and finally wrote about my grief musically. The song included a lot of elements. First and foremost a sense of 'place', which is what has dominated this narrative you're reading. It is something that has always made sense to me with my feelings and emotions, I attach them mentally to a specific physical place. The song also includes some resolution (lyrically and musically), and ideas of memory and ghosts. It talks about a knowledge of pride, and feeling it emanates from people, despite them having left this world. It has themes of movement, moving to a new place physically and mentally. Most of all, I sang of love. So much love.

> *I feel at home*
> *As the waves break down below*
> *I feel you here*
> *You're coming through loud and clear*
> *You tell me you're proud*
> *Your voices echoing out so loud*
> *Across the cliffs*
> *As I see your smiles,*
> *This weight starts to lift...*

Here, the weight truly did start to lift. As grief and emotion poured out of me as I tried to record a demo of the song, I suddenly felt yet another shift beneath my feet. By looking back at the turning tide I felt in Whitby and expressing it in a way that I really know how, I had made some progress. I felt proud and knew my grandparents would be proud too. Not quite closure, it felt like a big step forward. I thought that this would be the end of this chapter of my journey, a nice conclusion. But there were a few surprises still to reveal themselves.

### Bratislava, Slovakia – August 2023

> As I walk along the ancient city walls, a sign tells me of a one-time resident of the city who wrote the book on Romanian history which inspired Bram Stoker to write Dracula. I have a flash of memory. A few days previously, in Vienna, I saw a bookshop called 'Erlkönig'. This is a character from German folklore, the king of fairies, immortalised in a poem by Goethe. This was a big strand of narrative in *How Pale the Winter Has Made Us*, the book which accompanied me in the early days of my grief. In the book, The Erlkönig stalks Isabelle as she grieves. Seeing the bookshop made me stop for pause, but now seeing Dracula once more makes me wonder if he is my Erlkönig, whether he is the allegory for my grief. This bloodsucking monster, draining my lifeforce across the continents. From Romania to Whitby and now to Slovakia, he has followed me. Or am I just overcomplicating my grief again? Pulling on too many strands that lead nowhere? I choose to appreciate the coincidence and move along.

## Zadar, Croatia – August 2023

The hot weather took me back to childhood trips to Spain. My role as organiser on a group trip made me feel close to my grandpa, as I found myself using phrases and tones of voice that were originally his. Sitting on a balcony in scorching heat, looking at the mountains in the distance, the fig trees in the foreground, I reflected on how he kept it all together. How he balanced keeping everyone else happy and enjoying his holidays himself. Above all, I felt immense gratitude. To voice this, I turned to haiku, where I could focus on the beautiful nature around me while also exploring my emotions.

> *Humid and buzzing*
> *Crickets singing to the dusk*
> *I missed nights like this*
> *Craggy mountain range*
> *Blaring sunlight on my skin*
> *These bring you to mind*
> *Thoughts of Spanish heat*
> *Clouds in my mind, not the sky*
> *Old mixes with new*

As the trip ended, I found myself once more sitting with a row to myself on a flight. Outside, through the cloudless sky, I was treated to an unbelievable view of the Alps. With the help of a beautiful song, I once more found myself with hot tears falling down my face. My journey with understanding my grief through travel began with a tear-filled flight. Now, here I am once more crying above the clouds.

As the plane passes over the Alps, I am struck by their majesty. How could something so jagged and so harsh be so beautiful? The dark crags, sometimes dusted with bright white snow, climbed up as if reaching towards us. Putting down my book I meditated on them. We do not have mountains like this back home. Looking at them, I'm not sure there are mountains quite like these anywhere.

Here, I feel close to the heavens, perhaps because of the beauty below me. I am struck by an image of my grandparents. Flying, hand in hand, looking at all the beauty that the world has to offer. Following bends of rivers. Up and down, across the curves and dips and troughs of mountains below. Exploring. Appreciating.

They flow through city streets, seeing majestic buildings from any angle they wish. Invisibly, they drift through the art galleries of the world, freed from all the earthly pains the rest of us endure.

They are everywhere, all at once. Energy that flows around us all, constantly. In each beautiful vista, there they are. Enjoying it through my eyes.

As the rocks below (for their beauty exists only in my mind) haze and distort behind tears, I feel a familiar burning in my cheeks. I have cried many litres this last year, yet this is the first time it has felt like *this* since that plane journey to Romania, the one that sparked the idea for this writing. It is as if the tears have been warmed before being released down my hot cheeks, so hot that it feels that the tears might evaporate upon them.

Trying to understand the significance of this physical sensation, I choose to believe it is signifying of a new beginning. A fresh chapter. Time to close this one.

This felt like symmetry. My first ascent to this exploration of grieving through travel began with a lonesome flight, filled with scorching tears of furious and brand-new grief. Now, grief and I know each other a little better. He is something of a friend. While the tears on the descent were just as hot, there was a companionship in them. I was seeing beauty, and that made me think of two wonderful people whom I miss.

This grief will continue to shift and change shape through time. I am not naïve enough to pretend that is not so. Yet, I was able to take this moment to appreciate what wonderful grandparents I'd had. To picture them happy, floating, on a journey together that we mortals cannot comprehend. I remain here to keep their worldly legacy going. Through my words, through my actions and values, through my music, and through the stories I tell.

## Addendum

A week later, I looked through a photo album at my grandparents' house. It was the first one to hand that I had grabbed. As I turned the pages, I saw it filled with photos of a trip to Austria, where they explored the Alps. Taken aback, I checked the photos I had taken from the plane window. While I couldn't say for sure that the peaks I saw were the same as those in these 20-year-old photographs, I found I didn't care. I had seen that mountain range and felt deeply emotionally connected to my grandparents, and now here were pictures of them posing and being silly in front of those same mountains as they hiked through them. That was good enough for me. My constructed meaning mattered much more than the facts. At this point, I finally chose to bring Dan in. I had kept all this thinking about grieving and taking journeys under my cap for the most part until now. Despite having been my main grieving and travelling companion, I had not shared any of it explicitly with Dan.

R:    *Do you think that if we'd had these conversations about my grief/journey idea as it came to me in early March it would have affected how you approached these trips?*

D:    Erm … I don't really know. Probably a little bit, because of having more awareness. But I think that without speaking explicitly about it, we both knew that we needed these new traditions and that we wanted to spend more time together. To plan and go on fun trips. I think you've put language to it, but what you have said very much fits how I have been seeing my world.

R:    *It did feel weird keeping it to myself. It was on my mind a lot, but I almost didn't want to put words or ideas of mine into your head. I suppose I didn't want to step on your toes, grief-wise.*

D:    You would have never stepped on my toes! Talking about them helps me process things.

R:    *I didn't know that.*

D:    I think I spend a lot of time thinking about them on my own. Me and you didn't really speak about it until recently, maybe because we weren't ready. But I love talking about them when I can, it's really comforting.

R:    *It was a huge relief when we finally had the conversation about this chapter. I was glad to hear you'd had the same thoughts and ideas as me about travelling and grief.*

D:    That stuck with me. It was like a revelation to hear we had been having the same thoughts. I think we often think in the same ways. Our ways of processing grief are quite different, but they are joined by that travelling context. It's almost quite funny that you felt relieved! I would have loved to hear about it sooner.

R:    *Maybe that says something about the way that I've been grieving.*

D:    Yeah, I didn't realise how much you wanted to talk about it, because neither of us really asked each other how we could approach this whole grieving malarkey together. We just found ourselves naturally gravitating towards certain things, especially travel.

R:    *Do you think our next trip will be different, now that it is out there and explicit?*

D:    No, I don't think so. In terms of processing the grief, I think it will be the same. But I think if it means that you talk about them more, it will help me talk about them more, which is what I want to do. It might go some way to helping me shift this block that I still have. It might sound weird, but I think I would like to cry with you more. It hasn't happened much, but those moments where it did felt precious. Maybe now we are more open, that will be easier.

R:      *The only question left, then, is simple. Where to next?*

*

## Acknowledgements

In loving memory of Patricia and Michael Russ. Incredible grandparents who shaped me into the man that I am today.

Also to my friends and family, for being with me on all of my many journeys through this grief – I love you all dearly.

# 10

# CULTURAL IMPACT ON PROFESSIONAL IDENTITY

## Struggling to Connect with Professional Titles

*Adeela Irfan*

### Introduction

I had trouble deciding how to put myself in relation to time, space, and subject, so that I could write this chapter in the present moment. What I'm thinking about is connected to what has been occurring to me ever since I went to another country, if not even before that, and some of what I imagine will be happening in the future. So, from whence do I plan to tell my story? From the inside, I look at the outer world, through the lens of the wanderer interacting with new environments.

My decision to relocate abroad was motivated by a combination of personal struggles, a professional desire to work as a clinical psychologist or psychotherapist, as well as a phenomenological and spiritual quest to understand who I am and where I fit in the world. I can't say that my lifelong passion has been psychology. When I was denied admission to medical school, I found my passion for psychology, being curious to look into, and analyse, people's attitudes and behaviours, as well as family dynamics and cultural links. I was invalidated and rejected by my parents for not pursuing medicine. This was the first time I felt the impact of being rejected and craving for validation of what I wanted to do professionally. In the middle of the 1990s, depression was regarded as a mental ailment exclusively for the wealthy in Pakistani culture, or as an 'issue of rich people'. It was considered stigmatising for people to admit they had mental health problems.

DOI: 10.4324/9781003408963-10

## Manchester

After moving to Manchester, my husband and I suffered a horrible racist attack. There was a group of ten boys, ranging in age from 14 to 20, who attacked with fists and kicks. I screamed for help in the dark, but no one could be seen on the road. I was so weak at the time and worried for my husband's life that I called out to Allah for help. Suddenly, I saw a few cars approaching. I waved, shouted, and screamed, but nobody stopped. A car abruptly stopped, and the boys fled. My husband was treated at the scene by a woman who identified herself as a nurse. He was covered in blood, and his nose was broken. While he was in physical pain, I was in emotional pain, wondering what I had done to deserve this situation,

My emotional suffering intensified. I became agitated and severely traumatised, avoided going out, and spent all my time at home because I was afraid of the dark. I recognised five out of ten boys the day after I first saw them in town. My blood began to boil, and I experienced rage inside me that I had never felt before. Unfortunately, I swallowed it all and suffered emotional pain for a very long time. However, this experience enabled me to comprehend my future clients' traumatic presentations, such as racist attacks and physical violence.

## Dublin 2000

Fast forward a few months from leaving Manchester, I went to Dublin, Ireland, and my son was born. I went through a difficult pregnancy and childbirth. In the beginning, it was a frightening and lonely experience, but my role as a parent gave me the courage to get up and restart, to heal myself. I started looking for work as a psychologist since I was genuinely passionate about assisting those who were struggling with depression, anxiety, and relationship issues. I was told that I needed to update my qualifications because, despite my desire to work clinically with patients, my foreign qualifications were seen as not good enough to get into these roles or work with clients. My professional identity seemed gone as life became harder and more difficult for me. Everything appeared pointless, even depending on my professional career which had served as my identity, professional identity being a construct that affects how people think and act.

However, I have learned to embrace diversity and appreciate the beauty of different cultures. This has also taught me to be more resilient and adaptable in unfamiliar situations. I had to learn to adapt to new ways of communication and working styles, which challenged my preconceived notions. I embraced these differences and opened myself up to learning from others. As I navigated through unfamiliar customs and norms, I began to appreciate the diversity and richness of the new environments. Through my struggles, I gained a new-found resilience and adaptability that have served me well in both my personal and professional life. My persistent battle and additional training assisted me in reconstructing my professional identity. My earliest experiences contained fears about identity change in a new culture with Western values. However, although frightening, this was also thrilling because of being on my own in this journey, going into an area I'd never been to before.

There have been many nightmares along the route to attaining a career in clinical psychology, but one of the most important parts for me has been the support of my supervisors, both professionally and emotionally. Their modelling of compassion, understanding, support, and opportunity has been a ray of light and hope anytime the dream seemed to be fading.

I didn't have a professional network to call on in Dublin, which irritated me and made me feel disconnected from advancements in the profession. My next hurdle was to find a job – any work.

## My Little Laundrette in Dublin: December 2001

On a chilly morning, I was hurrying to open the shutters of the launderette where I had started working. I was anxious, and upon entering the launderette through the glass doors, I met my boss. She asked me 'Do you speak English? Do you understand English?' I was not expecting this question. Unaware that I was experiencing culture shock, I was in a foreign setting with a different culture, and I felt discriminated against because of my proficiency in English. It struck me as having done something wrong, and I felt guilty and not good enough for a culture where my proficiency in speaking and comprehending English was gauged.

My job before working in the launderette was as a psychology lecturer, and now here I was trying to comprehend the reality of standing in a small room full of dry-cleaning equipment and gadgets in addition to enormous industrial irons that I had never used before. This was definitely not a lecture hall! My mood was upbeat when I arrived at work, but as the day wore on, it began to drop into depression. I was questioning how I came to be this way while experiencing self-reflection and conflicted emotions. Although there is nothing wrong with working in a launderette, I never imagined that as a qualified psychologist I would find myself in one:

> *Since the morning, I've encountered several surprises – people, their remarks, new acquaintances, and their behaviour toward various cultures, people of different races, and people of different colours. My feelings have fluctuated, from confusion to irritability to hatred of myself, and thoughts that I am*

*finished and won't be able to escape this quicksand. I feel terrible hurt and rage at why this is happening to me. My lower abdominal ache distracts me from the emotional suffering I'm experiencing, and I notice that my legs are becoming sluggish. This reminds me that I had a caesarean section four months ago and that I still feel weak and in pain, but I need to demonstrate to my boss that I'm capable of working in a launderette, and I can't afford to lose this job.*

I continued working – my first day, followed by a second, a third, and so on, despite my bodily discomfort. And despite being judged on my accent, I learned that developing a deep sense of cultural awareness and understanding requires a continual effort to overcome those deeply entrenched life experiences that produce 'knee-jerk' reactions to events that are culturally new and different.

Success comes after an arduous process of thoroughly questioning lifelong loyalty to the presumed rightness and universality of a cultural worldview. I began to mix with the Irish community and became part of it. I started using phrases mostly heard in the community like 'walking on egg shells', 'a bag of Tayto', 'it's grand', 'I'm knackered', 'fair play to you', 'he's talking a load of Blarney', 'a pint of the black stuff', 'look at the state o' you!!' 'what's the story, horse?' 'what eejits!', and so many more. I started speaking their language, to show them that I had the ability to understand them.

That's how my little launderette became a mini-therapy corner where people came, offloaded their issues, and shared their problematic thoughts with me. I began to reformulate their difficulties, made people reflect on them, and helped them to find techniques that worked to resolve their issues. The whole process was occurring unknowingly, and customers liked to engage in conversations and find solutions together while their laundry was being sorted.

However, I came to understand that I'd been practising playing and disguising optimism in my head. 'I'm good; I can handle it'. The day began with me battling myself, and it finished with me becoming depressed. Due to my negative feelings, I became irritable with my husband, children, and extended family. I began blaming everyone for my difficulties and struggles. I couldn't figure out what the issue was? It appeared very difficult to discern who I'd become. Is this my bruised ego from being rejected by a new community and culture? Is this my attempt to assimilate Eastern ideals and completely different religious beliefs into the Western world? How am I going to get out of this quicksand, and where is it going to lead? As a clinical psychologist, I was worried about my own mental health due to career stress and new struggles in my professional and personal life.

## From Psychologist to a Psychotherapist

I decided that I couldn't continue working in a laundrette forever and I began looking for ways to advance myself professionally. I made the decision to look for appropriate psychotherapy training. During this, I started exploring: what happens when one learns to reflect on one's experiences, explore and challenge one's own distortions, and discard defence mechanisms that no longer serve a purpose? What happens when a person develops a sense of self that they can feel content with and often proud to achieve?

Karter (2002) argued that this creates an element of isolation. His investigations with trainee psychotherapists/psychologists revealed that many experience a change of goals, roles, needs, and wants. Many also experienced significant conflict within their families and in their personal friendships. Karter, Wheeler, and Richards (2007), reported that the trainee can develop a new-found way of interacting at a deep and meaningful level. However, equally, according to Karter (2002), the self-reflection element of training can destabilise one's own self, life, and functioning in the world. The self is an ever-changing expression of our narratives, a being-and-becoming through language and storytelling, as we continually attempt to make sense of our world and of ourselves (Anderson, 1997, p. 216). It is the cognitive component that facilitates self-evaluation, self-talk, self-reflection, and self-awareness, all of which can impact both positively and negatively on one's behaviours (Leary, 2004).

Reflexivity is a process of inquiry into one's subjective experiences and social behaviours. This process can liberate one's functioning, open one's experiences and choices, and create new opportunities and challenges. However, it is also the mental component that enables self-destruction. Negative internal dialogue, and reflection on negatively valued past experiences, or negatively distorted thoughts, beliefs, and attitudes, can obstruct success, damage relationships, and inhibit happiness (Leary, 2004). An inability to control the self and self-regulate one's thoughts can lead to personal sufferings – for example, depression, anxiety, anger, and addictions (Leary, 2004).

However, the constructive reflexivity process can be attained through developing one's self-awareness. Self-awareness is a term coined to contextualise and capture one's experience of understanding their existence, their choices, and their behaviours (Gleitman et al., 2006). As maintained by Nichols and Stich (2003), self-awareness enables one to process conscious and unconscious experiences. Working on this made it easier for me to take charge of my current emotions and behaviours. It aided in my development of adaptability to deal with problems in life and effective communication in the culture I was residing in, and learning. My self-awareness brought about clarity, which enabled me to make better decisions, lower my stress levels, and help me find life's pleasures.

I started working as a psychotherapist and gained experience of working with clients from different cultures in Ireland. I decided to do research on attitudes and beliefs of different cultures, and how this was handled in the therapy room by psychologists and psychotherapists. The idea of this research was developed from discussions with my clinical supervisor on the issues of multicultural clients, and from the realisation of the existing paucity of research in this area. My curiosity and clinical ability to form connections have caused me to think about and evaluate the competence of a therapist's knowledge, values/beliefs, and skills in a therapy room, with clients from other cultures. Arredondo et al. (1996) stated that multicultural therapeutic interventions refer to approaches that integrate multicultural and culture-specific awareness, knowledge, and skills into counselling practice. Cultural diversity is a fact of life in today's world, and psychologists and psychotherapists can no longer afford to ignore the issues involved when providing mental health treatment to culturally diverse people.

### Dynamics of Multiculturalism

Sue and Sue (2008) stated that humanistic psychologists have proposed the concept of ideal mental health as the criteria of normality. Such criteria stress the importance of attaining some positive goal. For example, the consciousness-balance of psychic forces (Freud, 2001; Jung, 1960), self-actualisation/creativity (Maslow, 1968; Rogers, 1961), competence, autonomy, and resistance to stress (Jourard, 1964; White, 1963), and self-disclosure (Jourard, 1964) have all been historically proposed to be important. However, the discriminatory nature of such approaches is grounded in the belief of their universal application (all populations in all situations). This reveals a failure to recognise the value base from which the criteria are derived, and that the particular therapeutic goal is intimately linked with the theoretical frame of the references and values held by the practitioner.

As a novice autoethnographer and a clinical practitioner, I see the potential for my self-reflexive narrative to 'advance from the inside of the author to outward expression while attempting to take readers inside themselves and finally out again' (Holman Jones, 2002, p. 53). Grant (2023) reminds us that autoethnography is a strategy that fuses the social sciences with the humanities and respects empirical data. Gonot-Schoupinsky, Weeks, and Carson (2023) state that positive autoethnography or pragmatic autoethnography (PosAE), encourages autoethnographers to consider their own happy memories and optimistic future expectations. It is envisioned as being versatile and flexible. While writing or working together on their narratives, it enables writers to incorporate evidence-based positive psychology, and when necessary, to reframe their narratives to include positive psychology thinking that might transform their viewpoints in a good way. The goals of PosAE are to prevent an overly negative bias in the narrative while avoiding being too sanguine, and to promote positive valence, whether it is in the present or in the future.

In line with the above, I'm redefining myself by tying my past, present, and future together through sharing my story. Many of the topics I wish to explore regarding cultural aspects of human experience appear to be held at an unconscious level (Speicher, 2000). However, writing about my journey has caused me to become more aware of both the inner and outer worlds and how they are intertwined, as revealed by my experiences of travelling, living, studying, working as a psychologist/psychotherapist in other cultures, and engaging in dialogue with others with similar experiences.

## Private Healthcare

I travelled back and forth from Dublin to England with work in 2014. I started working in private healthcare. On my first day of work, I entered a tall building;

> *It's an open plan office. I can see so many heads busy working and hear noise. It's a shock to me that a Psychology service is based in an open plan setting. So many questions arise about confidentiality, call recordings, ethics, empathy, warm authority, autonomy, informed consent, therapeutic process, and the therapeutic relationship, etc. How do they manage?*

I was intensely interested in 'being someone I was not'… I was too concerned with fitting in and more than willing to shape my aspirations according to the relatively narrow, concrete things I saw in my fellow colleagues. I started following a narcissistic person but did not admit their narcissism at the time… In disbelief, I later asked myself can a psychologist be a narcissist? I was not ready to accept that it's possible that a person working in a caring profession can abuse others. I also realised that I had been a victim of institutional abuse and targeted bullying by this person, and that the institutional culture was a very favourable environment for a narcissist to make others 'dance to their tunes'. All Black and Asian ethnic minority practitioners working in the organisation were a target of abuse.

My internal struggles were around negotiating expectations of multiple cultures while at the same time reacting to others' attributions of those cultures. On the one hand, a light-skinned woman who could 'pass' for being white does not have to deal with everyday racism or prove her professional commitment compared with a more visible person of colour. I was a brown-skinned psychologist. I needed to prove myself as a clinical lead for the service through my commitment, my professionalism, my dedication to the community and, more so, my academic qualifications. I travelled from Dublin to Manchester, Sunday to Wednesday, every week for six months. When I finished the job at 6 p.m., I thought every single moment,

*Thank God another day I survived in a corporate setting, where meetings are held four five times in a day, particularly meetings about meetings, and another meeting about previous meetings.*

It was not really a psychology service, looking more like an organisation dealing with 'profit and loss', interested in saving money by reducing sessions or charging handsome amounts to commercial companies for the therapy sessions provided to their employees. I supported all the clinicians I managed and guided them with empathy, respect, and responsibility, whereas some colleagues managed the team by 'divide and rule', and tried to damage my reputation as a professional. I paid attention to the opportunities for growth because I felt it would be impossible to evolve if I had stayed with an organisation that could not control institutional abuse and bullying.

Fortunately, my reflections of the aftermath and embracing new clinical opportunities in this profession provided a foundation for growth and have helped me to explore how my experience changed my mindset. My religious faith has given me inner strength to overcome the hardships and struggles in my profession. Throughout my life, I have been constantly reminded that my racial and cultural heritage are quite different from many in this society. Some of these reminders in my professional life are quite pleasant and validating. Many however serve to invalidate, diminish, and strike at the core of my racial identity. As a professional from a foreign culture, and a person of colour, I have experienced prejudice, stereotyping, and discrimination. I've been able to develop both my professional and personal identities as a result of surviving racism and monoculturalism.

### The NHS

I started working in the NHS in 2017 as a psychologist in Healthy Minds, an enhanced service pathway with complex clinical presentations. Despite it being a temporary position, I felt honoured that one of the service managers who knew me from my work respected my abilities and offered me this opportunity. I noted that Asian professionals, such as psychologists, therapists, counsellors, and psychological wellbeing practitioners, were not permitted to choose between clients who were white or those who belonged to black ethnic minority, and that if they expressed this desire they would be criticised and attacked. Similarly, clients who were Black, Asian, or from another ethnic group were not given the option of choosing a clinician who was more like them or who spoke their language. Even if the clinician could deliver therapy in the common language that the therapist and client spoke, there was a policy in psychological therapies to use interpreters. In contrast, English clients were permitted to exercise their rights to decline working with Asian or African clinical professionals.

It's a tough world working in the NHS with fellow clinicians who are tired and frustrated with such discrimination. I get this message from time to time through peer supervision and through stories supervisees share with me. It is equally frustrating for me because I value caring and sense its vulnerability in the prevailing organisational culture. Although not widely known in the UK, there is a growing body of literature from the US on the crucial psychological concept of 'cultural mistrust' (for a review, see Whaley, 2001), which may help to explain why minority ethnic groups in the UK are afraid, distrustful, and reluctant to use psychological services. Although the concept has undergone various rephrasing over the past two decades (such as references to ideas of 'cultural paranoia' and 'paranoid ideation'), its connotation has remained constant. It describes the lack of trust or 'distancing' that minority ethnic groups may have towards specific cultures, organisations, and professionals (including their practices – e.g., the use of psychological therapies) in their encounters with them (Boyd-Franklin, 2002; Owusu-Bempah & Howitt, 2000; Sainsbury Centre for Mental Health, 2002; Sashidharan, 2003; Whaley, 2001).

As argued by Dooley and Farndon (2021), a mismatch between staff and users of the service reduces the efficacy of the interventions. The requirements of job posts are for Health and Care Professions Council (HCPC) registered Psychologists. Most of the registered psychologists are clinical psychologists and there is a neglect of other areas of expertise. Migrant psychologists have not been widely considered within HCPC registration and there are no clear guidelines or straightforward ways to get registered. HCPC staff are not psychologically trained to measure competency. This is comprised of huge amounts of paperwork to prove competency and getting further validation on paper from their country of origin. And if the psychologist is a refugee, and for some reason cannot return to their country of origin and is unable to contact their institution for further validation of their academic qualification, the dilemma is they cannot be registered in the profession.

Likewise, there is still a struggle for me to achieve chartered standard membership of the British Psychological Society (BPS), because I used my highest level of qualification towards Graduate membership, therefore

I need to have another piece of paper to prove that my qualification meets the standard. BPS standards may want to know how much I know, but they don't *care* how much I care. It's a bureaucratic system to award membership levels to assess paperwork and not, in reality, to consider the need for diversity in the field. Although lots of 'diversity tunes' have been played out loud, there has been no real dancing to these tunes.

## Diversity

I observed that diversity is a big issue in the psychology profession in the UK. As an Asian woman, I personally noticed that there is a lack of minority representation in the field of psychology in the UK, with a deficit of British Asians with doctorates in clinical psychology. I believe that there should be more cultural diversity in academic settings and more diversity in the people researching clinical/counselling psychology issues. The diversity within the population in the UK will continue to increase and it has been noticed that there is a growing demand for multicultural competence in counsellors, psychotherapists, and psychologists. There is need to address these issues at the levels of research, clinical practice, and national policies.

A wider range of titles has been established for over 25 years, and this was consolidated when the Health Care Professions Council took over regulation in 2009. A protected title is awarded to those who have completed registered courses, while for others it takes a long time for them to prove themselves worthy. I was kept in different NHS services with different titles because there was not any straightforward way to practice under the title of 'clinical psychologist' for a person who qualified outside of England. My battle to accept different titles with similar job descriptions as those of a clinical psychologist was quite hard.

The consequence of my patience and positivity has been posttraumatic growth, which has enabled me to embrace all the titles I received throughout my service with the NHS. Using multiple titles was initially a struggle, but it enhanced my role in the field of psychology, and my skills and experience became a need for the services in specialist areas like psycho-sexual therapy, and the diagnosis and assessment of autism. I am now working with adaptation in therapy for autism which is very satisfying for me.

However, working in a bureaucratic environment teaches people to be compliant, rule-governed, and not to ask questions (Day, 1993). This realisation puts me in conflict with dominant organisational values and makes me realise that unless the organisation is supportive of more collaborative ways of working it will be difficult for me to have an impact. I began to realise that supervision may be a step towards more collaborative working methods in practice or to obtain accreditations and registrations.

## Clinical Experience with Other Cultures

I have worked with people from various cultural backgrounds and have tailored clinical interventions to the client's needs. I have done this by combining my creativity with clinical psychology expertise for diagnosis, evaluation, and formulation, as well as psychotherapy expertise in case conceptualisation. I have always considered factors like colour, ethnicity, gender, age, socioeconomic level, religion, way of life, and sexual orientation. According to Pedersen (2000), this is important for forming a therapeutic partnership. Drawing from my unpublished study from my MSc in Psychotherapy, understanding the client's culture and values gives a clinician a conceptual framework that they can utilise to make interventions. Psychologists need to be conscious of their own assumptions and prejudices, and how these things could affect how they interact with clients who are from different cultural backgrounds.

## Manifesting an Authentic Existence: A Clinical Experience

One of my clients Kim (from Eastern Europe) and I worked together for a year. I asked Kim to concentrate on her emerging self for her career. She was a trained nurse and worried that she might fail. We reviewed the source of her present feelings, and I reminded her that in the process of self-creation she was free to choose her career, whether it be a teacher, artist, or a homemaker. I asked her to examine the implications of her emerging values for her career choice. Kim had begun the constructive process of self-creation. We examined how these choices may bring changes in her various relationships. She has started to actualise her possibility for living an authentic existence and has begun to change her actions to reflect her newly chosen values.

For Kim to live these new values and participate in the life process of building her true existence, she must first determine what is of the utmost importance to her. This decision, however, is not an end in and of itself; it is only a prelude for her living these new cultural values and engaging in the life process of creating her own authentic existence. Kim found it very reassuring to learn that despite her decision to view the world from a different perspective, she had developed thought-reaction patterns over the course of her 40 years of existence (Yalom, 1980), that influenced her feelings and behaviours.

In our clinical interaction I told her that implementing her desired changes would not be without difficulty, and tried to communicate that none of us are truly able to actualise completely the goal we set for ourselves. Eventually even the most determined of us will have to acknowledge our failures and limitations to become what we have envisioned. I introduced Kim to the idea of being compassionate and forgiving of herself when she does not always manifest what she has judged to be a worthy existence. She was encouraged to remain true to her chosen values and was made aware that occasionally circumstances and social stressors will prevent her from finding solutions to her problems, making her new behaviours and actions awkward and possibly failing to reflect the values she intended to express.

As Kim gained experience in acting out her values, she understood better the practical consequences of initial choices she made in envisioning her new self. She has made significant changes in her life, has taken ownership of her existence, and has established the trajectories that will lead to her future. The anxieties, ambivalence, and neurotic symptoms that brought her to psychological treatment have subsided and she has actively engaged in life tasks compatible with her chosen values and directions.

## The Art of Connection and Being Creative

Dialogue is a natural way of communicating. It must be learned, and by writing an autoethnography for the first time, I was able to reflect, listen, be honest with myself, strengthen myself, and engage in a parallel process of caring and healing by talking to myself.

As Pennebaker (1989) noted;

> *When given the opportunity people readily divulge their deepest and darkest secrets. Even though people report they have lived with these thoughts and feelings virtually everyday, most noted that they have actively held back from telling others about these fundamental parts of themselves...*

The extent to which people discuss or confront traumas after they occur is a crucial component of stress management. When trauma is spoken about with others, social relationships are strengthened, coping strategies are shared, and emotional support is given. Conversely, when a trauma is not discussed, it can be detrimental. According to Pennebaker (1989, p. 223), talking about traumatic experiences can be physiologically and psychologically beneficial. On the other hand, keeping important events to oneself is linked to a higher risk of sickness, rumination, and other problems.

On many occasions, I made appropriate self-disclosures to help clients to relate to the experience, which led to the clients opening up and sharing their most personal experiences. Many of my clients spoke openly about their childhood sexual abuse for the first time during our sessions. Regarding my capacity to connect with children through the language they use, for instance, Tony, a child in care who attends the therapy sessions but doesn't speak much, has always wanted to go back to his mother's house. He only cared about football and exercise. I started using fitness equipment with him to get him to open up, and it was successful. He began talking about his feelings and emotions while he played skipping and caught a stress ball.

I also worked with a clinically depressed Asian female, Saadia, who was in her late fifties. She attended therapy and didn't talk, though I was delivering therapy in her native language (Urdu). She was emotionless and numb in the sessions. I explored what she used to do when she was a teenager. She said she used to knit but now has no desire to do that. In the next session, I brought wool and needles and put them on the table in therapy room. She looked at them with bright eyes, grabbed them and start knitting despite denying the desire to do it the previous week.

Saadia started talking while knitting in the session. She spoke about her difficult marital life, her poor connection with men due to her emotionally distant father, and her trust issues with men. All that connection was formed to move out of a formal setting for therapy and reaching out through other methods. By letting go of such restrictive mental patterns, energy is released, enabling new levels of creativity and connection.

## Concluding Thoughts

Most of us are unlikely to change until we are uneasy, rattled, or compelled to go inward. Accepting our current situation and choosing the path of least resistance is much simpler. Rarely does one arrive at a fundamentally different self-conception by merely reading some theoretical writing. Rather, it takes a supportive and trusting environment in which people can properly bring their own preconceptions and feelings to consciousness and process their own experiences.

Gonot-Schoupinsky, Weeks, and Carson (2023) state that it is possible to describe mental health issues from the individual's own phenomenological perspective using autoethnography, moderated by self-reflection and including supporting research findings. PosAE can help us present these positive self-reflections. According to Carless and Douglas (2017), such storied inquiry can help positive psychology research by, for example, translating loss and isolation narratives into more hopeful, connected, forward-looking ones.

I discovered a new technique for writing about my experiences when I realised how PosAE could help. To go back and consider the suffering I experienced because of my battle to be accepted in the profession I now work in, took a lot of determination. Rogers and Freiberg (1994) noted that people are ambivalent to learn because any significant learning involves a certain amount of pain, either connected with learning itself or giving up previous learning. There are both negative and positive aspects of pain in getting through rejection and regaining validation. A good example of the former is a young toddler learning to walk. He stumbles, trips, injures himself, and endures a terrible process. Yet the satisfaction of developing his potential far outweighs the bumps and bruises. With Professor Carson's assistance, I began writing my story. Now that I've finished it and I'm recovering from a heart condition that started while I was writing this chapter, I'm wondering if my psychological trauma turned into a physical trauma. Maybe, now that I'm in recovery, it's the path to a cathartic healing for my soul.

## References

Anderson, H. (1997). *Conversation, language and possibilities: A post-modern approach to therapy*. Basic Books.

Arredondo, P., Toporek, R., Brown, S.P., Jones, J., Locke, D.C., Sanchez, J., & Stadler, H. (1996). Operationalization of the multicultural counselling competencies. *Journal of Multicultural Counselling and Development, 24*(1), 42–78. https://doi.org/10.1002/j.2161-1912.1996.tb00288.xBoyd-Franklin, N. (2002). *Working with Black clients and families in therapy.* visiblity/invisibility. Conference Presentation. University of Leeds.

Carless, D., & Douglas, K. (2017). Narrative research. *The Journal of Positive Psychology, 12*(3), 307–308. https://doi.org/10.1080/17439760.2016.1262611

Day, C. (1993). Reflection: A necessary but not sufficient condition for professional development. *British Educational Research Journal, 19*(1), 83–93. https://doi.org/10.1080/0141192930190107

Dooley, C., & Farndon, H. (2021). We've got vacancies and we're missing out on the right people. *The Psychologist*, 8th February. https://www.bps.org.uk/psychologist/weve-got-vacancies-and-were-missing-out-right-people

Freud, S. (2001 [1901])). *The psychopathology of everyday life* (The Standard Edition of the Complete Psychological Works of Sigmund Freud. Volume VI). Vintage Classics.

Gleitman, H., Reisberg, D., & Gross, J. (2006). *Psychology* (7th ed.). W.W. Norton & Norton.

Gonot-Schoupinsky, F., Weeks, M., & Carson, J. (2023). 'You can end up in a happy place' (Voyce): A role for positive autoethnography. *Mental Health and Social Inclusion, 27*(4), 380–391. https://doi.org/10.1108/MHSI-02-2023-0021

Grant, A.J. (2023). Crafting and recognising good enough autoethnographies: A practical guide and checklist. *Mental Health and Social Inclusion, 27*(3), 196–209. https://doi.org/10.1108/MHSI-01-2023-0009

Holman Jones, S.H. (2002). The way we were, are, and might be: Torch singing as autoethnography. In A.P. Bochner & C. Ellis (Eds.). *Ethnographically speaking: Autoethnography, literature and aesthetic* (pp. 45–56). AltaMira Press.

Jourard, S.M. (1964). *The transparent self.* Van Nostrand.

Jung, C.G. (1960) The structure and dynamics of the psyche. In *Collected works* (p. 8). Princeton University Press.

Karter, J. (2002). *On training to be a therapist: The long and winding road to qualification.* Open University Press.

Leary, M.R. (2004). *The curse of the self: Self-awareness, egotism, and the quality of human life.* Oxford University Press.

Maslow, A.H. (1968). *Towards a psychology of being.* D. Van Nostrand.

Nichols, S., & Stich, S.P. (2003). *Mindreading: An integration account of pretence, self-awareness and understanding other minds.* Oxford University Press.

Owusu-Bempah, K., & Howitt, D. (2000). *Psychology beyond Western perspectives.* BPS Books.

Pedersen, P. (2000). *A handbook for developing multicultural awareness* (3rd ed.). American Counselling Association.

Pennebaker, J. (1989). Confession, inhibition, and disease. *Advances in Experimental Social Psychology, 22,* 211–244. https://doi.org/10.1016/S0065-2601 (08)60309-3

Rogers, C.R. (1961). *On becoming a person.* Houghton Mifflin.

Rogers, C.R., & Freiberg, H.J. (1994). *Freedom to learn* (3rd ed.). Merrill/Macmillan College Publishing Co.

Sainsbury Centre for Mental Health. (2002). *Breaking the cycles of fear: A review of the relationship between mental health services and African and Caribbean communities.* Sainsbury Centre for Mental Health. Breaking-the-Circles-of-Fear-2002. pdf (nhsbmenetwork.org.uk)

Sashidharan, S.P. (2003). From outside to inside: Improving mental health services for Black and minority ethnic communities in England. *Mental Health Review Journal, 8*(3), 22–25. https://doi.org/10.1108/13619322200300025

Speicher, M. (2000). Cultural and personal dimensions in human life. *Clinical Social Work Journal, 28,* 441–445. https://doi.org/10.1023/A:1005128208444

Sue, W.D., & Sue, D. (2008). *Counselling the culturally diverse: Theory and practice* (5th ed.). John Wiley & Sons, Inc.

Whaley, A.L. (2001). Cultural mistrust: An important psychological construct for diagnosis and treatment of African Americans. *Professional Psychology Research and Practice, 32*(6), 555–562. https://psycnet.apa.org/doi/10.1037/0735-7028.32.6.555

Wheeler, S., & Richards, K. (2007). *The impact of clinical supervision on counsellors and therapists, their practice, and their clients: A systematic review of the literature.* BACP. bacp-impact-clinical-supervision-on-counsellors-therapists-practice-and-clients-systematic-review.pdf

White, R.W. (1963). Ego and reality in psychoanalytic theory. *Psychological Issues, 3*(3, Whole No. 11), 1–210. Ego and reality in psychoanalytic theory (apa.org).

Yalom, I.D. (1980). *Existential psychotherapy.* Basic Books.

# 11

# A CONVERSATIONAL AUTOETHNOGRAPHY ON EXPERIENCING LOSS AND GRIEF

*Marcin Kafar and Justyna Ratkowska-Pasikowska*

## Marcin's Prologue: In Quest for a Common Ground of Autoethnographicity; The Dialogical and Experiential Foundations of Our Project

It's 24 April 2023, early morning. After waking up, I open my smartphone and find a Facebook notification that says: 'Alec Grant mentioned you in his post.' Intrigued, I went to Alec's timeline and found a graphic of a figure sitting behind a desk, imitating a philosopher lost in thought. On the one hand, the character is quite funny (s/he wears a fancy hat with long hair sticking out from under it; s/he wears glasses), on the other hand, his/her facial expressions indicate – that's how I understand it – a kind of preoccupation. The background of the graphic is filled with two clocks, a calendar, and crescents (Do they symbolize the dark side of the passing time?). Above the head of the figure, there in the central point of the graphic, is placed a sentence: 'Autoethnography is not a spectator sport.' It's easy to see who is expressing this and what it means when you get accustomed with the first two comments below the post: 'But it is sport?' asks Sarah Amir de la Garza, to which Alec replies:

> I was making an analogy. My intended, implied point is that you need to live autoethnographically; exhibit 'aut[o]ethnographicity' as Marcin Kafar puts it. I'm making a criticism of those who 'dip into' autoethnography without taking the approach at all seriously – who don't, in the case of narrative (as opposed to more explicitly arts-based autoethnography), read or write enough, and grapple with its assumptions philosophically.

DOI: 10.4324/9781003408963-11

I'm also having a dig at those who have done autoethnography in the past, but now sit in the sidelines or the stands and carp about other people's work.

So – 'sport' – you have to get seriously into the game.[1]

As I ponder this brief exchange of words, it becomes clear for me that in his graphic, Alec, as philosopher, has shown what true 'autoethnography' should be: a life permeated by 'autoethnographicity.' Alec treated my own original thought as a source of inspiration, and reminded me of an idea that appears in a piece entitled, *Traveling with Art Bochner and Carolyn Ellis or How I Became Harmonized with the Autoethnographic Life: An Autoformative Story* (Kafar, 2021, pp. 59–60):

'Autoethnographicity' is not the same as 'autoethnography.' We are prone to see autoethnography as exclusively tied up with research practices (in various types of reflexive acts), whereas autoethnographicity refers to common ideas, values, and beliefs of humanistic origin and which the concurrent gift of sensitivity, available only to a few of us, skilfully used to tell us about the inner and outer life of people. Thus … an authentically autoethnographic life must be permeated by autoethnographicity. At the same time, autoethnography that is devoid of autoethnographicity – which happens rather often, regarding the multiple understanding of 'autoethnography' coexisting today – should be understood as one of many 'dehumanized' cognitive tools of social sciences that function on the academic 'market.' Instead, an autoethnography that is imbued with autoethnographicity becomes a peculiar challenge that is able to transform reality by making life better, by participating in the process of negotiating meaning and making sense of experience.

The phrases like 'transform(ing) reality by making life better,' 'participating in the process of negotiating meaning,' and 'making sense of experience' belong to the classical autoethnographic vocabulary generated by its architects (see e.g., Bochner & Ellis, 2016). Those phrases show the potential of life as lived and active, not static. Autoethnographicity requires us to confront *human experiences* in constant motion – experiences that need to be to *listened to*, and *followed*. These are the conditions *sine qua non* for practicing good autoethnography, enabling us to *overcome schematic thinking and acting in favor of living through a meaningful life*.

Alec convincingly expresses the imperative of good autoethnography when saying, 'You have to get seriously into the game. Sure, Alec, you do 'have to,' but what might this mean? There is no universal answer to the above question because the character of the game changes each time we try to get into it. The game is not repeatable, and there are lots of games – all of them important.

Let's leave metaphors for a while and go back to real (autoethnographic) life. On 21 February 2023, my colleague and I received an e-mail from Alec, in which the three of us discussed the details of his arrival to the conference in Poland in June 2023. To my surprise, among the purely formal issues, there was a mention of him editing a publication, together with Professor Jerome Carson. Alec explained:

> I've recently spoken with Jerome with whom I'm currently editing the in-press Routledge volume, *Autoethnographies in Psychology and Mental Health: New Voices.* This will be a collection of autoethnographic chapters from people either in the discipline of psychology, as students or practitioners, or from people engaged in the mental health field as clients/ users or practitioners. We have two vacant chapter slots to fill (each 6,500 words), and we are both in agreement about inviting you or Marcin to think of two people from your universities, or associated with them, who could take up these slots. They would need to be new to autoethnography, with lived-experiential stories to tell.

I replied one day later;

Dear Alec and Jerome,

Thank you so much again for including me in your thinking about the book you two are working on. As you probably know, my home Department is part of the Faculty of Educational Sciences … and this Faculty is split between psychology and education (or more pedagogy as it is called in the Polish academic context). My disciplinary background is even more complicated – I did my PhD in the anthropology of culture and then migrated to education (mostly institutionally than mentally). So now, and for the last ten plus years, I've been situated at the margins of at least two different scopes of thought-orientations and I try to use the potential of my "betwixt and between" status. I could paraphrase here Carolyn [Ellis], who said elsewhere "It really doesn't matter what I'm called or what the *research* is called, it matters what the work does" (cf. Holman-Jones, 2004, p. 51). It is for this reason that my academic home is a transdisciplinary and meta-humanistic perspective, with an emphasis on the dialogic form of thinking and acting. Therefore, e.g., I am so close to autoethnography. I am expressing all of this not because I would like to tell you about my scholarly autobiography for its own sake, but because in the background of that story lies a partial answer to your proposal of finding someone who could take up a slot in your book, *Autoethnography in Psychology and Mental Health: New Voices*. Alec, reading your email immediately came to mind a friend from my faculty. Her name is Justyna Ratkowska-Pasikowska, and she was originally associated with psychology. Despite the fact that she hasn't had too many opportunities to connect to autoethnography, she is filled with "autoethnographicity". ...

As I mentioned, Justyna did not practice autoethnography *per se*, but she practiced "autoethnographicity," through a dialogue with me. The main point of reference for this particular encounter was a common ground of experiencing losing loved ones, as well as experiencing mourning and its role in our lives. Writing as a method of inquiry (Richardson, 2000), was an integral part of this process. Each of us wrote texts separately, but we were on the same page regarding e.g., therapeutic values of writing. For instance, Justyna published a volume of poetry devoted to dealing with dying and the death of her father, while many of my pieces repeat the motif of experiencing the end of life of my father, grandfather and grandmother. I tried to get to deeper meanings of life after death for those who are still alive; for example, when writing my first autoethnography 27 years after my grandfather's death, I realized that it was then that my mourning for his legacy began to become complete. It is a complex experience whose hidden dimensions to which we can get e.g., through our mediated relations with loved ones who have died, but also with those who, like Justyna and me, have experienced something similar.

These topics, as well as many others related to them, came back to me when I started to read Alec's email. I've spoken to Justyna and she agreed to co-operate with me. As a result, we would like to propose to you guys a kind of "conversational autoethnography" (to use your term, Alec (cf. Sørly, Karlsson & Grant, 2018) that will be presenting selected aspects of experiencing loss, with an emphasis on coping with it, thanks to what we call reflexive thinking. In this text we would be interested both in telling lived-experiential story/stories and showing how they might be composed due to their dialogic character of different sorts. On another level we would be able to connect our discourse with wider perspectives relating to already existing ... discourses that shed a light on the meanings of traumatic story/stories lived through by someone who is losing a loved one.

*(February 22, 2023)*.

Soon after, both Alec and Jerome responded enthusiastically to my/our proposal, encouraging Justyna and myself to take up the autoethnographic challenge, the results of which you, the reader, will be able to see below.

### Experiencing Loss and Grief: A Conversation between Justyna Ratkowska-Pasikowska and Marcin Kafar

In this part of our chapter, we will use the formula of 'dialoguing superimposed on dialoguing' (Kafar & Marynowicz-Hetka, 2021). This formula is both an idea and a methodological tool. As an idea, it refers to the vast, rooted in ancient European tradition, discovering knowledge through *meetings of voices*. Within this approach, 'dialogue' has a sense- and meaning-creating potential, emerging from moving in the space of the logic of *dialogue*, as opposed to *monologue*.

Therefore, we are interested in using a way of developing thoughts that aims at collisions, revealing contradictions, searching for hidden recognitions, but also discovering points of agreement, and deeper understanding. This leads to the creation of a specific *dyadic system*, expressed through the text (where two authors meet each other), and off-textual life (where authors become 'real people,' whose emotions, feelings and being are included in their shared socio-cultural reality). At the methodological level, the effect of our work is a dialogic text form, created as part of complex practices of knowledge generation and its multiple transformations. Hence, we want to talk about 'dialoguing superimposed on dialoguing.'

The individual layers of the dialogue contain elements of research conversations conducted by the two of us over several months in 2023. These were recorded, transcribed, and supplemented by our comments, which allowed us to wander in a spiral between individual threads and clues, specifying their interconnections in a hierarchy of importance. This made it easier for us to give titles to certain fragments of the text as presented below. Separately, we exchanged e-mails and attachments to them, where we had a chance to conduct a reflexive focused conversation about the process we are part of.

### From (Autoethnographic) Asymmetry to Symmetry and Back— Finding each other as Being on the Same Page

*Justyna Ratkowska-: Pasikowska (JUSTYNA)* — Marcin, before we move on to the main topics of our conversation, could you please explain in a few words what convinced you to invite me to start a dialogue with you?

*Marcin Kafar: (MARCIN)* — Thank you for this question, Justyna. I assume it is significant, not only within a horizon of what has been happening between us in recent months – you trying to find yourself as an autoethnographic novice, with me as a slightly more advanced autoethnographer. There is also a dimension of what makes

|  | an encounter like ours possible, including all results coming from it. Thus, I can see here the elements of the present, future and past as intertwining. In addition, it must be emphasized that these do not appear in a linear, but in a spiral correlation. |
|---|---|
| *Justyna:* | What does that mean? |
| *Marcin:* | It means that, for example, at any moment of our dialogue we can evoke or come across correlated tropes filled with meaning-creating potential. In parallel, one must consider that, each time, their specific location will open-up different spaces in the field of meanings that can be activated. So, I see a similar set of meanings as a kaleidoscopic configuration that is constantly transforming, and I believe this happens thanks to the ongoing conversation between the two of us. |
| *Justyna:* | What you're talking about is as intriguing in the abstract. Would you mind giving me a more concrete example of the idea you've just generated? |
| *Marcin:* | I will address the question you asked, namely, what convinced me that you are the right person to be in a dialogue with me? I am writing this passage on August 15, 2023, just after the end of our next meeting devoted to reflexive work on the experience of loss and grief. You probably remember how I said that 'Today I became convinced *again* that my initial intuition about you did not disappoint me.' |
| *Justyna:* | Yes, I do, Marcin. |
| *Marcin:* | Well, if I were to elaborate on that thought, I would say that there is a two-dimensionality in play here. We both find each other, first, as Arthur Bochner would put it, in the same 'fabric of experience' (Bochner, 1997), and, for some reason we are able to tune in perfectly to practice autoethnography together. On the other hand, it is a particular kind of autoethnography... |
| *Justyna:* | Conversational autoethnography... |
| *Marcin:* | Yes, but a term 'conversational autoethnography,' at least to some extent, is just a label that shows a lot, but also hides even more, and that 'more' is also to be discovered in the process of *being in a dialogue*. It is undeniable to me, but difficult to explain, that |

when Alec and Jerome approached me with the proposal of suggesting someone to prepare a chapter for a book they were editing, it was you who came back in my head like a boomerang. And I don't think it was only about being "new to autoethnography, with lived-experiential stories to tell."

Justyna: So, what was it about then?

Marcin: In short, about the power of autoethnographicity.

Justyna: If you were to sum up what 'autoethnographicity' entails as succinctly as possible, what would it be?

Marcin: I would certainly point to the ability to follow experience in a special way. It is something that cannot be trained from beginning to end; someone can excel in this practice, but above all, they must harmonize with what they live through. To be autoethnographically sensitized means to let yourself be immersed in a state of *truly* listening to the experience, no matter how demanding it could be, not escaping from it. And you, Justyna, in my opinion, have this rare ability. Later, of course, we take the next steps, but they are always secondary to what initially comes down to autoethnographicity.

Justyna: You referred to our conversation that took place a few days ago.

Marcin: Right, I did.

Justyna: From what I've just heard, I think there's a passage in the transcript of that conversation that perfectly illustrates following an experience.

Marcin: It sounds very interesting.

Justyna: Because it is.

Marcin: Isn't the passage the one that starts with my statement that, 'Despite the fact that we had quite a long break in working on our text, after just a few minutes of conversation, I had the feeling again that there was no break at all?'

Justyna: Yes, and I fully shared this feeling as well. It was astonishing, as I said to you earlier, here I will reach for another quote, 'Our text has been swirling in my head.'

Marcin: But isn't it a coincidence that you didn't really have the text as such in your head, but what allowed you to keep it with you?

| | |
|---|---|
| *Justyna:* | So we're back to the issue of the same 'fabric of experience'? |
| *Marcin:* | Exactly, but please notice that 'this same "fabric of experience"' is now connected with the very process of discovering in the dialogue the underlying links existing between, so to speak, pure experience and reflecting on it. While initially 'the same 'fabric of experience' concerned the common plane of experiencing loss and grief, later, and these are repeatable acts, we entered the sphere where we manage to alternately see the gap and cross it, to put it metaphorically. |
| *Justyna:* | That's right, Marcin. Now I clearly see we're on the same page. (*laughter*) |
| *Marcin:* | Definitely we are, Justyna. (*laughter*) |
| *Justyna:* | But there is one more aspect of the topics we're discussing. |
| *Marcin:* | What is it? |
| *Justyna:* | I would call it a dialectic of relational proximity and distance. You mentioned that in our project we play different roles – I am the 'autoethnographic novice' and you are the 'more advanced autoethnographer.' |
| *Marcin:* | Thanks to this, we meet the 'new voices in the field' editorial condition of the volume editors. I'd like to stress that not only you, for obvious reasons, present a new voice – I do also. You somehow force me to see well recognized things in a new perspective. As I mentioned, I will also use a quote from our last conversation, 'You encourage me to take paths that I would not need to explore as long as I already know them. However, statements you made lead me back to treat them as unobvious experiential-cognitional areas.' |
| *Justyna:* | Alec (Grant) suggested that you'd be my guide. |
| *Marcin:* | That's true. |
| *Justyna:* | But there are moments when I can audibly feel it (e.g., an inner voice tells me to censor myself). (**MARCIN**: And I am your imaginary censor?) Yes! [*laughs*] But there are also moments when I don't feel any asymmetry between us. |
| *Marcin:* | Both are inseparable from each other. |
| *Justyna:* | Correct! Autoethnography, or rather, in the nomenclature proposed by you, autoethnographicity reminds me of *authenticity*... |

| | |
|---|---|
| *Marcin:* | And of *being authentic* (Guignon, 2004)... |
| *Justyna:* | And of being authentic, of course, being true to yourself... |
| *Marcin:* | ...which is, among others, accepting your own experience somehow as something that is just as valid as any other type of experience. |
| *Justyna:* | You expressed it perfectly! |
| *Marcin:* | Thank you, Justyna. It seems to me that your being stuck in the middle of the dialectic of proximity and distance (including verbalizing this state) is a great exemplar of showing yourself to be authentic and therefore, consequently, also *becoming an autoethnographer.* |
| *Justyna:* | And so, in a somewhat roundabout way, we found ourselves on the same page again! (*laughter*) |
| *Marcin:* | It's so difficult for me to deny it. (*laughter*) |

## On the Role of Ritual in the Grieving Process

| | |
|---|---|
| *Marcin:* | Justyna, one of the better-known characteristics of autoethnography, proposed by Carolyn Ellis, is as follows: 'Autoethnography refers to writing about the personal and its relationship to culture. It is an autobiographical genre of writing and research that displays multiple layers of consciousness' (Ellis, 2004, p. 37). |
| *Justyna:* | What encourages you to recall this definition, Marcin? |
| *Marcin:* | I believe the grieving process is not unique in the sense that the intertwining of the personal and the cultural is perfectly manifested in its various expressions. Even just glancing at the transcripts of our conversations confirms the universal principle that an individual cannot detach himself/herself from the external – cultural – world. These tacit connections occur in the form of specific patterns of behavior. What is more, the latter has a direct impact on his/her perception of the experience. As a cultural anthropologist, I am convinced that single cultures, embedded in their respective times and spaces, act as filters, turning what is potentially accidental into what ultimately has little to do with chance. In this way, human life is shaped, which each time takes a hybrid form, being a mixture of individual choices made from the available repertoire of cultural conventions of thinking and acting. |

*Justyna:*      I agree with you, Marcin, but the open question is how your observations fit with our work?

*Marcin:*      What comes to my mind first is your small story about communing within death experiences in childhood through participation in funeral rituals. It was hearing this story that prompted me to share with you some observations about the connections that exist between individual and cultural areas.

*Justyna:*      If my memory doesn't cheat me, I told you this story during our second conversation.

*Marcin:*      That's right. Could you please redo it now?

*Justyna:*      Actually, I can cite it for you:

I've always had contact with death. In my large family, attending funerals was something completely normal and natural. My first experience of this kind was when I was five years old. Later, my father always took me to funerals. Not my mother, not my older sisters, only I represented our house during these celebrations.

*Marcin:*      Your story is exceptional at least by the fact that its content is a bit 'off the road.' Your experience of communing with death by actively participating in rituals such as funerals falls outside of mainstream behavior. Currently, in Western cultures, children are effectively isolated from what is transient, which could tune the child's imagination positively with death as something, as you put it nicely, 'normal and natural.' On the contrary, death is treated as highly absent, and this creates certain problems. Within this horizon, one can reflect on the transformations that individual consciousness undergoes against the background of cultural changes. I believe, in this respect, rituals play a significant role, although it is sometimes not obvious.

*Justyna:*      You're right, Marcin, this 'non-obviousness' also emerged in our conversations, for example in the fragment where I confide in you... (**MARCIN**: that you felt the funeral rituals were 'terrible and terrifying'?) Yes, for the purposes of our 'dialoguing superimposed on dialoguing,' I jotted down the following passage:

To this day I remember the village rituals, which for me are so terrible and terrifying. In retrospect, I seem to trivialize death – for example, I feel like I can't concentrate on sadness at funerals. I don't like going to funerals at all now because I feel like I don't fit in with the sadness, suffering, and grief others feel, even though I'm going through the same thing myself. There's a mystery to it, and I can't quite figure it out.

*Marcin:*     Sometimes it is enough to assume that things are as they are, but in the case of dealing with death rituals and the ambivalence that is inevitable from experiencing it personally, there is something that reveals our specific cultural situatedness (**JUSTYNA**: and probably not only ours, that is, yours and mine); obviously…

*Justyna:*     Do you think about the past colliding with the present?

*Marcin:*     That's it. It is worth recalling the French historian, Philippe Ariès, who created the well-known concept of 'tamed death' *versus* 'feral death' (Ariès, 1974). Ariès argues that over the centuries we have reached a point where death and dying, and consequently also experiencing loss and grief, have become highly troublesome for humans. Currently, this state (I am going a bit beyond Ariès) causes great tensions, with which we try to cope more or less effectively. Perhaps the mystery you mentioned contains some element of these processes involving great mental changes that we face, whether we like it or not.

*Justyna:*     There's definitely something hidden in it. Especially when I compare my experiences to yours. My dilemmas are not isolated.

*Marcin:*     Sure they are not! In my life I can easily find not so much *similar accents* as yours, but *clear traces*, incidentally leading me directly to practicing autoethnography. As you know, I published a series of pieces dedicated to the death of someone dear, including my grandmother and grandfather. The mourning of my grandfather lasted many years, which was not a typical state. The more I think about it, the more convinced I am that I have become one of the many victims of the 'feral death.' My grandfather was dying in hospital isolation, I did not have the opportunity to say goodbye to him. Our relationship didn't have a chance to get closure. The fact that his body was brought home to the province where I lived, and then the funeral was held there, didn't help me much. I suffered immensely and only writing about it more than two decades later allowed me to deal with the loss.

*Justyna:*     And what about your grandmother?

*Marcin:* Initially, I felt the same loss, but it lasted much shorter. Grandma was dying at the family home and each of us, her relatives, had the opportunity to prepare for her passing. It's a huge difference.

*Justyna:* The farewell ritual is very important?

*Marcin:* In some ways, I even consider it crucial.

## On the Importance of Finding Support While Experiencing Loss and Grief—from "Root Metaphors" to Encountering Others

*Justyna:* I would like to start this part of our 'dialoguing superimposed on dialoguing,' with the death of a crocodile (a bit perversely), which refers to the story of Peter Pan, and for me is a metaphor for the passage of time. Once the crocodile stops ticking, life is over. When you find out about cancer in your family, you start having this crocodile with a ticking clock on a leash. He's been ticking since diagnosis, and you don't know how long he'll be ticking. Cancer is a diagnosis that does not always end happily. From the very beginning of the diagnosis in my home (**MARCIN**: Your dad was diagnosed, right?) Yes, and from that moment on I only had one metaphor in my head – a crocodile. I'm not a big fan of Peter Pan, but this metaphor highly influenced my thoughts, or more broadly, the perception of reality.

*Marcin:* The "crocodile" metaphor allowed you, Justyna, to at least pre-order your new world. Due to your father's diagnosis, you began to live in the 'kingdom of the ill' (Sontag, 1991, p. 3).

*Justyna:* Not so much to live as simply to belong to it. By the way: I'm glad that you use the language of Susan Sontag, which I like, because you probably refer to her...

*Marcin:* Correct! Please note that again, involuntarily, we found ourselves in the 'the same "fabric of experience".' We both know that Sontag was also dying of cancer...

*Justyna:* Well, that's right: by writing about illness, she allowed herself and others to understand better, or understand at all, what is difficult to comprehend or simply is unbearable in the existential sense of the term...

*Marcin:* As a writer, Sontag had a rare gift. She managed to capture reality through accurate syntheses. With her writing, she organized what often escapes our control. An illness like cancer knocks us out of our usual types of conceptualization. Recognizing illness = entering chaos. Finding the right metaphor was the beginning of finding the azimuth again, it became the building of the cosmos, drawing a 'new map' (Frank, 1994, p. 1).

*Justyna:*   In my opinion, the writing about what we are experiencing, and what layers of meaning this 'something' has, is equipped with similar overtones. I'm going back in my memory to our initial correspondence about the project we are currently involved in.

*Marcin:*   What struck me there was the idiomaticity I came across in the stream of consciousness flowing from you to me. You shared intimate notes with me, revealing what you thought was important. At the same time, I had the impression that I'm not sure I have the key to the door in front of which I suddenly stood.

*Justyna:*   I often return to that correspondence, because it is very disturbing, and thus provokes further thinking, as in your note, 'I wrote a moment ago,' "I asked Justyna for her texts containing reverberations of the loss of a loved one, her Dad." I got these texts in e-mail attachments, but first I decided to open a document entitled "thoughts in the margins" and… I was let into an intimate world. There I found concise phrases such as "me, death and a crocodile," "Do you believe in the power that commands you to be in a certain place?," "he died for me," "Justyna has cancer on a leash (cf. Kotoro)," "You came for me?–she asked–I've been with you since you were born, just in case" (Wolf Erlbruch, *Gęś, śmierć i tulipan* [*Goose, Death and Tulip*], 2008), "when cancer came to live with us, I was already an adult woman, wife, mother," "without truth until death," "why try to tame death?," "death pornography." These phrases reflect the "reverse" dimension of experience, they indicate the existence of a sphere impassable for an outsider, but– in parallel–they can probably be deciphered when we start talking about them. Then what was previously hidden (for me) will become a *passage* connecting *mine* with *Her*, *His*. These lapidary phrases are an extract of meanings, a fabric soaked in a substance capable of causing an experiential vertigo – now indicating a gap *between us*, the existence of a kind of doubled idiosyncrasy (would I also have my "me, death and crocodile" – I have no doubt about it!). I wonder if – and why – it would be worth crossing it? To get closer to the doubled *Self*? To get closer to *Your-Self*? To search for this and discover what is common and therefore universal in this symmetrical movement 'from-to'? (Where would be the limits of this 'universality'? When writing this text, I thought that our (Justyna's and mine) voices would be metonymic in relation to other voices from Central Europe, Poland – a woman and a middle-aged man, both raised in the provinces, but also, for some time, living in a big city; is this background important here at all?)...'[2]

*Marcin:*      Thank you for that reminder, Justyna. Fortunately, we already know what the 'crocodile' is all about. (*laughter*)

*Justyna:*      Yes, but despite the ongoing conversation between us, I get the impression that more things are still hidden than uncovered...

*Marcin:*      I think they are, but I wouldn't value them, and if I did, I would value them positively. Elsewhere in the correspondence cited above, I uttered the words to which I strongly identify,

The point is to be able to reflect again and again on the fundamental issues that open us up to each other: What is the death of a loved one (for me)? What does it mean to mourn? How to deal with loss? Why would I want to think about it with Justyna? I don't know, but I can find out about it...

*Justyna:*      When I listen to you, Marcin, it starts to dawn on me – the common denominator for the knowledge we generate.

*Marcin:*      What is it?

*Justyna:*      That something is capturing the moment when *the solitude of the experience turns into its shared experience.*

*Marcin:*      And in it we will always come across *otherness*, which takes us back to *solitude*. Like the story about your relationship with your dad where you told me you had a hard time recognizing your dad.

*Justyna:*      My dad died on September 17, 2017, and I was in the process of moving to another city then. The last time I saw him was September 10. When I left my father, he was in a wheelchair. He talked to me. He already had trouble walking, but he was communicative. After a week he was already in the hospice. And when I entered the hospice room, I couldn't recognize him.

| | |
|---|---|
| *Marcin:* | Was there such a big difference after a few days? |
| *Justyna:* | Yes–it was pretty dramatic. I just couldn't believe what had happened. I really couldn't recognize him. |
| *Marcin:* | The person you love changes. However, usually such changes happen slowly enough for you to keep up with them. In your case, however, the turnaround is radical. Changes are accelerating so much that they exceed your perceptual abilities. You leave where your dad is. After a few days you come back and see someone you can't recognize. How did you feel then? |
| *Justyna:* | You know, there were actually a few things that shocked me. First, when I found out that *this* man is my beloved father. At the starting point, I didn't feel any specific emotions, other than a great surprise. Then I began to feel distinctly that I was losing him, that he was beginning to slip away from me. |
| *Marcin:* | Did you say goodbye to him then? |
| *Justyna:* | I don't think I did, even though I was there when he died. I was with his last breath. I saw it, but I don't think it's a goodbye. |

## On the Imperative of 'Living up to Death'

| | |
|---|---|
| *Marcin:* | Justyna, I suggest, if you agree of course, that in the last part of our 'dialoguing superimposed on dialoguing,' we raise the subject of a special triad, which looks like this: *life-death-life*. The hyphen between the words 'life' and 'death' indicates the moment of transition. Before death comes, there is a process of dying. And after the word 'death' there is another hyphen that brings us back to 'life.' This is how the circle is closed, not the linear process completed… |
| *Justyna:* | What you just said reminds me of the book *Żyć aż do śmierci* (*Living Up to Death*) by Paul Ricoeur (2008). |
| *Marcin:* | Right! This is a very important book for me. |
| *Justyna:* | It is for me, too! Our thoughts became concurrent again as you can see, Marcin. You probably remember very well that in the *Introduction* to this publication, Oliver Abel reminds us that in his *Memory, History, Forgetting*, Ricoeur quotes one of Hanna Arendt's statements, namely, 'People are not born to die, but to start' (Ricoeur, 2006, p. 646; after Abel, 2008, p. 13). Abel goes on to write, 'There is |

therefore a profound connection between joy and mourning, lamentation, and praise. Just as mourning oscillates from denial to consent, joy oscillates between struggle or appetite for life and the grace of carelessness.'

*Marcin:*      For Ricoeur, as important as himself ('living up to death') are others, loved ones who stay and who are also burdened with the task of 'living up to death.' In Ricoeur's philosophy this is strongly symmetrical, and this attitude results from the fact that Ricoeur, apart from being a philosopher, was also a Protestant Christian.

*Justyna:*     So like me, because I am also a Protestant.

*Marcin:*      I didn't know that.

*Justyna:*     Yes, I have a lot in common with Ricoeur. (*smile*) That's why the thought, or –better to say – the attitude he declares and implements is close to my heart.

*Marcin:*      What specific 'attitude' are you thinking of?

*Justyna:*     I mean the attitude of living 'in hope,' which has a deeply Christian connotation. It is leaning towards what follows 'after.'

*Marcin:*      And 'after' means 'life-death-.'

*Justyna:*     This is exactly where we-human beings come to: the horizon of life 'here' fills up and is crossed. Ultimately, the most crucial things happen when we cross the threshold.

*Marcin:*      So the imperative of 'living up to death' is fulfilled with *the hope for…*

*Justyna:*     Ricoeur has been saying from the very beginning that we should ask ourselves the same questions. Where are all the dead people? Where are they going? I think what I find phenomenal about him is the juxtaposition of joy and death. It is an unusual combination of these two thoughts, which is rarely seen. And you're right, Marcin, it probably has something in common with Ricoeur's deep faith.

*Marcin:*      Theoretically, if you have a deep belief that your life does not end after death, the latter should become something completely unproblematic. On the other hand, a careful reading of Ricoeur's testimonies (he himself calls them *Fragments*) did not save him from doubting…

*Justyna:*     Well, yes, it is very significant, and it is also so human.

*Marcin:*      The hope that Ricoeur lived by was alternately lost and regained. He wasn't afraid to show it, and that's what the greatness of a man is all about. Moreover, his last notes, later arranged in the book *Living Up to Death*, he left to others; those who remained were to decide whether it was worth publishing, when and in what form. In my opinion, this is also what being authentic means – being true to yourself and trusting others, those to whom I leave my testament. So, there is such an inclination towards life as well. Mourning is a very difficult moment to define. Mourning for someone close to us is obvious, but at the same time we are also willing to mourn for ourselves. And then we become someone other than we were before. Maybe that's why we won't be able or even should not go back to the life we had when we had then with us 'here and now' – our parents, grandparents, etc. I realize that what I'm saying may be controversial, but...

*Justyna:*   It touches me a lot what you say, Marcin. My memory wanders to the children's book, *Death, Goose and Tulip.* This is a great story. There's a thread in there that we're talking about. Goose asks death, 'Did you come for me?' and death replies, 'I have been with you since your birth, just in case.'

### Epilogue: A Few Words about the Power of Conversational Autoethnography

As we began to delve into our shared experiences of loss and grief, we quickly realized the depth of emotions and insights that could be revealed through the process of autoethnography. Through our dialogic exchanges, we uncovered moments of intense vulnerability and reflection that we might not have explored otherwise. We also discovered how writing could be a cathartic practice, providing an outlet for our grief and a means of creating meaning out of the painful experiences we had endured.

In our conversational autoethnography, we sought to convey not only the details of our individual experiences but also the shared themes and insights that arose along the way. Topics such as the role of ritual in the grieving process, the importance of finding support from others, the need of searching of a new vocabulary in expressing what one feels that should be expressed, etc., were all present in our stories. We used our conversing-writing tools to explore these topics in depth, drawing on our own experiences and on the perspectives of scholars and thinkers who had influenced our thinking.

As we worked on our project, we felt a growing sense of engagement and purpose. We were not simply conversing-writing to fulfil an academic obligation; we were engaging in a process of personal exploration and healing. Our autoethnography allowed us to confront our grief head-on, to give voice to the emotions and thoughts that had previously felt overwhelming and incohate. And we hoped that our work might also be helpful to others who were struggling with similar experiences, providing a source of comfort and insight that they might not find elsewhere.

Looking back on our project now, we are struck by the power and potential of conversational autoethnography as method of inquiry. By foregrounding personal experience and reflexive dialogue, this kind of autoethnography allows us to engage with our subject matter in a deep and meaningful way. It opens new avenues of insight and understanding, helping us to explore the complexities of human experience in all its richness and nuances. As Alec Grant said in his graphic, 'Autoethnography is not a spectator sport.' And indeed, it is not. It is a process of an interpersonal involvement, reflection, and transformation – a means of deepening our understanding of ourselves and the world around us.

## Notes

1 https://www.facebook.com/alec.grant.39 (April 24, 2023).
2 This note is dated March 14, 2023.

## References

Abel, O. (2008). Wstęp [Introducion]. In *Żyć aż do śmierci oraz fragmenty [Living up to death]* (pp. 5–25). (A. Turczyn, Trans.). Universitas.

Ariès, P. (1974). *Western attitudes toward death: From the middle ages to the present* (P. M. Ranum, Trans.). Johns Hopkins University Press.Bochner, A. P. (1997). It's about time: Narrative and the divided self. *Qualitative Inquiry, 3*, 418–438.

Bochner, A. P., & Ellis, C. (2016). *Evocative autoethnography: Writing lives and telling stories.* Routledge.

Ellis, C. (2004). *The ethnographic I: A methodological novel about autoethnography.* AltaMira Press.

Erlbruch, W. (2008). *Gęś, śmierć i tulipan [Death, Goose and Tulip].* (Ł. Żebrowski, Trans.). Wydawnictwo Hokus Pokus.

Frank, A. W. (1994). *The wounded storyteller: Body, illness, and ethics.* The University of Chicago Press.

Guignon, C. (2004). *Being authentic.* Routledge.

Holman-Jones, S. (2004). Building connections in qualitative research. Carolyn Ellis and Art Bochner in conversation with Stacy Holman-Jones [113 paragraphs]. *Forum Qualitative Sozialforschung / Forum: Qualitative Social Research, 3*(5), Art. 28.

Kafar, M. (2021). Traveling with Carolyn Ellis and Art Bochner, or how I became harmonized with the autoethnographic life. In T. E. Adams, R. M. Boylorn & L. M. Tillmann (Eds.), *Advances in autoethnography and narrative inquiry: Advances on the legacy of Carolyn Ellis and Arthur Bochner* (pp. 48–63). Routledge.

Kafar, M., & Marynowicz-Hetka, E. (2021). O "przepływach intelektualnych": spotkania dialogueowe [On "Intellectual Flows": Dialogue Encounters]. *Nauki o Wychowaniu. Studia Interdyscyplinarne [Educational Sciences. Interdisciplinary Studies]*, *2*(13), 251–274. https://doi.org/10.18778/2450-4491.13.15

Richardson, L. (2000). Writing: A method of inquiry. In N. Denzin & Y. Lincoln (Eds.), *Handbook of qualitative research* (pp. 516–629). Sage.

Ricoeur, P. (2006). *Pamięć, historia, zapomnienie [Memory, History, Forgetting]* (J. Margański, Trans.). Universitas.

Ricoeur, P. (2008). Żyć aż do śmierci oraz fragmenty [Living Up to *death and fragments]* (A. Turczyn, Trans.). Universitas.

Sontag, S. (1991). *Illness as metaphors and AIDS and Its metaphors*. Penguin Books.

Sørly, R., Karlsson, B., & Grant A. (2018). My mother's skull is burning: A story of stories. *Qualitative Inquiry*, *9–10*(25), 1–11. https://doi.org/10.1177/1077800418787547

# 12

# PANDEMIC DETECTIVES

## 'A Phone Corpse on the University Campus'[1]

*Dariusz Kubinowski and Oskar Szwabowski*

### Introduction

The interior of a police car. Two detectives-partners inside. Behind the wheel, Dar is in a visor and latex gloves. Next to him sits Os without a visor, mask, or gloves. Outside, the city during the epidemic. Almost empty streets. Deserted. The detectives drive past the queues in front of shops and a chemist. Os – sad, with a philosophical frown on his face – observes the places and frightened people that they pass.

Dar     (concentrated on driving the car, notices the frown and asks): What are you fantasizing about in your fucked up scientific mind?

Os:     Don't start again, you won't win with me anyway. Look, the epidemic was supposed to be over, and now the second wave has turned out to be worse than the first one. People will never learn. They are only waiting to go back to old habits. To that normality of theirs. They accept everything the government tells them – there is an epidemic, there isn't an epidemic. And there is still no proper apocalypse here, just creeping boredom and a constant appearance of what we call normality. Look, they are standing in those lines as if queuing to a temple. The whole point of this normality – consume, work and die. I think I'll go crazy with such normality, like the professor.

Dar:     Come on, you always have to put me in a bad mood first thing in the morning, and it's my wife's birthday today.

DOI: 10.4324/9781003408963-12

*Os:*     Great. That's the reason to celebrate, right? Give her my regards!
*Dar:*    Get lost!

## The Opening Credits of the Series with Suggestive Music

Music in the background. Two policemen escort a teenager; they push her. Empty shelves in shops. Queues in front of shops. Faces on the monitor screen. Empty streets. A car of the Military Police. End of entertainment programme, news. Empty parks. A person at a bus stop in the evening. Shadows on the walls. Blocks of flats – lights in windows. The face of a person in front of the monitor. A burnt phone (Figure 12.1).

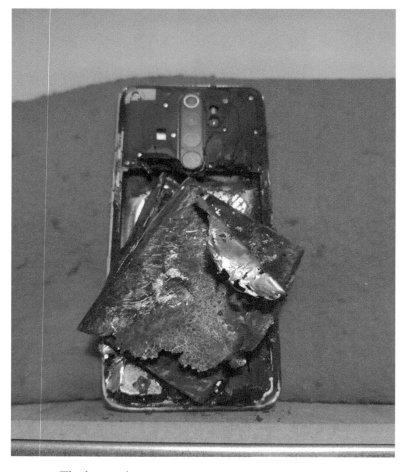

**FIGURE 12.1**   The burnt phone.

## Scene 1

The interior of a room with university emblems in the background; a table, at the table three people (the chairwoman, the first man, and the second man) in masks and gloves (the disciplinary committee); a video camera on a tripod; Dar opposite, wearing a visor, gloves and a tie, upright, disciplined, looks at the committee.

A committee member asks a question: Half a year ago you were part of the investigative team conducting the enquiry code-named 'Phone'. How did it start?

| | |
|---|---|
| *Dar:* | To this day, I cannot understand all this; how could you deal with a man like that. How inhuman the institution must be to destroy all the values our civilisation is based on, our humanism, just for bureaucratic reasons and using the pandemic. After all, the humanism is the basis, the foundation, right? |
| *Committee member:* | I can understand your emotions, but please come back to the point; we want to clarify everything. |
| *Dar:* | Now you want to clarify everything, and where were you when all that pathology at your university started? |
| *Committee member:* | Please keep to the facts. |

## Scene 2

The same room with the same committee, but opposite sits Os, without a mask or visor, keeping his distance, leaning against his table, his legs apart; he looks scruffy and anxious.

A committee member asks a question: Who informed you about the found phone?

| | |
|---|---|
| *Os:* | Do you mind if I smoke? |
| *Committee member:* | You cannot smoke here. |
| *Os:* | Forget your health fetishism. You will lose your breath one day anyway. Besides... (Os pauses, looks around the room, smacks his lips), besides, without nicotine I won't tell you the story. I'm already beginning to shake. And I'm a guest here, I suppose. What about your academic manners? |
| *Committee member:* | Regulations... |
| *Os:* | Come on, it's you who want to close the case. To find the culprit and show that the institution is clean. Spotless. |

The chairwoman passes a cup from the side: We are willing to hear your side of the story.

Os lights up a cigarette, takes a puff, and says: It's pure psychedelia, a completely normal case; it's only a pity about the man, isn't it? (he looks at the committee and smiles)


## Scene 3

Ruins of a building on university campus. A few figures in overalls. Police cars. Blue roof lights illuminate the area.

| | |
|---|---|
| *Os, (V.O.)* *(Voice Over):* | It was a wonderful time of quietness. It seemed to me that the world would finally stop. Streets without cars, cities without people. A better world. Something we can achieve only thanks to an apocalypse because we have already lost hope for any change. Man has programmed himself into what is already there, so you can only wait till his own habits finish him off. Unfortunately, even at that time bad things happened. |
| *Dar (V.O.):* | God finally got angry and sent that damned coronavirus to make people come to their senses and stop destroying the planet and each other, so that nature would take a break from the shit of human civilization. There was no other way out; millions of people have to die so that the rest can finally start changing the world for the better. All arguments failed, so God sent the apocalypse... Not everyone is getting it yet, but soon it will be too late... |


## Scene 4

Dar and Os stand next to a kid's corpse. His head is smashed. Nearby lies an almost completely burnt phone.

| | |
|---|---|
| *Os:* | Are you thinking the same as me? |
| *Dar:* | That you already know the culprit? |
| *Os:* | I have a theory. |
| *Dar:* | You always have a theory that explains everything. |
| *Os:* | I don't have that yet. |

## Scene 5

Dar in the disciplinary committee's room.

| | |
|---|---|
| *Dar:* | Everybody would think that the robbery had failed. Times of crisis. So, violence returned to the streets. Though emptier, but all the more dangerous. |
| *Chairwoman:* | Was the phone destroyed? |
| *Dar:* | Smartphone.Yes. Burnt. This is what didn't make sense. |

## Scene 6

Dar and Os stand at the edge of ruins behind the university building.

| | |
|---|---|
| *Os:* | It's quite a wasteland. The nearest blocks are over there. I suppose nobody would have seen anything. |
| *Dar:* | What was he doing here? And why is the phone burnt? |
| *Os:* | An upmarket smartphone. Judging by the kid's clothes, it can't have been his. |
| *Dar:* | You know, these days such gadgets are important to kids… |
| *Os:* | But in the clothes of his older brothers, he wouldn't have avoided mockery anyway. |
| *Dar:* | Maybe he was with someone. He destroyed the other kid's phone and got his head smashed in return. |
| *Os:* | Maybe. The other can't have been a kid. Look at that piece of stone. You would have needed quite a lot of strength. And the blow came from above. |
| *Dar:* | Let's wait to hear what the technicians say. There might be something on the phone. Maybe the phone will give us something. Some finger prints, data… |

Os lights up a cigarette: Whatever it was, he wouldn't have left the phone. Even the destroyed one.

| | |
|---|---|
| *Dar:* | Unless he got scared away. |
| *Os:* | Ok, let's wait. Though I tell you there won't be anything on the phone. We also need to identify the kid. Maybe someone reported him missing. He's been lying here for at least 24 hours. If it hadn't been for the old man with a dog, he would be lying longer. It's strange that the area hadn't been secured. It's a dangerous place. You may easily get killed here. |

## Scene 7

Os in the room of the university disciplinary committee: The phone turned out to be clean, as I had thought. A new thing. Unused. The technicians found fingerprints. Some matched those of the dead kid. Others belonged to two other people. One – a person with a criminal past, a paedophile after a stretch in jail. The other is unidentified. That immediately set us on the track before we came to you. But first, we had to visit the boy's family. Routine. Though it was the first time I told a mother that her kid was dead. Have you ever done that?

## Scene 8

**Dar before the committee:** It was a good lead. Good but gloomy. There were no signs of sexual abuse, but you know, things could have gone wrong early on.

## Scene 9

The interior of an old tenement house. Dar and Os go up the stairs. They walk over to the door. They knock. A middle-aged woman opens.

| | |
|---|---|
| *Dar:* | Have you got a son, nine or ten years old? |
| *Woman* *(her voice trembling):* | Yes, what's the matter? |
| *Dar:* | Is he at home now? |
| *Woman:* | No, he isn't. |
| *Dar:* | And where is he? |
| *Woman:* | He went out. I don't know. Maybe with friends. |
| *Os:* | But there is the epidemic, and you are in quarantine. |
| *Woman:* | Maybe to a shop? |
| *Os:* | When? |
| *Woman* *(starts crying):* | I don't know. He was hungry. We all were. His brother took him somewhere. They were supposed to find something. I don't know. I was exhausted. Since the epidemic started, I haven't got my salary, I haven't got a job. You know, I had a temporary contract, so I got the sack. I receive a welfare benefit for the boys. The rent itself went up so much that there is hardly anything left after I pay the bills. My husband worked illegally abroad. |

| | |
|---|---|
| | And now what? The borders are closed. And he's in hospital with suspected coronavirus. It would be easier for him to find a job. And he would earn more. What can I do? And the children... |
| *Os:* | So what, did you get rid of the kid? |
| *Woman:* | What do you mean 'get rid?' He's with his brother who's sixteen. He can sometimes bring home something. Was I supposed to make them sit and starve to death...? |
| *Os:* | Better if they die in the street, right? |
| *Dar:* | Where is the older son? |
| *Woman:* | I don't know... |

## Scene 10

Dar and Os in the car.

| | |
|---|---|
| *Os:* | I tell you, normality will come back when we lock up those swindlers from the government. Welfare. Very funny. We haven't had such a neoliberal acceleration for a long time. They allegedly support families, but in a mafia style. Their own. Look what that woman got from her life. Now she won't have much of it left. They will end up starving. Coronavirus victims... (a phone call interrupts Os' monologue. Dar answers it, listens, switches off the phone). |
| *Dar:* | OK, we have the details of that paedophile. |
| *Os:* | I feel like throwing up. |
| *Dar:* | Shall I stop? |
| *Os:* | What, is the world coming to an end? |

## Scene 11

A house in the suburbs. Rubbish on the lawn. Some windows broken. The notice on the fence: 'Get the fuck out of here!!!!!'

| | |
|---|---|
| *Os:* | I can see that they know you here. |
| *Paedophile:* | I'm in quarantine. Hence the notice. You'd better keep your distance. |
| *Os:* | And I thought it's because you hurt children. |
| *Paedophile:* | I've got the virus. I'm something that needs to be removed. This is the greatest crime now – to be ill. |

| | |
|---|---|
| *Dar* | (shows a smartphone in a plastic bag): Have you lost a phone by any chance? |
| *Paedophile:* | Not me... I found it in the street. I thought it worked, but it had already been broken. I threw it into the rubbish bin. |
| *Os:* | Where? |
| *Paedophile:* | Near that university. |
| *Dar:* | What were you doing there? |
| *Paedophile:* | I worked nearby. Where the sheet metal shop is. I was on my way to collect my last wages. That was before they diagnosed me. |
| *Os:* | Do they employ people like you? |
| *Paedophile (shrugs his shoulders):* | Illegally, below the minimum wage... I have hands and a bit of strength, that is what counts. Nobody looks into your papers. It's not a government job. And what is it about that phone? |
| *Os:* | It's about a child... |
| *Paedophile:* | It was destroyed; seriously, I don't know what's on it. |
| *Os:* | Bad things. Dead body. |
| *Paedophile:* | I, I... I only took it; I thought someone had lost it, I wanted to return it. |
| *Dar:* | Good citizen. |
| *Paedophile:* | I've served my term. I undergo therapy. I'm trying to live my life. |

## Scene 12

Dar before the committee: There were no traces of him on the body. There was no evidence that he was there. We couldn't do anything to him. Anyway, at the time of the murder he was in hospital. He couldn't have had a better alibi. But there was another lead. On the day when the kid lost his life, a young woman notified the police that her father, an aged professor at the same university, was missing. She phoned from abroad saying that he hadn't answered the phone for two days, and she couldn't come due to the pandemic. We had his address, so we went there immediately.

## Scene 13

In the car Dar and Os, they drive along empty streets and pass an elderly man with a shopping bag, leaning on a walking stick, going slowly; he barely breathes, they stop by him.

Dar opens the car window and asks: Are you OK? Do you need help?

*Man:*   I'm fine, thanks. I have to rest a bit, I have problems breathing because of the mask. But I still have to buy strawberries for my sick wife.

Dar closes the car window and starts the car.

*Os:*   Fuck, what a sacrifice, look. The guy loves his wife so much that he's ready to risk his life to please her, and he can barely stand up on his own. I also like strawberries, and now it's the season. (He turns to Dar) And how are your parents in this fucking isolation?

*Dar:*   I wanted to go to their place, it's over 400 kilometres. But my father told me he wouldn't let me in because they are both in the risk group. They are nearly eighty. I tell them the pandemic may last even 10 years, and we may not see each other again. And my dad replies – we don't let anyone in.

*Os:*   Your old man has to choose – either love or death. That's a fucking great choice. I would choose love. I'm not afraid of death. But luckily, I don't have children.

## Scene 14

Dar rings the doorbell of the old professor's flat. Nobody answers. Os presses down on the door handle and the door opens. They enter the hall. He's not at home. After a while they notice the professor's wife lying in bed; next to it, on a stool – medicine and food. The woman is silent and looks at them strangely. A mess around, a neglected apartment.

Suddenly the professor's wife asks: Are you from the university? We are waiting for a parcel.

*Dar:*              From the police.
*Professor's wife:* I rarely come here; my husband and I come on Sunday.
*Dar (V.O.):*       I was trying to make contact, a conversation, but it didn't work. There was something wrong with her. In the meantime, Os was checking the rooms.

Os walks around a small two-room apartment, enters the other room, and sees an old-style professor's office – library, desk, typewriter, TV set and VCR, videotapes, binders, souvenirs, diplomas on the walls, a photo of the professor from some conference.

He takes it off the wall, walks over to the woman and asks: Is this your husband?

She starts humming a sad, strange tune ... and cries.

| | |
|---|---|
| *Dar to Os:* | Okay, let's go; we won't find out anything here; you see there's no contact with her. |
| *Os:* | We need to report this to social services or the woman will die in that bed without help... |

## Scene 15

Rector's Office. Os and Dar stand in front of the desk. Administration clerk behind the desk. Pictures of rectors on the wall. A row of professors looking like kings of a small state.

Administration clerk (flings a dossier on the desk): These are all the documents. See, quite a number of them.

| | |
|---|---|
| *Os:* | Of what? |
| *Administration* | Of complaints. He was problematic. And he didn't conduct classes. Disciplinary dismissal. The epidemic is not a holiday. We also work. Everybody works. |
| *Dar:* | Something serious? (Dar points at the dossier) |
| *Administration clerk:* | I don't know. But the dossier is thick, isn't it? Anyway, those old professors are the worst. They don't understand that the times have changed. You have to beaver away or you drop out. Only this counts – work, work, and once again work. (the woman takes a sip of coffee) |
| *clerk:* | You work a lot, don't you? |
| *Administration* | Yes, a lot. All the time. (after a while, when Dar and Os are at the door) Nowadays nobody is immune from regulation. Especially now. Fewer and fewer of us are needed. |
| *Os:* *clerk:* | Nobody is needed, madam. We are all redundant. |

## Scene 16

The detectives Skype with the professor's friends.

Os and Dar in front of the monitor. A blurred face on the screen. Os takes notes. He says something to the screen. Faces are changing. Dar takes notes. He asks about something. A mug of coffee. A smouldering cigarette. Faces of academics, faces of the detectives. Flashing fluorescent light.

| | |
|---|---|
| *Dar (V.O.):* | We started routine interrogations. Besides, we didn't know what to do next. The case got stuck. Os |

|  |  |
|---|---|
|  | multiplied theories which seemed less and less likely. Though some of his conjectures turned out to be true. Otherwise you wouldn't have invited me here. |
| *Os (V.O.):* | Those were long and tiring conversations. Very informative. Especially that the administration kept their mouths shut. And here it was a stream of words as if they only waited till they could speak. |
| *Chairwoman (V.O.):* | We all had a difficult time then. We weren't prepared… |
| *Os (V.O.):* | You weren't, indeed… |
| *Dar (V.O.):* | We had to talk to people. There wasn't much in the dossier. Admonition for going to an international conference without the consent of the authorities. Admonition for finishing classes 10 minutes before the time. Applications for funding. Requests for the justification of the refusal of funding. Requests for a reply to a submitted letter. Nothing special. Assessment. Good, with distinction, but there's always a BUT from the committee: not active enough organizationally, not enough conferences, lack of social impact, lack of grant. The usual thing. |

## Scene 17

The face of Academic 1 on the monitor screen. More faces appear. Only for students, there are initials in black circles instead of faces.

|  |  |
|---|---|
| *Academic 1:* | At the beginning I was glad. The epidemic, classes online, few things to do, a lot of time at home. I thought I would finish texts, I would write something. It turned out things didn't work like that. I hadn't done anything for a month. Only teaching. Teaching and the related problems. I had a feeling I wasn't coping. And the constant frightening with the epidemic. From social media, from television – the media stopped being friendly. They didn't allay the fear any more. |
| *Female* | I have children at home. There's nowhere to send them to. I don't do classes online. I record them and send them to students. I do it at night when the children go to bed. |
| *Academic 1:* | Students even prefer that. Many are in a similar situation. |
| *Academic 2:* | I don't know, he hasn't answered my email for a week or more. I know he had some technical problems. Now that's the norm. The network is overloaded, it slows down, computers can't cope. One can hardly manage. And those superiors of ours decided that everything should happen on that corporate platform because some contracts had been signed. |

It's obvious though that it's a matter of control: who logs in, how much time they take, whether they do the classes. The fact that nothing works properly is of no importance. Students complain that this is bad software, teachers also complain, the admin can't see any problem, everything works fine for them. And my computer is more dead than alive, it grew a few years older during the quarantine. Me too. I have a feeling that it's going to burn soon.

| | |
|---|---|
| *Os:* | **(O.S.) (in the scene location, but at a distance):** Burn? |
| *Academic 2:* | Yes. |
| *Os* | **(O.S.):** Interesting. |
| *Academic 2:* | I mean it will burn out, go. Sometimes it's all hot when I'm working with that programme. And I had a better software, light, fast, without disruptions, even with a poor connection. But our authorities didn't know how to control me there. They didn't even know that software. So why should they check if it fits into their vision of online education? Just between you and me, they didn't have any vision. We kept receiving contradictory information. Things kept changing. I decided on something with students, and soon I had to explain that we couldn't do that, that we should do it differently because of a new regulation, then another. I never corresponded with students so much as I do now. Pity it's not about academic issues; I do it as a corporate worker with two jobs. |
| *Os (O.S.):* | Have they transferred you to another job? |
| *Academic 2:* | No, no. Only we had so much work. Administrative. I haven't seen such organizational chaos in a long time. And here, just think, no materials, no access to libraries. Everything has to be adjusted somehow. And it was still unclear if they would recognize those online hours or not. The ministry itself was not sure. The minister kept saying different things, and then he resigned. |
| *Dar (O.S.):* | I guess nobody liked him? |
| *Academic 2:* | Some did, some didn't. But at such a time. Simply, lack of responsibility. |
| *Academic 3:* | In what regular job can you do nothing? Some teachers didn't send anything to students, they didn't do classes. And they have teaching positions. But they do neither teaching nor research. And me? Lots of classes, and writing academic texts on top of that. It's good |

that there is control. University can no longer be a shelter for the lazy. Because of such people we slip down the rankings. I do a lot, and there are those who do nothing. It's not fair.

*Dar (O.S.):*     The professor was one of them?

*Academic 3:*     Maybe yes, maybe no. I don't know it in this case. I speak generally. Without names.

*Female*     I don't care if they record my lectures and classes or
*Academic 2:*     not. I say the same things in the same way anyway. The fact that some people don't feel like doing anything is another problem. I don't see anything wrong in it. Especially that it is the requirement of the ministry. And if someone doesn't have the equipment, they can go university; there are work stations, there is good Internet connection.

*Student 1:*     Old folks who cannot switch on the computer, not to mention being proficient in using apps during online lectures, shouldn't work at university at all!

*Female*     And it even suited me because there were no classes,
*Student 1:*     and then they gave us credits with very good grades because they are afraid to lose students due to the pandemic.

*Academic 3:*     No, recording is a very bad idea. This is too much of control. Knowing the reality, it's going to be used for political purposes. All these scandals now. On the left, on the right, that someone was laughing at the church, that someone was making fun of sexual minorities. This is bad for science. I stay away from that – I don't joke in class.

*Academic 4:*     I work in the car. Several hours. At home children, wife – two rooms. No chance. Everything goes slowly because of that. I hope we get back to normal work soon.

*Female*     It's not just about technology. It all came so suddenly.
*Academic 2:*     One day I am in class, in the classroom, in the crowd, and the next day, alone in the room, in front of the monitor. And get on. And write reports on how you are doing. And no matter how you are doing, you can't cope. But you can't admit this. And, you know, I have already had a nervous breakdown. This is really exhausting. You talk to yourself, you talk to yourself.

| | |
|---|---|
| *Academic 1:* | You talk to yourself. |
| *Female* | On the screen, only initials. |
| *Academic 1:* | |
| *Academic 1:* | Only initials on the screen. |
| *Female* | Without faces. |
| *Academic 2:* | |
| *Academic 2:* | And silence. |
| *Female* | You talk to yourself. Nobody answers. It wears me out. |
| *Academic 2:* | It saps my energy. It makes my work meaningless. |
| *Female* | And why should I switch on the camera if I can do |
| *Student 2:* | something else in the meantime? |
| *Academic 3:* | You talk to the computer. |
| *Academic 4:* | Normal work. |
| *Academic 2:* | I talk to myself. |
| *Student 2:* | Those online lectures turned out to be a parody. I split my sides laughing with the mic turned off. |
| *Academic 1:* | There are no others. |
| *Female Academic 2:* | There are no faces. |
| *Academic 3:* | There's no dialogue. |
| *Academic 4:* | Normal work |
| *Academic 2:* | Just to survive. |
| *Academic 4:* | Just to survive. |
| *Female* | Just to survive. |
| *Academic 2:* | |
| *Academic 1:* | Because things should be as if nothing has changed – from this to that hour, on this and that day, things from the syllabus, nothing more, nothing less, nothing different, nothing better. The plan must be implemented and assessed – transmission, control. No pirate educational networks,[2] you would have to take over the curriculum[3] for that. No, the technological, transmissive model must be preserved. As one band sang: "There won't be any revolution here". |
| *Female* | The ministry was afraid that we might start criticiz- |
| *Academic 1:* | ing the government. For what they do, and they do really bad things. For me, it's a kind of soft dictator- ship. Recording lectures, controlling the administra- tion, adding deans to the list of class participants – this has nothing to do with the quality of education. Does anyone know what this quality is all about? It is set- tling on things in such a way that we, humanists, social |

|  |  |
|---|---|
|  | researchers, are to keep quiet, cite textbooks, and check if the students have memorized that. And that's it. The next stage of destroying academic freedom. |
| *Os:* | And was he some kind of a political freak? |
| *Academic 3:* | I don't know. Now it's difficult to say what is excessive politicisation and what isn't. If you say that gender is constructed culturally, are you already a rotten Western leftist? I don't know. I'm trying to do my own things. I still have a conscience. The remnants of the intellectual ethos too, I suppose. |
| *Academic 4:* | Lectures and classes are meant to spread knowledge, and not stir up agitation. I really don't like the fact that some people hold rallies in their classes. There shouldn't be such things. So recording is not a bad thing, but it is checking that the academic ethos is not being violated, that students are getting the product we promised them. |
| *Female Student 2:* | I miss everybody. The university. The lecturers. |
| *Academic 3:* | David Grabaer writes about work without sense (Graeber, 2018). I have the impression that there is much more of it now. Patching holes, filling reports. I laugh that I write more about what I do than I actually do. |

*INTERMEZZO*
*Where are our bodies*
*where are our faces*
*glued to the monitor*
*frozen*
*like in the classroom*
*words, words, words*
*the silent depth of the monitor*
*normal work*
*echo of quotes from textbooks*
*without bodies*
*without faces*
*talking didactic machines*

## Scene 18

Os before the committee, puts out the cigarette: Not everybody wanted to talk. You are probably well aware of that. The fucking conspiracy of silence or maybe just fear. I can feel it within these walls. How come that those pseudo-intellectuals are afraid so much? One tells me that it's about very unclear relationships. Because somebody can be good once, but the other time they can't. And it's difficult to figure out who to side with and who to avoid. Conspiracies, as if you were really fighting for something important. And in fact, it's just an illusion that you have something to say, that you mean something. Now you are probably playing something as well. Though I know, I know, you are preserving some values. You don't have to recite them. Though you probably know them like a prayer. Mechanically uttered every night, and a penny to salvation, right?

| | |
|---|---|
| *Committee member:* | You are insulting us. |
| *Os:* | Really? I simply don't think that you are better than others. And I don't hold your species in high esteem. It's simply the same shit as in other corporations. Only the earnings are lower, I heard. |

## Scene 19

Dar and Os sit at the desk.
*Dar:*  What do you think about this?
*Os:*  That it leads us nowhere. I have no idea what the professor had to do with that kid.
*Dar:*  Maybe nothing? Maybe it's a coincidence.
*Os:*  Too many coincidences.

## Scene 20

Dar before the committee: We managed to find the kid's brother. He hid at a distant cousin's place. In the beginning, he didn't want to cooperate. You know, who would talk to the cops? But when Os put the screws on him and told him he was getting pinched for murder, the boy cracked up. It turned out they went to collect scrap metal, and when they were pulling out some rod, a piece of the construction broke off. That's all. Bad luck. He panicked and ran away. Os didn't seem entirely convinced. As always, he claimed there was more to it than that.

## Scene 21

Os before the committee: They found the smartphone in the bin. They thought that something could be taken out. Maybe we didn't have a murder, but we had the missing professor. At least some lead. A strange case – you burn your phone, a new one, pretty spendy, and you disappear. You abandon your sick wife. Something was wrong. I could feel that on my tongue. The sticky sweetish taste of pus oozing from an unhealed wound. The world is full of that. This world was sick long before coronavirus. But we got stuck. Again. And then I remembered the video tape. You may consider it a revelation. The taste led me along the greasy path of the festering wound. And we opened it. This is the only possible way of rescue. You need to clean the wound, sometimes cut something out or cut something off. And not necessarily fascism. Foucault[4] said so. I read him when I couldn't sleep. Do you know him? But he wasn't right. Fascism itself is condensed, boiling pus. Lots of it is now accumulating in the gashed, dying world. There's something sticky inside us which tells the boy to shout that he's someone because he pulled the trigger, because he killed. Agency. The sense of agency in the world where we have the appearances of democracy, appearances of activity, appearances of life – virtual interrogations, families, and classes.

## Scene 22

Dar and Os in the car.

| | |
|---|---|
| *Os (V.O.):* | There's something sticky inside us which tells the boy to shout that he's someone because he pulled the trigger, because he killed. Agency. The sense of agency in the world where we have the appearances of democracy, appearances of activity, appearances of life – virtual interrogations, families and classes. |
| *Dar:* | Bullshit. We have no access to weapons. |
| *Os:* | And just as well. Otherwise we would have the fucking war zone here. |
| *Dar (V.O.):* | It was a long way, and I had to listen to him. It's not easy, believe me. |
| *Os (looking through the window, smoking a cigarette):* | Everything is so fragile. We thought we were immortal, that our civilisation would soon make death disappear from our life. Long life, good life. TV series, shops, a house with a garden, weekends in supermarkets, sweets, and fat chickens. We, the champions, the super Western civilisation, the source of wisdom and wealth. And here comes one little bat, and bang – the illusion is shattered. We are fragile beings, and that fulfilment of ours |

was merely an attempt to escape from the awareness of fragility. We gobbled it up so as not to face
the necessity of death. That's why we said – climate
change – the leftist invention of eco-terrorists. We
are too cowardly, too stupid to understand how
temporary we are, and to start living instead of trying to survive. This is good: wash your hands, and
you'll be safe. Be afraid of door handles. Be afraid,
and maybe you'll survive. You know, we need contempt for survival. Maybe then we can start healing ourselves, others and the planet, which I don't
know why is still putting up with us.

## Scene 23

Dar before the committee.

*Chairwoman:* How did you get to the professor's recordings?
*Dar:* Os remembered that when we were in the professor's
flat for the first time, there was a VCR in his study, and a
video tape with some notice was lying on it, but then we
ignored it.

## Scene 24

Os before the committee, in a haze of cigarette smoke.

*Committee member:* Do you have to smoke all the time? You know we are
*mocking smile):* in the pandemic, and heavy smokers suffer from bad
cases of COVID-19.
*Os (with a* And maybe some of you are already ill?

The first man makes a gesture of being clearly offended.

*Chairwoman:* So, in the end, what's the mystery of the burnt phone
about? What did you discover in the professor's flat?
*Os:* When I realised there might be something on that tape,
we went to the professor's flat immediately. The tape was
lying in the exactly same place. And the notice on it said,
"My last will"! That was a shock. We could think of one
thing only...

## Scene 25

The professor's flat. Dar and Os sit in front of the television screen and watch the last fragments of the professor's recorded lecture on the consequences of climate change. Professor from the recording:

> ...If humanity doesn't come to its senses, we are going to face an ecological disaster, an economic crisis on an unprecedented scale, mass infections with unidentified viruses that will multiply and mutate; part of the planet will be depopulated due to very high temperatures; migrations will cause social chaos and political instability. That won't be another epoch-making change, but the end of civilization, and perhaps an apocalypse that will come sooner than we expect now. Thank you for your attention.

*Dar:* Wise words, but maybe we can manage to rescue something?
*Os:* Bullshit, can't you get it through your head that what's going on already is an apocalypse?

There will be no coming back to what we know as normality... But focus on the investigation, because we're looking for the professor. Fast-forward the tape!
Dar fast-forwards and stops the tape after a while as the professor's image appears.

*Os:* Rewind it, there's something else here.

Dar rewinds and replays the professor's confession.
The emotional speech of the professor from the video recording:

> 'I'm speaking to my wife, daughter, family, and university, saying good-bye, and asking for understanding and forgiveness. I can't live like that anymore; I simply can't cope; it's too much for one old man. It will be better if I'm gone. When the pandemic started, and my daughter couldn't help me because she lives abroad, I started to have problems at work because I didn't have the appropriate equipment for online teaching which the university demanded from me. I couldn't afford a modern laptop because I have a low salary, my wife has a pension, we're in debt, and medicines are very expensive. Anyway, I don't know if I would manage to learn all that because at work I have an old PC without the camera or microphone, which I used for sending emails. There was supposed to be

a training, but it was on some platform. So, you needed to log in, to have access. I didn't know how to do that. The administration sent me back to the training when I told them I didn't know how to do things. Anyway, I don't want to talk about that. The communication … so much humiliation. If I can't do things, it's my problem. I wasn't born with a tablet in my hand. I've never had a laptop. When, after a month, more reminders and disciplinary threats came from university, my daughter told me that I could buy a good smartphone with all modern applications. So, I sold my old mobile, after I had opened its case and taken out the SIM card, and my daughter ordered a new smartphone for me, delivered by the courier service, for half of my university salary. It was my last money this month. When the parcel arrived and I paid the courier, I immediately opened it. Unfortunately, the instruction manual was written in small print, and my eyesight is poor. I took out the phone; it seemed so beautiful to me, shining, and smelling new. I immediately decided to open it – the way I had done it so far – by removing the back cover. I couldn't manage, so I took a thin knife from the kitchen and started to prise open the case in order to put in the card. Suddenly, the phone burst into flames in my hands, my palms got burnt, and I nearly started a fire in my flat. When I saw the charred remains of my brand-new phone, I broke down in tears. I thought that was the end. I have no money, I have no phone, I have no energy, I have no will to live. To make things worse, at that moment, the postman delivered me a registered letter from the university with the termination of the employment contract due to the failure to perform teaching duties during the pandemic. I have no way out, my days have come to an end; I'm redundant waste of civilization, a piece of rubbish polluting the academic environment. I only appeal to all the people of good will who will be the first to watch this video, to notify social services so that they take care of my beloved wife'.

In the recording, you can clearly see tears rolling down the professor's cheeks.

*Dar (with fury):*   Shit, what a crap-fest this university is to destroy an outstanding academic like that, only because nobody could help him with technology. Dark powers rule this inhuman world.

*Os:*   I need a drink... I'm going for a smoke, and you take care of the lady and call the boss to tell him we've solved the mystery of the phone. I'm only wondering where the professor is, or his body.

**At that moment the detectives hear the voice of the professor's wife (O.S.):** Did you remember about strawberries?

They turn abruptly to the door and see the professor standing in the entrance, unshaved, stooped, with a bag in his hands, looking at them in a way indicating that he'd been watching the recording with them.

He speaks to them with tears in his eyes: And I wanted to do such a stupid thing.

He walks over to his wife and takes her in his arms.

| | |
|---|---|
| *Professor's wife:* | And my strawberries? |
| *Professor (smiling through tears):* | I've got them, I've got them, darling, I'll fetch them in a moment. |

The detectives watch the scene and look at each other smiling.

| | |
|---|---|
| *Os to Dar:* | You see, no matter how gloomy it is in the dark, there may always appear a great power of a small light … love. |

FADE IN

## Notes

1  This script, devoted to life in the times of the epidemic, is performative writing. The production is closer to the conception of Denzin (2018a) than to the traditional vision of Saldaña (2011, 2006; Teman & Saldaña, 2019). Although we think like artists – or so it seems to us – we still think like researchers, whatever that means. Hence the references in our text which indicate the sources of ideas and thoughts, or relate to specific, real events. We mix real events with fiction. Fictitious elements are supposed to reflect the mood, and to act as a metaphor, emphasizing what seems important to us. To be clear – no one was killed on the set. Well, apart from the phone, which was indeed a victim of the new regime of academic work in the times of the epidemic. While preparing to write, we looked for inspiration in the area of popular culture. The first pair of detectives we considered was Holmes and Watson. However, we found the Holmes method to be too scientific and not suited to the nature of our inquiry. After some research, we came across the first season of the True Detective series. We chose this series as an inspiration and a way to connect with viewers-readers for several reasons. First, we are not dealing with a manifestation of scientific ideology. Second, the investigation is an excuse for going deeper into our self. The self that is not isolated from others, but connected – with others and with the world. The self which will not find peace and salvation until social problems are resolved. Third, the heroes struggle with darkness there – the darkness within them, and the darkness that has fallen over the world. During the pandemic, neoliberal darkness has intensified (Szwabowski & Wiecław, 2021). The series suited our autoethnographic sensitivity very much, as well as being a metaphorical reference

to the times in which we live. We wanted to transfer this type of sensitivity and mood to our script, using it to intensify our experiences. You can judge for yourselves whether this series pilot deserves the entire season. The first episode of our series focuses on the issue of academic education. The epidemic did not open up new forms of cooperation with students, but it intensified technological aspects of teaching (see Malewski, 2010; Szwabowski, 2019). It also became a pretext for tightening local and state control over teaching. These changes took place when, from the perspective of critical pedagogy and critical qualitative research (Kincheloe, 2003; Kincheloe & McLaren, 2005; Denzin, 2017, 2018a, 2018b, 2020; de Oliveria, 2018; Ulmer, Kuby & Christ, 2020) intervention in public space becomes a pressing necessity – it is a time of an intensified, alarmist "pedagogy of urgency" (Morris, 2012; Giroux, 2016). Our text is an attempt at such an intervention and an appeal for the quest of an online education formula that will respond to the challenges of not only today's epidemic, but also of the apparent demise of democracy and the threat of a global disaster.

The production of the series started on the initiative of Author 1. For three months we kept epidemic journals, recording experiences and collecting materials. For obvious reasons – isolation, online classes, online events – our (auto) ethnography became virtual (Dunn & Myers, 2020). We drifted in different areas for hours, experiencing other-ourselves and other-us (Spry, 2016; Denzin, 2018a).

2  Lewis, 2012.
3  Neary and Amsler, 2012.
4  Foucault, 2003.

## Bibliography and References

Denzin, N. K. (2017). Critical qualitative inquiry. *Qualitative Inquiry, 23*(1), 8–16. https://doi.org/10.1177/1077800416681864

Denzin, N. K. (2018a). *Performance autoethnography: Critical pedagogy and the politics of culture.* Routledge.

Denzin, N. K. (2018b). Constructing new critical inquiry through performance autoethnography. *International Review of Qualitative Research, 11*(1), 51–56. https://doi.org/10.1525/irqr.2018.11.1.51

Denzin, N. K. (2020). Performing critical pedagogy in a politicized public sphere. *Qualitative Inquiry, 26*(2), 283–241. https://doi.org/10.1177/1077800419879082

de Oliveria, W. F. (2018). Freire and the construction of new critical qualitative inquiry. *International Review of Qualitative Research, 11*(1), 22–27. https://doi.org/10.1525/irqr.2018.11.1.22

Dunn, T. R., & Myers, W. B. (2020). Contemporary autoethnography is digital autoethnography: A proposal for maintaining methodological relevance in changing times. *Journal of Autoethnography, 1*(1), 43–59. https://doi.org/10.1525/joae.2020.1.1.43

Foucault, M. (2003). *Society must be defended.* Picador.

Giroux, H. A. (2016). Toward a politics of revolt and disruption. Higher education in dangerous times. *The Radical Imagine-Nation, 1*(1), 19–40. No DOI

Graeber, D. (2018). *Bullshit jobs. A theory.* Simon & Schuster.

Kincheloe, J. L. (2003). *Teachers as researchers. Qualitative inquiry as a path to empowerment.* Routledge.

Kincheloe, J. L., & McLaren, P. (2005). Rethinking critical theory and qualitative research. In N. K. Denzin & Y. S. Lincoln (Eds.), *The SAGE handbook of qualitative research* (Third Edition, pp. 303–342). Sage Publications.

Lewis, T. E. (2012). Exopedagogy: On pirates, shorelines, and the educational commonwealth. *Educational Philosophy and Theory, 44*(8), 845–861. https://doi.org/10.1111/j.1469-5812.2011.00759.x

Malewski, M. (2010). *Od nauczania do uczenia się. O paradygmatycznej zmianie w andragogice (From teaching to learning. On paradigm shift in andragogy)*. DSW.

Morris, D. (2012). Pedagogy in catastrophic times: Giroux and the task of critical public intellectuals. *Policy Futures in Education, 10*(6), 647–664. https://doi.org/10.2304/pfie.2012.10.6.647

Neary, M., & Amsler, S. (2012). Occupy: A new pedagogy of space and time? *Journal for Critical Education Policy Studies, 10*(2), 106–138. http://www.jceps.com/PDFs/10-2-03.pdf

Saldaña, J. (2006). This is not a performance text. *Qualitative Inquiry, 12*(6), 1091–1098. https://doi.org/10.1177/1077800406293239

Saldaña, J. (2011). *Ethnotheatre: Research from page to stage*. Left Coast Press.

Spry, T. (2016). *Autoethnography and the other. Unsettling power through utopian performatives*. Routledge.

Szwabowski, O. (2019). *Nekrofilna produkcja akademicka i pieśni partyzantów [Necrophilic academic production and partisan songs]*. Instytut Pedagogiki Uniwersytetu Wrocławskiego.

Szwabowski, O., & Wiecław, M. (2021). The Covid-shock doctrine: Under the tutorship of CoV-2, the voice(s) from Poland. *Cultural Studies ↔ Critical Methodologies, 21*(2), 187–193. https://doi.org/10.1177/1532708620931144

Teman, E. C., & Saldaña J. (2019). Stop thinking like a social scientist and start thinking like an artist. The research-based aesthetic product. *International Review of Qualitative Research, 12*(4), 453–475. https://doi.org/10.1525/irqr.2019.12.4.453

Ulmer, J. B., Kuby, C. R., & Christ, R. C. (2020). What do pedagogies produce? thinking/teaching qualitative inquiry. *Qualitative Inquiry, 26*(1), 3–12. https://doi.org/10.1177/1077800419869961

# 13

# A PHOENIX RISING

## Journeys through Childhood Trauma

*Kirsty Lilley*

### Introduction

I have lived for many years in a kind of no man's (sic) land – a liminal space, directionless. At once, I was permanently aged by the heaviness of abuse and yet trapped within a childlike universe. Secrets and family shame bear a unique weight on a tiny frame, escape being virtually impossible. I dreamt of escape often and would fantasise about the prospect of rescue, knowing neither of these things were likely to happen. I became inured to remaining invisible, a ghost to those around me. People often ask why I didn't disclose earlier, but I was disclosing constantly, behaviours being my chosen medium of communication. With the help and support of trusted others, I have spent the last few years relaying the foundations of my life, putting flesh on withered bones, and carving out another life. At the time of writing, I am 52 and life begins again, rising like the phoenix, pulling treasure from the wreckage.

My life overall has been difficult and painful. Despite challenges, I thought I would never overcome, I have developed the capacity with the enduring support of others to talk of, and share, my story. Although there have been joyful and meaningful experiences within the difficulty, and achievements of which I am proud, these have mostly been lived through the lens of enduring grief, shame, and very often a sense of exclusion. Fear is an all-consuming companion, rendering the ability to notice joy almost unreachable. Power dynamics have often reduced my ability to speak up and be heard by others. It is all too easy to fall headlong into the stories other people have narrated about my life and give up the chance to craft my own

DOI: 10.4324/9781003408963-13

testimony. Autoethnography and related representational forms have given me the opportunity to write extensively about the continuing impacts of childhood trauma and make sense of what happened to me, and the legacy it left. Whilst the impacts of early life trauma and relational disruption are well documented, what is less well documented are the narratives of those who have lived through these experiences and managed the ongoing effects within a society that has an ever-tightening and narrow perspective on what constitutes normal functioning.

\*\*\*

## Trust

I find it difficult to trust. Given the details of my story, this is unsurprising. The ability to trust arises from the trustworthiness of people and organisations. It is a learned capacity, developed through experience. When the shifting sands of untruths and secrets are all that one has known, it is a difficult task. We inhabit a post-truth society in which lies ooze from the lips of the powerful like grease from a half-roasted pig. The media print salacious attention-grabbing headlines which bear little resonance with the article they are attached to, and social media sites disseminate information unchecked for any grain of veracity. This can be testing for those of us who have a need for certainty and control which arises from disorganised and temperamental early life environments.

Trust is a fragile companion. She weaves in and out of life silently, building on the thoughts, words, and deeds that pass between people until she begins to form a patchwork quilt, keeping us warm and nourished throughout the bleakest of storms. There are parts of the cloth that inevitably become threadbare with the stretching of boundaries, and without warning, she is gone, whipped away by high winds and out of reach. What often takes years to craft vanishes in an instant, leaving a trail of empty promises and lies. My relationship with trust has been fleeting. Glimpses of her ethereal presence have shone through in the most abstract of places and lit up the room with a warm glow. Like a 'will o' the wisp', she has illuminated the way ahead, dancing around the flames and never getting too close. She has a quiet, musical quality, but on days when she leaves abruptly, a misdemeanour or two becoming too hard to bear, she takes with her the last remaining traces of oxygen and the light fades. She cannot co-exist with betrayal; one cancels out the other.

I have sharp memories of all the times that trust has deserted me. They remain clear in my mind as though they happened just yesterday. I can trace outlines of every scene and remember words that were spoken, especially the tone – sharp and condescending. I can often hear the same tone in the people around me now, but sometimes it's not clear whether it is just a ghost revisiting from the past. Past and present energies sometimes entwine with each other and obscure a clear view. It is difficult to distinguish timelines when this happens, like being trapped in a time machine with an agenda of its own. There have been so many occasions when trust has floated in only to be extinguished by a sharp blast of reality, and the current view of life has splintered into a million different shards. I could almost build a patchwork quilt of my own with these memories, but I doubt it would keep me warm at night. They seem to have layered upon each other as life has unfolded, a kaleidoscope of betrayal from people, places, and institutions in which we have little choice but to place the last remaining vestiges of faith.

> *It held the prospect of an enjoyable day but as many of these days did it turned out to be sour and unforgiving. We travelled in the car on a family excursion to the nearby beach. The sun was shining, and a picnic nestled in the boot of the car replete with favourite sandwiches and a bag of crisps each. I remember they were salt and vinegar. These details take on significant meaning when they are linked with such disturbing memories. After an enjoyable time playing in the dunes the time came to return home. On the way, we were to visit a current client of my father's building business to check on the progress of the extension being built. The house stood on palatial grounds, with what seemed like a never-ending driveway. We were given an ice cream by my father's client, and after ripping the wrapper off excitedly, I made the childlike but fatal mistake of dropping it on the pristine gravel much to the ire of my father. He screamed violently at me in front of everyone – belittling, nasty comments, and all hope and trust that he would care for me melted away like ice cream on a hot summer's day. I knew all too well what would follow when we arrived home.*

My relationship with trust has been built on these foundations. It is no surprise that it is easily ruptured, for this was just one of many similar experiences which were deftly shaping my sense of myself and the world around me. Life is difficult without trust; her absence makes life hard and unrelenting. I found it difficult to breathe in social situations which demand a level of trust for someone to move forward and develop. I spent many hours looking over my shoulder, checking that I had not done anything wrong, and this made it difficult to face forwards and take life by the reins. I would hold back, living in the shadows mostly. Opportunities for friendships, support from teachers and mentors slipped by, and the void was filled by manipulators who sense a certain kind of vulnerability. I carried a constant sense that something bad was always waiting around the corner. I became tired of asking for help and receiving the same old jaded replies, especially from those who I imagined might reasonably rely on. The notion that they might help me to rebuild a shattered sense of trust seemed anathema to them.

After many more of these experiences, I had no trust left – the well was dry. The type of trust that lies between oneself and other people had been eroded to an almost invisible line sketched onto the pavement – like one that might remain after a long-gone game of hopscotch, virtually washed away by rainwater. Trust between myself and organisations had long since diminished but the most pernicious and damaging of losses was the loss of trust in myself. I was almost blind and deaf to myself. I could not feel myself moving around in the world at times. I was a ghost in the lives of other people, hardly taking enough oxygen to be noticed. It slowly dawned on me that this is what I needed to discover, rebuild, and reset, if I were to have a chance at life, and so this became my task.

I started very slowly and in the smallest way I could. I have always been observant and so I tuned to those people around me within whom I could find an inkling and growing sense of safety, and watched from the sidelines how they spoke, what actions they took, and whether they were congruent. Whether the cloth that held their promises could hold the weight of my expectations. Slowly, remembering to breathe along the way, I gathered a small community of people around me, and within the spaces between us trust grew and opened like snowdrops pushing their way through the frozen ground. Trust began to melt away the frozen edges and she danced between myself and situations which would offer me a new way forward. She was light-footed and easily distracted at times, but persistence brought with it a certain kind of confidence and my wings began to unfurl.

Betrayal etches deep marks in the soul, and scar tissue leaves small fissures where the pain is still felt. Memories surface even in the happiest of times of the rug being pulled away from under my feet. It is at the pinnacle of joy that I most fear its loss. I need to steady myself on occasions, even now. Even so, there is a newfound balance in life, a confidence that comes from building things up from scratch with little more than a notion of what is needed to overcome the lack of something. Life is contradictory and para-doxical at times, and therein lies the beauty and the adventure. I have lately found myself sharing intimate details of what my life has been with virtual strangers and delighting in the freedom to choose this path for myself. My skin grows stronger and more durable by the day. Developing trust in one-self and others is not a fixed destination but an often-circular process that requires reflection, insight, courage, and most of all hope. Learning to trust brings many gifts including a growing sense of stability in the world, an ability to take opportunities as they present, and a net that will catch you after you leap. I have no prescriptive formula for developing trust, but I do know it is necessary, as necessary as breathing. Learning to trust is a vital investment in the future if we are to craft ourselves free from the bitterness that can emerge from perpetual rejection.

\* \* \*

## Shame

We live in a society saturated by shame. Although we pride ourselves on being tolerant, inclusive, and welcoming, only a chosen few are given the power to speak, make decisions, and create dominant cultural narratives. Public mistakes are often berated with a venomous force that is a poor match for the misdemeanour committed. Accountability and holding those in power responsible is vital, but often the beating that people experience is laced with viciousness and spiteful condemnation. Against this backdrop it is little wonder that the fear of speaking up in public is so widely experienced. In the gladiatorial ring of capricious public opinion, the crowd can be swayed one way or another depending on the zeitgeist of the time. I have a story to tell, but being all too familiar with the condemnation and judgement this can bring from others I am often reticent to speak up in public places, preferring the power of the written word. We live in a paradoxical world, one not easy to navigate. At once encouraged to speak up and be authentic while often being silenced by those unwilling to listen. Some of us are more burdened than others to find creative and often 'acceptable' ways to talk of, and express, the experiences responsible for cultivating a toxic sense of shame that continues to pervade life long after those experiences have gone.

Shame is a trickster, a beguiler of sorts. An all-seeing eye with an ability to detect its prey unrelentingly. Even when I am alone, I have the constant sense of being observed by its contemptuous gaze. As opportunities to connect disintegrate, it encourages me to hide in the shadows, holding the promise of protective anonymity. Exposure and being seen is my greatest fear. Like a sea snake, it wraps its body around my legs, choking off any feeling and rendering me immobile, stuck, and drowning in equal measure. As its vicious mouth makes its way up my back, I can feel its hot breath against my skin which begins to prickle and flush. I long to escape, to disappear, but I am held still by its strong grip whilst others get on with the daily activities of life, busy in their endeavours. I open my mouth to scream but no sound emerges, and no one seems to notice that I have fallen prey to its duplicity. Alone once again, I am now longing to be seen and heard but without the strength to cultivate the opportunities. There is a persistent desire to escape alongside an inability to do so, which has often left me confused and frustrated.

I have been told that shame is a necessary emotion, a protector of sorts to fend off a rejection from the group. An antidote to the risk of engaging in certain behaviours that will lead to social expulsion. This is the dichotomy; that it is simultaneously a protector and destroyer of relationships. A necessary evolutionary function to keep ourselves part of the group, but a cruel and corrosive mate to those who live alongside its presence. For me, it has meant wanting to disappear at any given opportunity of spending life avoiding connection, even with myself. Even when I am invited in by the kindly and supportive gestures of others, I am fixed, rooted to the spot, and all their exhortations to join them are met with a pale and insignificant smile. Behind the smile is a creeping sense of fear that once I am known they will see that I am at fault, unclean in some way, and unwanted. It is much better, wiser in fact, that I remain outside. The risk is too great to bear and another failed attempt at connection will be the undoing of me. Though supportive relationships are what we need to thrive in life, shame leaves us with the inability to form and enjoy them in any meaningful way.

*A particularly painful memory comes to the front of my mind of a time when I was sitting, vulnerable, and exposed in a bath of shallow water. I was a young girl on the brink of blossoming into early puberty and rendered terrified and assaulted by the vicious words of my father describing how dirty I was. I had not cleaned myself in the way he insisted upon and as I sat in the bath naked and helpless, I felt all essence of myself collapse under his scrutiny. It was as if the very bones of me were dissolving, my spine unable to hold the weight of my head which collapsed downwards. I felt this collapse many times in the face of his other equally rageful and brutal assaults. At that moment as my mother sat and watched I became object and not subject.*

There is an existential terror in being viewed so contemptuously by those who are supposed to extend the hand of loving parental care. Out of these experiences, I developed patterns of people-pleasing so insidious that I did not recognise them myself, preferring to see them as the marks of a 'nice person'. I know better now and have restructured my inner self, ensuring that my needs are heard and in many ways centre stage when needed. This is not an easy task as the first experience of ourselves is that which is reflected to us through the eyes of the other. If this is a damaging misrepresentation, those impacts linger long after we see this distortion for what it is.

Shame is a snake-like creature, with an ability to entangle itself around its victim, weaving tendrils of doubt and insecurity as it goes. Childhood abuse removes all sense of self. Bodily and emotional autonomy disappears at the demands of others, kept secret by threats and other methods of coercion. I have always needed to justify my existence in relation to how I was helping or assisting others. This is an enmeshment of sorts, a fusing of boundaries between one person and another with primary responsibility landing firmly in one camp. This arose due to the constant sense that I was merely an extension of others and not an individual in my own right. It took courage to decouple and carve out my sense of self, such is the terror of abandonment and isolation. I spent many moments wondering what it would be like to launch my own rescue mission, grab hold of the fraying rope and pull myself up from drowning waters to face the full glare of the midday sun. A kernel of an idea took root and the grit within my bones began to fortify and harden in readiness for the journey ahead. It was not an easy voyage, but I was not yet ready for a watery grave however safe and comfortable it might have been.

Looking back, I am not sure when I met with shame. It almost feels that it was born alongside me, waiting to catch me as I made my way and emerged into life. I felt unseen at home, unknown by those who professed to care, and exposed to situations that overwhelmed my childlike sensibilities. I unravelled to all intents, and any core I might have developed was replaced by a swirling sense of anxiety and watchfulness. I spent my early life tiptoeing around my father, dreading the sound of anything that would snap under my weight and wake him from his slumber. I learned to tread carefully. The roar was deafening when he did wake, shouting obscenities and accusations often directed my way. Without the necessary capacity to understand that I had done nothing to warrant this vicious onslaught, I spent hours trying to figure out which bit of me was bad. I concluded that it must be all of me. I wondered why no one else noticed or seemed to care, but I now know that others around me were themselves in the fixed grip of shame listening intently to the drip of its vicious lies. Head down at all costs, ignorance, and denial being the best policy.

I tried to escape on many occasions, but wherever I went shame followed me. I saw my father everywhere, in anyone I needed, rendering the possibility of asking for support impossible. His shadow would appear across the most well-meaning of people and I would retreat once more. Shame-induced behaviours often distorted how others saw me. Teachers were influenced by these distortions and my behaviours at school were seen through the prism of 'disengaged', 'a tell-tale', 'stupid little girl'. I was desperately trying to communicate that I was suffering in ways I could not yet understand, but every door remained closed. This pattern followed me throughout much of my life and each time I have spoken up I was viewed with disdain and misunderstanding. In the end, I gave up, and retreated, losing all hope and voice. What is the point of voicing anything when the very words are snatched from your mouth by those more powerful and cast adrift on the wind? Doors shut in front of me like the feeling of dominoes, creating a new path that would lead me into the arms of a life displaced from everything I wanted.

I plunged headfirst into despair and took refuge in the soothing arms of alcohol. Outwardly everything looked fine. I was well dressed, functioning to a point, the very epitome of success. Inside I was crumbling; shame choked off my air supply and squeezed tighter each day and it became a constant struggle to leave the house. I would return at the end of the day eager to screw the top from the wine bottle. It gave me a way to escape myself and the feelings I was experiencing. It also gave me the opportunity and reason to avoid other people and prove their views about my character correct. There is self-destruction inherent in the experience of shame, a desire to escape, even from oneself.

This went on for some time, years I think, until some light began to weave its way through the murky depths of existence. It certainly was not a eureka moment – I am often suspicious of those – but a slow dawning, a nagging feeling that there had to be something other than this. There is often an inbuilt drive and need to survive, even throughout the most difficult of times. After some positive relational experiences in which others expressed what I meant to them, that they believed in my potential, and witnessing first-hand how important I was to them, I began to consider a different path. I had been estranged from family long enough to have a different view of myself reflected to me, and this gave me the much-needed motivation to slowly move forward.

I began to sit with the frozen child inside me and listen intently to all she had to say. She had dreams and wishes for her life amidst a million memories shaded with fear and anxiety. This girl knew kindness, small acts of support bestowed by a loving grandmother which had been forgotten and covered by the weight of loss and grief. This girl had once held hope and felt its tiny feathers nestled in her hand. We met often, this girl and me. It was deeply uncomfortable to be witness to all that I heard, and the realisation that this was my story sat heavily upon my chest. Each time another story was raised to the light and spoken of, the weight began to lift and I took deeper breaths filling my whole lungs with air previously denied. Shame has the potential to disintegrate if held in the loving gaze of another. It is the contemptuous gaze that is the most damaging aspect of shame, a feeling of being held as inferior in the mind of another. Sometimes we laughed, this younger self and I, at the absurdity of it all, and poked fun at the ridiculous responses of others who in their wisdom decided I had some brain disease or other. We knew that we had a sophisticated bag of coping skills, employed to keep us living through all the pain. We did agree that this collection had served its purpose and was in desperate need of updating, a new world view needed.

I formed new relationships with all the parts of me that have been unheard and banished. They were mostly keen to speak, although some needed more encouragement than others and the reassurance of a calm witness. I am glad to say that I now have others who are willing to sit alongside me and listen. Unhurried, without an agenda, therapy has been lifesaving and life-giving. Developing new relationships has required a vulnerability that I have at times resisted, but with patience and nurturance, they have grown. Learning to repair relationships is uncomfortable; learning to set new boundaries a constant challenge. This is just part of life for those who have endured betrayal and hurt at the earliest of times.

This is a long journey and an unfinished tale. There will be many obstacles, crevices into which we, who have endured such experiences, will fall no doubt, and long spells in which we will need to rest and replenish. The grief of opportunities lost will overwhelm at times. There will also be periods of connection, love, and deep friendship. It will require courage, and all the strength which previously helped us to survive.

* * *

## The Black Sheep

*Black sheep are the outliers: forged from exclusion yet tenacious enough to survive.*

I have always felt different. As a young child who longed to be part of the group, this was a difficult experience to counter, especially in a world that purportedly celebrates difference but often demands 'groupthink' and conformity. Being the 'black sheep' is intimately linked to feelings of shame and exclusion, and is a mantle worn by many who find themselves in similarly less than inclusive environments.

My black sheep label arose from an early intuition that events happening in the family system were deeply toxic but in not having the language to express this knowledge. My behaviours became my 'language'. On many occasions and in many circumstances these behaviours were admonished rather than understood in context. This left me with a difficulty in trusting my own judgement and recognising my own needs. Although I have learned to celebrate my differences and diversity, the black sheep costume has often felt heavy indeed.

*I am a small child once more, staring up at the night sky; mesmerized by bright stars embedded in a black silky ocean. I twirl and twirl until dizziness overtakes me, collapsing onto the cool ground below hoping that I awake in another world, another scene. My eyes open slowly and the cold wet grass underneath me seeps into my light cotton nightgown. Leaves from the trees around me sway in the breeze and the rustling sound brings me back to the present, lying in the garden of my family home. I lie very still, hoping that I remain unnoticed; it is safer that way. I am, it seems, a disappointment, an oddity of sorts, in that I refuse to see the world in the same way that others more powerful than me see it. I am reliably informed that there is only one way to be in this world and only one point of view to continually adopt. Life is a game, a chess board in which the rules have been laid out for me. The fact that I do not subscribe to these rules is a constant source of consternation and angst to those that create them. I have always felt different, on the outside of things. I am a black sheep in a child's clothes and human form.*

I have grown into this role over the years, perhaps it has grown around me, moulded by the opinion of others. There are times when it has been exquisitely painful to be thought of in this way when it has arisen from merely having a different opinion, a different way of life than one which was prescribed. After many years I decided to seize my beautiful, black sheepskin and sweep it around myself in all its glory. It has kept me warm through the long nights of familial and social exile. Disapproving and contemptuous stares from those who you long to be embraced by have a fierce iciness that strikes at the heart and leaves one perpetually frozen. Protection from this comes from a warm cloak that marks me as different and propels me towards others who wear similar apparel. We form our friendships – a family of sorts – and understandings pass between us with a warmth that begins to melt the frost. It is a uniquely formed intuitive sense of how life has been for us. There is camaraderie in that.

I never really enjoyed any of the things that were deemed appropriate for me, or followed the paths that were laid down in front of me. When I did take tentative steps along pre-ordained routes there seemed to be so many barriers and obstructions presented that I often fell by the wayside. It would be a while before I picked myself up and started to navigate my way forward, and even now it is sometimes a struggle to wade through the difficulties that life events have left in their wake. Grief, abuse, and shame all leave their wounds, which despite various coverings gape open at times. I reflect on my schooldays and remember a self that struggled to fit into the small groups that naturally formed. I was always flitting between one group and another, never quite nailing my colours to the mast, a chameleon of sorts.

Of course, this behaviour is often the result of growing up in an environment in which it was imperative for survival to be quick to adapt to the moods of others, sensing when trouble was coming long before it arrived. Whilst everyone at school was enjoying the latest in new romantic and electronic music that the eighties heralded, I was enjoying opera and classical music, much to the amusement and derision of my peers. This does not sound on first reading like a radical act, but it is enough to mark someone as different and for the bullies to begin to circle like vultures around vulnerable prey. Once, mistaking the rules of rounders, I managed to score my whole team out which saw me relegated to the bottom of the social pile, bullied, and pilloried for weeks. I was forced to endure the bus trip on the next school outing in a seat by myself. Alone I sat, friendless, hot tears rolling down my face, as others sang and cheered at the back of the bus enjoying lovingly made packed lunches.

These may seem tiny anecdotes and inconsequential, but they are enough to start forming a view of oneself as different, an outsider to the pack, especially against the backdrop of regular familial exclusions. I once sat in the kitchen alone for hours whilst the rest of the family retreated to the living room and entertained themselves by the fire. I had taken an uninvited stand against my father in response to his scathing remarks directed towards my young brother, who had missed his shot at goal in his school football match. I can still see my father's eyes bulging with rage and protruding from his ever-reddening face – a tiny vein twitches on the side of his temple, and a small piece of spittle quivers on the end of his chin. My interjection was unwelcome, and I was told to remain alone in the kitchen to contemplate my disrespectful nature.

Society in general chooses and exalts those who conform, who say just enough of the right things, in the right way, with the right look and tone of voice. Even in the age of seeming diversity, there is little room for those who have a different life and story to tell. Often those who take the mouthpiece and the stage have conformed in subtle and not-so-subtle ways to what is expected. Mostly, a person must be recovered to speak of distress, or a professional to speak of what is helpful, whilst those of us who have experienced, who are still on the long winding road of healing, are left to wait patiently to be heard. The powerful and the entitled still do the choosing and the rest of us must queue up in line. That is, of course, until we learn to value and step into the difference we possess, seeing it as a mark of a life forged out uniquely with all the merits that this brings. We possess intuition and a certain kind of wisdom rare in those who have not known the searing pain of early abandonment.

In the end, I chose to go my own way. I became tired of rejection and not being seen. I have been estranged from family long enough now to see myself differently, to make better choices and grow in healthier ways. If this brings with it the title of 'black sheep' then I willingly accept the mantle and wear it with pride. It may not have led me to the marks of what is considered a conventional and approved life, but it is the life I have and there is much more yet to come. Of course, there is pain and disappointment woven into the experience of being different which can exclude us from many of the accolades that others achieve. I struggled to adapt to the demands of educational establishments largely because I was dealing with the heavy burden of early adversities, the effects of which were still largely unknown to me.

I did not have a language to articulate what I needed and how I saw the world, and I did not have the fortune to meet a mentor or tutor who would see my potential. Although many hail life's successes as the direct result of individual exertion, when we dig into the architecture and foundation of their stories, we often reveal a fabric of relational support holding an individual whilst they achieve. We have created a dominant narrative of individual success when these things are always co-created, arising from supportive relationships. Black sheep learn in their own way, and while we may not hold the certificate of societal approval we have our own knowledge, hard-earned.

\*\*\*

## Motherhood

The last bastion of societal standing is motherhood, revered and unsupported in equal amounts. This is a title that still comes with certain rules in terms of how it is to be fulfilled. A mother's role is not created on her terms but often by the opinions of a thousand bystanders, all too keen to advise, inform, comment, and condemn. My own experience of motherhood marked me out as different in many ways, enforced on me by a court process that takes little into account other than the carefully chosen presentations of those who have the skills and resources to be heard above all others. I have been stripped of many of the accoutrements of motherhood and admonished for it by those who know little of the deep injustice that many women suffer. I was left with a haunted motherhood that rendered me cast adrift from those who enjoyed permanent residency with their child. My only crime was a wish to take my son to another location and gain much-needed support after years of isolation, but this was twisted into a different story by parties with long-held agendas previously unknown to me. The court process will all too readily reveal the depths of cruelty that people will inhabit to get their way. The decision, taken out of my hands dictated that my son would live primarily with his father so he could continue to attend the school with which he was familiar. We shared residency on paper, but my time with him was sparse. It seemed the mantle of the black sheep would follow me into the realms of motherhood. It is a heavy mark to carry, especially at the school gates where other mothers congregate and stare. These experiences tear holes in the fabric of relationship between mother and child but we have done our best to weave them back together with patience and love.

Over time I have shed some of the marks of the black sheep and even gained some of the acquisitions of a life deemed acceptable. I own my property and hold down a small and independent freelance career. It is amusing to watch people change their attitudes towards me as I suddenly become more acceptable to them, earning a seat at the table because of my apparent conformity. In my heart, I will always feel the odd one out despite my outer representation and I have come to value being different. Walking the road less travelled has introduced me to people I may not have met in another version of life. Black sheep have the uncanny ability to recognise each other in all types of social situations even though we might on the surface blend into the crowd.

There is beauty in meeting like-minded souls, and they offer the potential of healing from earlier relational disruptions when I was reminded of difference rather than being celebrated for it. I have made a patchwork quilt from all the memories of the times I have spent with others who feel similarly less than included, they have been remarkable people each in their unique way. In my mind's eye, I return to the young child twirling in the garden in the dead of night, free from the constraints of overbearing and controlling others. This vision brings with it a freedom that has sometimes eluded me when I have been desperate to weld myself tightly to the world and its much-wanted acceptance. These memories remind me that I still possess the qualities inherent in this young girl who dreamed of escape and liberation. In many ways, I have achieved a certain sense of liberation and no longer cleave to dreams of fitting in, instead delighting in the difference and my warm and reliable sheepskin coat.

* * *

## Coda

Writing has given me many things. A way to express what I have experienced – my story if you will – without the interruptions so often given by those who find it difficult to listen. It has helped me to shape a new understanding of my experiences and the ability to carve a new way forward. It has given me a way to speak to power, so often denied, without the fear of my words being corrupted and misspoken by others. Above all, it has brought a new sense of peace, a peace that arises from knowing I have left a written legacy that will hopefully help others to tell their own story. I have a place now, in the written word. My writing is a physical demonstration that I have survived.

# 14

# CATCHING 'SLIDING DOOR' MOMENTS

## Finding Purpose in Life, and Maintaining Love, Compassion and Mental Wellbeing

*Mats Niklasson and Irene Niklasson*

### Prologue/Epilogue

When we began the journey of writing this manuscript 11 months ago, we didn't know where the process would lead us. Reading the chapter retrospectively we can't help having a feeling of 'kinship' with Vladimir and Estragon, the main characters in Beckett's play *Waiting for Godot* (Beckett, 1956). We recognize their endless discussions. Their 'love as companionship, a bonding that will last as long as the protagonists survive' (Calder, 2001, p. 59) flourish while waiting for Godot, who never comes. Our 'Godot' didn't turn up either, but our journey brought about three themes, each of which we consider as highly valuable for a keeping-up of love and mental health; the walking and talking cure; the sitting and talking cure; and the writing and talking cure.

### Part I

### An Invitation

*Mats:* 'Irene,' I said, 'I have been invited to write a proposed chapter in a book on "Autoethnography and Mental health"' The book is supposed to provide a platform for new autoethnographic writers in the field of mental health and psychology.'

*Irene:* 'It sounds good but how could you possibly contribute?'

*Mats:*

During discussion 'the story of Vestibularis' was suggested, which seemed fine to me. However, after at least another second of thinking I realized

DOI: 10.4324/9781003408963-14

that writing such a chapter is not for me to do by myself. You and I are used to acting as one. That story is our story.

*Irene:*

Wait a minute. Do you say that we should write together? You know that I'm not keen on writing in English. Swedish and partly German are my languages. I remember when you and Ulrika wrote your collaborative paper and how fluent she was when explaining herself (Hansson Blomkvist & Niklasson, 2022) and that is not me.

*Mats:*

Well, let's take one step at the time. According to the instructions I am, or rather, we should use an autoethnographic approach – that is, collaborate autoethnography (CAE) if we intend to write together. However, you are a bit reluctant concerning your writing and that makes it a bit complicated. When it comes to CAE, Bochner and Ellis (2016) wrote, "researchers write individual autoethnographies and simultaneously contribute their individual findings for collective analysis in a series of standardized steps" (p. 174). This was how Ulrika and I wrote our paper. Anyhow, further investigations have brought me to "two-person autoethnography,' which mostly stem from existing relations. Such an approach is called 'duoethnography" (DE) and is an example of a complete two-person dialogue model of CAE (Chang et al., 2013). Norris and colleagues (2016, p. 9) described DE as, "a collaborative research methodology in which two or more researchers of difference juxtapose their life histories to provide multiple understanding of the world. "

*Irene:*

Very tempting especially as we, in fact, are in some ways different from each other. You are a man, although sometimes more like a woman in your holistic mind set. While I am a woman, somewhat older than you and often more logical in my way of thinking and quicker when it comes to making decisions. Good so far, but what about the juxtaposition? As far as I understand the concept means some kind of tension, for example between opinions as in thesis and antithesis. Although we have had different opinions in various situations during our 34 years of running our Clinic 'Vestibularis', one reason why we have survived mentally as persons, and physically as an establishment, is that we have discussed and reached agreements and synthesis.

*Mats:*

You are right and we are facing a couple of problems here. First, according to DE (Norris et al., 2016) the stories told should rest on juxtaposition, i.e., your view and mine are standing on their own but alongside each other, creating a third space which opens up for the reader to be a part of the story and in their own mind create a synthesis. Second, Breault (2016) discussed the possibility that familiarity between authors/researchers could create a "meta-narrative" which prevents transformation and thereby dismisses the option to break new grounds.

Irene:     'Meta-narrative, what do you mean?'
Mats:

The concept "meta-narrative" was coined by the French post-modernist Jean-François Lyotard (1979) as a critique of the modernist belief that there are all-inclusive and overarching truths, that is "Universals." Putting it together it seems to me that a transformation is supposed to occur in a third space, that is, in the mind of the reader as a result of the authors/researchers unresolved discussion. This justifies the post-modern idea that there are no absolute truths, all is relative.

Irene:     'None of us think like that.'
Mats:

I agree, and I presume that's why we negotiate on almost everything. In line with that there is one point of importance which I know is of interest for us both. That is the voice and the face of the Other as it has been elaborated by Emmanuel Levinas (e.g., Moyn, 2005). According to DE (Lund et al., 2012), when the Other is included in a dialogue neither can claim universal truths or dominance. However, to me there is more to that. In our paper "The social worker as the Good Samaritan" (Blomkvist Hansson & Niklasson, 2022), Ulrika and I tried to grasp an everyday meaning of the concept 'the Other'. Ulrika told her story about meeting James, a homeless drug addict, in London and how, despite his initial resistance but with her tireless and undemanding care, a friendship evolved which transformed both their lives. Without mutual respect and the reaching of a synthesis – that is James moving from London to Sweden and leaving the drugs behind, the transformation had never come true. In a recent paper Sawyer and Norris (2015), the founders of DE, pondered over the method's evolution and concluded that, "Ultimately, duoethnography is underpinned by the hope that we can learn to be with each other, not just in tolerance and understanding but in dialogic growth."

Irene:     'Very clever. That sentence describes the very essence of our work and life together.'
Mats:     'Yes, and I think it could legitimize our use of DE because we have grown together both in tolerance and in understanding, very much due to a constant dialogue.'

*Irene:* 'Have you found out more about DE?'

*Mats:*

Yes, the method uses the concept 'currere' (Norris et al., 2016), which means that a person's life is looked upon as a curriculum, experienced in tandem with the Other. This conception goes back to Levinas who claimed that a person has to dwell in the present of another to really understand oneself. DE is not ultimately about self, as in autoethnography (AE); the story told is reciprocal and mutual and becomes "a report of a living." All in all, the method seems to be a reliable candidate for us to use.

*Irene:* 'Wait a minute, you just said that we should write this chapter?'

*Mats:* 'Yes, I think it would be an opportunity for us to tell our story. Isn't it amazing what we have achieved?'

*Irene:*

Okay, you are right, but you said that the chapter should focus on psychology and mental health. As a result of our clinical work and publications you were awarded a PhD in psychology so that part is sort of the essence in our life and work. I am more concerned about the mental health part.

*Mats:*

Don't worry, we have a lot to share in that area not the least when it comes for us to explain how we have been able to survive, for so long, both as a couple and as equal business partners. After all, Vestibularis could easily be viewed as a "total institution" – we live there, work there, eat and sleep there. It is somewhat like Goffman's theories about asylums (1991), but quite different of course.

*Irene:* 'Fine, I am in. What do we do next?'

*Mats:*

First we have to agree on the method. I suggest that we keep mainly to DE but because we are in constant dialogue and mostly think and act as one, we have to make that synthesis viable, which brings us somewhat in line with CAE. In accordance with DE, we are also expected to present a critique of cultural phenomena. The concept is difficult to comprehend but according to an anonymous source I found on the internet, a cultural phenomenon "occurs when certain individuals behave (in) a certain way merely because other individuals do as well. It also occurs when something or someone gains widespread popularity". We'll see later if it would be suitable in our story. One of DE's strengths is the power of the narrative, but to me it seems to be of importance to also bring in psychological and philosophical theory when suitable. Therefore, I suggest that our method should be a triangulation between DE, CAE and a narrative psychology approach. (e.g., Crossley, 2011)

*Irene:*

Sounds good, let's get started, but to begin with I think it is of importance that we introduce ourselves by telling how we met and how Vestibularis came about. Coming back to me as being a bit unsecure when it comes to write in English, I suggest that you use the "pen," with me sitting beside you, checking.

## Part II

### How We Met

It is really true what philosophy tells us, that life must be understood backwards. But with this, one forgets the second proposition, that it must be lived forwards.

*(Sören Kirkegaard)*

We met rather late in life. We were both married, Irene with three children and ten years my senior. Both of us were working as Physical Education (PE) teachers, Irene in a communal public school and me (Mats) at the Department of Teacher Training at the University College in Kalmar, Sweden. Our mutual interest was basically not sports, rather sensorimotor development. In the late 1980s, as a proposed way to enhance children's cognitive abilities, sensorimotor training gained a lot of interest in Sweden, foremost among teachers. In line with my suggestion, sensorimotor development was to be included as a part of the student's PE curriculum at the University College. My students were very interested in the subject and their enthusiasm spread to many of their supervising teachers in the surrounding public schools.

This increased interest among local teachers enabled the University College to offer public classes with me as the teacher. In 1988 Irene was one of my students, and this became the start of our future life together. However, divorcing is not an easy task, especially not when children are involved. Our love affair was met with both anger and joy from friends and colleagues. We received some anonymous threatening letters which were rather scary, and we got to learn that, as adults we should know better - crushes are for teenagers not adults. Some said, 'Let's see where you are in three months when the crush is gone.' When the turbulence faded our love was still there, but old friends were gone. On the other hand, we found some new ones. In retrospect we sometimes find it strange that we were able to endure the strain and the stress during, mainly, the first year. However, without knowing it at the time we intuitively developed, finding a way to tackle our difficulties and, honestly, also our joys. This became a way to 'therapeutically' treat our past as well as a way to plan our future.

## The Walking and Talking Cure

*Every day, I walk myself into a state of well-being and walk away from every illness. I have walked myself into my best thoughts, and I know of no thoughts so burdensome that one cannot walk away from it. Thus, if one just keeps on walking everything will be all right.*

*(Sören Kirkegaard)*

Of course, *this way* – walking – is nothing new. The Greeks realized the value of combining movement with intellectual activities, and Friedrich Nietzsche is quoted to have said that 'Only thoughts reached by walking have value' (Platt, 1976). More recently Rebecca Solnit (2001) wrote about how walking and culture, as well as walking and thinking, are tied together, and she argued for the slowness that walking brings. For us walking became *our way* to sort out blurry thinking, and a way to heal ourselves and keep-up our mental health. We were and still are lucky to live close to the Baltic and we spent and still spend hours upon hours walking along the water, talking, and talking.

## The Sitting and Talking Cure

We do not agree with this quotation by Hitchcock. Besides walking and talking during the day, we have spent, and are still spending after more than 34 years together, countless evening hours sitting and talking over a nice meal, and sometimes also with a good wine. It seems that we always have something to discuss, and the subjects will obviously never cease. However, it is not unusual that we repeat what has been discussed so many times before. It is a bit strange that we still endure to listen to each other repeating. Most probably this is *another way* to re-live the past to be able to cope with the future. Although we, already from the beginning, viewed ourselves as twin-souls, mostly acting as one, our love and friendship have grown over the years which has made us even stronger and secure.

## 'Ikigai' Or Having a Purpose in Life. The Development of the Vestibularis Clinic

The Japanese concept 'Ikigai' has no thoroughly comparable term in English but could be understood as the goal and joy of living, something to live for, i.e., a purpose in life (Tanno et al., 2009; Wilkes et al., 2022). To find a purpose in life predicts not only longevity and health it also seems to facilitate recovery from trauma and stress (Schaefer et al., 2013). We met in 1988 and already a year later we were allowed to start what came to be our 'life project' and purpose in life, that is, the Vestibularis Clinic. The Clinic (hereafter only Vestibularis), named after the balance system in the inner ear, started as a pilot project within my Physical Education Department at The Teacher Training College, very much due to the support from the prefect. At the time Irene had been affiliated to the department to assist me, and she was soon to give up her appointment in the public school due to our workload.

The aim of the pilot project was defined as twofold. We were supposed to assess and train pupils with sensorimotor problems from surrounding public schools, and I was expected to use gained knowledge when teaching my students about child development. Thus far, we had used assessment and training methods developed by the Danish physiotherapist Britta Holle (1981), but we thought we could do better as something was missing. Holle's method did not include vestibular stimulation (e.g., Ayres, 1973), which we realized should be of importance for even better training results.

Already in the late 1970s I, Mats, had heard about a method for assessment and intervention of sensorimotor problems developed by the psychologist Peter Blythe, active in Chester, UK. In 1988, I attended a conference in Stockholm hosted by Blythe's Institute for Neuro-Physiological Psychology (INPP) and got interested in his work. We wanted to improve the training we could offer and received the College's permission to attend INPP's courses both in Sweden and in Chester. We learned a lot and the training took another direction. The improvements made a difference and Vestibularis' reputation grew nationally. As a result, we were asked to assess and train school children from different parts of Sweden, and we were also frequently asked to give seminars all over the country. At around this time we also got to know the Finnish professor and brain researcher Matti Bergström. Over the years he became increasingly involved in our work, not the least due to his valuable collaboration in the development of our method 'Retraining for Balance' (Niklasson, Niklasson & Norlander, 2009).

Nothing lasts forever. After a couple of years, we were met with internal critique – from colleges but not from the administration. We realized, however, that our days were numbered and decided to ask the administration for permission to leave the College and bring Vestibularis and its clients with us, to start our own business. The administration was very supportive, although surprised. The situation was complicated. I had once promised the Dean to put all my effort into the building of an attractive PE department which made it impossible for me to have any secondary activity. As for now, I could stay in my position as a PE teacher, leaving

Vestibularis behind. You (Irene) were only temporarily employed and connected to the pilot project, which meant that you either could run Vestibularis alone or look for other employment. We acted as one and declared that we couldn't compromise with our conviction which was (and still is) that Vestibularis work had made, and could make, a difference in a lot of children's lives (Figure 14.1). We quit, but I honour the administration which gave me two years leave and a welcome back 'if you find that you can't run a business on your own.' When the decision was made, one college colleague told me that, 'You ought to understand that if all of us

**FIGURE 14.1**   Sebastian Blank, 'Lake walk', 2016.

(By kind permission of the artist).

at the College were to become as popular as you and Vestibularis have become, how would that look like?'

*Laying down a path in walking.*

*(Varela, Thompson & Rosch, 1993, p. 237)*

## Where Do We Go from Here?

We had made the decision to start a private establishment and were commercially lucky to bring our old clients. That was a good start. However, we knew that we were good practitioners but as entrepreneurs we were almost completely unexperienced. For us, Sebastian Blanck's painting 'Lake walk' defines the very essence of how our situation and our feelings were in the autumn of 1993.

## Part III

*Ultimately, the bond of all companionship, whether in marriage or friendship, is conversation, and conversation must have a common basis.*

*(Oscar Wilde)*

## Towards a 'Third Culture' Perspective

*Mats:*

I think it is fair to say that we have managed to stay together not only through love but also, because we have communicated almost every experience, good and bad, as well as every decision we have had to take. We haven't always agreed but we have finally managed to conclude that we have a purpose in life, and that is to use our experience and knowledge to do good. It might sound a bit smug to some but not to me.

*Irene:*

Not to me either and it is amazing to look back realizing how much time we have spent discussing, especially some issues, without reaching a synthesis. Issues which still are "thorns in our mental life," although more often in yours, and which we perpetually have to return to.

*Mats:* 'What specifically are you thinking about?'
*Irene:*

I am thinking about, for example, the resistance we and Vestibularis have met, not the least, from the medical community and how we sometimes have been badly treated, but there have been other 'windmills' to conquer as well. Our lived experience makes me every now and then feel like you and I are a bit like Don Quixote and Sancho Panza.

*Mats:*

An excellent comparison. I might be more of an idealistic personality, like Don, and yours more practical and hands on, like Sancho's. You are not a sidekick to me as little as I am a sidekick to you. Our different personalities are complementary and mold together well, which makes it easy and natural for us to act as one.

*Irene:*

You mentioned before that we, following DE, are expected to present some critique of cultural phenomena but as far as I understand we could also, according to Breault (2016), extend that to examine the economic or political situation on the self.

*Mats:*

Yes, that is correct, and I agree to what you just said about the "thorns in our mental life." We ought to elaborate on them further. So far, we have kept most of them to ourselves, but what about using our writing as a 'healing' narrative? This will be another way to come to terms with the issues by letting our feelings out. In line with post-modern theory, so influential on DE, we own our stories, and they could be used as cultural critique, but do we dare to do it?

*Irene:*

Wait a minute, postmodern theory? We have discussed Mohnkern (2022) and his opinion that many stories or narratives we read today widen the gap with reality, that is the gap between subjectivity and objectivity. It seems like every human is entitled to write their own story, regardless of its interest to others, or not. As I understand him his view is closer to ours, that there are too many 'writers,' not authors, who claim to own the truth. Everybody experiences reality differently. Shouldn't we, then, like Mohnkern wrote, leave the storytelling to the literature and true authors?

*Mats:*

I agree with your point concerning Mohnkern's view but let's "surf the wave." This might be an opportunity. If we could write down some of our experiences, I imagine that it would be a relief for us, and also what we write would be applicable to both DE and to the aim of this chapter.

*Irene:*

Oh well, I remain a bit sceptical but open for negotiation. However, you are probably right when it comes to writing down some clashing issues we have experienced with people from different parts of society. We have already explained how important it is for us to talk and to discuss and how we feel that speaking, very much but maybe not fully, has contributed to us keeping our mental health. The importance of being able to articulate feelings strongly applies to children and adolescents as well. Over the years we have experienced many clients, regardless of age, who at our first meeting have had difficulties speaking out and expressing themselves verbally. Instead, they have been frustrated and angry, using their fists when words faded. Their parents and their teachers have reported that they often got short replies to their questions. However, following training according to Sensorimotor therapy (SMT), clients in general developed their ability to express what they meant, wished, and felt. Clients who initially were easily frustrated and who had tantrums became more able to express themselves, to negotiate and to control their anger, using tears only when necessary. This experience of ours sends a message to parents and teachers: be aware when children show signs of delayed language abilities (Niklasson, Niklasson & Norlander, 2010). To you and to me it is obvious that the ability to verbally express oneself is of prime importance for our sanity.

While speaking, my scepticism concerning the writing has waned a bit. However, I can't grasp why you suddenly seem to be positive about postmodern theory.

*Mats:*    During the process of writing this chapter I have been thinking about a 'middle way' where modernist and post-modern theory could meet. I have re-read a book by an American professor, Karlis Racevskis, whom I met at a conference many years ago. We spoke a lot and he kindly sent me his book *Postmodernism and the search for enlightenment* (1993). The book isn't an easy read but if I understand him right, and I think I do, he asks the reader to compromise and think about how post-modern theory, in a positive and dynamic way, can influence modern thoughts. This brought me to what C.P. Snow wrote (Snow, 1963, pp. 70–71) when he extended his theory about the two cultures – on one hand the literal intellectuals and on the other the scientists:

*It is probably too early to speak of a third culture already in existence. But I am now convinced that this is coming. When it comes, some of the difficulties of communication will be softened: for such a culture has, just to do its job, to be on speaking terms with the scientific one. Then, as I said, the focus of this argument will be shifted, in a direction which will be more profitable to us all.*

In what you and I consider to be our most important publication so far (Niklasson, Niklasson & Norlander, 2010) we were able to validate our qualitative results using quantitative methods, which is as far as I know rather unusual. Both methods together came to be of importance for the final result. They, in a way, found each other in the middle. According to Professor Torsten Norlander, this paper turned sensorimotor training into sensorimotor therapy (SMT), which made further research possible within the field of psychology.

*Irene:*

> What comes to my mind is that you and I in our positions as therapists most probably have been and still are, a sort of 'middle way,' or a 'human third culture,' between parents who know their child intimately and teachers or the medical community who get to know a child very much through their scientific schooling. Maybe this holds for many therapists working privately. If so, it must be of even greater importance that practitioners such as us
> should have someone to 'bounce' experiences off.

*Mats:*

> Not a bad idea, I haven't thought about it that way. Our experienced issues have almost never been with the parents; they have been with schools and the medical community. When we earlier described the importance of communication in keeping good mental health, we should have added all positive feedback we have received from clients and their parents. Without their support, it would sometimes have been difficult to cope and endure despite us being together.

*Irene:*    'Many parents we have met over the years have asked for our help because their child has been misunderstood by their teacher and/ or because the medical community has failed to give appropriate support and help.'

*Mats:*

> Speaking about the medical community not giving support. I read a paper (Sibeoni & Revah-Levy, 2023) about a psychiatrist, one of the authors, coming back to work after recovering from mental illness and how she was met by coldness, distance, and embarrassment. The authors do not blame her colleagues, they rather raise questions about values and stigmatisation. That paper gives me courage to reveal a couple of our bad experiences but not with the aim to blame – rather for us to just write down bad experiences in a 'human third culture' perspective as a *third* way to progress our 'mental healing'. This might give us yet another

perspective on our own role in certain situations which hopefully could help us ponder on what we could have done better.

*Irene:* 'Your suggestion sounds good, but you didn't mention the critique of cultural phenomena which belongs to DE.'

*Mats:*

You are right, but we declared initially that our chapter should use a triangulation between the methods of DE, CAE and a narrative psychology approach. As our manuscript evolved over time, I happened to remember C.P. Snow's theory about a 'third culture'. My elaboration of the concept brought about your idea that *we* might have been and still are acting somewhat like a 'human third culture'. I think that is brilliant.

My suggestion is that we place ourselves in the middle of the story and use some cultural phenomena as mirrors. Then a narrative psychology approach might suit us best. According to Crossley (2011), this stands in contrast to the post-modern approach. The former aims at an understanding of an individual's specific experiences and is therefore concrete and less theoretical, while the latter tend to be more theoretical and abstract.

## Part IV

*Attend to yourself; turn your eye away from all that surrounds you and in towards your own inner self. Such is the first demand that Philosophy imposes upon the student. We speak of nothing that is outside you, but solely of yourself.*

*(Johann Gottlieb Fichte)*

## The Writing and Talking Cure

*Irene:*

I agree that a narrative psychological approach would serve our purpose well. However, but we should also continue to keep up our discussion and be as true as possible to the tenets of DE. I suggest that we divide our bad experiences or issues into two parts. First, the story about the *internal conflicts* which made us leave the University College. Then one section about a couple of negative experiences with the medical community: *external conflicts.*

*Mats:* 'Above, we briefly mentioned that we left the University College because we couldn't compromise with our conviction, that sensorimotor training could make a difference for some children. That's true, but there are more details to add.'

## Internal Conflicts

*Mats:*

At the time when the interest for sensorimotor training was at its peak among students at the University College, the staff were joined by a new, highly educated – PhD – colleague. Most of us had only our teacher's exam, but new winds had begun to blow because the Swedish Government had proposed that University Colleges should primarily employ people with PhDs. We all knew the responsibilities we had when teaching at the University College and I remember that we all tried to keep up as good an academic standard as possible. As mentioned above, I ran evening classes for several years, teaching mainly from Holle's books. Scientific papers and books on sensorimotor training were scarce since the field was rather new. Right from the beginning our new colleague became suspicious about my courses. When the reference list for my next course was discussed at the program committee's meeting, they succeeded in stopping me by convincing some of my non-academic 'colleagues' that what I taught was unscientific and did not belong at the College.

*Irene:*  'I remember that the whole situation made a huge negative impact on you.'

*Mats:*

Yes it did, in one way I might have been able to understand the PhD colleague, but I felt 'backstabbed' by my old 'friends'. Thinking back, it might not have been just the accusation of unscientific teaching that brought them against me; it might as well be what I was told later: "*What I taught had become too popular.*"

*Irene:*  'There was a meeting a couple of days later between the new prefect, you and the PhD where the new prefect joined sides with the PhD and you reacted very strongly.'

*Mats:*

Yes, I did. Unfortunately, the meeting was the day after I had a wisdom tooth removed. Some say that it is equal to losing a body part – very anxiety-ridden. I fully agree with that. I don't remember most of the meeting, I felt so sick. Certainly, the lost tooth affected my temper. I do remember that I was very resistant and childish and acting that way didn't improve my chances for a settlement.

*Irene:*   'What could you have done differently?'

*Mats:*

That is both an easy and a difficult question to answer. The easy answer is that I obviously should have behaved like an adult. On the other hand, Vestibularis, the pilot project, and my courses were interwoven. They were my 'babies' and I remember thinking that if I lose one, I might soon lose the others. Anyway, from that day on there was no return, and gradually our decision to leave the College matured. Since then, I have blamed the PhD for our departure.

*Irene:*   'What? I can't see why they should be blamed. Imagine that their opinion was more right than wrong and that you too quickly 'played the victim'.

*Mats:*   'A good point. We have discussed this issue so many times before, but you haven't said so before. It makes a difference for me. I know I'm still rather easily hurt which makes your suggestion plausible.'

*Irene:*

We often speak about "sliding door" moments which to us mean "scenarios" (Gottman, 2012), that is, *"what, if?", "what, if not?"* Their opinion made us leave the College, and in doing so we were free to develop Vestibularis into a Clinic, a private establishment, which later made your own PhD possible. Would this have happened had we stayed? Put another way, maybe you should be grateful that they made us go.

*Mats:*   'Wow, that would really be something. You have touched on this idea before but not as direct as now. Doing so, would let me make peace with that part of my past.'

*Irene:*   'Think about it, and we will discuss it further when walking or over dinner. Now let's move to section two.'

## External Conflicts

*Mats:*

Although I was accused for using unscientific literature in my teaching, I have always strived for scientific rigour, which eventually led to my own PhD. In my opinion we have mostly been respectfully met by MDs but sadly not by physiotherapists. I remember the day I was invited by an association of physiotherapists to present Vestibularis' results. Full of good intentions I arrived at the hospital just to find that more associates than previously told had been invited. I came in a hurry and had skipped lunch to be in time. In the crowded room participants were having sandwiches and coffee but no one offered me anything. I was asked to be seated in the middle of a round stage and started my presentation. Before I had finished my first sentence, I was interrupted by a vicious remark obviously intended to be a question. I answered as politely as I could and continued but I was immediately interrupted. This time my answer was less polite and more serious, "*Would you like to listen to what I have to say or should I go?*" From then on, the situation was tense, but I was given what I consider to be an (un)fair chance to finish my presentation.

Sometime later I was invited to speak at a national conference on orthopedics, but a couple of days before my presentation I was contacted by the organizer who told me that a strong group of physiotherapists had contacted him and, as he said, yelled at him: "*Don't you dare to let Niklasson speak. If you do, we will see to that participants will withdraw their presence*". Of course, I withdrew. These are two occasions I can't let go. They have become thorns in my mental life. How could educated people act like that? We have talked about them a lot but what should I have done?

*Irene:*

I find it difficult to give a fair answer, the situations were complicated. However, now the word is out and public. This is your story and hopefully will writing it down help you to leave it behind make a difference for you in the future?

## References

Ayres, A. J. (1973). *Sensory integration and learning disorders.* Western Psychological Services.
Beckett, S. (1956). *Waiting for Godot.* Faber and Faber Limited.
Blomkvist, U. H., & Niklasson, M. (2022). The social worker as the Good Samaritan: When my heart did the thinking. *Social Work and Social Sciences Review, 23*(2), 36–52. https://doi.org/10.1921/swssr.v23i2.2091
Bochner, A., & Ellis, C. (2016). *Evocative autoethnography: Writing lives and telling stories.* Routledge.
Breault, R. A. (2016). Emerging issues in duoethnography. *International Journal of Qualitative Studies in Education, 29*(6), 777–794. https://doi.org/10.1080/09518398.20161162866
Calder, J. (2001). *The philosophy of Samuel Beckett.* Calder Publications UK Ltd.
Chang, H., Ngunjiri, F. W., & Hernandez, K. A. C. (2013). *Collaborative autoethnography.* Routledge.
Crossley, M. L. (2011). *Introducing narrative psychology: Self, trauma, and the construction of meaning.* Open University Press.
Goffman, E. (1991). *Asylums: Essays on the social situation of mental patients and other inmates.* Penguin Books.
Gottman, J. (2012). *What makes love last?* Simon & Schuster.
Holle, B. (1981). *Motor development in children: Normal and retarded: A practical guide for sensory motor stimulation.* Blackwell Scientific.

Lyotard, J. (1979). *The postmodern condition: A report on knowledge.* University of Minnesota Press.

Lund, D., Sawyer, R. D., & Norris, J. (Eds.). (2012). *Duoethnography: dialogic methods for social, health, and educational research.* Left Coast Press.

Mohnkern, A. (2022). *Gegen die erzählung. Melville, proust und die algorithmen der gegenwart.* Verlag Turia + Kant.

Moyn, S. (2005). *Origins of the other: Emmanuel Levinas between revelation and ethics.* Cornell University Press.

Niklasson, M., Niklasson, I., & Norlander, T. (2009). Sensorimotor therapy: Using stereotypic movements and vestibular stimulation to increase sensorimotor proficiency of children with attentional and motor difficulties. *Perceptual and Motor Skills, 108*(3), 643–669. https://doi.org/10.2466/pms.108.3.643-669

Niklasson, M., Niklasson, I., & Norlander, T. (2010). Sensorimotor therapy: Physical and psychological regressions contribute to an improved kinesthetic and vestibular capacity in children and adolescents with motor difficulties and concentration problems. *Social Behavior and Personality, 38*(3), 327–345. https://psycnet.apa.org/doi/10.2224/sbp.2010.38.3.327

Norris, J., Sawyer, R. D., & Lund, D. (Eds.) (2016). *Duoethnography: Dialogic methods for social, health, and educational research.* Routledge.

Platt, M. (1976). Nietzsche on Flaubert and the powerlessness of his art. *Centennial Review, 20*(3), 309–313. https://www.jstor.org/org/stable/23738373

Racevskis, K. (1993). *Postmodernism and the search for enlightenment.* University Press of Virginia.

Sawyer, R., & Norris, J. (2015). Duoethnography: A retrospective 10 years after. *International Review of Qualitative Research, 8*(1), 1–4. https://doi.org/10.1525/irqr.2015.8.1.1

Schaefer, S. M., Morozink Boylan, J., Van Reekum, C. M., Lapate, R. C., Norris, C. J., Ryff, C. D., & Davidson, R. J. (2013). Purpose in life predicts better emotional recovery from negative stimuli. *PLoS ONE, 8*(11), e80329. https://doi.org/10.1371/journal.pone.0080329

Sibeoni, J., & Revah-Levy, A. (2023). A psychiatrist returning to work after a severe mental illness. *The Lancet Psychiatry* (published online August 24). https://doi.org/10.1016/s2215-0366(23)00296-1

Snow, C. P. (1963). *The two cultures: And a second look.* Cambridge University Press.

Solnit, R. (2001). *Wanderlust: A history of walking.* Penguin Books.

Tanno, K., Sakata, K., Ohsawa, M., Onoda, T., Itai, K., Yaegashi, Y., Tamakoshi, A., & JACC Study Group. (2009). Associations of Ikigai as a positive psychological factor with all-cause mortality and cause-specific mortality among middle-aged and elderly Japanese people: Findings from the Japan Collaborative Cohort Study. *Journal of Psychosomatic Research, 67*(1), 67–75. https://doi.org/10.1016/j.jpsychores.2008.10.018

Varela, F. J., Thompson, E., & Rosch, E. (1993). *The embodied mind. Cognitive science and human experience.* The MIT Press.

Wilkes, J., Garip, G., Kotera, Y., & Fido, D. (2022). Can Ikigai predict anxiety, depression, and well-being? *International Journal of Mental Health and Addiction*, 1–13. https://doi.org/10.1007/s11469-022-00764-7

# 15

# BUILDING RESILIENCE FROM BAD EXPERIENCES

## An Autoethnographic Account

*Nawal Saleh*

### Introduction: Autoethnography

The use of autoethnography as a form of self-study results in knowledge that otherwise may never have been considered (Grant, 2023; Soni, 2020). My complex upbringing has left me with confusion surrounding social norms and values (Kimbrough & Vostroknutov, 2016). As an individual attempting to integrate with society, being part of the community without this knowledge would be impossible. Providing the world with a knowledge perspective only achievable through an individual's series of unique experiences makes autoethnography invaluable, regarding the impact society has on an individual and vice-versa (Chang, 2016).

There are a wealth of criteria suggested to ensure the elevation of the quality of autoethnographic accounts. Grant (2023) deconstructs this information in a concise and informed way, providing enough information to start the autoethnographic journey while also providing essential resources for those intending to participate. The requirement that autoethnography be both evocative and credible (Grant, 2023; Richardson & St. Pierre, 2018) might suggest that lived experiences must be worth writing about for them to qualify for autoethnographic representation. It is worth noting, however, that while experiences may not be viewed by some as 'worth writing about', they can be the things that need the most exposure (Grant, 2023).

With the above in mind, the complexity of my childhood experiences, and the overlap of my special variety of trauma, parental buffering, and situational perception, has left me in a unique situation. This is one where I am

DOI: 10.4324/9781003408963-15

psychologically unable to open up to counsellors, feel very little relation to the culture I experienced growing up, and received no empathy from people who had no idea what I was and still am going through, leaving me essentially my own therapist (Bouldin, 2017). The accumulation of these factors, and many more which I may or may not be aware of, has given me, as a psychologist and a future counsellor, a respectful appreciation for autoethnography.

My story will address the issues I have faced growing up in an Egyptian home, while navigating the Western world, in an environment where corporal punishment was normalised, and what happened in the house stayed in the house (Burt et al., 2021).

It is important at this point to describe my approach to honouring relational ethics. When necessary, I got the opinions of both my older brother and my mother, both of whom are mentioned in this account. This was to ensure they were both being represented fairly and accurately, as well as affirming the actions of my father. As I am in non-contact with my father, his permission and approval were not sought; although there is very little chance he would take responsibility for these actions in any case (see Grant & Young, 2021). I counteract this by making a conscious effort to be factual in his portrayal, and to deliver an honest and genuine account of his actions. It is my opinion that anything less than an apologetically honest account of my father's behaviours would be an insult to those who had to endure it.

## From Egypt to England

My family emigrated from Egypt in 2000. My mum stayed in close contact with her parents and siblings, with Skype being an important and familiar lifeline in a strange and foreign country (Jang et al., 2016). In retrospect, my mother was completely alone. She was trapped in a relationship with a man she didn't like, in a country where the only other person she knew was over 100 miles away, and responsible for children who needed protecting.

Social support networks can have both positive and negative impacts on mental health (Guruge et al., 2015). While my mother had been in contact with her sisters to help her through a difficult time, it was her brothers who forced her to settle for my father, a testament to the power men have in Egyptian culture. My mother's reasons for staying with an abusive partner are not mine to tell, although the impact it had on my siblings and myself were quite significant. Nothing compares to the impact this relationship had on her. Along with a quadruple limb surgery (surgery on both arms and both legs) carried out before I was three years old, and expectations set on her by a culture she left and a religion she deeply believed in, my mother was left physically and mentally vulnerable (Oosterhuis et al., 2019). Although not perfect, she did the best she could in the circumstances we were in (Namy et al., 2017). She was under a large amount of stress, having moved countries under duress, and finding herself married to an awful, abusive man in a foreign country (Shaw & Starr, 2019).

The first house we stayed in was in Nottingham. Number 1, Port Arthur will be something that my inner child clings onto. It is my first memory of any kind of stable environment in which we were raised. As is typical, I experienced many firsts in this house. The first time I recognised myself in a mirror. The first time I had a meltdown because my brother was doing something I wasn't allowed to (first of many). The first time I remember my dad losing his temper and 'disciplining' me, was because I had taken the bookmark out of his Qur'an. I had taken a pretty piece of thread that had been hidden or caught in the book to display it on the outside where it could be appreciated. But it was not – I clearly recall my father grabbing my hair and lifting me by the ponytail, and me wondering what I had done wrong.

While I harboured great resentment and fear towards my father, the way he was acting was normalised, especially in my father's village. My negative feelings were always viewed as unjustified, because that is how children are supposed to be raised. What I had not normalised is being in situations where complete strangers were being racist to us.

I've lived in both the UK and Egypt and have witnessed the social attitudes in both countries towards smacking children. While I lived in my father's village from 2007 to 2010, my experience was that if children were viewed as a nuisance it was any adult's right to discipline them (Straus, 1991). While this can seem horrifying to Westerners, this tight-knit community we lived in allowed for all adults to be in constant communication with each other. The adult would discipline the child for misbehaving, inform the child's parents why they disciplined them, and the child would proceed to get a beating at home for misbehaving in public and embarrassing the parents. It was a flawless system for parents to guarantee their children would still fear them despite them being miles apart. While this may seem that I am condoning this behaviour, I am simply trying to explain an Egyptian practice that may seem foreign to Westerners, and trying to portray why this method of discipline was so popular (Whipple & Richey, 1997). The African Proverb 'It takes a village to raise a child' is taken into a different light when personal experience skews the meaning to 'It takes a village to discipline a child' (Reupert et al., 2022).

My father's distribution of physical punishment only built resentment and anger, leading on my part to *realistic estrangement* (Bernet et al., 2020). This is distinct from parental alienation, which is parental rejection with no legitimate justification (Poustie et al., 2018). Realistic estrangement is for the benefit of the child. On occasions when my mother hit me, I knew I had crossed a line and had always considered this discipline, as opposed to my father's wanton abuse (Poustie et al., 2018; Whipple & Richey, 1997). Even when my mother was hitting me out of anger rather than discipline, I still took the beatings and grew to appreciate that my mother rarely lost her temper – and when she did, I was definitely being a terror.

By the time I was in reception class, we had moved schools and houses to a five-story house in Nottingham, one that was a 'fixer-upper', but we fixed it up as a family. New floorboards were put in, we removed the wallpaper and painted the walls ourselves, and my brother and I even got to share the best room, the attic. While we were able to fix all the faults in the house, the faults in the wider community were becoming more and more audacious. What started as name-calling and crossing the road to get away from us, morphed into throwing rocks at my mother while she was with her children and stepping on her abaya from behind to trip her up, all of which my mother had been putting up with from a young age. Her wearing the Niqab has caused issues in her past, and with the aid of age and wisdom, she was able to rise above it (Ellefsen et al., 2022).

## Domestic Abuse: The Consequences of Keeping It Under Wraps

My father, who is Nubian by birth and born in the south of Egypt, was raised in one of the oldest cities in Egypt. Although it had a rich history, like many other locations in Egypt it eventually succumbed to poverty. Thirty minutes each morning was reserved for wiping the dust off the car, stray dogs owned the street, and litter was a regular part of the landscape. Although my father experienced corporal punishment from his father in the form of being tied up to the bed, he was orphaned at a young age and raised by his older half-brother, a retired military officer, and his wife.

When my father excelled at school and became an interior designer, he became the family's main breadwinner. As a result, the people who raised him became somewhat dependent on him, flipping the power dynamic in a way that favoured my father and possibly resulting in the onset of his narcissistic traits. The abuse my father experienced at the hands of my paternal grandfather was regularly brought up as examples of how better off we were, although it should be noted that as my father's abuse escalated, these examples were surpassed.

Life at home was extremely difficult, but school was not much better. Having moved around quite frequently, I found it difficult to make long-term meaningful relationships, a difficulty that has followed me into adulthood. The ability to make friends came so much easier to my brother than it did to me, a consequence of my father's constant reminders of how inadequate and annoying I was. I discovered too late that these outbursts had nothing to do with me, as I had already internalised his words which resulted in the current shambolic state of my self-esteem (Yun et al., 2019).

I was under the impression that my brother had gone through the same abuse I did, but when we got older and started confronting my dad for a resolution, my mother pointed out that my father had always been a lot harder on me – a point confirmed by others. Not to invalidate it, the abuse my brother experienced was different, with distinct impacts on his own mental health, but it would be wrong of me to not explicitly mention that I was treated worse than my brother – because of the simple fact that I was a girl.

The important thing to mention is how much both parents stressed the idea of 'what happens in this house is no one else's business'. 'Social services will put your dad in prison and take you away from us', we were told. During my entire childhood, there was always anxiety that I might slip up, say something to the wrong person and get my father into trouble, not because he would be in trouble, but because of what he would do to me when he got out. This anxiety was multiplied due to my turbulent tendency to over-share. If I was careful what I said around adults, in my mind, I could tell my friends everything.

However, I learned quite quickly that just because you can tell your friends something, this doesn't mean they'll believe you. After meeting my charismatic and friendly dad, their opinions of him were formed and did not correlate with the version of events I was addressing. I was left confused as to why *my* friends would believe my father's façade over my recollection. Little did I know that this was something he had been practising his entire life.

## Experiences in Schools

My difficulties with oversharing only grew from there. No matter how private I tried to be, or how quiet and mysterious I wanted to appear, oversharing with 'friends' had always been a problem for me. It was not until I looked back that I recognised my profound loneliness and need for admiration (Shabahang et al., 2022). Having moved around a lot due to temporary housing, by the time I reached Year seven, I had gone to 12 schools and lived in 24 different houses. At every school we would attend, my brother thrived at making friends straight away, while I was left feeling awkward in class, focusing on the schoolwork, and looking forward to playtime where I would be reunited with him. When I did manage to build those relationships, it was a race to get to know them and get them to like me before it was time to move away. This probably contributed to my obsessive need to overshare significantly, along with my lack of understanding that a lot of time is needed for other people to trust you.

It was not typical for me to stay in one school for a prolonged period. Consequently, when I finally graduated from primary to secondary, I made no effort at the start of the school year. This sudden change in behaviour may have been a result of attending an all-girls school, leaving me without my brother and the social support that came with him. Ironically, I had given up on the one occasion when everyone else had been in the same boat as me. My opinion of people had been jaded by my past failed friendships and the bullying I experienced at schools, along with the inherent belief that I would be gone soon. I no longer suffered fools. I would answer back to every snarky quip thrown at me, mirror their dirty looks, and had gotten into a few physical fights during my time in secondary school. Despite my behavioural issues, I was one of the highest achievers in our year. The combination of my unkindness towards my peers and always coming top of the class increased their resentment towards me. I am now old enough to acknowledge that I was not a likeable person during my secondary school days, which mostly stemmed from my hatred towards myself.

I was often vindictive and felt like the world was against me because no one understood my pain. Whenever anyone would raise their voice at me, my involuntary reaction was to cry. I became very familiar with the eyeroll followed by an incredulous, 'Here come the waterworks'. I resented this, I was angry at myself for crying in front of a teacher, I was angry at them for assuming I was faking it, and most importantly, I was angry at my family because I could never tell any of the teachers what was happening at home. Had I done this, I may have received more support from the school, they may have been more accommodating with my behaviour, and I may have had someone trusted to talk to. However, the racism and discrimination I experienced from the teachers because I was Egyptian and Muslim makes me reconsider whether they were the correct authority to go to.

## Inability to Escape Abuse

A few years after finally 'settling' in Nottingham, we moved to London. My mother's condition had worsened, so we were staying with my uncle until the council found us a house. The housing we received was always temporary, so we moved frequently around London. With each new house followed a new school, new friends, and the same old story. I would go to school, feel uncomfortable around my classmates, and opt to stay around my brother as much as I could. I always remember having difficulty with people in my age group. Those older than me were always kinder to me, but this could also be because I was 'Mohamed's little sister'.

Meanwhile, at home, my mother was trying her best to repair the breaking relationship between my father and me. In our household, my father's ideal parenting style was 'destroy and repair'. My father destroyed our will to do 'the bad thing' by beating the desire out of us, and then my mother would come in and explain why he was doing it. 'It's for your benefit to discipline you. He hates hitting you as much as you hate being hit'. It was what was expected of her – she was the 'good cop' to his 'bad'. She put his behaviour in context to ensure we understood it was not malicious. My mother's failure at this was largely due to what I understood to be her belief that my father was 'not a bad guy', something that always frustrated me growing up. I now understand that this was not only a cultural expectation; doing right by your husband is an Islamic duty. Everything she did towards my father was socially and morally honourable, leaving very little to criticise in terms of wifely duties.

She would always encourage me to be open and honest with my father, in the hope that I would strengthen my relationship with him. When I was around 5–6, I tried to somersault and hit the television with my foot, knocking over the antenna. When I was unable to restore the image on the television, I hid under the covers out of fear that my father would punish me. When my mother found me, she told me that he was a reasonable man. If I was honest and forthcoming, he wouldn't hit me. I believed her, so I nodded when she asked if she could invite my father into the room. I had barely finished the sentence when I felt his fists landing. My father had already pushed my mother to the side for better access to me. My mother instantly came between me and my father, and after a few seconds of scrambling he stopped trying to reach me and turned his attention to punishing my mum for disturbing his discipline. That was probably the moment I knew unequivocally that I could never trust my father.

## Confusion and Divorces

I would like to say at this point that due to the sheer number of things that happened in my childhood, it is difficult for me to accurately gauge ages and timings. If readers are sometimes left a little confused about the chronology of events and circumstances, this is because I am confused.

My parents have married and divorced each other twice. They were married two years before I was born and, while the marriage was abusive, they stayed together until we moved to Egypt. My mother was empowered by the physical presence of her social circle and felt secure to divorce him. They divorced around 2008 when I was nine years old, but had already separated when I was eight. We moved – just me, my brother and my father – into his dad's house, and my younger siblings stayed with my mum. I had to take care of my father and my brother with the aid of our neighbour from ages eight to ten. We lived in Nottingham I was around 2–4, and I was five when we moved to London.

My parents divorced for the first time while we were living in Egypt. In the event of a divorce, the children will go into the father's custody. Similarly, if the father dies, the children do not go to the mother, even if they were still married at the point of his death, but will go to the father's oldest living brother. My father worked full-time, so had allowed my younger siblings to live with my mother, who together with her sanity and independence, took them back to England. As the oldest daughter and the only female in the house at the time, my role had turned from child to housekeeper. I was expected to do things around the house, from keeping it clean to taking my father's shoes off when he came back from work. We had a neighbour who had helped raise my father back when he was orphaned. She was forced to help me make the food as I was terrified of lighting the gas stove. My father looked down on her because of her social status and would always berate me for being unable to handle the cooking by myself. 'People your age get married and have a house to keep', is something I would hear often, followed by, 'If you ever get married, your husband will return you within the week'.

This living arrangement continued until one day during the winter break, my father approached me. He informed me that he would be asking my maternal grandfather for my mother's hand in marriage, I exclaimed excitedly while hugging him, 'For the first time in my life, I love you'. The second divorce was more permanent. My mother was grieving the loss of her brother. To put this in context, her brother was 21. He had been celebrating his Egyptian equivalent of a 'stag do', when a gun misfired and shot him in the left eye. He was taken off life support on his wedding day.

Soon after the shooting, my father abruptly showed up to the hospital room to inform my mother that she had to go back to England so we could start school. He was flying out of Egypt the next day and there had to be someone with us going back. He refused to change his own ticket and insisted that my mother buy him a new one if she 'demanded' to stay. His utter indifference and lack of compromise or sacrifice in a difficult situation for not only his wife, who had just lost her youngest brother but also his children, who had lost their favourite uncle was a true testament to his narcissistic traits. My mother refused to leave until her brother either left the hospital or was buried. My mother was at her brother's hospital bed for a full week, but left his bedside to find my father a ticket back home. She would not find out until she returned that her brother had passed away while she was not present.

My brother's experience was more direct. He, along with our cousins, heard shots fired. Moving towards the noise, they ran down, only to find our youngest uncle lying on the floor. Stunned, my brother watched as my uncle was carried into the back of the car, numbly clambering in after him. After visiting multiple hospitals in the area and being turned away due to the hopelessness of his condition, someone paid for a motorcycle to take my brother back home. He was 14 when he saw his uncle dying.

Afterwards, my father hurriedly pointed out to my mother that as her brother was dead it was time to go back to England. He did not attend the funeral, despite us being in the country at the time, and refused to send his condolences after the fact. Neither my family nor my mother was on the receiving end of any empathy or mercy from my father, and to this day he has not expressed any condolences for my uncle or my grandfather. Quite the opposite, he is constantly and openly verbally abusive towards my late uncle and grandfather, and often says that my grandfather is burning in hell.

When my mother refused to come back after the burial – a choice he openly expressed his disapproval of, my father criticised my mother for staying in Egypt to take care of her parents, when she had siblings in Egypt as well as a family that needed taking care of in England. When she came back to England, her depression had hit a new level; she had spent most of her time crying and was unable to get out of bed most days. In response, my father served her with divorce papers and asked her to leave his house, and my role as the housekeeper was reinstated.

My father had now lost his primary target for abuse, and since I was already doing most of my mother's duties, the new target became clear. My older brother was now big enough to fight back, and my siblings were young enough to not hate him yet, so his attention had turned almost entirely to me. The physical, emotional, and mental abuse I was being bombarded with left me affectionately fantasising about my suicide. When it would be too much and I would not be able to handle it anymore, I would ask if my mother could move back in. I don't recall how easy these transitions were, but no matter how long my mother was back, we would always get to a point where we could not afford to live comfortably.

My mother always wanted the best for us. While she was always impressively thrifty, when it would get to the point where she was struggling to provide she would be wracked with guilt and feelings of inadequacy. This had a large impact on her already fragile mental health, and I would make the executive decision that I could put up with the abuse, for as long as my younger siblings were getting the life my mother wanted for them. And so, the cycle continued until my mental health had declined so much that I considered self-admission to a mental health hospital. I went as far as to Google what hospitals were on my route to school but quickly reconsidered it in case it impacted my chances of employment in the future. Finally, I confessed to my mother that I couldn't get the thought of killing myself out of my head. I would never do it because my siblings were quite young, and I did not want to add that to the list of traumas they experienced. I told her that I couldn't stay here anymore, and if I did, I might convince myself to go through with it.

My mother resolved to have a 'sit down' with my brother, my father, and me. We would air our grievances and look for ways to resolve the issues. This was one of many sit-downs my mother had instigated in the hopes of building a better relationship with our father. Her conviction that he was a reasonable man was desperately misguided, but her intentions were never malicious and always for the benefit of her children. As a result, I cannot hold this against her. After attempting to have a civil conversation, my mother finally said, 'Your daughter is thinking about killing herself, you need to change something or we'll lose her', to which his response was, 'If she wants to kill herself, that's her choice; it's one less mouth for me to feed'.

The next day, he drove me to school, not out of kindness but control. He said my mother had poisoned my mind against him and shocked me with, 'Name one bad thing I've done to you?' I was dumbfounded, but he took my silence as a response. 'See, you can't think of a single thing!' Once I arrived at school, I waited for his car to drive off and left school. I had no phone since he had taken it, so I texted my mother and father from a payphone telling them not to expect me back any time soon. I spent the rest of the day walking around mosques, libraries, and parks. After finishing a prayer at a mosque, I settled down to read when a dark figure walked in. I absentmindedly looked up and instantly sat at attention. Despite her niqab covering her face, I instantly recognised my mother's eyes. The second I was in view, she started running towards me. Had I not already resolved to never go back to the house with my father again, I would have once again been afraid for my life. Running away from home reflects badly on the family and tarnishes the name, something my father would not stand for.

My mother brought me into a deep embrace, explaining how worried she had been. She then updated me up on recent events. When she received the text, she called my father to ask him where his daughter was. After I did not arrive home after school that day, his indifference did not falter. My mother learned of this and instantly acted. I was taken home and my father was never allowed to enter that house again.

## Volunteering and Discovering Abuse

Severe corporal punishment in Egypt is a regular method of parenting, while in the UK it is illegal and a form of abuse, at least to the extent that my father administered it. The significance of this is something I finally managed to put into words using an example I came across from my 'behavioural psychology' module. It was indicated that when young children hurt themselves, they react differently based on their environment. When left to their own devices, they will look stunned but will ultimately move on. When surrounded by adults, it is the shock or concern that scares them (Lansbury, 2020). Had I been receiving the same treatment in another environment (Egypt, where no one bats an eye if a child is getting slapped across the face in public), the impact that it had on me would have been different. When I turned 16, I started applying to volunteer to work with children and vulnerable adults. I was trained in being able to identify different forms of abuse and how they might present in the people we would be working with. My heart sank as my eyes scanned through the list and I found a summary of my father's behaviour. My training had turned into a checklist of all the terrible things my father had put me through. A 'bouquet of cruelty' came to mind when thinking of my father's behaviour, but with time I came to understand that I would not have gotten a better example of a wide range of abuse anywhere else. My father *was* the textbook.

In Egyptian culture, corporal punishment is still the prevalent means of discipline in lower socio-economic groups (Abolfotouh et al., 2009). In these cases, while a feeling of upset or resentment could remain, there is a general understanding that parents 'do what is best for you' (Bornstein et al., 2018). Parental behaviour becomes more understandable when our experience puts their actions into context (Zou, 2021). 'You'll understand when you're older', was a frustrating rebuttal to my inquisitive, unsatisfied objection (Khilkevich, 2014). As I grew older, I experienced the things my parents had (for example, paying bills, having a full-time job, and even being a guardian to my younger siblings).

When reflecting on their respective parenting styles, I quickly understood the difference between my father's controlling maliciousness and my mother's misguided benevolence (Mabbe et al., 2018). I vilify my father and idolise my mother, despite both being categorically psychologically controlling parents, in addition to them delivering corporal punishment.

## Adulthood

Every bad experience is an opportunity to build resilience and my life has been rife with opportunities. Despite this, I consider myself quite successful in my adulthood (Abdel-Fatah, 2021). Identifying adverse childhood experiences (ACEs) (Hughes et al., 2017), and learning their effects on adults, has been a large part of my growth journey, as well as increasing my self-awareness surrounding personal adverse experiences (Whitworth,

2016). Understanding how my personality is an accumulation of defence mechanisms and maladaptive behaviours has aided towards my self-acceptance and resolving alienating diffidence (Yazdanparast & Spears, 2018).

All of this has aided my journey of self-discovery in a potentially decades-long investigation of myself. I was always interested in psychology. My drive and curiosity propelled me into my future, where I learned that I did not become the person I am today *despite* my dad. I became the person I am because I saw an example of everything I didn't want to be (Brassett et al., 2021; Schubert et al., 2016). My negative experiences directly corresponded with the character strengths required to survive, and I have become a better person because of it (Emerson, 2018; Goodman et al., 2016).

While my ACE score is high, the outcomes associated with these have been mediated by coincidental and haphazard aspects of my personality and upbringing (Abdel-Fatah, 2021; Hughes et al., 2017; Wickham et al., 2016). My Islamic upbringing discouraged substance abuse, making it easier for me as an adult to resist the temptations of drugs and excessive drinking (Boppre & Boyer, 2021; Healey et al., 2014). Almost by accident, my attendance at an Egyptian school on Saturdays aided in my educational progress despite constantly moving houses and schools. Perhaps the advanced curriculum gave me an advantage in future years (Gerring, 2014; Sutherland, 2015)? Additionally, the stability of attending the same Egyptian school on a Saturday could have mitigated the effect of moving state schools on my education.

My curiosity allowed me to seek comfort in learning and expanding my knowledge, maturing my self-awareness, and welcoming self-acceptance, in addition to inspiring my future degrees and career (Gruber & Ranganath, 2019). My inquisitive mind has forced me to reflect on my lived experience constantly, whether out of self-pity or an improvised defence mechanism to process the chaotic events of my life, a lot of which still confuses me (Burt et al., 2021).

### Reflections

Writing this autoethnography has been one of the most therapeutic forms of reflection. Rather than rumination and speculation, the research has given me evidence-based explanations for my thoughts, feelings, and actions (Allen et al., 2020; Blanke et al., 2020). Experiencing adversities that many have not also allows me to empathise better with others and be more mindful of what other people may be experiencing. It has also resulted in the patience and support I provide to my family and friends (Greenberg et al., 2018; Sheridan & Carr, 2020).

My mother has also been a great source of inspiration for me (Bernet et al., 2020; Ellefsen et al., 2022). Despite the difficulties she has faced, her unconditional positive regard for people does not falter (Goodman et al., 2016). She has set an example of kindness, genuineness, and warmth. Irrespective of changes in our socio-economic status, my mother would go above and beyond to provide the high-quality life she experienced for her children, with an impressive amount of thriftiness and a healthy dose of religiosity (Doherty & Scannell-Desch, 2023).

My father has been a source of resentment and hatred for a long period, but upon reflection, my relationship with my siblings, as well as my relationship with my mum, would never have been as strong as it is now without experiencing these adverse events together and supporting each other (Effiong et al., 2022; Qazi et al., 2022). In direct rebellion against our father's alienation tactics (Bernet et al., 2020), we communicate our love for each other regularly, ensuring that none of us feels unloved again.

## References

Abdel-Fatah, N. A. (2021). Determinants of severe physical disciplinary practices against children in Egypt. *Child Abuse & Neglect, 111,* 104821. https://doi.org/10.1016/j.chiabu.2020.104821

Abolfotouh, M. A., El-Bourgy, M. D., Seif El Din, A. G., & Mehanna, A. A. (2009). Corporal punishment: Mother's disciplinary behavior and child's psychological profile in Alexandria, Egypt. *Journal of Forensic Nursing, 5*(1), 5–17. https://doi.org/10.1111/j.1939-3938.2009.01025.x

Allen, S. F., Wetherell, M. A., & Smith, M. A. (2020). Online writing about positive life experiences reduces depression and perceived stress reactivity in socially inhibited individuals. *Psychiatry Research, 284,* 1–9. https://doi.org/10.1016/j.psychres.2019.112697

Bernet, W., Gregory, N., Rohner, R. P., & Reay, K. M. (2020). Measuring the difference between parental alienation and parental estrangement: The PARQ-Gap. *Journal of Forensic Sciences, 65*(4), 1225–1234. https://doi.org/10.1111/1556-4029.14300

Blanke, E. S., Schmidt, M. J., Riediger, M., & Brose, A. (2020). Thinking mindfully: How mindfulness relates to rumination and reflection in daily life. *Emotion, 20*(8), 1369. https://psycnet.apa.org/doi/10.1037/emo0000659

Boppre, B., & Boyer, C. (2021). "The traps started during my childhood": The role of substance abuse in women's responses to adverse childhood experiences (ACEs). *Journal of Aggression, Maltreatment & Trauma, 30*(4), 429–449. https://psycnet.apa.org/doi/10.1080/10926771.2019.1651808

Bornstein, M. H., Putnick, D. L., & Suwalsky, J. T. (2018). Parenting cognitions→parenting practices→child adjustment? The standard model. *Development and Psychopathology, 30*(2), 399–416. https://doi.org/10.1017/s0954579417000931

Bouldin, A. S. (2017). Reflection is not reflexive. *American Journal of Pharmaceutical Education, 81*(9), 7–9. https://doi.org/10.5688/ajpe6832

Brassett, J., Browning, C., & O'Dwyer, M. (2021). You've got to be kidding: Anxiety, humour and ontological security. *Global Society, 35*(1), 8–26. https://doi.org/10.1080/13600826.2020.1828298

Burt, S. A., Clark, D. A., Gershoff, E. T., Klump, K. L., & Hyde, L. W. (2021). Twin differences in harsh parenting predict youth's antisocial behavior. *Psychological Science, 32*(3), 395–409. https://doi.org/10.1177/0956797620968532

Chang, H. (2016). Autoethnography in health research: Growing pains? *Qualitative Health Research, 26*(4), 443–451. https://doi.org/10.1177/1049732315627432

Doherty, M. E., & Scannell-Desch, E. (2023). Posttraumatic growth in women who have experienced intimate partner abuse. *Journal of Psychosocial Nursing and Mental Health Services, 61*(8), 34–41. https://doi.org/10.3928/02793695-20230222-01

Effiong, J. E., Ibeagha, P. N., & Iorfa, S. K. (2022). Traumatic bonding in victims of intimate partner violence is intensified via empathy. *Journal of Social and Personal Relationships, 39*(12), 3619–3637. https://doi.org/10.1177/02654075221106237

Ellefsen, R., Banafsheh, A., & Sandberg, S. (2022). Resisting racism in everyday life: From ignoring to confrontation and protest. *Ethnic and Racial Studies, 45*(16), 435–457. https://psycnet.apa.org/doi/10.1080/01419870.2022.2094716

Emerson, A. M. (2018). Strategizing and fatalizing: Self and other in the trauma narratives of justice-involved women. *Qualitative Health Research, 28*(6), 873–887. https://doi.org/10.1177/1049732318758634

Gerring, J. P. (2014). Moving: Its impact on the child. *Journal of the American Academy of Child & Adolescent Psychiatry, 53*(2), 138–140. https://doi.org/10.1016/j.jaac.2013.12.006

Goodman, L. A., Fauci, J. E., Sullivan, C. M., DiGiovanni, C. D., & Wilson, J. M. (2016). Domestic violence survivors' empowerment and mental health: Exploring the role of the alliance with advocates. *American Journal of Orthopsychiatry, 86*(3), 286–296. https://psycnet.apa.org/doi/10.1037/ort0000137

Grant, A. J. (2023). Crafting and recognising good enough autoethnographies: A practical guide and checklist. *Mental Health and Social Inclusion, 27*(3), 196–209. https://doi.org/10.1108/MHSI-01-2023-0009

Grant, A., & Young, S. (2021). Troubling Tolichism in several voices: Resisting epistemic violence in creative analytical and critical autoethnographic practices. *Journal of Autoethnography, 3*(1), 103–117. https://doi.org/10.1525/joae.2022.3.1.103

Greenberg, D. M., Baron-Cohen, S., Rosenberg, N., Fonagy, P., & Rentfrow, P. J. (2018). Elevated empathy in adults following childhood trauma. *PLoS One, 13*(10), e0203886. https://doi.org/10.1371/journal.pone.0203886

Gruber, M. J., & Ranganath, C. (2019). How curiosity enhances hippocampus-dependent memory: The prediction, appraisal, curiosity, and exploration (PACE) framework. *Trends in Cognitive Sciences, 23*(12), 1014–1025. https://psycnet.apa.org/doi/10.1016/j.tics.2019.10.003

Guruge, S., Thomson, M. S., George, U., & Chaze, F. (2015). Social support, social conflict, and immigrant women's mental health in a Canadian context: A scoping review. *Journal of Psychiatric and Mental Health Nursing, 22*(9), 655–667. https://doi.org/10.1111/jpm.12216

Healey, C., Rahman, A., Faizal, M., & Kinderman, P. (2014). Underage drinking in the UK: Changing trends, impact and interventions. A rapid evidence synthesis. *International Journal of Drug Policy, 25*(1), 124–132. https://doi.org/10.1016/j.drugpo.2013.07.008

Hughes, K., Bellis, M. A., Hardcastle, K. A., Sethi, D., Butchart, A., Mikton, C., … Dunne, M. P. (2017). The effect of multiple adverse childhood experiences on health: A systematic review and meta-analysis. *The Lancet Public Health, 2*(8), e356–e366. https://doi.org/10.1016/s2468-2667(17)30118-4

Jang, Y., Park, N. S., Chiriboga, D. A., Yoon, H., Ko, J., Lee, J., & Kim, M. T. (2016). Risk factors for social isolation in older Korean Americans. *Journal of Aging and Health, 28*(1), 3–18. https://doi.org/10.1177/0898264315584578

Khilkevich, S. V. (2014). The experience and wisdom is the key to success in education. *Polylinguality and Transcultural Practices*, (4), 18–21. https://journals.rudn.ru/polylinguality/article/view/1972

Kimbrough, E. O., & Vostroknutov, A. (2016). Norms make preferences social. *Journal of the European Economic Association, 14*(3), 608–638. https://doi.org/10.1111/jeea.12152

Lansbury, J. (2020, January 29). *The most helpful response when your child gets hurt (4 Guidelines)*. Retrieved from www.janetlansbury.com: https://www.janetlansbury.com/2020/01/the-most-helpful-response-when-your-child-gets-hurt-4-guidelines/

Mabbe, E., Soenens, B., Vansteenkiste, M., van der Kaap-Deeder, J., & Mouratidis, A. (2018). Day-to-day variation in autonomy-supportive and psychologically controlling parenting: The role of parents' daily experiences of need satisfaction and need frustration. *Parenting, 18*(2), 86–109. https://psycnet.apa.org/doi/10.1080/15295192.2018.1444131

Namy, S., Carlson, C., O'Hara, K., Nakuti, J., Bukuluki, P., Lwanyaaga, J., … Michau, L. (2017). Towards a feminist understanding of intersecting violence against women and children in the family. *Social Science & Medicine, 184*, 40–48. https://psycnet.apa.org/doi/10.1016/j.socscimed.2017.04.042

Oosterhuis, T., Smaardijk, V. R., Kuijer, P. P., Langendam, M. W., Frings-Dresen, M. H., & Hoving, J. L. (2019). Systematic review of prognostic factors for work participation in patients with sciatica. *Occupational and Environmental Medicine, 76*(10), 772–779. https://doi.org/10.1136/oemed-2019-105797

Poustie, C., Matthewson, M., & Balmer, S. (2018). The forgotten parent: The targeted parent perspective of parental alienation. *Journal of Family Issues, 39*(12), 3298–3323. https://doi.org/10.1177/0192513X18777867

Qazi, W. I., Shahzad, S., & Waheed, T. (2022). Critical discourse analysis of trauma bonding in female victims of intimate partner abuse: A phenomenological constructivist approach. *Sustainable Business and Society in Emerging Economies, 4*(4), 727–734. https://doi.org/10.26710/sbsee.v4i4.2496

Reupert, A., Straussner, S. L., Weimand, B., & Maybery, D. (2022). It takes a village to raise a child: Understanding and expanding the concept of the "Village". *Frontiers in Public Health 10*, 756066. https://doi.org/10.3389/fpubh.2022.756066

Richardson, L., & St. Pierre, E. (2018). Writing: A method of inquiry. In N. K. Denzin & Y. S. Lincoln (Ed.), *The SAGE handbook of qualitative research* (5th ed., pp. 818–838). Sage Publications.

Schubert, C. F., Schmidt, U., & Rosner, R. (2016). Posttraumatic growth in populations with posttraumatic stress disorder—A systematic review on growth-related psychological constructs and biological variables. *Clinical Psychology & Psychotherapy, 23*(6), 469–486. https://doi.org/10.1002/cpp.1985

Shabahang, R., Shim, H., Aruguete, M. S., & Zsila, Á. (2022). Oversharing on social media: Anxiety, attention-seeking, and social media addiction predict the breadth and depth of sharing. *Psychological Reports, 127*(2):513-5301–18. https://doi.org/10.1177/00332941221122861

Shaw, Z. A., & Starr, L. R. (2019). Intergenerational transmission of emotion dysregulation: The role of authoritarian parenting style and family chronic stress. *Journal of Child and Family Studies, 28*, 3508–3518. https://psycnet.apa.org/doi/10.1007/s10826-019-01534-1

Sheridan, G., & Carr, A. (2020). Survivors' lived experiences of posttraumatic growth after institutional childhood abuse: An interpretative phenomenological analysis. *Child Abuse & Neglect, 103*, 104430. https://doi.org/10.1016/j.chiabu.2020.104430

Soni, S. (2020). Personal narrative of mental illness within the family: A mental health professional's autoethnography. *Journal of Psychosocial Research, 15*(1), 69–76. https://doi.org/10.32381/JPR.2020.15.01.5

Straus, M. A. (1991). Discipline and deviance: Physical punishment of children and violence and other crime in adulthood. *Social Problems, 38*(2), 133–154. https://psycnet.apa.org/doi/10.1525/sp.1991.38.2.03a00010

Sutherland, A. (2015, January 25). *How education influences our experience of parenting*. Retrieved from Institute for Family Studies: https://ifstudies.org/blog/how-education-influences-our-experience-of-parenting

Whipple, E. E., & Richey, C. A. (1997). Crossing the line from physical discipline to child abuse: How much is too much? *Child Abuse & Neglect, 21*(5), 431–444. https://doi.org/10.1016/S0145-2134(97)00004-5

Whitworth, J. D. (2016). The role of psychoeducation in trauma recovery: Recommendations for content and delivery. *Journal of Evidence-Informed Social Work, 13*(5), 442–451. https://doi.org/10.1080/23761407.2016.1166852

Wickham, S., Barr, B., & Taylor-Robinson, D. (2016). Impact of moving into poverty on maternal and child mental health: Longitudinal analysis of the Millennium Cohort Study. *The Lancet, 388*, 4–10. (thelancet.com)

Yazdanparast, A., & Spears, N. (2018). The new me or the me I'm proud of? Impact of objective self-awareness and standards on acceptance of cosmetic procedures. *European Journal of Marketing, 52*(1/2), 279–301. https://doi.org/10.1108/EJM-09-2016-0532

Yun, J. Y., Shim, G., & Jeong, B. (2019). Verbal abuse related to self-esteem damage and unjust blame harms mental health and social interaction in college population. *Scientific Reports, 9*(1), 5655. s41598-019-42199-6.pdf

Zou, J. (2021). The effect of parenting pressure on children's internalizing problem behaviors and its mechanism. *Work, 69*(2), 675–685. https://doi.org/10.3233/wor-213508

# 16

## LOCATING AND DECENTRING PROFESSIONAL EXPERTISE AS A FEMINIST CRITICAL PSYCHOLOGIST IN INDIA

*Sonia Soans*

### Introduction

Psychology as a discipline has come to dominate the Indian education and cultural scene, offering everything from quick fix solutions, self-help, and therapy. The discipline enjoys popularity amongst the many university courses on offer. Psychology is not, however, neutral, objective, or devoid of social and cultural prejudice. My experience with the discipline over two decades has changed through time, from a passive consumer to an active creator of knowledge. This transition brings with the power and authority to declare legitimacy over understanding human behaviour. Decentring the notion of professional expertise through a feminist, service user, and mad studies framework, I will map my experience as a student and as a lecturer. Using these theoretical standpoints as the basis of my analysis, I want to both critique my role and discuss how psychologists play a role in validating ethno-nationalist claims. In an independent India, reclaiming the past as a space of authenticity and spiritual superiority has meant that postcolonial and decolonial psychologies have become a means of suppressing subaltern/Dalit critiques. As a critical psychologist, I am constantly working to analyse hegemonic discourse within the discipline of psychology. This chapter will attempt to answer the question: How can autoethnography become a means of creating an astute critical psychology in the Indian context?

### Demystifying Psychology

The discipline of psychology has become a popular subject in many countries, at school and university, in the past few decades. India is no exception.

DOI: 10.4324/9781003408963-16

The subject is offered from high school courses right through doctoral studies. Short courses and diplomas are equally popular. However, the discipline is not without its flaws. Its popularity is owed to several factors, which will be discussed in this chapter. Growing neoliberalism in education, underfunding, right-wing extremism, and growing ethnocentrism are some of the issues that have affected the ways in which psychology operates. This list, whilst not exhaustive, is a means to offer critiques of psychology through personal experience and various antioppressive theoretical frameworks. The chapter will attempt to answer this question: *How can autoethnography become a means of creating an astute critical psychology in the Indian context?*

Using autoethnography, I will trace my trajectory in the field to make sense of my personal experience in the context of academia and praxis. This chapter will focus on my experience as a psychology student studying in India and the United Kingdom and my subsequent career in both countries. I will be centring my experience to write a reflective account of my career. In using autoethnography, I am attempting to provide a commentary on psychology as an academic discipline and its many social and cultural implications in Indian and wider global society. Through writing, I am attempting to verbalise discomfort and use this as a means of transformation. This is an idea I am borrowing from black feminist writer and activist Audre Lorde (1984).

Additionally, the chapter will use the feminist theory and mad, neurodiversity and disability studies perspectives to challenge notions of objectivity and neutrality. The inclusion of these two theoretical positions is personal, and the intention is to provide both a critique and an intervention that challenges the hegemonic position of psychology's assumptions. Both theoretical standpoints are also a means of providing intervention and contextualising personal experiences and both are activist-driven and accessible. In summarising my experience over a 20-year period, I hope to capture changing cultures and acknowledge my own constantly shifting position. Rather than an exercise in self-indulgence, this autoethnographic approach will serve to articulate the complexities, nuances, contradictions, and ambiguities in the discipline at a macrolevel.

## Autoethnography

Autoethnography is a qualitative method of research that has a few defining features. Grant (2019, p. 88) defines it as follows:

> Autoethnography is a form of narrative qualitative inquiry which values subjectivity, emotions, relationships with others, and epiphany and other

strong personal experiences as research resources. The approach focuses on self-culture intersections, in connecting the auto- biographical with the socio-cultural.

Grant (2010, p. 113) makes a case for autoethnography as a means to capture the transient:

> The individual story leaves traces of at least one path through a shifting, transforming and disappearing (multi-) cultural landscape. This could be viewed as either a quest for stability in an era of rapid change or a story of instability and ambiguity.

It is precisely this shifting landscape that will be explored through the aforementioned theoretical standpoints. Qualitative methodology allows for the possibilities of exploring data that is not easily quantifiable. Unlike an autobiography, autoethnography is a means of retelling one's story, with critical enquiry and theoretical standpoints woven into an analysis.

### Psychology in India: Two Cultures

The discipline of psychology was introduced to India during the colonial era in the early 20th century (1916). Two key figures were responsible for the direction the discipline took: Girendershekhar Bose and Narendranath Sen. Bose's work focused on psychoanalysis and therapy. Sen, by way of contrast, approached psychology more as an academic discipline than a psychotherapeutic one. Both of them wanted to create a psychology that was informed by Indian culture and looked for parallels and concepts in ancient Hindu scriptures. In recent years, their position has been critiqued for its casteist assumptions and centring Indian identity in an ancient precolonial past (Soans, 2024).

The Department of Psychology at Calcutta University, where Narendranath Sen became a Professor, continues to be a respected educational institute in India. Psychology in India lives in two dichotomous cultures, which are heavily influenced by the prevailing zeitgeist. The first is the American-influenced, quantitative, positivist, neuro-biological culture, and the other culture seeks cultural authenticity through the past. It would be unwise to assume that either of these cultures is unchanging or neutral. American psychology, which was produced in the middle of the 20th century, has come to be seen as a template for psychologies across the world. The influence of this psychology can be seen through the methodologies and concepts produced, there being seen as a universal template (Kayaoğlu & Batur, 2013). A solution to this psychology is often thought to be found in centring culture and indigenous perspectives. Whilst on the surface, it might seem like a logical solution, it is not without critique. 'Indigenous' can be a nebulous term that might affirm ethnocentric and nationalist ideas as natural. The term 'culture' is equally problematic in the way in which it gets applied to non-White societies, presented as unchanging, all pervasive, without individual variations.

Whenever I encounter the 'culture' term in the Indian or global context, I find it frustrating. In the Indian context, I often find it excludes people like me whose ethnic and religious identities are at best considered inauthentic and at worst dangerous. Following Anzaldúa (1987), my standpoint position in critical psychology is formed as a result of the tensions produced within these cultural borderlands. 'Borderlands' is a space that is externally seen with suspicion, its inauthentic nature perceived as threatening. Yet this duality allows for the creation of cultures – a queer, biracial, bicultural one in Anzaldúa's case and an intersectional feminist critical psychology in my own. By eschewing a call for authenticity and obeying academic rules, I am able to create and recreate psychology. The critiques are not limited to binaries but are constantly invested in deconstructing hegemonies.

Psychology, as I have experienced it, often validates commonsensical ideas about issues such as birth order, gender, and most importantly, normalcy. It is not uncommon to see mental health service users described in derogatory terms in literature or in everyday university department discussions. Anxieties about minority, oppressed, and psychiatrised groups often find themselves being reified through psychology, which has come to symbolise a moral authority.

### Becoming a Psychologist

My studies in psychology began as an undergraduate in 2002. At this time, psychology represented the prospect of a career in therapy or counselling. For most students, psychology is associated with some form of therapeutic intervention. Along with psychology, I also had to study Sociology and English Literature as major subjects. The course included the usual introductory concepts, experiments, and statistical modules. For many of us, this formal introduction to psychology was a disappointment, dramatically different from the pop psychology that had piqued our interest. Therapy, mind reading, serial killers, hypnotherapy, and other sensational ideas that are often associated with psychology were not part of the course, which focused exclusively on establishing the scientific and objective nature of psychology.

My master's degree was a means of achieving my goal of becoming a clinical psychologist. This rigorous two-year course began with an intense study of statistics, experimentation, and theoretical modules that focused on the biological, universal, and objective nature of psychology. This was followed by work in a rehabilitation clinic in a large South Indian metropolis city, followed by an MPhil, followed by a job as an assistant professor in a Bangalore college – this representing the academic and professional pattern of the collegiate system in some Indian universities. All of this happened whilst I felt unease with the psychology I was teaching. It is naïve assumption that we were helping people only made my discomfort stronger.

I finally applied for a PhD in the United Kingdom. I had met my professors, Erica Burman and Ian Parker, on their trip to India, and they articulated the things I thought but lacked the language or courage to articulate. Mesmerised by critical psychology, I took a course on it with my professor, Diptarup Chowdhry, during my MPhil. Being able to discuss ideas outside of psychology, narrowly defined, was exhilarating. These sessions and reading as many varied texts as my professors (Kenneth McLaughlin, Rachel Robbins, and Martin King) could give me and provided me with the means of refining my arguments. Arriving in Manchester in the dead of winter and meeting people from all over the world in this university town helped me in many ways. Living in a city that was mixed and has a history of activism with open seminars, protests, concerts, and art exhibitions almost every day reshaped and broadened my own worldview. Being treated as an intelligent grownup by my professors helped me think critically, and their constant challenges to my arguments helped me refine my thinking.

On my return to India, I have held various positions, some permanent and some precarious. However, I experienced intellectual loneliness – not being able to be immersed in art, culture, and discussions in a way I once was left me feeling isolated. Intent on helping myself, I decided to start my own network where I could meet scholars like myself. In the past year, organising and networking as Afro-Asian Critical Psychology has helped me feel less lonely, and it has also sharpened my intellect. Meeting precarious scholars and activists who are challenging systems has revitalised me intellectually. Many of us critical psychologists and activists in the Global South and Global North live and work in isolation. Precarity and threat of neoliberal academia impose a sterile camaraderie between colleagues, which is exacerbated by the fact that our ideas are not always welcome.

In the following sections, I will discuss my discontentment with the status quo in Indian psychology whilst delving into my personal history. I will connect my experience to theoretical positions that will help explain how autoethnography and critical psychology can provide an intervention and a means of creating psychologies that are striving towards justice.

## Discontentment with Therapy and Psychology

*Psychology as a Discipline of Power*

> My batchmates and I are standing in a small hospital room in scrubs. A middle-aged woman is lying on an operating table, hooked up to various machines. Nurses and doctors come in and check on her. We stand in the back of the room, waiting for the psychiatrist to come in. When he does, he talks about the patient's condition and why we are administering ECT. He asks us various questions about the procedure and why it is used. The 'patient' is spoken about as if she is not there. I wonder what she makes of us in the anesthetised state she is in. What does she think of five or six young students in the room who stood watching her talk about her 'condition'? Does she want us there, watching over her? Does she want this ECT? Was that lady who was given an ECT in front of a few psychology students really so 'mentally ill' that the only option was to give her a shock? Was the young man who claimed his food was poisoned and could hear voices dangerous and too far removed from reality?

During the final semester of my master's, I was introduced to antipsychiatry theorists, such as Thomas Szasz, Michel Foucault, and R.D. Laing, casually in a discussion group. We were asked by the professor leading the group if we thought psychotherapy could do no harm. We were amused as a class: the idea of therapy, the kind where people reveal the innermost burdens of their souls whilst being guided by a benign therapist, seemed absurd to us. However, after working as an intern in the psychiatric ward, this question began to feel less absurd. Psychologists didn't do harm after all – we entered the profession with the intention to help. Besides, we weren't qualified to prescribe medications or check on people in psychiatric wards. Talking was all we did, and it was harmless, or so we thought. As aspiring therapists, we had learnt how treating mental illness had come a long way from torture. With their emphasis on talking, psychotherapy and counselling were kind methods. In a positivist worldview, talking to a therapist for an hour was an inevitably kinder way of dealing with mental illness. The everyday indignities of being labelled, corrected, and pathologised never entered into our discussions.

The days of shackling people and burning them for daemon possession were over; that happened in a different era. Psychotherapy and psychiatry we were taught (in 2005–2007) were products of objective and scientific expertise. The witch trials and other acts of violence were things that happened far away, in northern, eastern, and rural India, not in Bangalore, an international IT city. Psychological violence was hard to categorise, as the language and means to describe it came from a place of discomfort and not socially validated expertise.

Antipsychiatrists with their bold claims made me question what I had learnt. Antipsychiatry, unlike clinical psychology, was not adamant in its claims of knowing the human mind completely. I did not claim to know exactly what mental illness was or how it could be categorised and treated. This is a discomfort I have gradually come to respect and understand as a space for discovery.

After my master's degree, I began work in a drug and alcohol rehabilitation clinic. This facility, like many others in India, was run on the 12-step principles of Alcoholics Anonymous (AA) and Narcotics Anonymous (NA), mostly run by people who were in different stages of recovery. I was an expert by education, not by experience, in this place. Through my work here, I quickly learned of the gendered and power-structured nature of psychology and psychiatry in the way they operated and manifested themselves. Scientific objectivity was trumpeted as a means of silencing arguments that, in any way, contradicted the realities of experts through lived experience.

Terms such as 'objectivity' started unravelling very quickly when I encountered everyday practice. There was no denying that some of the clients had difficulties with alcohol and drug consumption, which led to several problems with studies, employment, and interpersonal relationships. However, their addiction existed within a particular cultural context. The stereotypical young male addicts who listened to rock music, drove motorcycles, and went to raves existed alongside middle-aged men in office jobs and large families. They, in turn, existed with young and old Indian women: the cool women with tattoos who went to parties, and the aunties who cooked three meals a day, dressed in conservative saris, raised children, and visited places of worship. In Indian culture, addiction is rarely thought of as a female problem or a problem affecting Indian women. Our ideas of addiction are based on images and research on male subjects. Encountering Indian women as addicts brought with it prejudices and misogyny that made their way into the way the women were treated. Whilst diagnostic categories brought about their own form of abuse, so did 'culture'. It is in these everyday practices that the notion of neutrality can be deconstructed. When victim life stories are de-privileged, knowledge systems perpetuate structural disadvantage. In doing so, she points out how unequal such systems of knowledge create a structural disadvantage.

In related terms, it is, in fact, exactly on these terms – neutrality, objectivity, and rationality – that psychology most forcefully assumed its position in the apparatus of social control in apartheid and capitalist South Africa (Böhmke & Tlali, 2008, p. 122). Tlali's challenge to neutrality opens up the discussion about the material and political conditions in which psychology builds up a corpus of scientificity. For many years, I could not express my discomfort with certain aspects of scientific objectivity that psychology proposed. Numerically validated evidence in the form of quantitative research was the basis of most psychology I had studied. Yet, it rarely represented my reality. Studies conducted in 1950s America on a white, male, university-educated population felt alien at times. Whilst human experience transcends time and space, there are times when these studies fail to acknowledge the culture in which they emerged. Prejudice and well-being might be universal in some ways; however, the history and social context in which they exist is what makes them unique and a topic of study through several eras and social conditions. Whilst my sociology modules engaged with the everyday anxieties of India, my psychology modules did not reflect that. This decontextualised psychology has done little to address the imbalances of everyday life in India or provide structurally sound solutions to what ails us as a society (Matthew & Pellissery, 2024).

## Section 3: Feminist Interventions

Feminism has been a significant force to reckon with in the 20th century. As a movement, it has challenged notions of gender that are thought of as natural and biological. Perhaps the triumph of feminism has been in the way it has leant itself to activism, academia, and everyday interventions. Feminism's strength lies in its reflexivity and attention to social, political, and cultural change.

My introduction to feminist theory came in the form of seminars and workshops on the issue during my MPhil. Whilst I was aware of feminism and its arguments; it is safe to say I did not engage with it cerebrally, as I have come to do so now. However, it was my PhD that really introduced me to theoretical feminism and local activism, which have come to shape so many interventions in the last few decades. My supervisor introduced me to several feminist authors and arguments that challenged various notions of womanhood and gender. Being immersed in literature, which was critical, opened up a new avenue into psychology and the social sciences. Feminism gave me the language to articulate ideas that I could only vaguely construct in my mind. Feminism, as Audre Lorde (1981) points out, helps articulate anger and thoughts that are often written off as personal discomfort. Lorde's work was accessible and struck a deep chord in me. Her brand of intersectional black feminism addressed dissonance that was felt but rarely articulated.

Whilst it is widely noted that psychology departments are mostly made up of female students and lecturers; this does not exempt us from gendered politics. Kagan and Lewis (1990) noted how psychology departments are made up of women students and staff, but positions of power remain in the hands of men. They went on to discuss the emotional labour that is associated with psychology, which makes it a discipline associated with women. This has been my experience studying and working in India and the United Kingdom. I have taught numerous courses that are dominated by women students; a similar situation exists in the staff room too, whilst the Head of Department and Dean's office are a different story.

> A young colleague calls me to the college cafeteria in tears. She has been checked for wearing bright makeup, jewellery, and clothes. She is advised by the older female management that she is attracting inappropriate attention. Another colleague joins us, complaining that she has been checked for not wearing any make-up or jewellery, and her unmarried status is brought into question. I share a similar story of being checked for being unmarried and childless as a psychology lecturer; my minimal make-up and jewellery are brought into question too. Being unmarried and childless in my 30s, they explain, makes me incapable of understanding people and psychology. In order to ensure women teachers are respected and look professional, they have to wear a sari. No other national dress is permitted. This particular garment, as stated in various circulars from the national university regulator tells us, will ensure students treat us as mature educators and help maintain a national identity. Sitting in the cafeteria, the one place without CCTV cameras, which are dotted all along the classrooms and staff rooms, we get to talk freely. Much of the system is geared for surveillance of staff and students, with technophilia being upheld as a means of progress and justice. In the United Kingdom, no one asks me personal questions or comments about my life choices. Back in India, my personal life is dissected in order to question my credibility.

Women, by their very presence in psychology, do not guarantee a feminist solidarity. Psychology departments in India and the United Kingdom that I have worked in are not feminist by virtue of identity. Most of us in the field are homogenous when it comes to our backgrounds: middle class, urban, upper caste, cisgendered, and heterosexual. We often perpetuate the status quo and sexism that come with our position. Whilst there is a point to be made about psychology being heavily dominated by western thought; it is in everyday conversations about femininity, marriage, and childrearing that psychologists assert normality as gatekeepers of cultural hegemony. I would argue that these transmissions of normality make their way uncritically into positivist psychology, which critical psychology attempts to deconstruct. Our inward beliefs are imposed on the world around us through banal studies on well-being, stress, and personality types. This lack of self-interrogation has meant that we are often upholding the very structures that oppress us and other women less privileged than us. Feminist critiques of psychology are not merely about identity or inclusion without attention to politics.

> The complexity and breadth of feminist aims mean that feminist psychology should not be like any other field of psychology. It should criticize not just psychological objects, methods and theories, but also the institutional and wider social and political situation of psychology.
>
> *(Squire, 1990, p. 77)*

Squire's recommendation leads to a deeper examination of feminist aims, such as power, culture, and zeitgeist. This line of enquiry takes us to larger issues beyond identity and leads us to introspect about how systems uphold a status quo. At a time when we are talking about the neoliberal university and the emotional labour of women in the workplace, a feminist analysis helps us peel away notions of professionalism, institutionalism, and epistemic sexism.

Applying Squire's analysis to my experience, I can see the way in which I played into the idea of being able to help people deal with emotional issues through my own position in society. As a middle-class woman who has some amount of caste privilege, my very appearance has been managed by the educational system. The mandatory sari dress code, no sleeveless allowed, reifies the dominant culture. My femininity must follow certain contradictory norms; for example, make-up and jewellery are frowned upon if present, and I may equally be ticked off for not wearing any and looking impoverished. Those ideas permeate the classroom and the staff-room alike. Bold assertions about Indian families as curative, that give scant regard to heteronormative, casteist, and classist assumptions, make their way into psychology teaching, research, clinical practice, and eventually into policy.

## Decolonisation Is Not Enough

In the grand narrative of decolonising psychology and mental health, the micronarrative of 'debhaminising' has been erased or written off as being anti-Indian. Decolonisation is not Debrahminisation. The everyday indignities to the erasure of Dalit and other marginalised people's histories in India are not allied to the decolonisation claims that seek the restoration of Brahminical supremacy. Dalit people make up the lowest caste in the Indian caste system, with all manner of abuse perpetrated against them, coupled with social and legal neglect. Brahmins, on the other hand, occupy the top-most caste in Indian society. Scholarship by Dalit people focuses on deconstructing hegemonic ideas. The postcolonial/ decolonial scholarship based on ethnonationalist and Brahminical claims fails to address the plurality of Indian history and communities that are deemed inauthentic. Perpetuating orientialist fantasies, these psychologies promote the idea that cultural differences exist and that they are unchanging in India and the Majority of the World. Dalit scholars, such as Braj Ranjan Mani (2005), talk about debhaminising history as a means of understanding epistemic, social, cultural, and political violence in India. Debrahminisation attempts to decentre uncontested narratives about India and its history by providing alternative perspectives from Dalit histories.

## Deconstructing Ethnocentrism through Feminism

Feminist intervention in psychology would need to consider how gender can be used to perpetuate ethnocentricism and religious nationalism. Claims of tradition, authenticity, domesticity, and spiritual superiority are tropes of nationalism; they are, as McClintock (1993) points out, invariably gendered and dangerous. The dissemination of this ideology into everyday life and academia has meant that certain narratives about the nation can be told with scant regard to their veracity. In India's case, nationalism has been a part of the postcolonial and decolonial narrative since before independence. Framing women through a spiritual and domestic lens has ensured that they have been seen as bearers of national culture (Chatterjee, 1989). This has meant that women are both keepers and reproducers of culture, and also its scapegoats. Embodying this duality of being both tyrants and victims has meant that women and feminists rarely question their role in the perpetuation of caste, class, heteronormative, and ableist ideology. In upholding 'postcolonial myths' (Ubale, 2020), we have created the idea of an unchanging India, which was disrupted by colonialism, returning to the imagined past. It is no surprise, then, that indigenous, postcolonial, and decolonial psychologies insist on trauma, loss, and nostalgia. Applying an intersectional framework that feminism already possesses can help deconstruct the category of woman and peel away layers of privilege whilst addressing how multiple oppressions play a role in women's lives.

*Critical Feminist Psychology*

In leading itself to intersectionality, reflexivity, and activism, feminism allows for discourse to constantly evolve and adapt. Critical feminist psychology, as I envision it, would then be constantly examining sources of power, privilege, and how the psy-complex disseminates into everyday life.

Feminism has a unique position in society. On the one hand, feminists (myself included) are seen as dangers to society, destroying families and instigating women. On the other hand, we are seen as an anachronism – elitist or completely untrained – when it comes to including our perspectives in academia. My PhD supervisor, Dr Rachel Robbins, would often say that feminism's strength lies in the diversity of thought it reflects upon the diversity of the feminists. It is through these diverse arguments and plurality of experiences that I found feminist writing and activism deeply stimulating.

Fears of critiquing non-western societies and their cultures exist within western academia and western feminism – a legitimate fear based on historical factors. However, liberal ideologies, such as feminism, mad studies, neurodiversity, and disability studies, need to be consistent in their critiques of abuse and not allow culture to be weaponised against marginal groups. In conceptualising the Majority of the World as driven by culture, western scholars and activists have allowed for various bad-faith arguments around culture to dominate discourse, which has drowned out the voices of minorities. Anzaldúa's feminist critique of culture(s) looks at the ways in which 'traditional' cultures are gendered and transmitted.

> Culture forms our beliefs. We perceive the version of reality that it communicates. Dominant paradigms, predefined concepts that exist as unquestionable, unchallengeable, are transmitted to us through the culture. Culture is made by those in power - men. Males make the rules and laws; women transmit them. How many times have I heard mothers and mothers-in law tell their sons to beat their wives for not obeying them, for being bociconas (big mouths), for being callejeras (going to visit and gossip with neighbors), for expecting their husbands to help with the rearing of children and the housework, for wanting to be something other than housewives?
>
> *(Anzaldúa, 1987, p. 38)*

Anzaldúa's autoethnographic work maps the 'Borderlands' she encounters in her everyday life. Cultures, which claim legitimacy and purity, reject her for not being completely authentic. However, her queer feminist critiques are interventions against cultural hegemony. Extending feminist intersectionality into other avenues, I will now turn to discuss how alliances can be formed through mad, neurodivergent, and disability perspectives.

*Section 5: Decentring Expertise Centring Mad Perspectives*

After a busy day at work, driven to tears by yet another seminar on schizophrenics being difficult to treat, I come home and start scrolling through alternatives to schizophrenia treatment. I think an old issue of Asylum Magazine had an article about the Hearing Voices Network. I stumble upon a YouTube video called 'A doctor who hears voices'. Someone called Rufus May is talking about alternatives to hearing voices. He explains how to work with someone who hears voices; he asks questions about the voices and how they make the person hearing them feel, and he listens attentively. At some point in the documentary, he reveals he heard voices as a teenager and confronts his former psychiatrist about not listening to him. A few years later, during my PhD, I would organise a seminar with Rufus May as a speaker.

### Mad Studies as an Alternative and a Means of Challenging the Hegemony of Psychology

Mad, neurodiversity, and disability studies represent a paradigm shift in how we think of a group of people who have historically been seen as noncredible. The 'abnormal' mind and body' have been and continue to be a site for curing. The power of psychiatric diagnosis has often been written through cases of abuse, which, whilst true, often forgets that this is symptomatic of a larger structure. Subtle forms of abuse and everyday indignities often go unrecognised, whereas sensational cases of abuse and violence grab limited attention. Cases of extreme violence where the victim is proven beyond a doubt to be innocent are believed. Gender, sexuality, past history, dress, lying, and any kind of behavioural infraction on the part of the victims make them less believable and more deserving of their abuse. Outrage that follows against psychiatric abuse sees these extreme cases as an aberration whilst ignoring the daily abuse that is built into the system.

From this point on, I will use the term 'Madneurodis' studies to collectively refer to the three perspectives, for ease of the reader, rather than clubbing each of these areas as one. Psychology and psychiatry have often reinforced that through everyday practices and more formal systems such as diagnostic taxonomies. Through my studies and work in a rehab, I saw a way in which I could wield power and hold a claim to truth by virtue of being 'a professional'. This dichotomy of sane versus insane has meant that the everyday injustices, infantalisation, and exclusion of a group of people were justified as being for their own good. Thus, the epistemic and hermeneutic injustice perpetrated on this group could be justified not out of cruelty but on grounds of kindness and therapeutic intervention. In seeing mad, queer, and feminist perspectives gaining momentum, I feel a sense of pleasure. The agency that has been denied to several psychiatrised people has found its way in activism, academia, and social media.

> Mad studies which has evolved from the activist histories and thinking of mad people ourselves in conjunction with allies.
>
> *(Reaume, 2021, p. 100)*

In being able to shatter the propriety of 'correct procedures', we have been able to move beyond artifice and towards a psychology of justice. I consider this a *paradigm shift*, as these perspectives have challenged the way we think about issues of scientific credibility and knowledge in psychology in the following ways.

### Expertise

Madneurodis studies and activism decentre expertise from psychologists, policymakers, and people who have traditionally held power when it comes to making decisions about those who are psychiatrised. White's (2021) vision of mad liberation is based on challenging epistemic hermeneutic violence that has devalued the voices of service users on the basis of their identity.

### Educational and Institutional Validation

Whilst madneurodis studies are academically respectable, and some of its proponents work in traditional academic or clinical jobs, those aren't necessarily considered a benchmark for these perspectives to flourish.

### Solidarity on the Basis of Lived Experience

There is recognition of common experiences of marginalisation that binds the madneurodis movement together. The three movements are built on the recognition that formal systems of knowledge weaponise care. Whilst there may be different levels of agreement over diagnosis and intervention, there is a common thread of solidarity and recognition that lived experience provides an insight and level of expertise into one's own condition.

### Human Difference as a Space for Change and Understanding

In mainstream psychology, different behaviours and bodies have been written about as pathological. These differences have been seen from the perspective of people who have been considered normal. Psychology's ideas of normality are rarely challenged. Chapman (2022), in making a case for 'Neurodivergent Marxism', points out how hyperableism and normality are propagated through the valourisation of productivity. In linking behavioural traits with capitalist, ideals of work certain neurodiverse traits are used to strengthen ableism.

### Variations of Human Experience

In decentring certain kinds of minds and bodies as normal, Madneurodis perspectives place contextual normalcy as existing within oppressive social and material conditions. This isn't to say that difficulties arising from disability, neurodiversity, and mental illness are imagined and can be cured through reasonable adjustment. It is, however, a recognition that there is much to be learned through changing our ideas about normalcy and ways of being.

Centring perspectives of those with lived experience have broken the binary between positivist psychology and indigenous psychology (Soans, 2022). The polar debate between positivist psychology and indigenous psychology speaks about the mad, neurodivergent, and disabled individual as if they have no agency. In the many seminars, I have attended, speakers have spoken of the burden 'these people' are or how their relatives need constant care. Constant infantalisation of 'these people' has meant that psychology has been able to speak for people in ways that are unhelpful. Mad movements have perhaps answered the question my professor asked all those years ago about psychotherapy causing harm.

### Lived Experience and the Plurality of Ideas

Service users are not a monolithic group, nor are their perspectives, which contain ambiguity and contradiction. This does not invalidate the movement, far from it, as by acknowledging plurality of perspectives mad studies and service users are able to reconcile the contradictory nature of behaviour and psychology. This stands in stark contrast to the kind of psychology that often studies behaviours in isolation in laboratories, and that produces contradictory results because of this.

### Writing Critical Psychology in Challenging Times in the Wake of Nationalism and Everyday Violence Against Scholars

At the time of writing this chapter, I have met and worked with academics who are in precarious positions. These are caused by neoliberal conditions, which have meant that their work is devalued in many academic circles or is difficult to produce. Another precarious group is made up of scholars whose work has been met with criticism and sanctions due to its critiques of nationalism and state power.

Thought is under attack, too. Criticism, debate, and discussions are taboo as far as the ruling dispensation is concerned. Whilst many institutions of higher learning, research, and academic excellence find their future under threat, many women are being cruelly threatened, intimidated, and viciously targeted because not only do they dare to take on the Sangh Parivar[1] but also because women today are highly visible in the struggle against them (Ali, 2017, p. 215).

In using my experience as a means of autoethnographic writing, I hope to have effectively challenged assumptions I have in the past held about psychology and my role in furthering various oppressive hegemonies. Turning towards critical psychology has helped me articulate my discomfort with psychology. Foster's explanation of what critical psychology is sheds light on what critical psychology critiques.

> Critical psychology is critical in two main senses. First, it is critical of the field of psychology itself, its theories, assumptions, methods, techniques, practices and research problems. In this regard it targets two main problems of mainstream psychology, the ontological issue of 'self-contained individualism' and the epistemological issue of positivism–empiricism. Second, it is critical in a dedication to large-scale political projects, a concern with social transformation, justice, human rights and welfare; it proposes values which are directed towards human betterment, helping those denied a voice, those with little power. Put more abstractly, its interests are emancipatory.
>
> *(Foster, 2008, p. 92)*

In applying autoethnography – a critical qualitative method of inquiry – to my experience, I have attempted to critique the discipline of psychology, its methodologies, and its assumptions. In locating myself within my national and academic culture, I have attempted to ground my critiques in the zeitgeist and wider culture that exists and forms a circular relationship with psychology. Using autoethnography in writing this critique is a personal and political decision. The devaluing of qualitative research as a legitimate method of inquiry is a political choice psychologists have made. The limited space for qualitative research in Indian psychology is no accident; it has legitimised the claims of psychology being a legitimate science. Allying itself with neoliberal ideology and psychology in India often reaffirms cultural biases and ideas.

> Qualitative research in psychology opens a space for turning mere academic investigation into prefigurative political practice, for turning qualitative psychology into something that is challenging and transformative.
>
> *(Parker, 2005, p. 131)*

Parker's call for transformation can be interpreted in the following ways for me: first, I map out my transformation though looking back at my career and noticing what brought about changes in my position. Second, it involves using my standpoints and the theories that have influenced me to create a critical psychology that attempts to address socio-political issues. Looking inward and applying the critical gaze required of autoethnography challenges several assumptions about objectivity and neutrality. In locating oneself as a research subject, researchers turn their gaze inward towards themselves. In writing this autoethnography, I am eschewing standard practices of psychology by scrutinising my own thoughts as research data.

## Note

1 The Sangh Parivar (family of RSS) is a term referring to the collection of right-wing organisations allied to Hindutva ideology. This movement represents a nationalist ideology and has militant supporters who have taken to vigilantism to combat what they perceive as national threats.

## References

Ali, S. (2017). Patriarchy, caste and neoliberalism: violence against women in India. *WOMEN PHILOSOPHERS' JOURNAL: Intellectuals, philosophers, Women in India: Endangered Species, 4–5*, 202–216. (9) (PDF) "Intellectuals, Philosophers, Women in India: Endangered Species" - Revue des femmes philosophes JOURNAL ISSUE N° 4–5 / December 2017 (researchgate.net)

Anzaldúa, G. (1987) *Borderlands/la frontera: The new mestiza*. Aunt Lute Books.

Böhmke, W., & Tlali, T. (2008). Bodies and behaviour: A history of scientific psychology in South Africa. In D. Painter & C. Van Ommen (Eds.), *Interiors: A history of psychology in South Africa* (pp. 125–151). Unisa Press.

Chapman, R. (2022). Towards neurodivergent Marxism. *Asylum Magazine, 29*(3), 13–14.

Chatterjee, P. (1989). Colonialism, nationalism, and colonialized women: The contest in India. *American Ethnologist, 16*(4), 622–633. https://www.jstor.org/stable/645113

Foster, D. (2008) Critical psychology: A historical overview. In C. van Ommen & D. Painter (Eds.), *Interiors: A history of psychology in South Africa* (pp. 92–124). UNISA Press.

Grant, A. (2010). Autoethnographic ethics and rewriting the fragmented self. *Journal of Psychiatric and Mental Health Nursing, 17*(2), 111–116. https://doi.org/10.1111/j.1365-2850.2009.01478.x

Grant, A. (2019). Dare to be a wolf: Embracing autoethnography in nurse educational research. *Nurse Education Today, 82*, 88–92. https://doi.org/10.1016/j.nedt.2019.07.006

Kagan, C., & Lewis, S. (1990). "Where's your sense of humour?" Swimming against the tide in higher education. In E. Burman (Ed.), *Feminists and psychological practice* (pp. 18–32). Sage.

Kayaoğlu, A., & Batur, S. (2013). Critical psychology in Turkey: Recent developments. *Annual Review of Critical Psychology*, *10*, 916–931. turkey-ii-916–931.pdf (wordpress.com)

Lorde, A. (1981). The uses of anger: Women responding to racism. *BlackPast.org.* https://blackpast.org/1981-audre-lorde-uses-anger-women-responding-racism

Lorde, A. (1984). *Sister outsider: Essays and speeches.* Crossing Press.

Mani, B. R. (2005). *Debrahmanising history: Dominance and resistance in Indian society.* Manohar.

Matthew, L., & Pellissery, S. (2024). Peasant psychology: A preamble to indigenizing Indian psychology. *Annual Review of Critical Psychology*, *17*, 60–74. 0-covercontentseditorial.pdf (wordpress.com)

McClintock, A. (1993). Family feuds: gender, nationalism and the family. *Feminist Review*, *44*(1), 61–80. https://doi.org/10.2307/1395196

Parker, I. (2005). *Qualitative psychology: Introducing radical research.* Open University Press.

Reaume, G. (2021). How is mad studies different from anti-psychiatry and critical psychiatry? In P. Beresford & J. Russo (Eds.), *The Routledge international handbook of mad studies* (pp. 98–107). Routledge.

Soans, S. (2022). A critique of the romanticisation of pre-psychiatric systems of care in the Global South. *Asylum Magazine*, *29*(1), 30–31.

Soans, S. (2024). Challenging decolonisation and postcolonialism in India and South Asia: Directions for critical psychology. *Annual Review of Critical Psychology*, *17*, 200–211. (wordpress.com)

Squire, C. (1990). Feminism as antipsychology: learning and teaching in feminist psychology. In E. Burman (Ed.), *Feminists and psychological practice* (pp. 76–88). Sage.

Ubale, A. (2020). Culture question: Western and Indian context. *Epitome: International Journal of Multidisciplinary Research*, *6*(10), 1–10. Abstract (epitome-journals.com)

White, W. (2021). Re-writing the master narrative: A prerequisite for mad liberation. In P. Beresford & J. Russo (Eds.), *The Routledge international handbook of mad studies* (pp. 76–89). Routledge.

# 17

# MENTAL HEALTH AND THE BODY

## An Autoethnography of Neuralgia, Migraine, and Insulin Resistance

*Colette Szczepaniak*

### Introduction

Emotions are primary in the body. One first experiences bodily emotions and then recognizes them. However, it is not a 'zero–one' situation,[1] since experiencing the body is culturally filtered and socially controlled (Konecki et al., 2023). When it is culturally filtered and socially controlled too much, you start denying your emotions, which leads you to feel that you are invisible and not seen by others, including those who should be closest. And when that happens for 30 years, your body gives you painful signs that there is one person you must take care of: yourself. Our felt bodily emotions are socialized in the same way as our behavior. Some emotions are socially accepted, and others are not. This means that experiencing bodily feelings is socially regulated.

This chapter presents a somatic phenomenological autoethnographic inquiry (Bentz, 2016). 'Through somatic phenomenological inquiry, we are able to release the personal accumulations of power distortions such as trauma, ego, money, and sensual decadence, thereby opening the space to plug in to the transcendant' (Bentz, 2016, pp. 60–61). I look at this work as an 'auto – work on identity' (Konecki, 2007). Which means that, for me, it works in the service of the development of my self-image and identity in respect of the specific social world in which I am immersed (Konecki, 2018). Moreover, my aim as a woman is to finally write myself: a woman 'must start writing about women and introduce women to the world of writing, from which they have been forced out as violently as they have been forced out of feeling their bodies' (Cixous, 1993, p. 147). Since, 'We can

DOI: 10.4324/9781003408963-17

only write from the space of the personal, about our own bodies, feelings, hungers, desires, hopes, dreams, fears' (Denzin, 2011, p. 11).

---

## VIGNETTE 1  Neuralgia

I believe today that we can choose what constitutes our 'family'. For me, those are my friends and people I care about, and they care about me. They are always ready to help, don't judge, and we are always willing to spend time together. However, I was taught and socialized to spend Christmas and other important events like anniversaries or birthdays with people related to me by blood. Spending Christmas with the blood family was one of their expectations I had to meet.

For a few years, we spent Christmas and other events at my house. My husband is at sea.[2] Everyone is talking; I hear somebody's saying that it's 'the most wonderful time of the year', like in the song. Everyone is laughing and enjoying their time, except me. I feel like I am watching my life through aquarium glass and that I'm the fish without a voice. I'm sitting there and watching while someone tells me that the food I prepared is not so tasty and that the room somebody's sleeping in is not warm enough. Sounds and gestures are reaching me in slow motion. I think that this is the moment I start to realize something is wrong, but I don't yet know what it is. What I do know is that I miss my husband; I regret that he's not with us, with his children. No one cares, and no one asks about my feelings and emotions. Nothing new. I feel alone.[3] My feelings and emotions were never important to anybody from the blood family.

All the Christmas food is ready. We are sitting at the table and starting to eat, and when I want to take the very first bite, I suddenly feel that I can't swallow anything. 'By censoring the body, one also censors breath and speech' (Cixous, 1993, p. 152). I feel pain in the front of my neck, in the esophagus. I can't even swallow the saliva; the pain is that strong. No one cares—as usual. 'Take a throat pill', someone says. 'Yeah, sure', I respond, but somewhere inside me, I want to scream that I feel empty, that I feel lonely.[4] I feel that way, but how can I say it out loud? Should I say something like: 'Hey, family, I feel lonely with you?'[5] If I wanted to be honest, I should say something more like: 'You omit me, you omit my feelings, emotions… You've done this for years'. I feel that the only things they care about Christmas are the decorations and the tree. For me, Christmas was about feeling good about the people you're spending the Christmas with. Neuralgia was evoked by my inability to say my thoughts out loud. 'A voiceless soul/Trapped in the body' (Metta, 2010, p. 120). I didn't know about it when it happened for the first time.

I don't remember in what circumstances this happened to me again, but when it did, I went to the laryngologist. He looked into my throat and said: 'everything is all right, it's typical neuralgia. Do you have much stress right now? 'Stress?, I asked. 'I write my PhD and have two little kids, and my husband is a seaman'. 'Don't you have a family to support you?', he asked. I thought then that I had a family, and for the whole life I'd heard that 'family is the most important thing in life'. Now I know that it's not true. The most important is *a person* in *my* family. He prescribed me a medicament with pregabalin. After, when I met with my blood family, usually experiencing this neuropathic pain, I took this pill, and the pain was gone. But then I felt dizziness and a balance disturbance and had to ask someone to drive me to my children's creche because I wasn't able to drive the car. Another time, I took pregabalin after a meeting with my blood family, and I got a terrible rash on my chest. At one session, I told my therapist about it, and she said: 'But you know why that is?' 'What, the rash?', I asked. She nodded. I held my breath: 'because I am allergic to this medicament?' 'Because your body gives you signals and you try to ignore them by taking a pill', she responded.

When I told somebody from the blood family that I had neuralgia, I heard: 'Neuralgia! And what is that? Another invention from the modern medicine?' or 'Oh, come on! I am sure the doctor is not right about the diagnosis!' Or at best: 'Yeah, you have so much stress with writing PhD'. 'What is wrong with me?'—this was my first thought, which has always accompanied me through most of my life and was caused by me constantly dismissing my true self and fighting with the person I really was. But hopefully the next thought was more like: 'What is my body trying to tell me?' This was my first step to healing.

---

\* \* \*

I have often felt surrounded by people whom I regard as narcissists, which disturbs me. In modern psychology and sociology, the concept of narcissism is widely examined, written about, and talked about. Intuitive understandings may suggest that a narcissistic person is characterized by self-adoration (Sennett, 2009). This is driven by Greek mythology about Narcissus, who was so impossibly handsome that he fell in love with his own image. However, narcissistic people are more self-hating than self-loving (although they would never admit that to themselves). Narcissists don't recognize the needs of others. Their feelings of magnitude conflict with their feelings of emptiness and narcissism.

Giddens (2012) argues that consumption and consumer capitalism contribute to the development of narcissism on a large scale. According to him, the creation of an educated and discerning public collapsed long ago under the pressure of consumerism—the 'society of semblance'. Sennett similarly argues that one of the causes of the spread of narcissism in contemporary society is that its public sphere is 'dead'. So, in their private lives, people are searching for something which is lacking in the public sphere (Sennett, 2009). Complementing Giddens and Sennett, Lasch (1980) contends that narcissism is a defensive response to fear and feeling guilty, related to the threats posed by the modern world. According to Lasch, narcissism reflects indifference toward the future and the past, 'destroying' both of them in the context of the fear of threats from current reality.

One reason I couldn't speak out loud is that narcissistic people can play the victim very well. Playing the victim allows the ego to remain intact by searching for 'guilty others'. Narcissists blame the world and, in some cases, seek validation from people who are prepared to rescue them (McCullough et al., 2003). Children growing up in narcissistic environments can dismiss their 'True Self' as defective or unlovable, instead forming a 'grandiose' self to overcompensate (Tanasugarn, 2022).

\*\*\*

When I realized that my body gave me signals that something was wrong, without me knowing what exactly was wrong, I started long-term therapy. It took me some time to understand that I always felt dissatisfaction about me and my actions from my blood family. I could always do better; I always felt not good enough, but I thought that was 'natural'. I was raised in the feeling of being 'not enough': not enough smart, not enough pretty, not enough hard working. Even when I was alone in a new place of living, with two kids at the age of two and six months, doing my PhD, taking care of the dog, house, and the garden all alone. I could be still better: thinner, not so thin, more cheerful, more passionate. Even when I write all this, I feel gentle prick on the left side of my throat. It reminds me that I am important. My feelings, opinions, and the truth about me and being fine with myself is important. The most important thing in my life.

Knowing this, I stopped spending Christmas and attending other events with my blood family. Now I spend my children's birthdays and celebrate other events with the family I have chosen: friends and people who are open to the person I really am and not the definition of perfectionism they want me to be.

\* \* \*

Claude Lévi-Strauss (2012) suggests that the nature of family relations is determined in particular types of society by the types of social structure. The cultural anthropologist Lewis Henry Morgan argued that words used to describe family members, such as 'mother' or 'cousin', indicate the rights and responsibilities associated with particular family members within households as well as the larger community. Those titles or labels, like father or aunt, describe how a person fits into a family as well as the obligations he or she has to others (Gilliland, 2018). The concepts of status and role are crucial for thinking about the behaviors that are expected of individuals who occupy various positions in the family. Different cultures may define the relative statuses involved in families differently. 'Role' refers to the set of behaviors expected of an individual who occupies a particular status. Roles, like statuses, are cultural ideals or expectations, and there will be different understandings of how family members meet these expectations. Statuses and roles change within cultures over time (Gilliland, 2018). The American researcher David Murray Schneider (1980) pointed out that family affinities are primarily a cultural construct and are not everywhere expressed in genealogical relations.

It is worth emphasizing that in Polish culture there is a strong Catholic Church influence on society and, without a doubt, there is also corresponding Biblical support for the traditional family designed by God. The Bible defines the family structure and rules for family members and also emphasizes the importance of the Church family as an essential component of healthy growth.[6]

---

## VIGNETTE 2   Migraine

I am alone at home with my three-month-old daughter, doing the dishes in the kitchen. I look at her lying on the floor and I see only half of her face. This is weird, I am winking twice—nothing changes. I look somewhere behind her—it's like only one eye is working. I ignore it and start putting the cups into the cupboard. One cup turns out to be too heavy for my hand and falls. I can't feel my right hand now and still can't see out of my right eye. 'Something is going on', I think, and now this terrible headache comes. I feel neck, teeth, tongue, and head pain, like all the muscles in my head have tightened. I must lie down. I put my daughter in the trolley, leave her on the terrace, open the window to hear her, and lie on the couch. I fall asleep and I wake up two hours later panicking, with a thought in my mind: 'where is my daughter?!' I run to the terrace window, look into the pram, and see that she is sleeping as if nothing has happened. I go to the kitchen to take a pill. The standard headache pill, like ibuprom or paracetamol, doesn't work. I feel very bad for the next three days. I have a headache, I feel very weak, and I get cystitis, which is usual in migraines with auras. I don't do much—just the basic and necessary things. However, taking care of a baby with no chance of help from anyone is exhausting enough.

This is happening in the pandemic, and the only chance to have contact with the doctor is via an online visit. I visit the neurologist, and after listening to my symptoms, she states that this is a migraine with aura. She prescribed me sumatriptan, which I must take just when I feel predictive symptoms. These usually include visual disturbances in my right eye, such as flashes of light, lines, stars, or waves. When I feel the migraine is coming, I take this pill, but if I don't notice predictive symptoms, it will be too late and no drug will work. I will suffer much pain. My migraines taught me to be mindful about the signals my body gives me. I am now much more attentive to what I feel in my body. It happened that I missed predictive symptoms once, but I didn't allow myself to do it again because I knew that the way I felt was important.

I inherited migraines from my dad, who has never taken care of himself, and his greatest pleasure in life is overworking. He didn't even go to the doctor with his migraines—he preferred to suffer and play the role of a hero: 'look, I have a headache and I still work!' Do I have to live like this? Do I have to accept my life with migraines and aura?

---

\*\*\*

Is there a chance for an individual to develop her or his 'true self' in the face of the conventionally expected status and role for an individual? We are not self-contained atoms but social individuals. Hopefully though, a family doesn't live on a desert island, and there are also other circumstances influencing the development ourselves. Those are neighborhood, social contacts, social class, gender, ethnicity, religion, and the beliefs and values in which we are educated. 'Those who surround us will judge, influence and mirror an image of our self-back to us in many different ways' (Burkitt, 2008, p. 4). *Self is something that has to be made and to discover.* As Grant (2010, p. 580) writes:

> The act of social self-making is an active one, drawing on biographical and narrative resources, and an individual becomes a self in so far as s/he can take the attitude of others and act towards her or himself as others act.
>
> *(Grant, 2010, p. 580)*

According to Mead (1962), no individual could be reflective without first becoming an object to herself or himself. The capacity to differentiate and to establish a dialog between a personal 'I' and a social 'me' is acquired mainly through language. The social self is also an object for others in terms of their ability to confer or deny identity.

---

## VIGNETTE 3    Insulin Resistance

Something has been wrong for months—I made some changes concerning my way of life; for example, I introduced meditation and regular therapy, but it appeared it wasn't enough. I gained 8 kg in four months; I felt very sleepy and exhausted every morning after a night with eight to ten hours of sound sleep. I felt tired every minute of every day. I was exhausted and therefore grumpy and dissatisfied with everyone and everything. I started to exercise, and after two months of doing regular sports, I gained another 4 kg, but I felt that something was not okay with my body. I had a blood test to see if my thyroid works well and went with the results to the endocrinologist. She said that everything looked fine, but the symptoms I had indicated insulin resistance.

After this visit, I told my husband what the doctor had said. His response was: 'You?! Insulin resistance?! I don't know... That's another new disease?!' 'Let's firstly check it because I think you've made it up'. I had the blood test again to verify my insulin and glucose levels after one and two hours, and the insulin level turned out to be much higher than it should be. I showed my husband these results, and he said: 'I am sure that this means nothing. Go to the diabetologist and you'll see that it's nothing wrong with you'. I went to the diabetologist, the next day, and after seeing those blood test results and hearing about my lifestyle, doing a PhD with two little kids and a seafarer husband, she said: 'Too much cortisol in your life! One night without sleep doubles cortisol levels'. 'I haven't slept through the night for 3 years', I respond. 'My recommendation for you, from a mother to a mother, is not to work. Little children are exhausting enough and if you have no support from anybody...' she didn't end. 'But writing and doing research makes me happy. This is something I was made for. It is not work and doing PhD which exhausts me. It's a family life', I thought; however, I didn't say it loud because I realized that this doctor was very conservative, and she also tried to convince me not to use any pharmacological protection against pregnancy. Besides giving me this advice, she also prescribed me an insulin-lowering drug and gave me a list of foods I should and shouldn't eat. She also told me not to do very hard workouts and not to overload my body. Just a

30-minute walk every day. 'Wow', I thought, 'in the world where you should always try harder to overcome your barriers I am not supposed to do that. Just walking for 30 minutes. I like it. I don't need to prove anything to anybody'. I was supposed to take metformin three times a day and an additional one before I went to sleep. 'Nice', I thought, 'I've turned 30 and my day resembles the day of a drug addict'. The doctor's suggestion to eat more raw vegetables, less white wheat, and no alcohol made me feel relieved. This was something I hadn't thought about concerning my lifestyle. 'So, that's a fact', I thought,

I really have too much stress, and I really don't care of myself, I don't eat well, I don't sleep well, I don't rest. What else can I expect? I really needed this kind of confirmation from the third person, a doctor?

\* \* \*

I could take pills one after another to live and not bother about why my body gives me those signals. I would function with all of those pills, wouldn't I? However, I preferred to see my body as both the chasm and the link to my recovery (Metta, 2013). It was my guideline to pull me through. I started to meditate and stay silent. Staying in silence brought me solutions and enabled me to hear my body's signals and what I really wanted. It appeared that, even though I denied it, I still served other people's expectations or my imagined speculations of what those expectations were. Young mothers are particularly burdened by a certain tradition and idea of who a mother is (Rich, 1986). I pretended that I lived the way I wanted, but in fact, I still related it to society's expectations of me as a woman, mother, wife, and researcher. Polish conservative culture and society, in which women and men are supposed to be 'this or that' instead of what they really are, wasn't helpful either. I think that there were two crucial aspects that made me unable to speak and feel well: Polish sociocultural conservatism and my narcissistic social environment. My body had to speak for me.

Fortunately, I had my writing, which helped me in my healing process. Cixous writes: 'Write yourself; your body must make itself heard' (1986, p. 97). I wrote articles about the social pressure on young mothers and the constant criticism which rendered them vulnerable.[7] I had a strong internal need to write and accept that, 'women's lifewriting has many socio-cultural and political implications for the ways we read history, construct knowledge, and imagine future generations…' (Metta, 2010, p. 29).

Months of being on a diet and walking alone every day passed. I've tried myself to find my own balance between family life, work, and entertainment. I started laughing more, taking care of myself, and not caring what people might say; to have more fun, to live and not just exist. I lost 10 kg and started to feel well. I don't feel tired anymore. I've gained strength to the point that I could save someone's life. And this was my deepest, truest, and most honest desire: to not only work and have a family but also to engage myself in aid actions. I feel I must leave this world better than I found it.

Let me end with Cixous's words:

> An act that will commemorate a woman's speaking out, and therefore her breakthrough entry into history, which has always been based on her denial. By writing, forge a weapon against the antilogos. Write to finally be able to take the initiative in your case, to have a right and a place in the entire symbolic system, in the historical process. It's finally time for women to leave their mark in written and spoken language
>
> *(Cixous, 1993, pp. 152–153)*

## Notes

1 This is a literal Polish translation of the English 'black or white situation' term: cultural and societal influences mediate between the experience and recognition of bodily sensations.
2 He's a seafarer.
3 Alec Grant wrote about feeling alone in 'normal' daily social situations: 'I feel alone (no surprises there boy: you've felt like this since 1952)' (Grant, 2010, p. 579).
4 Hills et al. (2016, p. 135) state that: 'Controversy and confusion surround terms such as "psychosomatic" and "psychogenic" – with existing evidence suggesting that these terms still imply that symptoms are "all in the mind" and thus that "there's nothing wrong with you"' (Leone, Wessely, Huibers, Knottnerus, & Kant, 2011; Ricciardi & Edwards, 2014). Many people dread such a diagnosis because the implication is that their symptoms will no longer be taken seriously (Hinton & Kirk, 2016; Mobini, 2015). Some strongly resist and fiercely reject the idea of a psychological element to their symptoms/experience and may even believe their symptoms indicate that something is seriously wrong but is being missed' (Hinton & Kirk, 2016).
5 When working on this paper, I had a dream that I was at the research seminar and I was presenting the paper I wrote in front of a group of people I work with, and when I started reading my very well-prepared article out loud, I made many mistakes and got lost, and confused as if I were reading the text for the first time. In that dream, I have a similar feeling of 'not being in the right place' or 'not playing the right role' like in the situation I describe.
6 Of course, the models of modern families have changed in the modern world, and we can observe different types of families nowadays, but describing this wider in this chapter is not the right place for this.
7 Szczepaniak, C. (2021). Autoetnografia trudów macierzyństwa. [Autoethnography of the difficulties of motherhood], *Ars Educandi*, *18*(18), 83–103. https://doi.org/10.26881/ae.2021.18.05; Szczepaniak, C. (2022). W 'mikroświecie macierzyństwa' – doświadczanie samotności macierzyńskiej w badaniu autoetnograficznym. [In the 'microworld of motherhood'– experiencing the loneliness while being a mother. Autoethnographic study] *Przegląd Socjologii Jakościowej*, *18*(4), 152–167. https://doi.org/10.18778/1733-8069.18.4.06.

## References

Bentz, V. M. (2016). Knowing as being: Somatic phenomenology as a contemplative practice. In: V. M. Bentz & V. Giorgino (Eds.), *Contemplative social research. Caring for self, being and lifeworld* (pp. 50–79). Fielding University Press.

Burkitt, I. (2008). *Social selves: Theories of self and society.* SAGE Publications Ltd.

Cixous, H. (1986). *The newly born woman.* University of Minnesota Press.

Cixous, H. (1993). *Śmiech meduzy. [The laugh of the Medusa].* Teksty Drugie : Teoria literatury, krytyka, interpretacja nr 4/5/6 (22/23/24), 147–166. Śmiech Meduzy - Instytut Badań Literackich PAN (rcin.org.pl)

Denzin, N. (2011). Foreword: performing autoethnography: Making the personal political. In: T. Spry (Ed.), *Body, paper, stage: Writing and performing autoethnography* (pp. 11–13). Left Coast Press, Inc.

Giddens, A. (2012). *Nowoczesność i tożsamość. „Ja' i społeczeństwo w epoce później nowoczesności [Modernity and Self – Identity. Self and Society in the Late Modern Age].* Warszawa: Wydawnictwo Naukowe PWN.

Gilliland, M. (2018). Family and marriage. In: N. Fernandez & D. Amory (Eds.), *Perspectives: An open invitation to cultural anthropology.* Available online: https://courses.lumenlearning.com/suny-esc-culturalanthropology/

Grant, A. (2010). Writing the reflexive self: An autoethnography of alcoholism and the impact of psychotherapy culture. *Journal of Psychiatric and Mental Health Nursing, 17*(7), 577–582. https://doi.org/10.1111/j.1365-2850.2010.01566.x

Hills, J., Lees, J., Freshwater, D., & Cahill, J. (2016). Psychosoma in crisis: An autoethnographic study of medically unexplained symptoms and their diverse contexts. *British Journal of Guidance & Counselling, 46*(2), 135–147. https://doi.org/10.1080/03069885.2016.1172201

Hinton, D., & Kirk, S. (2016). Families' and healthcare professionals' perceptions of healthcare services for children and young people with medically unexplained symptoms: A narrative review of the literature. *Health Soc Care Community, 24*(1), 12–26. https://doi.org/10.1111/hsc.12184

Konecki, K. T. (2007). Działanie przedsiębiorcze. Auto – praca nad tożsamością a społeczny proces konstruowania motywacji do działania przedsiębiorczego [Entrepreneurial Action. Auto – work on identity and the social process of constructing motivation for entrepreneurial activity]. In: J. Leoński & U. Kozłowska (Eds.), *W kręgu socjologii interpretatywnej. Badania jakościowe nad tożsamością* (72–115). Szczecin: Uniwersytet Szczeciński – Economicus.

Konecki, K. T. (2018). *Advances in contemplative social research.* Łódź-Kraków: Wydawnictwo Uniwersytetu Łódzkiego.

Konecki, K. T., Płaczek, A., & Tarasiuk, D. (2023). *Experiencing the body in yoga practice: Meanings and knowledge transfer.* Routledge.

Lasch, C. (1980). *The culture of narcissism.* Abacus.

Leone, S. S., Wessely, S., Huibers, M. J. H., Knottnerus, J. A., & Kant, I. (2011). Two sides of the same coin? On the history and phenomenology of chronic fatigue and burnout. *Psychology & Health, 26*(4), 449–464. https://doi.org/10.1080/08870440903494191

Lévi-Strauss, C. (2012). *Elementarne struktury pokrewieństwa [Elementary structures of kinship].* Warszawa: Oficyna Wydawnicza Volumen.

McCullough, M. E., Emmons, R. A., Kilpatrick, S. D., & Mooney, C. N. (2003). Narcissists as 'victims': The role of narcissism in the perception of transgressions.

*Personality and Social Psychology Bulletin, 29*(7), 885–893. https://doi. org/10.1177/0146167203029007007

Mead, G. H. (1962). *Mind, self and society.* University of Chicago Press.

Metta, M. (2010). *Writing against, alongside and beyond memory: Lifewriting as reflexive poststructuralist feminist research practice.* Peter Lang.

Metta, M. (2013). Putting the body on the line. Embodied writing and recovery through domestic violence. In: S. Holman Jones, T. E. Adams & C. Ellis (Eds.), *Handbook of autoethnography* (1st ed., pp. 486–509). Routledge.

Mobini, S. (2015). Psychology of medically unexplained symptoms: A practical review. *Cogent Psychology, 2*(1), 1–10. https://doi.org/10.1080/23311908.2015. 1033876

Ricciardi, L., & Edwards, M. J. (2014). Treatment of functional (psychogenic) movement disorders. *Neurotherapeutics, 11*(1), 201–207. https://doi.org/10.1007/s13311-013-0246-x

Rich, A. (1986). *Of woman born. Motherhood as experience and institution.* W.W. Norton & Company.

Sennett, R. (2009). *Upadek człowieka publicznego* [The fall of public men]. Warszawa: Muza.

Schneider, D. M. (1980). *American kinship: A cultural account.* University of Chicago Press.

Tanasugarn, A. (2022). *The consequences of growing up with a narcisst, How growing up with narcissistic parents can affect our sense of Self.* Available online: The Consequences Of Growing Up With A Narcissist | by Annie Tanasugarn, PhD | Invisible Illness | Medium

# 18

# SPURIOUS EMOTIONAL UNDERSTANDING

## What Do 'Ordinary' People Know about Entrapment in the Bubbly, Fizzing, 'Hung-Before' Feeling?

*Siw Heidi Tønnessen*

### The Opposite Way Around

I started drinking alcohol in my teens, as do many people. I stopped drinking alcohol when I was 39, as do few. I spent almost 25 years trying to drink alcohol with control. I took for granted that the way my friends and society control their drinking was also possible for me, only to discover that it is the opposite way around: alcohol controls me.

### Writing (Grapy) about I (Auto) in Culture (Ethno)

I feel a responsibility to start this chapter by saying that my standpoint is in critical analytical and evocative autoethnography (Adams, 2017). Autoethnography can be described as the art and science of critically representing one's life in relation to cultural expectations, beliefs, and practices through writing. This is done in order to demonstrate and call out the lack of public awareness of the power of dominant cultural discourses and narratives (Adams & Herrmann, 2023; Grant, 2022). There is a fundamental link between the 'auto' and the 'ethno' because what something means to an individual is dependent on the cultural discourses available to them (Grant, 2010). Autoethnography can be used to subvert a discourse through providing an 'insider' alternative to dominant narratives and offering narratives that critique the social situatedness of the self (Grant, 2022; Spry, 2001).

DOI: 10.4324/9781003408963-18

There is an ongoing debate about no-criteria/criteria for good (enough) autoethnography (see, for example, Adams, 2017; Adams & Herrmann, 2023; Grant, 2023; Szwabowski, 2019). I will not debate this, but I stress that I support the criteria of using theory (Grant, 2019, 2023, 2024) in my autoethnographic analytic writing. I believe, with Grant (2019), that theory-free zones may display the 'naïve realist assumption that (the writers) particular world *is the world* in universal sense' (p. 89, my brackets). Because transparency is vital in all my writing, I locate my theoretical epistemological position within social construction, specifically discourse theory.

Discourses can be understood as ways of speaking and acting that are taken for granted within a situated context (McNamee, 2015). There are always such things taken for granted ways in any social context (Gergen, 2015, 2020; McNamee, 2010). Zerubavel (2018) named the ones in general cultural use as 'unremarkable', as opposite to 'markable'. The unremarkable ways of speaking and acting can be understood as the expressions of dominant discourses, whereas the markable are expressions of more marginal discourses. The 'ethno' of autoethnography is about challenging unremarkable, taken for granted, dominant discourses. This applies to both the *dis-courses* – the smaller aspects of how meaning-making takes place within situated practices – and the *Discourses*, the broader historical governing narratives (Bager, 2019; Herrmann, 2022).

## When I Drink

'When I drink' is the title of a poetry collection by a Norwegian poet (Svedman, 2019). For me, the title alludes to the fact that *if* I start drinking again, the same mechanisms as described below will hit me – thus, the present tense style in my writing.

Alcohol structures my emotions, my thinking, and my acting 24 hours a day. Depending on where I start to tell the story (in the morning, at lunchtime, in the afternoon, in the evening, at night, or at dawn), the telling will give a different emotional starting point. Dawn equals anxiety. Morning equals a little less anxiety (maybe because of some relief from having given myself the promise of not drinking in the following evening). When I reach my lunch break, the voices in my head start to debate: *'how about just one more, just one more bottle of red wine, and then you can stop tomorrow?'* versus *'no, remember the fear and anxiety from when you woke up this morning'.*

My favourite time of day is the afternoon. At that time, the 'just-one-more-time' voice has overpowered and silenced the fearfully nervous voice from the break of dawn. I know that I am going to drink again this evening. This decision fills my body with a bubbly fizz that is almost as good as the first glass. Or maybe even better.

> *There is a meeting at work, and I engage in a conversation with my colleagues. At the same time there is a 'meeting' going on in my head, the all-too-familiar discussion about whether to drink or not today. I don't know if other people have the same ability to pretend to focus outwards, while actually focusing inwards – probably, because I am hardly that special. Anyways, I have a well-known feeling in my stomach, a feeling of a nearby turning point. My thoughts move steady towards this point parallel with my colleagues ongoing discussion. There! I make the decision to buy a bottle red wine to bring home after work. Probably a quite familiar thing for many to decide, but a decision that set me off from the top of a roller coaster. The suction in my stomach is so good, so varm and so intense. My skin tingles. The fizz starts in my neck and spreads all over my body. I breathe calmly, in long breaths. My face relaxes. My skin fits. I am less stressed, less restless. My colleagues are suddenly less irritating. Even though I have no clue about what they are talking about, I nod, and I smile. If they ask for my opinion on whatever I will agree regardless of what I agree to. Because to be honest, I don't care. I only care about the fact that my thoughts, once again, have saved me. When I drink, my everyday revelation is not about swallowing the first sip of wine; my everyday revelation is thinking about swallowing the first sip of wine. This is my addiction. My entrapment.*

As years go by and my drinking progresses, the fizz decreases. Maybe because my tolerance for alcohol increases until there is more and more of an overlap between the urge to drink and the shame of drinking again. This means that alcohol doesn't work for me anymore. I hit rock bottom (Bateson, 1971; Denzin 1987a, b), and I ask for help because even though alcohol doesn't work anymore, shame certainly does. The only joy I now find in relation to alcohol is the few seconds of fizz in the 'hung-before' (as an equivalent to 'hungover') prior to the point when the desperate feeling of shame hits. My possibility to get high on the hung-before fizz has been taken away from me, with severe consequences for my mental health.

## My First Therapist

Regarding my drinking problem, there are two therapists who have done their best to help me. My first therapist I got to know was in 2011, and we spent an hour a week together for about a year. I can't remember every detail in his approach to my problem, but I do remember our joint action for making me able to drink with control. He wrote the pro and cons of drinking on a flipchart. Together we planned for the following week: when to drink, when not to drink; how much to drink, how much not to drink; and so on. Even though I tried my very best to help him to help me, I failed. I drank on evenings we had agreed should be without wine. After a whilst my therapist suggested for me to try Antabuse. For months, I stayed sober on this medication on weekdays and drank at the weekends. As I was controlling the number of glasses, the glasses got more and more hold of me. I was a caught in a symmetrical, escalating fight with the bottle (Bateson, 1971), which I was doomed to lose.

In *The cybernetics of "self": A theory of alcoholism* (1971), Gregory Bateson argues that an alcoholic (who still drinks) has an everyday unpleasant state of mind due to his ever-present symmetrical battle with the bottle. This symmetrical relationship is to be understood as a relation between two battling states of mind: one directed to drinking, with the other opposed to this. The alcoholic's response to this is to get drunk. Bateson suggests that the only lasting solution to the drinking problem is what he refers to as a 'complementary surrender' – that is to quit the battling with the bottle by stopping drinking alcohol. This requires a shift from a symmetrical to a complementary relationship, a relationship that builds on dissimilarity and mutual fitting together instead of battling and accepting always to be defeated by the bottle.

Today, I understand that there was something wrong with the premises of my therapist's approach to me. He assumed that I could learn to drink like most people—with control. Elsewhere, I have written about the presence of the 'drinking with control' discourse in the therapy room (Tønnessen, 2023).

Maybe my therapist knew about the bubbly, fizzing feeling following a decision to drink. I never asked him. I am, though, quite sure that he did not *know* ('know' understood as self-experienced bodily – 'brainly' – and heartfelt knowledge) about the emotional imprisonment of alcohol. If he himself had been held in captivity, I am quite sure that he would not suggest the learn-to-drink-controlled approach. Said another way, my therapist and I have different situated knowledge concerning alcohol drinking. Wylie (2013, p. 31) writes that the

*Social location systematically shapes and limits what we know, including tacit, experiential knowledge as well as explicit understanding, what we take knowledge to be as well as specific epistemic content.*

Social location is defined structurally by a hierarchically structured system of power relations. At the time I met my therapist, he was a psychology specialist with his situated knowledge, and I was a drinking alcoholic with my situated knowledge. I will not try to describe my therapist's situated knowledge in detail, but I trusted his therapeutic competence and subjected to his way of helping me. At the time, all I wanted was someone to provide me with a solution to my problem – a problem situated in my knowledge that I can describe as a 24-hour emotional captivity by alcohol, which controls my life in a mundane, routine way. This imprisonment is quite stable, providing me with the same ups and downs in the way I feel guided by my alcoholic clock. Detached from the things happening in my life and my children's lives – whether it is summer, winter, birthdays, Christmas, and so on. The authenticity of the smiles I give to people I meet in my everyday life is dependent on whether I have secured an appropriate amount of wine for the evening or not. When I am captured by alcohol, I have a foggy distanced way of being in life. I have my secret thoughts of when to drink next, always (every single day and all year long) planning for having enough to drink, but not too much. As a consequence of my lack of control, I have to control my drinking in advance when I am not intoxicated. When I start drinking, I always want more. I share this knowledge with my therapist – a knowledge he has probably heard hundreds of times.

## Spurious Emotional Understanding

*As I sit down on the subway, I think about today's session with my therapist. He is an experienced and well-educated psychology specialist. I have been seeing him for some months now, but I am not sure if it actually helps with my drinking problem. He seems pleased though – and it is a nice feeling to help him to a feeling of helping me. I ignore the grumbling in my stomach that tells me that something is wrong. We have so much in common, my therapist and I. I philosophize and use a 'professional language' (I am also a therapist by education) when we talk. Our conversations are intellectual, smart, and funny – and they flow. I feel that he understands me.*

After a year of therapy, I still drink alcohol. Maybe with some degree of increased control; Antabuse on Monday–Thursday, drinking on Friday–Sunday. I still go to therapy once a week. Not all of the things the therapist says fit with me, but I choose to overlook the things that do not fit. This is because I believe that he must be able to help me and because I would really like to help him to help me. I want to make him believe that he is helping me – maybe out of cowardice, maybe out of courtesy, or even out of desperation.

At a certain point, my therapist discharged me. I am not sure whether it was a decision rooted in my 'progress' or was more to do with the number of therapy sessions allocated to me by the 'system'. Regardless, I left my therapist's office to progress my drinking for two more years.

In *The Recovering Alcoholic*, Norman K. Denzin (1987b) writes about what he calls 'spurious emotional understanding'. He says that there are inter-actional moments when individuals mistake their own feelings and under-standings for the feelings of others and interpret their feelings as the feelings of others. Spurious emotionality arises in those situations where interactants refuse, or are unable, to enter into the other's field of experience. In spuri-ous emotionality, the individual thinks she can understand and feel the pain and suffering of others, but she cannot. She applies the wrong interpretive framework – when she views the other's experiences not from the other's point of view but from her own. This leaves the other feeling that they have not been understood, and resentment towards the one interpreting might be produced, and perhaps good intentions rejected.

*Sitting at my office at the University and writing this manuscript makes me wonder about what the therapist thought of me at that time. Did he feel that he succeeded with me? Does he even remember me? Maybe I shall send this manuscript to him when it is finished? He will maybe react negatively to my claim that he has a 'spurious emotional understanding' of my drinking prob-lem. I don't like to make people feel bad about them themselves, but maybe it is important for his practice to know the things I now know? I don't know.*

## A Spurious Colonization of the First-Person Perspective

The first-person perspective is a well-known term within recovery-oriented practice and research (Davidson et al., 2008; De Ruysscher et al., 2017; Ness et al., 2014; Oute & Jørgensen, 2021). The term underlines how researchers and professionals want to acknowledge the person behind diagnoses or dis-orders. Davidson et al. (2008, p. 273) writes, '(...) *we need to accept that it is the people with these experiences who know best what is entailed both in living through and in recovering from these disorders*'.

I would like to reply to Davidson and his colleagues that we always have to keep in mind that the first-person perspective is (usually) not self-experienced by second persons. It is a perspective that practitioners and researchers borrow from alcoholics like me, but there is a thin line between borrowing and forgetting who you borrowed from, or even forgetting that you have actually borrowed in the first place. A peculiar thing about this 'second-person borrowing of my first-person perspective' is the way practitioners and researchers seem to overlook the fact that they are never able to understand the perspective from the actual first-person position (unless, of course, they themselves experience addiction and mental health challenges). People positioned in the second-person perspective will always have a spurious emotional understanding (Denzin, 1987b) of alcoholism. I know – because I used to be one of the second persons.

Another important aspect when the second person borrows is the risk that personal narratives can be interrupted, hi-jacked, and co-opted into other stories, often in ways beyond the control of the story owner (Grant, 2016). They can be filtered through researchers discourses and webs of meaning and in effect becoming culturally colonized (Grant, 2022); colonized by being used in contexts few 'first persons' themselves have access to, like scientific journals and communities. This risks exclusion from the right to ownership of one's own resources, a right lost on people with spurious emotional understanding. Perhaps this is in line with what De Ruysscher and colleagues (2019) warn about when questioning the 'professionalization of recovery'. Hunt and Resnick (2015) call this professionalization of recovery a well-meaning theft-through-adoption.

There are similarities between the first-person perspective and the standpoint theory.

---

**Standpoint theory:**

*The central claim of standpoint theory is that those who are subject to oppression and systems of domination possess an epistemic advantage with respect to understanding experiences of oppression and subjugation. As such, members of structurally oppressed groups can know different things – or know them better – than those who are comparatively privileged.*
*(Freeman & Stewart, 2020, p. 45)*

Standpoint theory is thus committed to the situated knowledge thesis and argues that members of historically and systemically marginalized groups have more credibility with respect to recognizing and identifying instances of oppression than others who are not members of those groups (Freeman & Stewart, 2020, p. 36).

To know something about being controlled by alcohol situates me and provides me with an epistemic advantage, but those who occupy particular marginal standpoints do not *automatically* know more or know better. This means that just because I am a sober alcoholic does not indicate that I automatically know more or know better about alcoholism, but because of my marginal standpoint, I *can* know different things and I *can* know them better (Wylie, 2013). Failing to recognize this shortcoming can make me commit the error of colonizing the first-person perspective.

## A Hybrid Identity Position, 'Self-Help' and 'Other-Help'

*I am at the local pub, only minutes away from my house. On Tuesdays there are few people here. I make a point out of showing my book to the bartender, and lay 'The child protection act of 1992' on the counter as I order. I want all of the people present to know that I am more than a guest at the local pub. I am an 'A' college student soon to have my exam. I don't always show off like I do now, because at school I make an explicit point out of hiding that I drink alone several days per week. I lead a double life even though I am only in my twenties.*

Leading a double life might be conceptualized as what Grant (2016) calls a *hybrid identity position* – a merged position of simultaneously being an academic and a recovering alcoholic who has successfully negotiated former severe mental health challenges. This is quite similar to my own hybrid identity position – a position that grants me the possibility to commute between the first-person and the second-person perspectives.

I graduated in 2001 but started working as a social worker in 1997. I have done different forms of municipal youth work until 2022, and then I started teaching at the University within the fields of mental health, substance use, and addiction. I completed my master's degree in 2011 and started my PhD in 2019. So, it is safe to say that I know something about occupying a second-person position in doing, teaching, and researching practice. As a practitioner, I have, for example, tried to help many young people control their use of alcohol and drugs, both before and after I realized, and found a solution to, my own problem. Many of these people solved their problems completely on their own.

When looking from the dominant second-person perspective onto the marginal first-person, we tend to name such self-solving of a problem as 'self-help'. The term 'self-help' has no meaning if it wasn't for the term 'help'. If it weren't for 'help', taken for granted to be understood as 'professional-help', the term 'self-help' would be without meaning. In Zerubavel's (2018, p. 39) words, self-help is 'marked', and (professional-) help is 'unmarked' (taken for granted), with marked terms are typically introduced into the language only after their unmarked counterparts.

When I look from the marginal, marked first-person perspective onto the dominant, unmarked second-person perspective, I am tempted to name such professional-help: 'other-help'.

## Limitations of Other-Helpers

Inherent in the second-person position is a lack of authentic and genuine emotional understanding of what it *feels like* (e.g. to be entrapped and controlled by alcohol). This emotional understanding is thus doomed to be spurious and false because people speaking about alcohol, alcoholism, and recovery from the second-person, other-help perspective do not self-know about a 24-hour emotional prison. Or maybe, said differently, they can, of course, know about it if they have been told about it. But they do not *feel* about it. Other-helpers did their best to help me, but to be honest, even though I believe these people stretched far to help, they actually contributed to a worsening of my problem. Other-help groups of different professionals do not help me to stop my drinking.

I believe that this limitation inherent in the perspective applies to research done from the second-person perspective as well. Simply put, in data generation in qualitative research, we usually talk to a number of individuals, and when we analyse the material, we usually look for something that these individuals have in common. This is a nomothetic approach to science, looking for consistence, regularity, the 'law' (Crotty, 1998). Such commonalities between individuals can be used to shape a practice. An example is the recovery model 'CHIME', which is a conceptual framework for personal recovery which is 'theoretically defensible and robust synthesis of people's experiences of recovery in mental illness' (Leamy et al., 2011, p. 45). In such a theoretical synthesizing something must be lost. We are quick to assume that problems can be solved by the right therapeutic model (McNamee, 1996); however, models tend to simplify, and consequently something gets lost (Lauveng, 2020). Models build upon the abovementioned nomothetic approach to science, whilst in an idiographic approach, one seeks to isolate the individual phenomena in order to trace their unique development (Crotty, 1998, p. 68). These two approaches are often confused by second persons, maybe because of not being aware of the fact that models and persons are of two different logical types.

**The theory of logical types:** Following Russell's theory on logical types (Russell, 1910 in Bateson et al., 1956), Bateson and his colleagues argue for

*A discontinuity between a class and its members. The class cannot be a member of itself nor can one of the members be the class, since the term*

> *used for the class is of a different level of abstraction - a different Logical Type - from terms used for members. Although in formal logic there is an attempt to maintain this discontinuity between a class and its members, we argue that in the psychology of real communications this discontinuity is continually and inevitably breached.*
>
> *(Bateson et al., p. 251)*

Following Bateson and his colleagues, I argue for a discontinuity between the 'class' understood as the model and the 'members' understood as the persons. Persons and models are of different logical types; thus, when developing general, unpersonal, static models for dynamic, individually experienced, and personal recovery, something is lost. Models have limited power to change because change occurs in ongoing processes and not as a result of a battle between competing theories, models, techniques, or truths (McNamee, 2015). My therapist's way of addressing my drinking problem through his controlled drinking model might perhaps be interpreted as helpful in the way that it escalated my problem, which in turn expedited my mental collapse. The model helped me on my way to meeting my second therapist, and he helped me to make the choice to quit drinking alcohol.

## Authentic Emotional Understanding

> In *The recovering alcoholic,* Norman K. Denzin (1987b, p. 99) describes an 'authentic emotional understanding'. In order for deep, authentic, shared emotional understanding to be produced and understood, a common field of shared and shareable experience must be created. This allows each individual to locate herself in the experiential framework of the other.

I met my second therapist in 2014. He told me about his years of struggles with the bottle, about his self-delusion, and about the hundreds of broken promises he made to himself and the people around him. *'Sunday was my worst day of the week. Full of desperate regret, I promised my wife that I would never drink again. Only to find myself drinking the following weekend'.* I told him about my morning promises – promises that I always broke in the evening. He genuine understood my emotions, and I genuine understood his. This is because we are both alcoholics, and we share an authentic emotional understanding.

*When writing about this meeting I am struck by the power in it. He a man, older than me, from a completely different part of the country, with a completely different background, having a similar story to mine. Our talking was about quite similar feelings, and quite similar ways of acting (or not acting) – strange in the most positive way.*

## (Self-)Sustainable (Self-)Therapy

When I drink, I cannot solve my drinking problem. It is like trying to lift myself by the hair (Bateson, 1971). I need someone else to lift me up. My alcoholic therapist lifted me for a whilst and made me capable of becoming my own therapist (Denzin, 1987a). He helped me to construct a cybernetic, self-sustainable way of living my life by replacing the symmetrical fight with the bottle to a more complementary way of engaging in life (Bateson, 1971). By following some simple rules and by engaging in complementary relations with other alcoholics, I am safe. Engaging regularly with other alcoholics helps me to maintain my self-therapy. I am present in my life 24/7, all the time, every waking and sleeping hour for the rest of my life. An other-therapist will never be.

*It's the middle of the night and I wake up from a nightmare. A dream that has come back to me at regular intervals in recent years: I drink alcohol, but I am not drunk. Actually, I am never even close to being drunk. I drink just some sips of wine, a glass at most. The amount of wine is not the important issue. The important theme in these dreams is whether I should tell that I have had drops of red wine in my mouth, drops I have allowed to run down my throat. Or whether I should keep it a secret. It is the fear of the reaction from people around me that scares the shit of me. The anxious faces of my children, the silent and dismissive posture of my boyfriend. As I sweat in my bed, I try to instruct my self to breathing slowly – in – out – in – out. The urge to run out of bed, to scream in desperation, vanishes slowly, slowly. I become calmer. I can think clearer.*

## Feeling Threats to the Cybernetic Sustainable Self

*There is a break in a meeting at my workplace. Me and a colleague are talking about an upcoming summer party. He knows that I do not drink alcohol, and I sincerely believe he is only trying to be nice to me (and maybe to signal that he respects my choice of a sober way of life) when he asks how it is for me to be present at work events where people drink. The question makes me uneasy. I do not know why, but it does. I do not like this situation, but I do not understand why I don't like it. I want to leave the room, go to the toilet, or maybe even run outside. But I smile. I smile to my colleague. I nod, and in a friendly way help him do what he seems to want to do – to, in an equally friendly way, help me in what he interpreted as an upcoming uneasy situation for me (alcohol drinking at an event at work), when he actually is the one placing me in an uneasy situation. He continues to tell me how he thinks that alcohol should be less present in work situations. I explain that I am not that occupied with the politics of alcohol. This is a confusing situation, my colleague is only trying to be nice to me, but my gut feeling signalizes a treat. My colleague continues with his talking, and I do not know how to answer his attempt to voice his concern for me through giving arguments for stricter alcohol regulations by the politicians. Maybe my colleague has heard about the 'total consumption hypothesis'?*

> The total consumption hypothesis implies that 'normal consumers' of alcohol are also involved and influence the number of heavy consumers and thus the extent of alcohol problems in society. This underpins the strategy in Norwegian alcohol policy – namely, to try to reduce total consumption (Nordlund, 2003).

This theory has nothing to do with the way I drink. Politicians, regulations, and summer parties with or without alcohol have nothing to do with my problem. If I want to start drinking again, I will do so. And when I drink, I will find the means (red wine, whiskey, or any other ethanol) wherever I am. Maybe this is a fundamental difference between my colleague and I. A difference that I see more clearly than him because he has a spurious emotional understanding. My mentor and editor for this chapter, Professor Alec Grant – a recovered alcoholic – and I share an authentic emotional understanding of this matter. We experience and share the feelings of 'othering' and 'being othered'.

## The Gut Felt Feeling of Othering

The situation with my colleague is not unique. I have experienced it many times: situations where someone has a clear intention to be supportive but is neither perceived as nor felt to be supportive (Sommer, 2021, p. 335); or situations where well-meaning individuals still perpetuate oppressive norms (Freeman & Stewart, 2020, p. 42). How can I interpret that my gut signalizes treat instead of support from my well-meaning colleague?

Maybe Sara Ahmed (2014) can come to my rescue? She writes about the concept of 'othering', which I understand as a way of making an individual or a group different through the way one speaks. Zerubavel (2018) calls this mechanism a *politico-semiotic process with the purpose to establish and maintain social dominance*. Freeman and Stewart (2020, p. 37) refer to the act of defining someone as the 'other' as a mechanism of microaggression, writing:

> *A common example of a microaggression occurs when a person of color is asked "Where are you from?" and when they respond with, "New York, just like you," the questioner persists in asking, "But where are you really from?"* They explain: *This exchange is considered to be a microaggression, since it presupposes that there's an important difference between a white person and a person of color who are both from the United States. Even if unintentional, such a line of questioning sends the message to the person of color that they aren't a "true" American, or that they are really a foreigner or "Other" in their own country.*

With his questions, my colleague sends a gut-felt message to me, a message saying that I am different than him. Maybe not different in a bad way, but still different. Different in a deviant way because I do not manage to live up to the societal discourse that imposes on me the expectation to drink alcohol with control (Tønnessen, 2023).

## Closing, for Now

> *At work we are having the same discussion again. When someone uses the word 'normal' or the word 'normality,' someone else always react. If I understand those who react correctly, their reaction is premised on assumed moral and political aspects of the terms 'normal' and 'normality', because the terms include some people and exclude others. They talk about being tolerant towards people who do not fit into the 'normal' category. I always react to this discussion, but I have difficulties understanding why. I want to be normal, even if my colleagues 'allow' me to be abnormal. Maybe it has something to do with my wish to be unmarked. I have led a most abnormal double life for many years. Now, all I want is to live a simple, single tracked life. I do not want responsibility for the needs of people around me to be generous and tolerant by rejecting 'normal' and 'normality'. Maybe they should try living a marked life, instead of a life that's un-reflexively scrutinized – what Zerubavel (2018) calls the unmarked life of the white, heteronormative, 'abled' man.*

Members of marginal groups know different things than members of dominant groups (Freeman & Stewart, 2020; Wylie, 2013), but members of marginal groups do not necessarily share the same knowledge. Talking to Alec Grant gives me a feeling of us being alike, both in thinking and in feeling – in think-feeling, which I do not share with all sober alcoholics. So, if researching the first-person perspective from a second-person perspective, one has to keep in mind at least two things. First, there are things professionals and researchers are not able to grasp, like entrapment in the bubbly fizzing 'hung-before' feeling. Second, many but not all, alcoholics might be able to grasp this feeling because we alcoholics also differ from one another.

Grant (2023) writes about the relationship between the queer and the familiar. In this academic text, I use a queer resource (my nonacademic drunkenness) within a familiar space (the academic context) to write something more unfamiliar. Unfamiliar means *marked* in relation to the unremarkable and the taken for granted (Zerubavel, 2018). Autoethnography is a marked research methodology, which challenges discourses within the doing of qualitative research. I like it.

## References

Adams, T. E. (2017). Autoethnographic responsibilities. *International Review of Qualitative Research*, *10*(1), 62–66. https://doi.org/10.1525/irqr.2017.10.1.62

Adams, T. E., & Herrmann, A. F. (2023). Good autoethnography. *Journal of Autoethnography*, *4*(1), 1–9. https://doi.org/10.1525/joae.2023.4.1.1

Ahmed, S. (2014). *Cultural politics of emotion*. Edinburgh University Press.Bager, A. S. (2019). A multimodal discourse analysis of positioning and identity work in a leadership development practice: A combined dialogicality and small story analysis. *Communication & Language at Work*, *6*(1), 40–62. https://doi.org/10.7146/claw.v6i1.113911

Bateson, G. (1971). The cybernetics of "self": A theory of alcoholism. *Psychiatry*, *34*(1), 1–18. https://doi.org/10.1080/00332747.1971.11023653

Bateson, G., Jackson, D. D., Haley, J., & Weakland, J. (1956). Toward a theory of schizophrenia. *Behavioral Science*, *1*(4), 251–264. https://doi.org/10.1002/bs.3830010402

Crotty, M. J. (1998). *The foundations of social research: Meaning and perspective in the research process*. The foundations of social research. SAGE Publications Ltd. [PDF] The Foundations of Social Research by Michael Crotty eBook | Perlego

Davidson, L., Andres-Hyman, R., Bedregal, L., Tondora, J., Frey, J., & Kirk, T. A. (2008). From "double trouble" to "dual recovery": Integrating models of recovery in addiction and mental health. *Journal of Dual Diagnosis*, *4*(3), 273–290. https://doi.org/10.1080/15504260802072396

Denzin, N. K. (1987a). *The alcoholic self*. SAGE Publications, Inc.

Denzin, N. K. (1987b). *The recovering alcoholic*. SAGE Publications, Inc.

De Ruysscher, C., Tomlinson, P., Vanheule, S., & Vandevelde, S. (2019). Questioning the professionalization of recovery: A collaborative exploration of a recovery process. *Disability & Society*, *34*(5), 797–818. https://doi.org/10.1080/09687599.2019.1588708

De Ruysscher, C., Vandervelde, S., Vanderplasschen, W., De Maeyer, J., & Vanheule, S. (2017). The concept of recovery as experienced by persons with dual diagnosis: A systematic review of qualitative research from a first-person perspective. *Journal of Dual Diagnosis, 13*(4), 264–279. https://doi.org/10. 1080/15504263.2017.1349977

Freeman, L., & Stewart, H. (2020). Sticks and stones can break your bones and words can really hurt you: A standpoint epistemological reply to critics of the microaggression research program. In L. Freeman & J. Weekes Schroer (Eds.), *Microaggressions and philosophy* (pp. 36–66). Routledge.

Gergen, K. J. (2015). *An invitation to social construction* (3rd ed.). Sage.

Gergen, K. J. (2020). Introduction. In S. McNamee, M. M. Gergen, C. Camargo-Borges & E. F. Rasera (Eds.), *The Sage handbook of social constructionist practice* (pp. 3–14). Sage.

Grant, A. (2010). Writing the reflexive self: An autoethnography of alcoholism and the impact of psychotherapy culture. *Journal of Psychiatric and Mental Health Nursing, 17*(7), 577–582. https://doi.org/10.1111/j.1365-2850.2010.01566.x

Grant, A. J. (2016). Living my narrative: Storying dishonesty and deception in mental health nursing. *Nursing Philosophy, 17*(3), 194–201. https://doi.org/ 10.1111/nup.12127

Grant, A. J. (2019). Dare to be a wolf: Embracing autoethnography in nurse educational research. *Nurse Education Today, 82,* 88–92. https://doi.org/10.1016/j. nedt.2019.07.006

Grant, A. (2022). What has autoethnography got to offer mental health nursing? *British Journal of Mental Health Nursing, 11*(4), 4–11. https://doi. org/10.12968/bjmh.2022.0035

Grant, A. J. (2023). Crafting and recognising good enough autoethnographies: A practical guide and checklist. *Mental Health and Social Inclusion, 27*(3), 196–209. https://doi.org/10.1108/MHSI-01-2023-0009

Grant, A. (Ed.) (2024). *Writing philosophical autoethnography.* Routledge.

Herrmann, A. (2022). The future of autoethnographic criteria. *International Review of Qualitative Research, 15*(1), 125–135. https://doi.org/10.1177/ 19408447211049513

Hunt, M. G., & Resnick, S. G. (2015). Two birds, one stone: Unintended consequences and potential solutions for problems with recovery in mental health. *Psychiatric Services, 66*(11), 1235–1237. https://doi.org/10.1176/appi.ps. 201400518

Lauveng, A. (2020). *Grunnbok i psykisk helsearbeid: det landskapet vi er mennesker i.* [Basic book in mental health work: the landscape in which we are all human beings]. Universitetsforlaget. Scandinavian University Press.

Leamy, M., Bird, V., Boutillier, C., Williams, J., & Slade, M. (2011). Conceptual framework for personal recovery in mental health: Systematic review and narrative synthesis. *British Journal of Psychiatry, 199*(6), 445–452. https://doi. org/10.1192/bjp.bp.110.083733

McNamee, S. (1996). Therapy and identity construction in a postmodern world. In D. Grodin & T. Lindlof (Eds.), *Constructing the self in a mediated world* (pp. 141–155). Sage Publications, Inc.

McNamee, S. (2010). Research as social construction: Transformative inquiry. *Saúde & Transformação Social/Health & Social Change, 1*(1), 9–19. Redalyc. Research as Social Construction: Transformative Inquiry

McNamee, S. (2015) Ethics as discursive potential. *Australian & New Zealand Journal of Family Therapy, 36*(4), 419–433. https://doi.org/10.1002/anzf.1125

Ness, O., Borg, M., & Davidson, L. (2014). Facilitators and barriers in dual recovery: A literature review of first-person perspectives. *Advances in Dual Diagnosis*, *7*(3), 107–117. https://doi.org/10.1108/ADD-02-2014-0007

Nordlund, S. (2003). Totalforbruksteorien og dens betydning for alkoholpolitikken. [The total consumption theory and its significance for alcohol policy]. *Tidsskrift for Den norske legeforening*, *123*, 46–48. Totalforbruksteorien og dens betydning for alkoholpolitikken | Tidsskrift for Den norske legeforening (tidsskriftet.no)

Oute, J., & Jørgensen, K. (2021). Forord. Recovery-orienterede praksisser i velfærdsinstitutioner og civilsamfund [Recovery-oriented practices in health and social care and civil society]. In J. Oute & K. Jørgensen (Eds.), *Recovery-orienterede praksisser i velfærdsinstitutioner og civilsamfund [Recovery-oriented practices: In health and social care and civil society]* (pp. 9–23). Samfundslitteratur.

Sommer, M. (2021). Støtte som mulighet til unge med psykiske helseproblemer. [Support as an opportunity for young people with mental health problems] *Tidsskrift for psykisk helsearbeid*, (4), 331–342. https://doi.org/10.18261/issn.1504-3010-2021-04-03

Spry, T. (2001). Performing autoethnography: An embodied methodological praxis. *Qualitative Inquiry*, *7*(6), 706–732. https://doi.org/10.1177/107780040100700605

Svedman, M. (2019). *Når jeg drikker*. Dikt. [When I drink. Poem]. Cappelen Damm.

Szwabowski, O. (2019). Forget all criteria. *International Review of Qualitative Research*, *12*(4), 476–481. https://doi.org/10.1525/irqr.2019.12.4.476

Tønnessen, S. (2023). The meaningfulness of challenging the controlled drinking discourse. An Autoethnographic study. *Qualitative Social Work*. Online First https://doi.org/10.1177/14733250231200499

Wylie, A. (2013). Why standpoint matters. In A. Wylie (Ed.), *Science and other cultures* (pp. 26–48). Routledge.

Zerubavel, E. (2018). *Taken for granted: The remarkable power of the unremarkable*. Princeton University Press.

# 19

## DROPPING THE AUTOETHNOGRAPHIC SEEDS IN THE SOIL

*Marianne Trent*

### Introduction

The 1990s were responsible for lots of things, some of which have been significant for the woman and psychologist you will learn about here. My decision to study psychology at A Level and at degree level, for example, were all products of the 1990s. Also, my decision to branch out into becoming an author also unknowingly started as a kernel of an idea in the 1990s. Growing up at that time in a remote English village, it seemed I had a lot of free time and so had to get creative at how to fill it. Going to the closest library and getting my full allocation of seven books at a time was a genuine treat. There were also all kinds of postal services I dabbled with, including one called 'Jokes by Post', 'Britannia Music', where you could get four CDs for £1 each, and my favourite was an equivalent but for books! You see, I've always loved reading. For me, books are a chance to be part of something beautiful and, what I now know as a psychologist, the opportunity to be immersed in a truly mindful activity. So, in this book, scheme members got to choose six books for a really low cost and then would have to buy a number of full-priced titles across the following 18 months.

It was one of these first six books that would stay with me as a seed of an idea that would begin germinating almost 20 years later. Nancy Friday had published *Women on Top: How Real Life Has Changed Women's Sexual Fantasies* (Friday, 1991), and by the mid-1990s, it had found its way onto the book club catalogue. By that time, I'd read Judy Blume's *Forever* (1975), *More* Magazine, and my brother's *Loaded* Mags enough times that

DOI: 10.4324/9781003408963-19

I was ready for something a bit more real. It seems that, with hindsight, it was autoethnography I was ready for because *Women on Top* was a collection of first-hand descriptions of not only women's fantasies but their own thoughts, insights, delights, hopes, and fears associated with these fantasies. I was so taken by this honesty and rawness, and that you could be so immersed in these private and intimate thoughts of women you'd never meet and likely wouldn't tell them if they met you in the street.

Over the years that followed, I completed my A Levels, went to university, graduated, went travelling around the world, and did a load of relevant roles working with and learning about people before starting my training as a Clinical Psychologist and then qualifying in 2011. Somewhere along the way, possibly because of the great minimalist purge brought on by Carol Smillie's *Changing Rooms* television programme, *Women on Top* must have wound its way to the charity shop. I wish I still had it now. My husband probably does too!

## Starting to Germinate

If we fast forward a bit further, in December 2017, after a couple of years of being unwell, my dad died. During his diagnosis in 2016, I was pregnant with my youngest child, and then it seemed that I spent a couple of years nursing the baby to sleep whilst holding my phone in one hand. But what was I up to on my phone all this time? I hear you ponder! Well, during the last year of my dad's life and in the months after, I found myself to be in the incredibly fortunate position of having lots of fellow psychologists and professionals who understood grief, loved me, and knew that it was okay and important in fact to talk to me about grief – their own experiences of it – and how I was doing. I just knew that all these people who were messaging me via WhatsApp, text, and Messenger and making me feel so validated and supported at one of the most harrowing times of my life were doing the most incredible service to me. I also knew that most people going through grief would likely be doing it alone. I had the idea that it would be fabulous to put together a 'Nancy Friday style' collection of stories by real people who had grieved. I had already decided that I would call it 'The Grief Collective', but it seemed to just percolate there in my mind, waiting for the perfect conditions to begin to grow. At the start of the pandemic in September 2020, my colleague Tim Mahy, a Health Psychologist, challenged me, along with other colleagues, to write and publish a whole book. I realised that now was my time. The perfect occasion had arisen for me to let *The Grief Collective* (Trent, 2020) find its wings and take flight – to go out there and help support other people in the way that I had felt so held by my friends and colleagues.

So, now I had to start the task of attempting to advertise, write, curate, and publish a whole book in 30 days. It's fair to say that there were a lot of late nights and that my role of being a governor for a local school was unfortunately a casualty of this endeavour. But what I couldn't have anticipated was just what an utter privilege it would be to immerse myself in people's incredibly personal and poignant narratives. Many of the contributors were strangers to me and had responded to my social media requests. What I love about the book is how reading it feels like getting access to someone's deepest, most personal thoughts and feelings, many of which are incredibly painful. It also feels like a very welcoming and validating club, where grief is understood, and the reader doesn't feel like a social pariah for having a 'Hurty heart' and eyes that don't want to stop streaming.

When I was in these incredibly intense 30 days, I didn't actually realise that I was creating anything in any particular genre. I just knew that I thought it would be useful and that as such it was a job well worth doing.

The book was published in October 2020 and was received well by contributors and readers alike. It was hard to believe that a whole book had come together so quickly and so beautifully. To hold the first copy of the book in my hands made me feel immensely connected to my dad and to the people who had trusted me with their real lives. As I was holding that copy in my hands, which I chose to live stream, I'll admit to a heart-in-mouth moment when I realised, I had inadvertently signed off on a version with a format error – but I didn't let that show during the video, and the issue was thankfully quickly resolved. I felt, and still feel, proud that my own experiences with grieving for my dad allowed others to work through and feel supported and validated in some of their own pain. Contributors who wrote chapters also told me that writing their stories had also helped them to process their own experiences and to reflect upon this superbly challenging time in their lives. In fact, so many of the things that make me a good psychologist have come about from key experiences in my life.[1] I know I can't just leave that there in a book for enquiring minds, so let me cover some of the areas I mean:

- the experience of a poorly attuned supervision relationship;
- the breaking down of friendships and relationships;
- the loss of my own wonderful father;
- the growing, birthing, feeding, and coping with the sleeplessness of my two sons;
- the setting up and running of my business;
- and so many more.

And what I have learned is that people often won't be able to engage with or benefit from what you've got to say until they reach the time in their own life where they have been able to gain the insight and, in some cases, the necessary mid-20s frontal lobe development to be able to have our messages do anything but pass from one ear to the next. For me, I think the benefit of autoethnographic accounts means that we can put our stories down on paper at the right time for us and that they can be picked up at the right time for the person who needs to learn from them. In preparing to write this chapter for this text you hold in your hands, I asked my audience what autoethnography means to them.[2] Dean had something to say about the unique window of time and opportunity you have into someone's life with this style of reading and writing:

> As I have lived with Post-Meningitic Hydrocephalus since 1971, I am keen to read books with items on 'Living with an acquired brain injury and issues and difficulties we experience in everyday life'. I was asked by the Charity 'The Brain and Spine Foundation' to do an article myself on my disability, how I help others, what advice I give and the people I have found helpful. This has been a new learning experience for me, and I like knowing that others might be able to benefit from my story and it might help them navigate this tricky path too.
>
> **Dean Muslin**

## New Branches

I firmly believe that our own adverse experiences can lead to shifts in our empathy and abilities with the clients we serve. Before I was qualified, I remember worrying I wouldn't be life-experienced enough, adverse, or otherwise, to truly be a convincing psychologist. I wasn't alone in this concern; my peers and I feared that we would be called out as such by service users, but that didn't happen, which was a relief. It turns out that the role plays we did to practice those imagined situations weren't needed. Whilst generally during training, the teaching was of a high standard, my own and my cohort's favourite lectures, hands down, were those having videos of real client sessions in them and those that included case studies.

Somehow, being able to step into the client's world really helped us to connect with the content and then be able to be clinically helpful, either immediately or in the future. This is beautifully described by Izzy:

> Combining the knowledge, we hold as professionals and have collected over the years with an individual's account of their illness, their struggle and also their strengths - allows us to better meet them where they are at.
>
> **Izzy Bros**

## This Fruit Is Causing Reflux

This section is evoking memories of the first ever 'proper' psychology essay I wrote. It was late 1997, and I was probably humming Robbie Williams' *Angels* as I typed it. The assignment was to debate whether psychology is a science. There were for and against arguments, followed by the conclusion that yes, I decided it was. I think the same is going to play out here, but let's not give away any spoilers.

## A Beneficial Development

Autoethnography offers the unique ability to add context to the people, area, or population under scrutiny. We can see how things work in both theory and practice and, of course, allow for individual differences which will occur when we work with humans.

> *I liked being able to put experiences into a context - to explore a phenomenon both alone and whilst considering particular cultural influences. It feels more personal and relatable, with obvious real-world applicability.*
>
> **Erin Puttock**

I think upon reflection that's due to the personal feel of what is being learned, and this realisation started the cogs of another idea whirring for me. Many of my best ideas come to me either during exercise or whilst showering after. It was as I was washing my hair one day postrun that I thought to myself how incredibly useful it would be for aspiring psychologists to be able to read the accounts of Clinical Psychologists and how they got there. I figured that being able to step into the world of relatable people would help inspire and transform. So that's exactly what I set about doing with my next book baby: *The Clinical Psychologist Collective: Advice and Guidance for Aspiring Clinical Psychologists* (Trent, 2021).

This time I cut myself a little more compassionate slack by allowing almost six months from project launch to publishing date. I also drafted in some additional help with proofreading and so thankfully avoided the last-minute format errors! The book itself is a collection of 38 stories in an autoethnographic style written by psychologists. It allows people a similarly intimate, confidante, and companionable insight into the lives of real people and real psychologists at that! The thing about this style of writing is that it feels so deeply personal, like having people speak directly to you and in a way which feels like a two-way relationship. A reader review draws our attention to the unique relationship between the reader and the writer that this style of writing allows:

> *As an aspiring clinical psychologist who has followed Dr Trent for a while on socials, I bought this book to gain insight into the world of clinical psychology.*

*This book certainly awarded me that, along with a wealth of additional insight that I had not considered. I have always thought I would need to halt other life plans whilst working towards the DClinPsy. The stories that were told in this book have completely changed my outlook. As an older student, I knew that realistically I might not reach qualified status until my mid-thirties and had told myself I was willing to put starting a family on hold for my psychology dream. The stories in this book have taught me that there are limitless possibilities in terms of trajectories towards training and the take-home message I received was that really, anything is possible in this journey. This has made me so happy to learn and I can't thank the authors and collaborators enough for their storytelling. Would highly recommend to all aspiring psychologists.*

*Eden*

Another member of my network told me what resonated with her about autoethnography, and even referenced *The Clinical Psychologist Collective*;

*I have found it helpful to hear people's experiences first hand. It can be helpful to hear both the similarities and differences. There is something special about using the person's words rather than making sense of them or interpreting them. When trying to get onto the course it was great to hear people's journeys and put names and stories behind the DClinPsych process. Qualitative research that uses people's voices is also powerful. Again, I think it ensures we are not interpreting other people's experiences and taking away their voices. I think this can be empowering for the people whose voices are being recorded and also those listening. I think it can also be very therapeutic for the writers. Autoethnography makes peoples stories come to life and is probably my favourite way to learn about human experiences.*

*Kyah Sisulu*

I couldn't agree more, and I love people, their stories, and what we can learn from them, and very much like the Heineken Beer tag line from the 20th century, that *reaches the parts that other types of research just don't*! I really like how it allows us to balance theory and practice, and you can almost see and feel the personal case studies being laid down in our brains in a way that will be useful for us as professionals in the future, as Jack explains:

*I recently came across a collaborative autoethnography that explored mental health among college athletes (Gross et al., 2020). As someone who works in this area, I found it particularly poignant and unforgettable, largely due to the personal case that was discussed. The autoethnography recounted the story of a young rower who confided in a former college athlete, now a student-athlete service professional, about her suicidal thoughts. The article was a moving and thought-provoking read, enriched by insights from a counsellor that helped connect theory and research with the real-life story. The reflective points and studies were also powerful, making the article valuable to me as both an assistant psychologist and an academy football coach. While systematic reviews have their place, I found this article more emotionally engaging and thus, more memorable. Breaking down statistics is important, but hearing individual stories can have an even greater impact on readers. This autoethnography made me reflect more regarding my personal scenarios than other articles have and has made me more attentive to the young athlete's needs in my role as a coach.*

**Jack Griffiths**

I think what Jack also nicely describes is that autoethnographic research is of particular relevance to those of us who work in protecting, empowering, and understanding the mental health of other people. I guess that's why we are writing about this in a psychology book – after all, it's a fascinating and compelling style for those invested in and passionate about people. Michelle explains why she thinks autoethnographic stories pack the punch they do:

*The power of personal case studies, reflections and stories lies in the fact that, through reading about someone else's lived experiences, we are forced to question the universal themes they touch upon, how and where our own experiences intersect and what we may have done the same or differently. I think they are a critical element of positive mental health by normalising conversations around difficult subjects, encouraging others to share their own story and, ideally, to seek help.*

**Michelle Ewen**

I also see autoethnography as allowing us to be more responsive and holistic in addressing current issues and trends when working with clinical populations. This is a benefit also described by Addie:

*It honours the experiences of the person/people involved and supports the 'nothing about me without me' research framework that is becoming more common, particularly when working with vulnerable populations.*

**Addie**

In a similar vein, Jacob adds:

*Autoethnography is a really interesting method because it allows for in-depth authentic exploration of a situation from someone's own point of view. I like this because it means that the way in which the individual experiences a certain change or situation can be very well observed allowing you to forgo any inference in what things may have been or may be interpreted like in the kind of the experiencer. This is so important because it gives change-makers the opportunity to direct change with a great deal of efficiency and accuracy, spending less time on wondering how this change will impact those it will affect.*

*Jacob*

I think we also need to be incredibly mindful that the populations we serve don't always like to tell their stories on a grand scale. It can be hard to get enough participants on board for quantitative research, and instead, there is so much to be learned from the voice of individuals:

*I much prefer qualitative or mixed methods, anyway, given that qualitative really allows nuances and individual experiences to be picked up. Unique experiences i.e., of the 'hardest to reach' populations require most research and normed measures don't pick up their experiences as research isn't normed on them! So, it allows new findings to open new discussions to advance our reach and support those based on research done on them.*

*Diana Luk*

### Not All Fruits Are Delicious

There is most definitely no perfect way to do anything, and research and dissemination are no exception to that. Autoethnography isn't faultless, and not everyone likes it to begin with.

*It does not in my opinion offer the complete answer/solution to the question or problem I'm thinking about, but then RCTs don't necessarily either.*

*Lucy Georgiades*

It's not always seen as 'sciencey' enough. In fact, sometimes it isn't even sciencey at all; instead, autoethnographical accounts crop up in magazines. I have always loved reading weekly magazines, and even as a qualified psychologist, I sometimes learn my information on more unusual presentations or situations from first-person accounts in publications such as *That's Life* or *Take a Break*.

For me as a reader, I like this taking a 'pinch of salt' approach – just learning what I can, taking what I find helpful, and leaving what I don't. But not everyone likes this subjectivity:

*It can sometimes detract from the objectivity of the text and makes it sound more like a subjective opinion, which can make it less reliable as a source of factual information.*

*Elior*

*It may be hard to distinguish the truth from fiction if somebody is telling their own story from memory.*

*Helena*

What you may not realise about me is that over the last three years I haven't just enjoyed reading magazines, but I've extended my passion to actually writing for the media myself. During this time, I have learned some useful things along the way. I've also been able to try to consider how people might understand what has been written or said and have seen that, even when handled sensitively, some people may still be upset or feel misrepresented. That said, in some cases, when not handled well by writers or editors, some people are concerned that it could be potentially damaging to people's impressions of particular groups of people, as Michelle explains:

*I do not like personal stories that are irresponsible in tone or nature - glamourising harmful conditions such as eating disorders, entrenching unhelpful attitudes or behaviours, or stories that cause people to think unkindly of themselves or others. There is a great deal of power and responsibility associated with the telling of personal case studies which needs to be wielded with care. We also need to ensure that personal stories are told with an understanding of the potential consequences - which is especially important in an age of viral 'content'. Participants need to be aware that they could be trolled, have their original meaning or intent skewered or, at the riskier end of the spectrum, suffer reputational harm, financial lost or even unemployment.*

*Michelle*

As well as there being concern about the impact reading other's information might have on the reader, there are also concerns about what this level of honesty and attention might do to or for the person sharing, as Izzy so wonderfully surmises:

*A person's understanding of their experiences past and present may be limited by their mental health literacy, awareness of and comfort with reflecting on tricky and painful aspects of their life or family circumstances. Not everyone is ready for, able to, or even needs this level of introspection. However, it might be necessary to cover more in-depth formulations in learning tools such as case studies - the difference between a clinician's formulation and a person's account of their experience may be interesting in and of itself.*

*Izzy Bros*

It's fair to say that the time taken for the knowledge gained is also in indirect proportion:

*As everyone's experiences are unique, then a greater number of people willing to share their stories/experiences are needed in order to gain a richness of understanding - this can be very difficult to obtain and time consuming to analyse in comparison to, say, survey data.*

**Addie**

I am taken back to my A-Level studies when I consider the reliability of eyewitness testimony. My husband would also declare that my recall of events is not that reliable, but I would of course say the same of him! Ain't marriage grand?!

*I do think that autoethnography is slightly problematic in relation to false memory syndrome. The recalling of events that have happened and the way in which they made one feel is influenced not only by the immediate situation in question, but the reactions and actions of themselves and those surrounding them. I feel that this can sometimes present autoethnography with some challenges to overcome.*

**Jacob**

*As with any research type there are some ethical considerations for the research team themselves... There are of course also key factors for the researcher themselves which need to be addressed for any type of research...I find at times autoethnography can be subjective and sometimes lacks objectivity, as it relies heavily on personal experiences and perspectives. This can raise questions about the validity and reliability of the research and make it difficult to generalise findings beyond the individual author's experience. As a result, it can be challenging to assess the quality of autoethnographic research. I find as a reader, as it is often emotive, it can be difficult to remain rational as well as remember to be critical when such compelling stories of individuals are presented. I find there is also a risk of bias in autoethnography, as the researcher may be influenced by their own personal beliefs, values, and experiences. This can lead to a lack of diversity in the perspectives and narratives presented, as well as the potential for the researcher to overemphasise or overlook certain aspects of their experience. However, this can of course be the case in all research articles not just in autoethnography. I have found at times the focus on the author's personal experiences and narratives can lead to a lack of attention to wider social and cultural factors that may be influencing the topic being studied. This can limit the scope and depth of the research and may make it difficult to identify other important patterns or trends. The use of personal experiences and narratives can also raise ethical concerns, particularly when dealing with sensitive topics such as trauma or mental health. As a researcher, it is important to consider your own well-being and that of the participants involved and ensure that they obtain informed consent and protect the anonymity and privacy of those involved. I find as a reader too as these articles can often be emotive to consider your own wellbeing when reading such difficult stories.*

*Jack Griffiths*

## Growing for Pleasure

Many of us working in mental health also find a way to weave our personal passions into something work-related but fun and enlivening too. I know that when I consider my own journey, one of the most fun but beneficial things I did was volunteer as an activity coordinator for The Brownies. It allowed me to learn so much about the normal range in abilities and temperament in a non-clinical sample of children. Even over 15 years later, I still think of those incredible young people and the lessons they taught me about how to help them to give and to get the most out of their experiences. I am most certainly not alone in this either:

> *As a football coach and mental health professional, authoethnography has also helped me to better understand the experiences of my players, particularly those from different cultural or socio-economic backgrounds. This understanding has helped me to create a more inclusive and supportive team environment. Overall, authoethnography offers a unique and powerful means of exploring personal and professional experiences, as well as social and cultural phenomena. I like the combination of personal narratives and critical analysis as they also can provide a different means to challenge certain dominant narratives and power structures within psychology.*
>
> *Jack Griffiths*

## Identifying This Peculiar Fruit

Check me out bandying the term 'autoethnography' around like it was purposeful. If I am totally honest, I'll admit that it was only after I'd published the Clinical Psychologist Collective, yes, two books in, that I even realised I'd unknowingly been producing autoethnographical accounts. You see, Professor Jerome Carson, coeditor of this current book, got in touch with me to say:

> *Marianne, I just wanted to congratulate you on your book of narratives on the journey into clinical psychology. I will certainly be recommending it and citing it in any papers I write in the clinical arena. I found the sample*

*chapter for the grief collective very moving. I ordered a personal copy and one for a friend who recently lost her mother. Well done.*

Well, this did rather make me feel like Jeremy Clarkson (2020) on his farm when he declared, *'I did a thing!'*

It felt kind of surprising but wonderful to know that actually what I had created was actually science-y and was being revered by an actual proper professor! I sort of feel like I am just *doing my thing* because I think it will be helpful and because I know I would have found it helpful when I was at that life stage. It's wonderfully fulfilling when others feel the same. I also think that I am not alone in viewing interpretivist research this way, like it is somehow *not proper* because it's such a small sample. But of course, what we know is that there is so much to be learned about humanity and the human condition from small samples, as Elior explains:

> *I'm currently reading 'Man's Search for Meaning' by Psychiatrist Victor Frankl (1962), in which he writes about his scientific observations in almost an academic essay format but includes harrowing accounts of his own experience in concentration camps to help illustrate his points. It's a powerful example of autoethnography and shows how a relatively unique lived experience can play a powerful part in exploring human behaviour.*
>
> **Elior**

And yet, I keep coming back to my own felt sense that this is how I learn best. So, how come positivism gets all the kudos? How come the gold standard is still the randomised controlled trial? Perhaps it's time we looked at researching how students and subject enthusiasts actually learn best from the research they read. Lucy concurs:

> *Unlike formal randomised controlled trials, the voice of individuals involved in the research is heard. All the participants may have undergone the same intervention or life experience (for example, surgical procedure, rehabilitation centre care), but it offers real insight into people's personal values and aspects of how clinicians provide person centred care that just can't be captured by statistics and only looking at participants that fit neatly into homogeneous groups. It's real-life research.*
>
> **Lucy Georgiades**

This is all very well if the people signing off on your work see the style as relevant and robust. But, of course, that's not always the case!

Autoethnography is a great method for understanding culture and social issues. They provide deeper insights and unique perspectives that those who are not a part of the culture may fail to understand. I chose autoethnography for my master's dissertation. I was not taught about this by my lecturers; however, one of my supervisor's sent me research by Brett Smith and Andrew Sparkes to familiarise myself with the method. As I studied sport psychology, I actually had to defend the use of autoethnography and its relevance to the subject.

*Helena*

## How Our Life Learning Offers Helpful Branches for Others

Having now justified to myself and to many others that there is value in interpretive accounts when applied to psychology, in fact, really, it's meta-psychology because we are talking about psychology to psychologists! Anyway, regardless of what it is, the value is most definitely there! Having previously been an aspiring psychologist myself and knowing how hard it can be to get publications and also how marvellous it feels to see your own name in print, this experience and opportunity were something I also wanted to be able to create for others. I was also keen for people to be able to tap into an earlier stage of people's psychology career narratives whilst they were still in progress and not yet qualified psychologists. It was for these reasons that I wanted to create *The Aspiring Psychologist Collective* (Trent, 2022), described as 'a brick of a book' featuring 43 autoethnographic accounts by people on their way to getting qualified.

I didn't really mean to set out to brand myself as an expert in being and becoming a psychologist. I just did the things I enjoy and that feel like my so-called 'zone of genius'. I think it is easy for any of us to think that the things we are good at are easily achievable by everyone else we know. But we mustn't disregard our own expertise, as Amber explains:

*To me, autoethnography is acknowledging and celebrating we are all experts by experience. These experiences may be positive or negative, but they leave a mark on us.*

*Amber Hayday*

Creating the new book really was a recognition of my own shift to learning to sit comfortably as an expert in the field.

## Trying to Make Sense of All These Branches

The irony is not lost on me that during my studies I used to find research methods pretty boring as it all seemed pretty dry, and yet here I am in a research methods text book talking about positivism and interpretivism. Even the title 'positivist', describing quantitative research alone, feels potentially pretty disparaging. Surely, if it is a fact for that person, then it is still positivist?

I write this particular section on the day that Lucy Letby was sentenced and given a whole life term for her crimes of murder and attempted murder of young babies in the care of the neonatal unit where she worked. There has been public and professional uproar because she refused to attend the courtroom to receive her sentence. This means that she then effectively also chose not to hear the victim impact statements read out by families or their representatives. I think that for many, this has 'rubbed salt' in the already open, raw wounds of grief and trauma. This was the family's chance to have their own autoethnographic accounts heard by the guilty party and thus to feel validated and seen. Speaking as a trauma specialist myself, for some, it might have felt like a key part of the processing of their experiences, and this has been denied to them. For any laws to change, it would seem that a robust piece of qualitative research looking at the impact on victims of perpetrators not attending court for sentencing might well serve to pave the way for any changes whereby victim statements are played in the holding cell in the court.

## Future Saplings

So? What beckons next for me? I love the concept of autoethnography and am currently a coauthor on an exciting book project looking at health professionals' experiences of having Autism Spectrum Conditions. As I write, the podcast has just ticked over to its 50,000th MP3 download. I plan to continue to create podcast episodes. I am also part way through writing a generic mental health book, which would have been finished by now had I not broken my arm. The arm suffered its fate just as I was about to write the first draft for this chapter to submit to Professors Jerome Carson and Alec Grant. I should also use this space to thank them both for asking me to write this chapter and to Jerome, especially, for illuminating me to the idea that what I was creating was autoethnography. I also want to thank the people who offered me their thoughts on autoethnography and whose words also appear in this chapter. I hope this book will serve future generations of researchers well and that it injects some much-needed moisture to help further roots, shoots, and leaves to flourish. Also, a big thanks to my dad, who likely would never have listened to my podcast or read my books because they don't reference vintage motorbikes enough, but would have been so deeply proud and supportive nonetheless.

## Notes

1 Oh, now I've been hit by an attack of the self-critic monster encouraging me to think whether it would be better to write 'good enough' but no, I am going to resist and stick with good.

2 I hope that they love seeing their names in print here and that it pays rich dividends for them in any psychology applications in the future. In some cases, people gave me their full name, and in others, just their first name. I know that editorially it may look a bit disjointed to use a variety of name formats, but I'd like to honour those who wanted to be named by using their full names, so please forgive my editorial transgression.

## References

Blume, J. (1975). *Forever.* Bradbury Press.

Clarkson, J. (2020). *Clarkson's farm.* Expectation entertainment con dao productions. Amazon. Expectation Entertainment Con Dao Productions. Amazon. - Search (bing.com)

Frankl, V. E. (1962). *Man's search for meaning: An introduction to logotherapy.* Beacon Press.

Friday, N. (1991). *Women on top: How real life has changed women's sexual fantasies.* Random House.

Gross, K. D., Rubin, L. M., & Weese, A. P. (2020). College athletes and suicide prevention: A collaborative autoethnography. *Journal of Issues in Intercollegiate Athletics,* Winter 2020 Special Issue, 82–97. JIIAArticleGrossRubinWeese2020. pdfTrent, M. J. (2020). *The grief collective: Stories of life, loss and learning to heal.* KDP.

Trent, M. J. (2021). *The clinical psychologist collective: Advice and guidance for aspiring clinical psychologists.* KDP.

Trent, M. J. (2022). *The aspiring psychologist collective: Reflective accounts of mental health professionals on their way to qualification.* KDP.

## *Magazines Cited*

*Take a Break.* Take a Break

*That's Life.* That's Life Magazine (thatslife.co.uk)

# INDEX

Note: *Italic* page numbers refer to figures and page numbers followed by "n" denote endnotes.